standard catalog of ®

MUSTANG

1964-2001

Brad Bowling

Published by

krause publications

700 East State Street, Iola, WI 54990-0001
Telephone (715) 445-2214
www.krause.com

Please call or write for our free catalog. Our toll free number to place an order or obtain a free catalog is (800) 258-0929 or please use our regular business telephone, (715) 445-2214.

ISBN: 0-87349-244-7
Library of Congress Catalog Number: 2001086762
UPC: 046081002441

Front Cover: 1989 GT, 1967 Shelby GT-350, 1996 GT coupe
Page 1: 1967 GTA 2+2, 2001 GT
Page 3: 1970 Shelby GT-500 convertible
Page 4: 1967 GTA 2+2, 1983 GT, 1999 GT convertible
Page 5: 1965 Shelby GT-350, 1989 Saleen SSC, 1995 SVT Cobra
Page 6: 1993 SVT Cobra
Page 7: 1999 Saleen S-281, 1986 GT
Page 9: 1967 GTA 2+2
Back Cover: 1967 GTA 2+2, 2001 GT

About the Author

Brad Bowling began writing and photographing features for *Mustang Monthly* in 1985, while majoring in Public Relations at the University of Alabama. Upon graduation, he moved to Atlanta and became the editor of *Mustang Times* and sat on the Mustang Club of America board of directors.

In 1989 Bowling relocated to Anaheim, California, to be the public relations coordinator for Saleen Autosport. A year later he became assistant editor of *Mustang Illustrated*, just down the road from Saleen in Fullerton. Trading sunny southern California for arctic Iola, Wisconsin, in 1991, Bowling became the editor of Krause Publications' *Old Cars Weekly* for five years before taking a position as director of Web site development for the public relations department of Lowe's Motor Speedway.

The author has owned three Mustangs—a Vintage Burgundy '67 coupe, a Teal '95 GT convertible and a Zinc Yellow '01 GT coupe—but has been fortunate enough to drive more than 200 examples of the pony car. This is Bowling's fifth Mustang book. His Web site, www.bradbowling.com, contains many of his car-related articles and photography. He currently lives in Concord, North Carolina, with his fiancée Heather and their American Eskimo dog, Lizzie.

Photo Credits

All photos by the author unless indicated.

(FMC) Ford Motor Company
(JH) Jerry Heasley

(OCW) Old Cars Weekly
(PH) Phil Hall

Richard and Scott Wert were some of the great Shelby owners I encountered while researching this book. This 1970 GT-500 convertible is just one awesome car the father and son have collected.

CONTENTS

1964-1/2-1969

1970-1989

1990-2001

Shelby 1965-1970

Saleen 1984-2001

Cobra 1993-2001

Acknowledgments

Years before there was an Internet, there was a network of people, clubs, and companies devoted to the enjoyment and preservation of Ford's Mustang. Without those connections and links it would be impossible to assemble the information that makes up books like the Standard Catalog of® Mustang.

During the writing of this book, it was my privilege to spend three months in the world of Mustangs visiting with its friendly, enthusiastic citizens. While this list does not cover every person I spoke to in the course of my research, I hope it gives due thanks to most of the folks who steered me in the right direction, answered lots of trivial questions, or let me photograph their beautiful cars.

The ever-helpful Carolina Regional Mustang Club, of Charlotte, North Carolina, let me use its April meeting to plead for good photography subjects—and boy, did the members respond! You'll see examples of the club's cars owned by Norm & Karen Demers, Keith & Pat Suddeth, Johnnie & Rachel Garner, Dave & Gina Goff, Mike & Lori Rayburn, Larry Vandeventer and Bob Cox. To see even more gorgeous Mustangs from the Carolina group, visit the club's Web site at www.ponytales.org.

One of my favorite places to visit in Concord, North Carolina, is Morrison Motor Co., which is owned by Jimmy Morrison. Jimmy and I have spent many an hour deep in car-guy talk during the past 10 years, and there's always something on his lot that I really want to take home. Corvettes, Firebirds/Camaros, Vipers, Impalas, Jeeps, and Prowlers abound—always sprinkled liberally with Mustang GTs, Saleens, and SVT Cobras. In addition to the company's inventory, Jimmy's huge private collection includes a '71 Mach 1 with 429-cid power, a '69 Boss 302, a '69 GT coupe sporting a 428-cid V-8 and two never-driven '93 SVT Cobras. For the Standard Catalog project, Jimmy handed me the keys to all of his Mustangs and let me take off for parts unknown with more than a dozen really nice pony cars. Morrison Motor Co. is located at 1170 Old Charlotte Road, Concord, NC 28027. The phone number is (704) 782-7716, and the Web site is www.morrisonmotorco.com.

When I wandered into Daniel Carpenter's shop to see if he had any Ford literature I might photocopy, I had no idea he was an avid collector of Fox-bodied Mustangs. Seeing a '90 Saleen convertible (with the original window sticker in place) in his lobby gave me a clue that Daniel and I had something to talk about besides old shop manuals. His personal collection includes a '79 Pace Car Replica, '83 convertible, two '86 GTs and a '93 SVT Cobra R—none of which have ever been driven! Additionally, there is a 400-mile '89 GT, a 3,000-mile '93 LX convertible and a couple of Cobras running around his place with less than 4,000 miles each. Daniel was nice enough to prep the cars I needed for my photography so these largely unseen treasures could be shared with the readers of this book. Daniel is the son of Dennis Carpenter—the famous reproducer of impossible-to-find Ford parts. Daniel's new shop, which sits just down the

Jimmy Morrison opened his collection to the author for photography. His 1993 SVT Cobra has never been driven or dealer-prepped.

Mark LaMaskin had a room full of Saleen Mustangs waiting to be photographed, including this 1999 S-281 convertible with Speedster package.

street from his father's place, turns out rubber and plastic reproduction Mustang parts, often from original Ford factory molds. For information about the Mustang components his company produces, contact Daniel Carpenter Reproductions at 4310 Concord Parkway S., Concord, NC 28027 or (704) 786-0990.

When Saleen Mustang owners and enthusiasts found out I was including a section on Steve Saleen's cars, I received more information than I could possibly fit into a book of this size. Liz Summar, who runs Team Saleen (www.saleen.com), put me on to Greg and Laura Wackett, who know everybody who ever thought about buying a Saleen because they run a service locating cars for people (saleenlocator@yahoo.com), and they've been closely involved with all things Saleen since the beginning. The Wacketts introduced me to Mark LaMaskin, another expert who buys and sells Saleen Mustangs and SVT Cobras for a living through Performance Autosport (www.performanceautosport.com). Mark invited me to his shop in Richmond, Virginia, for an all-day photo shoot of his inventory; he's another collector who will gladly hand me a dealer license plate and a set of keys to a 300-horsepower supercharged Mustang with no questions asked. Mark can be reached at Performance Autosport, 12927 Plaza Dr., Ste. B, Richmond, VA 23233 and (804) 784-8851 or through info@performanceautosport.com. Mark and Greg agreed to proof this book's Saleen chapters for technical accuracy; their changes greatly improved the material's quality.

If there's a guy I would want involved in the Shelby section of this book, it's Howard Pardee. Howard bought a new Shelby GT-350 in 1965, drove it every day for nine years, then bought a second one. He has been intensely involved with the Shelby American Automobile Club (SAAC) since its inception and acts as 1965-66 GT-350 registrar for the group. His collection of Shelby literature makes him one of the foremost experts in the country of the short-lived, Mustang-based

supercar. After a chance online meeting, Howard agreed to pore over the Shelby chapters of this book; his corrections and up-to-date information have taken those pages to a much higher level of accuracy and interest. Howard can be reached by e-mail at 65-66registrar@saac.com. To contact SAAC, write to P.O. Box 788, Sharon, CT 06069.

Special thanks also must go to Jerry Heasley, a great friend and mentor for the past 15 years; my bride-to-be Heather, who didn't at all seem to mind having her spare bedroom converted into Standard Catalog Central for three months; my parents and grandparents, whose lifelong support gave me the confidence and ability to take on projects like this (although my father still has nightmares about the 1967 Mustang he bought me in 1984); and, of course, Jimmy Glenn.

Most of the cars in Daniel Carpenter's collection have never been driven. This 1986 Mustang GT is still wearing every label and marking from the Ford factory.

Introduction

World War II changed the lives of millions of people. For the purposes of this book, it is important to consider how it indirectly transformed the American auto industry.

Wartime exposure to automobiles in other parts of the world changed the views and interests of American car enthusiasts who served overseas. Many came back to the United States with a newfound love of the small, open sports cars they had driven in Europe and Great Britain. By the early 1950s, "dream cars" seen at auto shows began to look like Americanized renditions of the T-series MG or Jaguar XK-120. When the Chevrolet Corvette and Kaiser-Darrin hit the showrooms in 1953 a trend was set for the future.

Ford Motor Company followed the trend with its 1955 two-seat Thunderbird, which it promoted as a "personal car," rather than a sports car. Far more luxurious and weather-tight than an MG, Triumph, Jaguar, or Austin-Healey, the "T-bird" offered such amenities as a detachable fiberglass hard-top, an optional automatic transmission and powerful extra-cost V-8 engines (with a supercharger in some models).

Though far more successful in the showroom than competitor Chevrolet's Corvette, the Thunderbird was an expensive car to build as it shared few components with other Fords. Sales were respectable at 16,155 (for the '55), 15,631 ('56) and 21,380 ('57); however, the bottom line was always a small loss or a minuscule profit. It was not enough to offset the cost of building an exclusive car line with few production-volume efficiencies.

Ford's Robert McNamara decided to enlarge the Thunderbird into a four-passenger sports/personal model. This "Squarebird" had bucket seats and a center console, like many sports cars, but its larger size, big-car engineering, and rich appointments made it more of a luxury vehicle. It had an obvious sporty flavor, but was far from a sports car. It was also a profitable success; one of only two domestic car models to increase sales in 1958.

THE FALCON GETS SPORTY

During the early 1960s, Ford started adding sporty features to its compact Falcon in an attempt to win some of the former sports car buyers that Chevrolet's Corvair Monza was stealing from imported car dealers.

A 1962 version of the Falcon, called the Futura, got bucket seats and a four-speed floor shift; however, these minor changes did not put it on par with the radical, rear-engine Monza. It took little away from Chevy's growing market segment, which rose to 350,000 buyers. Ford was getting about one-third as many combined sales from its Falcon Futura and Mercury Comet S-22 sports models.

MEET THE FAIRLANE GROUP

Lido Anthony Iacocca began working for Ford Motor Company in the 1950s, where he passed up an engineer's job at the Dearborn, Michigan, factory for a sales job. A successful "$56 per month for a '56 Ford" campaign caught the eye of Robert S. McNamara, vice president and general manager of Ford Division.

Based largely on the strength of the '56 promotion, which Iacocca claims helped sell 70,000 extra cars that year, McNamara promoted "Lee" to the new position of truck marketing manager. Iacocca's career rocketed him through the position of car marketing manager and general manager of Ford until 1962, when he became vice president and general manager of Ford.

Iacocca was probably the most influential member of the Fairlane Group, a committee of eight to ten Ford managers and reps from the J. Walter Thompson ad agency. The group met each week at the Fairlane Inn in Dearborn, where they pondered the future directions of various Ford product lines.

MUSTANG I

During 1962, Iacocca and friends brainstormed, then built, an all-new prototype sports-competition car as an engineering exercise. The Mustang I was refreshingly different from many of the then-current Detroit experimental vehicles due to its ultra-lightweight and competition-ready components. It also had a distinctly European flair—no surprise when one realizes it was launched under the direction of Royston G. Lunn, a product planner who was a European transplant.

Lunn, whose résumé included time with Aston Martin and AC Cars in England, was given a budget, a clean sheet of paper, and the mandate to "build something sporty." Despite the complexity of the project, he did not start with an existing Ford chassis, a fact which helped emphasize its distinction from many other Detroit "dream cars" of the era.

Herb Misch, a former Packard designer, was tapped to be project engineer. During the summer of 1962, Misch helped design and build the Mustang I during an amazingly short period of 100 working days.

Under the direction of Eugene Bordinat, sketches of the car were transformed into a clay model in just three weeks. Despite the short turnaround, the impact of his work has stood the test of time. Bordinat had worked his way up through the General Motors' styling studios before moving to Ford in 1947 and over to Lincoln Division in the '50s. He became vice president and director of styling for the entire company in 1962.

Blessed with the drive of Iacocca, the skills of Lunn and Misch, and the luck of Bordinat, the project sailed along very smoothly that summer. The main factors in the initial concept for the car were drivability, performance, comfort, appearance, feature appeal, and flexibility of application. Though designed as a road vehicle, the Mustang I met all Federation Internationale de l'Automobile (FIA) and Sports Car Club of America (SCCA) competition regulations. It was decided to aim the vehicle at the 1.5-liter engine class, which was mid-range in the small sports car category.

An extremely lightweight machine, the Mustang I had a "space frame" constructed entirely of one-inch tubing, a body skin formed of .060-inch thick aluminum and an integral rollbar. Troutman and Barnes, the California body builders responsible for Lance Reventlow's Scarab race cars, fabricated body panels.

To design a sports car with low-cost potential, an existing driveline had to be utilized. It was determined that either the four-cylinder inline engine used in the English Ford or the German 12M Cardinal V-4 engine could be used. Both engines had over 1,500 cubic centimeters and were attractive for a sports car concept. However, the inline-four's dimensions would have necessitated a conventional, front-engine driveline arrangement, while the V-4 came with a transaxle unit that permitted a rear-drive layout with engine location ahead of the rear axle.

The front-engine approach allowed a shorter overall length and better luggage compartment, while the mid-ship arrangement allowed better drag characteristics and a lower center of gravity. Because a lower mass translated into the best roadability, the V-4 was chosen to power the project car.

Bordinat was given a 90-inch wheelbase platform to build on and a 48-inch front and 49-inch rear track. Overall length worked out as 154 inches. Overall width was 61 inches. The spare wheel, gas tank and battery sat up front, while a drop-in luggage carrier was designed for the rear decklid opening. Inside, the seats were fixed in place and driving controls were adjustable. Foldaway headlamps made the aerodynamic front possible.

The body skin was a one-piece "pod" riveted to the space frame where possible. It included the inside surface of the floor and toe board and the seat pans. All attachment brackets for the mechanical units were welded to the space frame. Built-in wheel arches, headlamp cans and other forms strengthened the body pod.

Including the seats as part of the body skin made the car stronger and allowed use of a clean, lightweight seat trim and built-in headrests. Safety belts were rigidly attached to the structure and could be made easily retractable, and a composite central console was constructed to provide easily accessible controls. Less floor trim was required and seat attaching and adjusting hardware was eliminated.

In addition to clutch/brake/accelerator pedals with four inches of adjustment, the interior featured an easily accessible gear-change lever, a fly-off hand brake, a horn, turn indicators and choke control—all located in the console. Large, easy-to-read instruments were mounted in a padded dash with a built-in grab handle.

While the prototype had a competition-type windshield, a road-going unit and several optional hard and soft tops were under consideration. All were designed to mate with the integral rollbar, which had a hinged or pivoted backlight.

In a paper on the car, Lunn described the engine/transaxle as the "power pack" and noted that it was the larger displacement version of a unit designed for the 12M German Cardinal. It consisted of the 1,500cc, 60-degree V-4 balance-shaft engine, a four-speed fully-synchronized concentric-drive manual transmission combined in a common housing with an axle unit and conventional clutch.

Changes made to upgrade performance of the production engine included a high-lift camshaft; high-pressure springs; a larger single-throat carburetor; an electric fuel pump; installation of a vacuum and centrifugally actuated distributor; and use of a gauze-type air cleaner. For competition applications, a new manifold with twin-throat Weber carburetors could be installed. A special gear-shift mechanism was fabricated, but a close-ratio transmission could not be developed within the 100-day deadline and widely-spaced standard gear ratios were used.

A two-radiator cooling circuit was designed for the car, with interior heating provisions. The side-mounted radiators had electric fans controlled by a thermostat.

The front suspension was a short/long arm (SLA) type and independent link rear suspension was used. The mid-engine configuration contributed greatly to good weight distribution, which enhanced the car's handling characteristics. Brakes were adapted from the Ford Consul model (built by Ford of England) and consisted of 9.5-inch discs up front and 9-inch diameter rear drums. The Mustang was designed for tires in the 5.30x13 to 5.50x13 size range.

Road versions of the engine generated 89 horsepower, which was good for a top speed of about 112.9 miles per hour. The Weber-carbureted track version produced 109 horsepower at the same 6,500-rpm maximum and about 13 more miles per hour of top speed.

The Mustang I made its first appearance at the United States Grand Prix, in Watkins Glen, New York, on Oct. 7, 1962. On October 20, it was seen at the Laguna Seca Pacific Grand Prix, in Monterey, California. It set the enthusiast world on its ear and whet an appetite for things to come.

Under McNamara, Ford made many profitable products, but few really exciting ones had been seen since the two-seat Thunderbird. European automotive journalists especially found the Mustang I refreshing. France's Bernard Cahier wrote, "The Mustang could put on a convincing performance (as a sports car)."

Eventually, the prototype served out its useful life. It was given to the Henry Ford Museum and Greenfield Village for safekeeping. Today, millions of visitors see it there, as part of the museum's "The Automobile in American Life" exhibit.

This 1967 GTA fastback belongs to Carolina Regional Mustang Club members Dave and Gina Goff.

1964-1/2 convertible
Owners: Johnnie and Rachel Garner

1964-1/2

The Mustang, the model that gave birth to the entire "pony" car phenomenon, was introduced April 17, 1964. Like a purebred racehorse it bolted from the starting gate and was halfway down the front stretch before the rest of the competition could catch up.

Debuting not at the traditional start of the 1964 model year but six months in as an "early" 1965, it combined sporty looks, economy, and brisk performance in a package that had a base price of $2,368. As a result of brilliant marketing and research Mustangs could be equipped to be anything from absolute economy cars to luxury sports cars. The Mustang, with its extended hood, shortened rear deck, sculptured body panels, and sporty bucket seats provided a family-size sedan for grocery-getting mothers, an appearance for those who yearned for another two-seat Thunderbird, and plenty of power and handling options for the performance Ford enthusiast.

A hardtop coupe and convertible were offered initially, with a 2+2 fastback model coming along by the official start of the 1965 model year. All three body styles had 108-inch wheelbases and overall lengths of 181.6 inches. The hardtop weighed 2,449 pounds and the convertible weighed 2,615 pounds. They were priced at $2,368 and $2,614, respectively. By comparison, Chevrolet's Corvair Monza Spyder coupe stickered for $2,599, the Corvair Monza Spyder convertible for $2,811, and the two-week-old 1964 Plymouth Barracuda fastback for $2,365.

The Mustang's standard engine was a 170-cid inline-six that generated 101 hp. The Monza Spyder's "pancake" six produced 150 hp, and the Barracuda offered a 225-cid "slant" six with 145 hp. Additionally, Ford offered V-8 power, initially displacing 260 cubic inches and boasting

164 hp when equipped with a two-barrel carburetor. While this was less powerful than the Barracuda's 273-cid, 180-hp extra-cost V-8, the Mustang had an appearance that more buyers preferred at the time. In a beauty contest, the Mustang won out over the Barracuda.

Part of the Mustang's success was no doubt attributable to the prosperous American economy enjoyed by the baby boom generation. In Ford's lingo, this was the "Mustang Generation," a phrase coined to express the enthusiasm of the time and the car that captured its excitement.

"This generation wants economy and sportiness, handling and performance, all wrapped up in one set of wheels," went the sales pitch. "There is a market out there searching for a car. Ford Motor Company committed itself to design that car. It carries four people, weighs under 2,500 pounds and costs less than $2,500." The Mustang just about hit its targets. Admittedly, it was a few pounds over the ideal weight and rear passengers needed to be short of average height to fit comfortably.

From six decades of experience selling cars, Ford's publicity machine was able to create a buzz about the Mustang the likes of which had never been felt in Detroit. In March, a full month before the Mustang's public introduction, the company had a member of the Ford family drive a black pilot model to a luncheon in downtown Detroit. There, the *Detroit Free Press* snapped "spy" photos and sent pictures out on the news wires, where *Newsweek,* among others, picked one up and ran it.

Although April 17 marked the car's first sales date, the American public began its affair with the Mustang a night before, when all three networks ran commercials showcasing the new pony car to nearly 29 million viewers. The following day, spectators attending the New York World's Fair saw the car up close and personal at a special unveiling ceremony. The pre-launch blitz worked beautifully, as 22,000 orders were taken for Mustangs on the first day, and by its first anniversary sales had reached 417,000 units.

Lee Iacocca can take credit for the idea of introducing the Mustang as a "midyear" model—a strategy he had employed for the debuts of the Falcon Futura and Galaxie 500XL Sports Hardtop. While playing with the schedule had the desired effect of shining a stronger spotlight on the Mustang, it has led to the idea that Ford produced a "1964-1/2" model—there's simply no such animal. To fill dealer orders Ford began pumping ponies out of its Dearborn, Michigan; San Jose, California; and Metuchen, New Jersey, plants.

Since a car named after a galloping pony conjures images of horsepower to spare, the Mustang was naturally able to keep pace with its direct competitors. When *Road & Track* tested Mustangs in its May 1964 issue, available engines were the 170-cid 101-hp six, the 260-cid 164-hp V-8 with two-barrel carburetor, and the 289-cid 210-hp V-8 with four-barrel carburetor. For real speed freaks, the 271-hp Hi-Po 289-cid V-8, introduced in the Indy Pace Cars, had a four-barrel carburetor, solid valve lifters, and 10.5:1 compression ratio. Later in the year, a 200-cid 120-hp six became the base engine, and the 170-cid six and the 260-cid V-8 were dropped.

By the end of 1964, the Mustang had scored 120,000

sales. Despite its late start, only a handful of established people-movers from Chevrolet (Impala, Bel Air, and Chevelle) and Ford (Galaxie 500) had outsold it. It even surpassed the Falcon, from which it was partly derived.

Interestingly, most early Mustangs were not "strippers." Only 27 percent had the base six-cylinder engine. Nearly half had automatic transmissions and nearly 20 percent had optional four-speed manual transmissions—a manual three-speed was standard. Other creature comforts included radios (78%), heaters (99%), power steering (31%), whitewall tires (88%), windshield washers (48%), back-up lights (45%), tinted windshields (22%), full tinted glass (8%) and air conditioning (6.4%).

1964-1/2 standard wheel covers

1964-1/2 data plate

1964-1/2 luxury interior

1964-1/2 luxury interior door panel

1964-1/2 D-code 289/4V V-8

DATA PLATE DECODING

Important encoded information is found on the Ford Motor Company data plate, located on the rear edge of the left front door. The data plate contains an upper row of code that reveals body and trim information plus (at center level) a Vehicle Warranty Number that reveals other important data.

BODY CODE

65A – hardtop coupe
65B – hardtop coupe, luxury
65C – hardtop coupe, bench seats
76A – convertible
76B – convertible, luxury
76C – convertible, bench seats

PAINT CODE

A   Raven Black
B   Pagoda Green
C   Pace Car White
     (special order)
D   Dynasty Green
F   Guardsman Blue
H   Caspian Blue
J   Rangoon Red
K   Silversmoke Gray
M   Wimbledon White
O   Tropical Turquoise
P   Prairie Bronze
R   Phoenician Yellow
S   Cascade Green
V   Sunlight Yellow
X   Vintage Burgundy
Y   Skylight Blue
Z   Chantilly Beige
3   Poppy Red

ASSEMBLY DATE CODE

The next group of symbols consisted of two numbers and a letter, which represent the assembly date code. The numbers give the day (i.e.: "01" = first day) and the letter designates month of year, following normal progression (i.e.: "A" = January; "B" = February, etc.), except that the letter "I" is skipped.

AXLE RATIO CODES*

1/A – 3.00:1
2/B – 2.83:1
3/C – 3.20:1
5/E – 3.50:1
6/F – 2.80:1
8/H – 3.89:1
9/I – 4.11:1

* number indicates conventional axle/letter denotes limited-slip unit

TRANSMISSION CODE

1 – 3-speed manual
5 – 4-speed manual
6 – C-4 automatic

VEHICLE WARRANTY NUMBER
MODEL YEAR

5 – 1965*

* Ford made no distinction between the early ("1964-1/2") and late (1965) models. Technically, there is no such thing as a 1964-1/2.

ASSEMBLY PLANT

F – Dearborn, Michigan
R – San Jose, California
T – Metuchen, New Jersey

BODY SERIAL NUMBERS

07 – hardtop
08 – convertible

ENGINE CODE

U – 170-cid 1-bbl. 6-cyl.
F – 260-cid 2-bbl. V-8
D – 289-cid 4-bbl. V-8
K – 289-cid 4-bbl. high-performance V-8

CONSECUTIVE UNIT NUMBER

Begins at 100001 at each factory.

ENGINES

170-cid 1-bbl. Inline Six

Valves . . . . overhead
Block . . . . cast iron
Displacement . . . . 170 cid
Bore and stroke . . . . 3.50 x 2.94 inches
Compression ratio 8.7:1
Brake hp . . . . 101 at 4400 rpm
Main bearings 7
Valve lifters . . . . hydraulic
Carburetor. Ford (Autolite) one-barrel Model C30F-9510-G
Code . . . . U

1964-1/2 wire wheel cover

1964-1/2 hardtop coupe (FMC)

260-cid 2-bbl. V-8

Valves . . . . overhead
Block . . . . cast iron
Displacement . . . . 260 cid
Bore and stroke . . . . 3.80 x 2.87 inches
Compression ratio 8.8:1
Brake hp . . . . 164 at 4400 rpm
Main bearings 5
Valve lifters . . . . hydraulic
Carburetor . Ford (Autolite) two-barrel Model C40F-9510E
Code . . . . F

289-cid 4-bbl. V-8

Valves . . . . overhead
Block . . . . cast iron
Displacement . . . . 289 cid
Bore and stroke . . . . 4.00 x 2.87 inches
Compression ratio 9.0:1
Brake hp . . . . 210 at 4400 rpm
Main bearings 5
Valve lifters . . . . hydraulic
Carburetor Ford (Autolite) four-barrel Model C4AF-9510-B
Code . . . . D

289-cid 4-bbl. High-Performance V-8

Valves . . . . overhead
Block . . . . cast iron
Displacement . . . . 289 cid
Bore and stroke . . . . 4.00 x 2.87 inches
Compression ratio 10.5:1
Brake hp . . . . 271 at 6000 rpm
Main bearings 5
Valve lifters . . . . solid
Carburetor Ford (Autolite) four-barrel Model C4OF-9510-AL
Code . . . . K

CHASSIS

Wheelbase . . . . 108 inches
Overall length . . . . 181.6 inches
Tires . . . . (with V-8) 7.00 x 13 four-ply tubeless
. . . . (with high-performance 289 V-8)
. . . . (with 7.00 x 14 four-plytubeless blackwall
. . (other models) 6.50 x 13 four-ply tubeless blackwall

OPTION LIST

Accent Group $27.70
Ford air conditioner $283.20
Heavy-duty battery $7.60
Front disc brakes $58.00
Full-length center console $51.50
Console for use with air conditioning $32.20
Equa-Lock limited slip differential $42.50
California-type closed emissions system $5.30
Challenger V-8 . . . . $108.00
Challenger four-barrel V-8 engine $162.00

Challenger high-performance four-barrel V-8 . . . . . $442.60
Early year only, 260-cid V-8 . . . . $75.00
Emergency flashers $19.60
Tinted glass with banded windshield $30.90
Banded, tinted windshield only $21.55
Back-up lights $10.70
Rocker panel moldings $16.10
Power brakes $43.20
Power steering $86.30
Power convertible top $54.10
Push-button radio with antenna $58.50
Rally-Pac instrumentation with clock and
    tachometer $70.80
Deluxe retractable front seat safety belts $7.55
Special Handling Package $31.30
Padded sun visors $5.70
Cruise-O-Matic transmission . . . . (with six) $179.80
. . . . (with 200-hp and 225-hp V-8s) $189.60
Four-speed manual transmission . . . . . . (with six) $115.90
. . . . (with V-8) $75.80
Hardtop vinyl roof $75.80
Visibility Group . . . . (includes remote-control mirror,
        day/nite mirror, two-speed electric wipers and
                        windshield washers) $36.00
Wheel covers with simulated knock-off hubs $18.20
Wire wheel covers, 14 inch $45.80
Styled steel wheels, 14 inch $122.30
Size 6.50 x 13 whitewalls . . . . (with six) $33.90
Size 6.95 x 14 tires . . . . (blackwall with six) $7.40
. . . . (whitewall with six) $41.30
    (whitewall with V-8s, except high-performance type) $33.90
    (black nylon, except with high-performance) V-8 $15.80
. . (Red Band nylon with V-8s except high-performance)
                        V-8 $49.60
. . . . . . (Black nylon or white sidewall nylon with high-
            performance V-8) no charge

NOTE: The MagicAire heater ($32.20 credit) and front seat belts ($11 credit) were "delete options."

OPTION POPULARITY

Automatic transmission 49.2%
Four-speed manual transmission 19.3%
V-8 engines 73.1%
Six-cylinder engine 26.9%
Radio 77.8%
Heater 99.1%
Power steering 30.9%
Power brakes 7.7%
Whitewalls 88.2%
Windshield washers 48.3%
Tinted windshields 22.4%
Tinted glass 8.0%
Back-up lights 44.6%
Air conditioning 6.4%

1964-1/2 MUSTANG PRODUCTION CHART

Model	Doors/Body/Seating	Factory Price	Shipping Weight	Prod. Total
07	2/hardtop/4	$2368	2449	91,532
08	2/convertible/4	$2614	2615	28,468

NOTE 1: Total series output was 120,000 units.

**1965 convertible
Owners: Keith and Pat Suddeth**

1965

One brand-new model and a number of minor revisions were seen at the start of the Mustang's first full year of production. A fastback body, known as the 2+2, joined the hardtop and convertible, creating an expanded stable of three pony cars. The fastback featured a larger backlight glass, a shorter trunk lid, functional fresh air vents on the B-pillar and a folding rear seat that turned the sporty car into a two-seater capable of carrying full-length snow skis or other outdoor gear. It was identical to the other two Mustang models from the window line down.

An alternator replaced the generator used on early cars. Otherwise, engine options remained the same, except that the small Falcon-derived six-cylinder (the 170-cid unit) was replaced with the 200-cid "big car" six.

A number of small changes and some new options were introduced on the later 1965 models. While C-type clips secured interior door handles on the earliest Mustangs, Allen screw attachments were a running production change adopted for later cars. The spacing between the letters in the lower bodyside nameplates was modified, giving them a five-inch measurement (about one-quarter-inch longer than before). The push-down door lock buttons were chrome plated, in contrast to the 1964-1/2 type, which were colored to match the interior. Front disc brakes were a new option.

A GT package was available that included the 225-hp V-8; three-speed fully-synchronized stick shift; special GT grille with built-in fog lamps; GT front fender insignia; a GT five-dial instrument cluster; a GT paint stripe (which could be deleted); a dual exhaust system with "trumpet" extensions; front wheel disc brakes; and a special handling package. For more money, the 271-hp solid-lifter high-performance V-8 and four-speed stick shift could be substituted.

New options were promoted with slogans like "Another 'unexpected' from Mustang ... new GT" and "Mustang Unique Ford GT stripe - badge of America's greatest total performance cars!" The new option packages allowed buyers to design a luxury Mustang or a sport Mustang. A luxury interior option was available for any hardtop, convertible or 2+2, featuring an instrument panel with wood-grained vinyl trim, new bucket seats with handsome, embossed inserts, a sporty steering wheel with chromed "rivets," and more little niceties including integral door armrests and door courtesy lights. The embossed bucket seats became known as the "pony" interior, as the embossment showed "herds" of stylized wild mustangs.

The FoMoCo Genuine Parts division offered a series of "Cobra Kits" that could be installed for better performance. Kits for the 221-, 260- and 289-cid Ford V-8s were marketed. They included extras from simple packages (such as chrome dress-up parts and a Cobra distributor kit) to harder-to-install engine performance kits, dual exhaust kits, cam kits, heavy-duty clutch kits, and induction kits with single four-barrel, dual four-barrel, and triple two-barrel carburetor setups.

Ford's advertising campaigns hit hard on the notion that the Mustang could be "factory-customized" to suit the individual buyer's needs. A series of Walter Mitty-themed advertisements appeared in leading magazines, recounting tales of how a bashful Midwest schoolteacher became a society darling after buying a Mustang, or how Wolfgang (a harpsichord player) changed his life after purchasing his sporty Ford. In almost all cases, the cars depicted were hardtops with full wheel covers, whitewall tires and V-8 badges. Not surprisingly, these options all had high installation rates in 1965.

The standard equipment list for 1965 was much the same as before, including heater and defroster; dual sun visors; Sports-type front bumpers; full wheel covers; vinyl upholstery; seat belts; padded instrument panel; automatic courtesy lights; cigarette lighter; front and rear carpets; foam-padded front bucket seats; self-adjusting brakes; Sports steering wheel; five 6.50 x 13 four-ply tubeless black sidewall tires; and six-cylinder engine. The 6.95 x 14 tires were standard in the Mustang V-8 series.

Along with a much-publicized Tiffany Gold Medal for excellence in American design during 1964, the 1965 Mustang was honored with a Bronze Medal Award from the Industrial Design Institute.

DATA PLATE DECODING

The Vehicle Identification Number is stamped on the top upper flange of the left front fender apron, visible with the hood open. The warranty number was at the top left-hand corner of the warranty plate (mounted on the driver's door). The data on the upper row of codes (body code, color code, trim code, etc.) was a narrow, unfinished band that crossed the data plate horizontally, nearly at its center.

BODY CODE

63A – fastback
63B – fastback, luxury
65A – hardtop coupe
65B – hardtop coupe, luxury
65C – hardtop coupe, bench seats
76A – convertible
76B – convertible, luxury
76C – convertible, bench seats

PAINT CODE

A	Raven Black	R	Ivy Green
C	Honey Gold	S	Cascade Green
D	Dynasty Green	V	Sunlight Yellow
F	Arcadian Blue	X	Vintage Burgundy
H	Caspian Blue	Y	Silver Blue
I	Champagne Beige	Z	Chantilly Beige
J	Rangoon Red	3	Poppy Red
K	Silversmoke Gray		

1965 convertible

1965 T-code 200/1V inline six

1965 upgrade wheel cover

1965 hardtop

M	Wimbledon White	5	Twilight Turquoise
O	Tropical Turquoise	7	Phoenician Yellow
P	Prairie Bronze	8	Springtime Yellow

ASSEMBLY DATE CODE

The "later" 1965 date codes were changed in regards to the letter used to designate a specific month. Code "N" designated January. Code "O" was not used and the remaining months ran in normal alphabetical progression from Code "P" (for February) through Code "Z" (for December).

AXLE RATIO CODES*

1/A – 3.00:1
2/B – 2.83:1
3/C – 3.20:1
5/E – 3.50:1
6/F – 2.80:1
8/H – 3.89:1
9/I – 4.11:1

* number indicates conventional axle/letter denotes limited-slip unit

TRANSMISSION CODE

1 – 3-speed manual
5 – 4-speed manual
6 – C-4 automatic

VEHICLE WARRANTY NUMBER MODEL YEAR

5 – 1965*

* Ford made no distinction between the early ("1964 -1/2") and late (1965) models. Technically, there is no such thing as a 1964 -1/2.

ASSEMBLY PLANT

F – Dearborn, Michigan
R – San Jose, California
T – Metuchen, New Jersey

BODY SERIAL NUMBERS

07 – hardtop
08 – convertible
09 – fastback

ENGINE CODE

T – 200-cid 1-bbl. 6-cyl.
C – 289-cid 2-bbl. V-8
A – 289-cid 4-bbl. V-8
K – 289-cid 4-bbl. high-performance V-8

CONSECUTIVE UNIT NUMBER

Begins at 100001 at each factory

ENGINES

200-cid 1-bbl. Inline Six

Valves	overhead
Block	cast iron
Displacement	200 cid
Bore and stroke	3.68 x 3.13 inches
Compression ratio	9.2:1
Brake hp	120 at 4400 rpm
Main bearings	7
Valve lifters	hydraulic
Carburetor	Ford (Autolite) one-barrel Model C5OF-9510-E
Code	T

289-cid 2-bbl. V-8

Valves	overhead
Block	cast iron
Displacement	289 cid
Bore and stroke	4.00 x 2.87 inches
Compression ratio	9.3:1
Brake hp	200 at 4400 rpm
Main bearings	5
Valve lifters	hydraulic
Carburetor	Ford (Autolite) two-barrel Model C5ZF-9510-A
Code	C

1965 2+2 (FMC)

289-cid 4-bbl. V-8

Valves . . . . overhead
Block . . . . cast iron
Displacement. . . . . 289 cid
Bore and stroke. . . . . 4.00 x 2.87 inches
Compression ratio 10.0:1
Brake hp . . . . 225 at 4800 rpm
Main bearings 5
Valve lifters. hydraulic
Carburetor Ford (Autolite) four-barrel Model C5ZF-9510-C
Code . . . . A

289-cid 4-bbl. High-Performance V-8

Valves . . . . overhead
Block . . . . cast iron
Displacement. . . . . 289 cid
Bore and stroke . . . . 4.00 x 2.87 inches
Compression ratio 10.5:1
Brake hp . . . . 271 at 6000 rpm
Main bearings 5
Valve lifters . . . . solid
Carburetor . Ford (Autolite) four-barrel Model C4OF-9510-AL
Code . . . . K

CHASSIS

Wheelbase . . . . 108 inches
Overall length . . . . 181.6 inches
Tires . . . . (V-8) 7.00 x 13 four-ply tubeless blackwalls
(high-performance 289 V-8) 7.00 x 14 four-ply tubeless blackwall
. . . (other models) 6.50 x 13 four-ply tubeless blackwall

OPTIONS LIST

Accent Group. . . . . (hardtop and convertible) $27.70
. . . . (fastback) $14.20
Ford air conditioner $283.20
Heavy-duty battery $7.60
Front disc brakes $58.00
Full-length center console. $51.50
Console for use with air conditioning $32.20
Equa-Lock limited slip differential. $42.50
California-type closed emissions system $5.30
Challenger V-8 . . . . $108.00
Challenger four-barrel V-8 engine $162.00
Challenger high-performance four-barrel V-8
   (including Handling Package and 6.95 x 14 nylon tires) $442.60
Early year only, 260-cid V-8 . . . . $75.00
Emergency flashers. $19.60
Tinted glass with banded windshield $30.90
Banded, tinted windshield only $21.55
Back-up lights $10.70
Rocker panel moldings. . . . . (except fastback) $16.10

Power brakes $43.20
Power steering $86.30
Power convertible top $54.10
Push-button radio with antenna $58.50
Rally-Pac instrumentation with clock and tachometer $70.80
Deluxe retractable front seat safety belts. $7.55
Special Handling Package . (with 200- or 225-hp V-8) $31.30
Padded sun visors $5.70
Cruise-O-Matic transmission . . . . (with six) $179.80
. . . . (with 200- and 225-hp V-8s) $189.60
Four-speed manual transmission . . . . . . (with six) $115.90
. . . . (with V-8) $188.00
Hardtop vinyl roof. $75.80
Visibility Group . . . (includes remote-control mirror, day/nite
   mirror, two-speed electric wipers and windshield washers)
   $36.00
Wheel covers with simulated knock-off hubs. $18.20
Wire wheel covers, 14 inch $45.80
Styled steel wheels, 14 inch $122.30
Size 6.50 x 13 whitewalls . . . . (with six) $33.90
Size 6.95 x 14 tires . . . . (blackwall with six) $7.40
. . . . (whitewall with six) $41.30
   (whitewall with V-8s, except high-performance type) $33.90
   (black nylon, except with high-performance V-8) $15.80
   (Red Band nylon with V-8s except high-performance
      V-8) $49.60
   (Black nylon or white sidewall nylon with high-
      performance V-8) no charge

NOTE: The MagicAire heater ($32.20 credit) and front seat belts ($11 credit) were "delete options."

OPTION POPULARITY

Automatic transmission 53.6%
Four-speed manual transmission. 14.5%
V-8 engines. 64.4%
K-code high-performance V-8 . . . . 1.3%
Six-cylinder engine 35.6%
Radio 79.9%
Heater 98.9%
Power steering 24.9%
Bucket seats 97%
Front seat safety belts 100%
White sidewall tires 83.6%
Windshield washers 47.3%
Tinted windshields 22.4%
Tinted glass 9%
Back-up lights 38.6%
Air conditioning 9.1%
Dual exhaust 3.9%
Limited-slip differential 2%

1965 MUSTANG PRODUCTION CHART

Model	Doors/Body/Seating	Factory Price	Shipping Weight	Prod. Total
07	2/hardtop/4	$2372	2465	409,260
09	2/fastback/4	$2589	2515	77,079
08	2/convertible/4	$2614	2650	73,112

NOTE 1: Total model year output was 559,451 units. This figure includes 5,776 luxury fastbacks; 22,232 luxury hardtops; 14,905 bench seat-equipped hardtops; 5,338 luxury convertibles and 2,111 convertibles equipped with bench seats.

NOTE 2: In figures rounded off to the nearest 100 units, the total included 198,900 sixes and 360,600 V-8s.

1966 2+2
Owner: Steve Markham

1966

"What do you do after you build a million Mustangs? Start on the second million!" joked an advertisement in 1966. This campaign best illustrates the enviable position in which Ford found itself concerning the second full year of Mustang production.

The Mustang continued to sell like hotcakes, in spite (or maybe because) of only minor restyling in the trim department. A revised instrument panel was designed to look less like the Falcon's. The grille retained its now-familiar shape, but had the Mustang horse emblem running in a floating "corral" with a background of horizontal metal strips. The 1966 side cove received more ornate trim with what many describe as a "three-toothed comb."

To spread the word about its successful offspring, Ford ran a beautiful three-panel advertisement in many popular magazines that trumpeted "One million Mustangs in two years!" The ads also noted the three best-selling new cars of all-time were all Fords: the Model A, the Falcon, and the Mustang. What the ads didn't mention was a slight price increase, $44 for the hardtop, $18 for the 2+2, and $49 for the convertible due to a 3.7 percent cost of living increase. When interest rates jumped to a record 5.5 percent, Americans' purchasing power went downward a full percent. Car sales, zooming at the start of the season, fell drastically in the second half of the year. This, combined with a shortage of V-8 engines, contributed to a sales push for the cheaper, more efficient six-cylinder Mustangs.

Ford's clever ad campaigns featured headlines such as "Six and the single girl" and "Now don't forget to wave when you pass your gas station." Ford's quick reaction to the war-weakened economy kept Mustang sales strong. Buyers received a personalized nameplate for purchasing any Mustang during the "Millionth Mustang Sale" promotion. There was also a discounted price on a specially-equipped Limited Edition Mustang with the 200-cid six, special wheel-covers, a distinctive accent stripe, a center console, an engine decal, and a chromed air cleaner.

Walter Mitty ads continued for 1966, such as one showing a "harried accountant" who changed his lifestyle to that of a relaxed-looking convertible owner through the purchase of a red Mustang ragtop. Another promotion offered a motorized Mustang GT toy car, which was available from Ford dealers for $4.95. Ford even took out a full-page ad showing a young boy pushing the car under his Christmas tree.

1966 was the first year of federally mandated safety standards and all Fords included front and rear seat belts; padded instrument panel; emergency flashers; electric wipers; and windshield washers as standard equipment. In addition, the list of regular Mustang features was comprised of the following: front bucket seats; pleated vinyl upholstery and interior trim; Sports-type steering wheel; five-dial instrument cluster; full carpeting; heater and defroster; left-hand door outside rearview mirror; back-up lamps; door courtesy lights; rocker panel moldings; full wheel covers; three-speed manual transmission with floor lever control; and 200-cid 120-hp six-cylinder engine. The fastback coupe also came with special Silent-Flo ventilation, and the base V-8 was the 200-hp version of the 289-cid engine.

Mustang was the third best-selling individual nameplate in the American industry, an outstanding achievement for a car only three model-years old. Despite the slowing economy, production of Mustangs peaked at 607,568 in 1966. Henry Ford II was Ford Motor Co. board chairman and Arjay Miller was the president. M.S. McLaughlin who held the titles of vice-president and general manager headed the Ford Division, which was actually responsible for Mustang sales.

DATA PLATE DECODING

The Vehicle Identification Number is stamped on an aluminum tab on the instrument panel, viewable through windshield. The warranty number was at the top left-hand corner of the warranty plate (mounted on the driver's door). The data on the upper row of codes (body code, color code, trim code, etc.) was a narrow, unfinished band that crossed the data plate, horizontally, nearly at its center.

VEHICLE WARRANTY NUMBER
MODEL YEAR

6 – 1966

ASSEMBLY PLANT

F – Dearborn, Michigan
R – San Jose, California
T – Metuchen, New Jersey

BODY SERIAL NUMBERS

07 – hardtop
08 – convertible
09 – fastback

ENGINE CODE

T – 200-cid 1-bbl. 6-cyl.
C – 289-cid 2-bbl. V-8
A – 289-cid 4-bbl. V-8
K – 289-cid 4-bbl. high-performance V-8

CONSECUTIVE UNIT NUMBER

Begins at 100001 at each factory

CODE NUMBERS
BODY CODE

63A – fastback
63B – fastback, luxury
65A – hardtop coupe
65B – hardtop coupe, luxury
65C – hardtop coupe, bench seats
76A – convertible
76B – convertible, luxury
76C – convertible, bench seats

1966 luxury interior, optional air conditioner with console

1966 A-code 289/4V V-8

1966 luxury interior

1966 luxury interior, folding rear seat, up

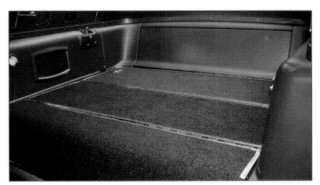

1966 luxury interior, folding rear seat, down

PAINT CODE

A	Raven Black	U	Tahoe Turquoise
F	Arcadian Blue	V	Emberglo
H	Sahara Beige	X	Vintage Burgundy
K	Nightmist Blue	Y	Silver Blue
M	Wimbledon White	Z	Sauterne Gold
P	Antique Bronze	4	Silver Frost
R	Ivy Green Metallic	5	Signal Flare Red
T	Candyapple Red	8	Springtime Yellow

ASSEMBLY DATE CODE

The next group of symbols consisted of two numbers and a letter, which represent the assembly date code. The numbers give the day (i.e.: "01" = first day) and the letter designates month of year, following normal progression (i.e.: "A" = January; "B" = February, etc.), except that the letters "I" and "O" are skipped.

AXLE RATIO CODES*

1/A – 3.00:1
2/B – 2.83:1
3/C – 3.20:1
5/E – 3.50:1

6/F – 2.80:1
8/H – 3.89:1
9/I – 4.11:1

* number indicates conventional axle/letter denotes limited-slip unit

TRANSMISSION CODE

1 – 3-speed manual
5 – 4-speed manual
6 – C-4 automatic

ENGINES

200-cid 1-bbl. Inline Six

Valves . . . . overhead
Block . . . . cast iron
Displacement . . . . 200 cid
Bore and stroke . . . . 3.68 x 3.13 inches
Compression ratio 9.2:1
Brake hp . . . . 120 at 4400 rpm
Main bearings 7
Valve lifters . . . . hydraulic
Carburetor Ford (Autolite) one-barrel Model C6OF-9510-AD
Code . . . . T

289-cid 2-bbl. V-8

Valves . . . . overhead
Block . . . . cast iron
Displacement . . . . 289 cid
Bore and stroke . . . . 4.00 x 2.87 inches

Compression ratio 9.3:1
Brake hp . . . . 200 at 4400 rpm
Main bearings 5
Valve lifters . . . . hydraulic
Carburetor. Ford (Autolite) two-barrel Model C6DF-9510-A
Code C

289-cid 4-bbl. V-8

Valves . . . . overhead
Block . . . . cast iron
Displacement . . . . 289 cid
Bore and stroke . . . . 4.00 x 2.87 inches
Compression ratio 10.1:1
Brake hp . . . . 225 at 4800 rpm
Main bearings 5
Valve lifters . . . . hydraulic
Carburetor Ford (Autolite) four-barrel Model C6ZF-9510-A
Code . . . . A

289-cid 4-bbl. High-Performance V-8

Valves . . . . overhead
Block . . . . cast iron
Displacement . . . . 289 cid
Bore and stroke . . . . 4.00 x 2.87 inches
Compression ratio 10.5:1
Brake hp . . . . 271 at 6000 rpm
Main bearings 5
Valve lifters . . . . solid
Carburetor Ford (Autolite) four-barrel Model C6OF-9510-C
Code . . . . K

CHASSIS

Wheelbase . . . . 108 inches
Overall length . . . . 181.6 inches
Tires . . . . 6.95 x 14 four-ply tubeless blackwall
(high-performance 289 V-8) 7.00 x 14 four-ply tubeless blackwall

OPTIONS LIST

Accent striping . . . . (less rear ornamentation) $13.90
Interior Décor Group (includes special interior trim, deluxe woodgrain steering wheel, rear window door courtesy light and pistol-grip door handle) $94.13
Ford air conditioner $310.90
Heavy-duty battery $7.44
Front disc brakes . . . . (with V-8 only) $56.77
Full-length center console $50.41
Full-width front seat with armrest
. . . . (for styles 65A, 76A only) $24.42

1966 hardtop (FMC)

**1966 convertible
Owner: Lenny Weiss**

Console for use with air conditioning $31.52
Limited-slip differential. $41.60
Closed crankcase emissions system
. . . . (except with high-performance V-8) $519.00
Exhaust emissions control system
. . . . (except with high-performance V-8) $45.45
GT Equipment Group
(with high-performance V-8 only, includes dual exhaust;
fog lamps; special ornamentation; disc brakes; GT rac-
ing stripes; and Handling Package components) $152.20
Challenger V-8 . . . . $105.63
Challenger four-barrel V-8 engine $158.48
Challenger high-performance four-barrel V-8
. . . . (in standard Mustang) $433.55
. . . . (in Mustang GT) $381.97
Tinted glass with banded windshield $30.25
Banded, tinted windshield only $21.09
Two-speed electric windshield wipers $12.95
Rear deck luggage rack . . . . (except fastback) $32.44
Power brakes $42.29
Power steering $84.47
Power convertible top $52.95
Push-button radio with antenna $57.51
Stereo tape player . . . . (radio mandatory) $128.49
Rally-Pac instrumentation with clock and tachometer $69.30
Deluxe retractable front seat safety belts and warning lamp $14.53
Deluxe steering wheel with simulated woodgrain. . . $31.52
Special Handling Package . (with 200- or 225-hp V-8) $30.84
Cruise-O-Matic transmission . . . . (with six) $175.80
. . . . (with 200- and 225-hp V-8s) $185.39
. . . . (with 271-hp V-8) $216.27
Four-speed manual transmission . . . . . (with six) $113.45
. . . . (with V-8) $184.02
Hardtop vinyl roof. $74.36
Visibility Group . (includes remote-control mirror, day/nite
mirror, two-speed electric wipers and windshield
washers) $29.81
Wheel covers with simulated knock-off hubs. $19.48

Wire wheel covers, 14 inch $58.24
Styled steel wheels, 14 inch . . . . (V-8 models only) $93.84
Size 6.95 x 14 tires . . . . blackwall $15.67
. . . . whitewall $33.31
. . . . nylon whitewall $48.89
. . . Red Band nylon with V-8s except high-performance
V-8 $48.97
. . . . Black nylon or white sidewall nylon with
high-performance V-8 NO CHARGE

NOTE: The MagicAire heater ($45.45 credit) and front seat belts ($11 credit) were "delete options."
NOTE: Air conditioning, three-speed manual transmission, power steering and U.S. Royal tires not available in combination with high-performance V-8. Power brakes and accent striping not available with GT Equipment Group. Full-width front seat not available in cars with Interior Décor Group or Model 63A or cars with console options.

OPTION POPULARITY

Four-speed transmission. 7.1%
Automatic transmission 62.8%
V-8 engines. 58.3%
Radio 79.3%
Heater 98.8%
Power steering 28.9%
Power brakes 3.3%
Vinyl top 9.5%
Tinted windshield 29.1%
All tinted glass 7.3%
Disc brakes. 6.7%
Dual exhaust 5%
Limited-slip differential 2.6%
Non-glare inside rearview mirror 17.9%
Whitewall tires 85.3%
Air conditioning 9.5%

1966 MUSTANG PRODUCTION CHART

Model	Doors/Body/Seating	Factory Price	Shipping Weight	Prod. Total
07	2/hardtop/4	$2416	2488	499,751
09	2/fastback/4	$2607	2519	35,698
08	2/convertible/4	$2653	2650	72,119

NOTE 1: Total series output was 607,568 units. This figure included 7,889 luxury fastbacks; 55,938 luxury hardtops; 21,397 hardtops equipped with bench seats; 12,520 luxury convertibles and 3,190 convertibles equipped with bench seats.

1966 standard interior, optional air conditioner

1966 standard interior, door panel

1966 trunk

1967 2+2 GTA
Owner: David and Gina Goff

1967

The sneak attack Ford made with the Mustang's introduction gave the company a sales advantage that ran out in 1967. Competition that year came in the form of Chevrolet's Camaro, Pontiac's Firebird (introduced six months behind its sister Camaro), and Mercury's Mustang-based Cougar, among others. Ford responded to the knowledge of these upcoming pony cars with a first-ever redesign of the Mustang featuring a jazzy new body, a wider track for better road grip, a broader range of engines, and a longer options list.

Styling was similar to the original in its theme, but everything was larger. The grille featured a more pronounced opening. The feature lines on the side led to a bigger simulated air scoop. The taillights took the form of three vertical lenses on each side of a concave indentation panel, with a centrally located gas cap. Overall, the appearance was more muscular. The wheelbase was unchanged, but overall length grew by nearly two inches. Front and rear tread widths went up by 2.1 inches and overall width was 2.7 inches wider at 70.9 inches. Especially low and sleek was the new 2+2 fastback. The roofline had a clean, unbroken sweep rearward to a distinctive, concave rear panel. Functional air louvers in the roof rear quarters became thinner.

With competition on the way, Ford pulled no punches in the performance department, offering a big-block V-8 for 1967. The 390-cid 320-hp powerplant provided neck-snapping street performance and some dragstrip bragging rights for only $264. The small-bore/long-stroke engine was a member of the Ford "FE" family, introduced way back in 1958. Otherwise, all 1966 engines were carried over.

One interesting distinction was made in the form of a 1967-only GTA option—the "A" indicating an automatic transmission. A Tilt-Away steering wheel; built-in heater/air-conditioner; overhead console; Stereo-Sonic tape system; SelectShift automatic transmission that also could be shifted manually; bench seat; AM/FM radio; fingertip speed control; custom exterior trim group and front power disc brakes were all extra-cost options.

Ford ads helped convince potential buyers that the Mustang was still the best pony car for the dollar. "The Mustang Pledge," where owners promised not to brag too much about their new cars, was the theme that seemed to hit the hardest. One advertisement, headlined "Strike a blow for originality," showed a giant boxing glove with the galloping pony badge and a red hardtop, pushing the concept that Mustang was the lowest-priced car of its kind with bucket seats. Another advertisement, aimed at women, showed a blue car and a blonde taking the pledge. "I will not sell tickets to all the people who want to ride in my '67 Mustang," was among her promises. "Bred first ... to be first," was another slogan used in several color ads.

1967 optional styled steel wheel

Ford's attempts to reach a more money-conscious buyer produced the Sports Sprint in the spring of 1967. For a special price, Sports Sprint buyers got sporty hood vents with recessed turn indicators; whitewalls; full wheelcovers; bright rocker panel moldings; a chrome air cleaner; and a vinyl-covered shift lever if SelectShift Cruise-O-Matic transmission was ordered. In addition, Sports Sprint buyers were tempted with a special price on factory-installed SelectAire air conditioning. Available in hardtop and convertible styles, it was offered in a "Ford's better ideas for sale" promotion that pitched "1968 ideas at 1967 prices."

The slowing economy hurt sales figures for American cars across the board, even for the still-popular Mustang. Instead of selling nine million units industry-wide, final sales figures would actually fall by a million units from the previous year. Total production for 1967 was 472,121 units. Ford managed to increase V-8 production by 20 percent for the year and, at the same time, the special promotions boosted air conditioning installations to 16 percent, a 6.5 percent increase.

Mustang standard equipment included all Ford Motor Co. safety features plus front bucket seats, full carpeting, floor-mounted shifter, vinyl interior trim, heater, wheel covers and cigarette lighter. The fastback came with wheel covers, special emblems and rocker panel moldings.

Henry Ford II was chairman of Ford Motor Co. Mustang's creator, Lee Iacocca, was an executive vice-president in charge of North American Operations and was definitely on his way up the corporate ladder, thanks to the success of his pony car.

DATA PLATE DECODING

The Vehicle Identification Number is stamped on an aluminum tab on the instrument panel, viewable through windshield. The warranty number was at the top left-hand corner of the warranty plate (mounted on the driver's door). The data on the upper row of codes (body code, color code, trim code, etc.) was a narrow, unfinished band that crossed the data plate, horizontally, nearly at its center.

VEHICLE WARRANTY NUMBER
MODEL YEAR

7 – 1967

ASSEMBLY PLANT

F – Dearborn, Michigan
R – San Jose, California
T – Metuchen, New Jersey

BODY SERIAL NUMBERS

01 – hardtop
02 – convertible
03 – fastback

1967 GTA grille, auxiliary lights

1967 GTA badge

1967 luxury interior

1967 GTA, Exterior Decor Group hood

1967 luxury interior, folding rear seat, down

ENGINE CODE

T – 200-cid 1-bbl. 6-cyl.
C – 289-cid 2-bbl. V-8
A – 289-cid 4-bbl. V-8
K – 289-cid 4-bbl. high-performance V-8
S – 390-cid 4-bbl. V-8

CONSECUTIVE UNIT NUMBER

Begins at 100001 at each factory

CODE NUMBERS
BODY CODE

63A – fastback
63B – fastback, luxury
65A – hardtop coupe
65B – hardtop coupe, luxury
65C – hardtop coupe, bench seats
76A – convertible
76B – convertible, luxury
76C – convertible, bench seats

PAINT CODE

A	Raven Black	T	Candyapple Red
B	Frost Turquoise	U	Tahoe Turquoise
D	Acapulco Blue	V	Burnt Amber
E	Beige Mist	W	Clearwater Aqua
F	Arcadian Blue	X	Vintage Burgundy
H	Diamond Green	Y	Dark Moss Green
I	Lime Gold	Z	Sauterne Gold
K	Nightmist Blue	4	Silver Frost
M	Wimbledon White	6	Pebble Beige
N	Diamond Blue		Springtime Yellow
Q	Brittany Blue		Bright Yellow
S	Dusk Rose		

ASSEMBLY DATE CODE

The next group of symbols consisted of two numbers and a letter, which represent the assembly date code. The numbers give the day (i.e.: "01" = first day) and the letter designates month of year, following normal progression (i.e.: "A" = January; "B" = February, etc.), except that the letters "I" and "O" are skipped.

AXLE RATIO CODES*

0 – 2.79:1	4/D – 3.25:1
1/A – 3.00:1	5/E – 3.50:1
2 – 2.83:1	8/H – 3.89:1
3/C – 3.20:1	I – 4.11:1

* number indicates conventional axle/letter denotes limited-slip unit

TRANSMISSION CODE

1 – 3-speed manual
5 – 4-speed manual
U – C-6 automatic
W – C-4 automatic

ENGINES

200-cid 1-bbl. Inline Six

Valves . . . . overhead
Block . . . . cast iron
Displacement . . . . 200 cid
Bore and stroke. . . . . 3.68 x 3.13 inches
Compression ratio 9.2:1
Brake hp . . . . 120 at 4400 rpm
Main bearings 7
Valve lifters. . . . . hydraulic
Carburetor. . . . . Holley 1-bbl.
Code . . . . T

289-cid 2-bbl. V-8

Valves . . . . overhead
Block . . . . cast iron
Displacement . . . . 289 cid
Bore and stroke. . . . . 4.00 x 2.87 inches
Compression ratio 9.3:1
Brake hp . . . . 200 at 4400 rpm
Main bearings 5
Valve lifters. . . . . hydraulic
Carburetor. . . . . Holley 2-bbl.
Code C

289-cid 4-bbl. V-8

Valves . . . . overhead
Block . . . . cast iron
Displacement . . . . 289 cid
Bore and stroke. . . . . 4.00 x 2.87 inches
Compression ratio 9.8:1
Brake hp . . . . 225 at 4800 rpm
Main bearings 5
Valve lifters. . . . . hydraulic
Carburetor. . . . . Holley 4-bbl.
Code . . . . A

289-cid 4-bbl. High-Performance V-8

Valves . . . . overhead
Block . . . . cast iron
Displacement . . . . 289 cid
Bore and stroke. . . . . 4.00 x 2.87 inches
Compression ratio 10.5:1
Brake hp . . . . 271 at 6000 rpm
Main bearings 5
Valve lifters. . . . . solid
Carburetor. . . . . Holley 4-bbl.
Code . . . . K

390-cid 4-bbl. V-8

Valves . . . . overhead
Block . . . . cast iron

1967 luxury interior, door panel

Displacement . . . . 390 cid
Bore and stroke . . . . 4.05 x 3.78 inches
Compression ratio 10.5:1
Brake hp . . . . 320 at 4600 rpm
Main bearings 5
Valve lifters . . . . hydraulic
Carburetor . . . . Holley 4-bbl.
Code . . . . S

CHASSIS

Wheelbase . . . . 108 inches
Overall length . . . . 183.6 inches
Tires . . . . 6.95 x 14 four-ply tubeless blackwall

OPTIONS LIST

200-hp V-8 . . . . $106
225-hp V-8 . . . . $158
271-hp V-8, included with GT Equipment Group $434
320-hp V-8 . . . . $264
Cruise-O-Matic three-speed automatic transmission
. . . . (with six-cylinder) $188
. . . . (with 200-hp and 225-hp V-8s) $198
. . . . (with 271-hp and 320-hp V-8s) $232
Four-speed manual transmission
. . . . (with six-cylinder or 225-hp V-8) $184
. . . . (with other V-8s) $233
Heavy-duty three-speed manual, required with
390-cid V-8 . . . . $79
Power front disc brakes $65
Power steering $84
Power top, convertible $53
GT Equipment Group, V-8s only $205
Limited-slip differential $42
Competition Handling Package, with GT Group only . . $62
Styled steel wheels, 2+2 . . . . $94
. . . . (other models) $115
Tinted windows and windshield $30
Convenience control panel $40
Fingertip speed control, V-8 and Cruise-O-Matic required $71

Remote-control left door mirror, standard 2+2 . . . . . . $10
Safety-glass rear window, convertible $32
Select-Aire conditioning $356
Push-button AM radio $58
Push-button AM/FM radio $134
Stereo-Sonic tape system, AM radio required $128
"Sport Deck" option with folding rear seat and access door
for 2+2 . . . . $65
Full-width front seat, not available with 2+2 . . . . . . $24
Tilt-Away steering wheel $60
Deck lid luggage rack not available on 2+2 . . . . $32
Comfort-weave vinyl trim, not available on convertible $25
Center console, radio required $50
Deluxe steering wheel $32
Exterior Decor Group $39
Lower back panel grille $19
Interior Decor Group for convertible $95
. . . . (for other models) $108
Two-tone paint, lower back grille $13
Accent stripe $14
Vinyl roof, hardtop $74
Wheel covers, standard on 2+2 . . . . $21
Wire wheel covers, 2+2 . . . . $58
. . . . (other models) $80
Typical whitewall tire option $33
Rocker panel moldings, standard on 2+2 . . . . $16
Magic-Aire heater delete option . . . . $32 credit

1967 convertible (FMC)

1967 hardtop (PH)

1967 convertible (FMC)

1967 MUSTANG PRODUCTION CHART

Model	Doors/Body/Seating	Factory Price	Shipping Weight	Prod. Total
01	2/hardtop/4	$2461	2578	356,271
02	2/fastback/4	$2592	2605	71,042
03	2/convertible/4	$2698	2738	44,808

NOTE 1: Total series output was 472,121 units including both sixes and V-8s.
NOTE 2: Series output includes 22,228 luxury hardtops; 8,190 hardtops with bench seats; 17,391 luxury fastbacks; 4,848 luxury convertibles and 1,209 convertibles equipped with bench seats.
NOTE 3: In figures rounded off to the nearest 100, the model year output of 1967 Mustangs included 141,500 sixes and 330,600 V-8s.

1968 convertible T-5
Owner: Johnnie and Rachel Garner

1968

There were no major styling changes for 1968. Under the hood, however, came a midyear offering that changed the Mustang from sporty pony car to dragstrip terror—the 428-cid 335-hp V-8! Other new engines included a 302-cid V-8 rated at 230 hp when equipped with a four-barrel carburetor and 220 hp when wearing a two-barrel. A 390-cid V-8 with 325 hp was a new "FE" family engine offered in the Mustang for 1968. The 200-cid six and base 289-cid V-8 were standard, but their ratings dropped to 115 and 195 hp, respectively.

Bucket seats, a floor-mounted stick, a sports steering wheel, and rich, loop-pile carpeting remained standard equipment. What few changes there were included a front end with the Mustang emblem "floating" in the grille; script-style (instead of block letter) Mustang body side nameplates; and cleaner-looking bright metal trim on the cove (replacing the previous "cheese graters"). There was a new two-tone hood that predicted the more radical coloring to come on the 1969 Mach 1s and Bosses. Despite minimal changes in the product, prices rose substantially, averaging about $140 more per model.

From the outside, the most obvious benefit to be had by ordering the $147 GT option was a choice of stripes—either the rocker panel type or a reflecting "C" stripe. The latter widened along the ridge of the front fender and ran across the door, to the upper rear body quarter. From there, it turned down, around the sculptured depression ahead of the rear wheel, and tapered forward, along the lower body to about the mid-point of the door.

The GT package also included auxiliary lights in the grille, a GT gas cap, and GT wheelcovers. On the 1968 Mustang, the extra lights no longer had a bar separating them from the corral in the grille. Front disc brakes were usually extra-cost, but were standard when big-block V-8s were ordered. A total of 17,458 GTs were made in 1968.

A very unusual package was promoted by West Coast Ford dealers in 1968—the Shelby-influenced GT/CS California Special. Available only in coupe form, the GT/CS included a Shelby-style decklid with a spoiler, sequential taillights, and a blacked-out grille (minus Mustang identification). Wheelcovers were the same ones used on 1968 GTs, but without GT identification. About 5000 Mustangs were produced with this package, although a similar High Country Special was sold in smaller numbers in Colorado.

As if to show that Ford was a company in tune with America's young folks and their various movements, ads invited 1968 car shoppers to "Turn yourself on, switch your style and show a new face in the most exciting car on the American road," in reference to the Mustang. One series of ads stressed a "Great Original" theme, highlighting the Mustang's role as America's original pony car. Still another urged customers to "Get hip to the great transformer ... Mustang makes dull people interesting, interesting people absolutely fascinating!" To appeal to its non-hip buyers, Ford told of the apocryphal Sidney, a white-shirt-and-tie type who spent his Sundays "seashelling at the seashore" before purchasing a red Mustang 2+2. We then see Sidney being "transformed" into a lifeguard with three bathing beauties clinging to his muscular arms.

While the Mustang was still the best-selling pony car in America, it slipped from second place in domestic auto production in 1965 to seventh palce in 1968. A 60-day strike against Ford from late September to late November of 1967 had a negative effect on Mustang sales and production.

DATA PLATE DECODING

The Vehicle Identification Number is stamped on an aluminum tab on the instrument panel, viewable through windshield. The warranty number was at the top left-hand corner of the warranty plate (mounted on the driver's door). The data on the upper row of codes (body code, color code, trim code, etc.) was a narrow, unfinished band that crossed the data plate, horizontally, nearly at its center.

VEHICLE WARRANTY NUMBER
MODEL YEAR

8 – 1968

ASSEMBLY PLANT

F – Dearborn, Michigan
R – San Jose, California
T – Metuchen, New Jersey

BODY SERIAL NUMBERS

01 – hardtop
02 – fastback
03 – convertible

ENGINE CODE

T – 200-cid 1-bbl. 6-cyl.
C – 289-cid 2-bbl. V-8
F – 302-cid 2-bbl. V-8
J – 302-cid 4-bbl. V-8
X – 390-cid 2-bbl. V-8
S – 390-cid 4-bbl. V-8
R – 428-cid 4-bbl. V-8

CONSECUTIVE UNIT NUMBER

Begins at 100001 at each factory

CODE NUMBERS
BODY CODE

63A – fastback
63B – fastback, luxury
63C – fastback, bench seats
63D – fastback, bench seats, luxury
65A – hardtop coupe
65B – hardtop coupe, luxury
65C – hardtop coupe, bench seats
65D – hardtop coupe, bench seats, luxury
76A – convertible
76B – convertible, luxury

PAINT CODE

A   Raven Black
B   Royal Maroon
D   Acapulco Blue
F   Gulfstream Aqua
I   Lime Gold
M   Wimbledon White
N   Diamond Blue
O   Seafoam Green
Q   Brittany Blue
R   Highland Green
T   Candyapple Red
U   Tahoe Turquoise
W   Meadowlark
     Yellow
X   Presidential Blue
Y   Sunlit Gold
6   Pebble Beige

**1968 standard
wheel cover**

1968 convertible T-5

1968 T-5 emblem

1968 grille

1968 fuel filler cap

ASSEMBLY DATE CODE

The next group of symbols consisted of two numbers and a letter, which represent the assembly date code. The numbers give the day (i.e.: "01" = first day) and the letter designates month of year, following normal progression (i.e.: "A" = January; "B" = February, etc.), except that the letters "I" and "O" are skipped.

AXLE RATIO CODES*

1 – 2.75:1	6/F – 3.20:1
2 – 2.79:1	7/G – 3.25:1
4 – 2.83:1	8/H – 3.50:1
5/E – 3.00:1	

* number indicates conventional axle/letter denotes limited-slip unit

TRANSMISSION CODE

1 – 3-speed manual	U – C-6 automatic
5 – 4-speed manual	W – C-4 automatic
6 – 4-speed manual	

ENGINES

200-cid 1-bbl. Inline Six

Valves . . . . overhead
Block . . . . cast iron
Displacement . . . . 200 cid
Bore and stroke . . . . 3.68 x 3.13 inches
Compression ratio 8.8:1
Brake hp . . . . 115 at 3800 rpm
Main bearings 7
Valve lifters . . . . hydraulic
Carburetor . . . . Autolite Model C8OF-9510-E 1-bbl.
Code . . . . T

289-cid 2-bbl. V-8

Valves . . . . overhead
Block . . . . cast iron
Displacement . . . . 289 cid
Bore and stroke . . . . 4.00 x 2.87 inches
Compression ratio 8.7:1
Brake hp . . . . 195 at 4600 rpm
Main bearings 5
Valve lifters . . . . hydraulic
Carburetor . . . . Autolite Model C8AF-9510-AF 2-bbl.
Code C

302-cid 2-bbl. V-8

Valves . . . . overhead
Block . . . . cast iron
Displacement . . . . 302 cid
Bore and stroke . . . . 4.00 x 3.00 inches

Brake hp 220
Main bearings 5
Valve lifters . . . . hydraulic
Carburetor . . . . Motorcraft 2-bbl.
Code . . . . F

302-cid 4-bbl. V-8

Valves . . . . overhead
Block . . . . cast iron
Displacement . . . . 302 cid
Bore and stroke . . . . 4.00 x 3.00 inches
Compression ratio 10.0:1
Brake hp . . . . 230 at 4800 rpm
Main bearings 5
Valve lifters . . . . hydraulic
Carburetor . . . . Motorcraft 4-bbl.
Code . . . . J

390-cid 2-bbl. V-8

Valves . . . . overhead
Block . . . . cast iron
Displacement . . . . 390 cid
Bore and stroke . . . . 4.05 x 3.78 inches
Compression ratio 10.5:1
Main bearings 5
Valve lifters . . . . hydraulic
Carburetor . . . . Holley 2-bbl.
Code X

390-cid 4-bbl. V-8

Valves . . . . overhead
Block . . . . cast iron
Displacement . . . . 390 cid
Bore and stroke . . . . 4.05 x 3.78 inches
Compression ratio 10.5:1
Brake hp . . . . 325 at 4800 rpm
Main bearings 5
Valve lifters . . . . hydraulic
Carburetor . . . . Holley 4-bbl.
Code . . . . S

428-cid 4-bbl. Cobra Jet V-8

Valves . . . . overhead
Block . . . . cast iron
Displacement . . . . 428 cid
Bore and stroke . . . . 4.13 x 3.98 inches
Compression ratio 10.7:1
Brake hp . . . . 335 at 5600 rpm
Main bearings 5
Valve lifters . . . . hydraulic
Carburetor . . . . Holley 4-bbl.
Code . . . . R

1968 T-code 200/1V inline six

1968 standard interior

CHASSIS

Wheelbase . . . . 108 inches
Overall length . . . . 183.6 inches
Tires . . . . 6.95 x 14 four-ply tubeless blackwall
 (E70-14 four-ply tubeless blackwall, with Wide-Oval
 Sport tire option)

OPTION LIST

289 cid/195 hp two-barrel V-8 . . . . $106
302 cid/230 hp four-barrel V-8 . . . . $172
390 cid/325 hp four-barrel V-8 . . . . $158
428 cid/335 hp four-barrel Cobra-Jet V-8 . . . . $245
SelectShift Cruise-O-Matic three-speed automatic
 . . . . (with six-cylinder) $19
 . . . . (with 289 V-8) $201
 . . . . (with 390 V-8) $233
Four-speed manual, not available with six-cylinder
 . . . . (with 289 V-8) $184
 . . . . (with 390 V-8) $233
Power front disc brakes, V-8s only, required with 390 V-8
 or GT Equipment Group $54
Power steering $84
Power top, convertible $53
GT Equipment Group, 230-hp or 325-hp V-8s with power
 brakes not available with Sports Trim Group or optional wheel covers $147

Tachometer, V-8s only $54
Limited-slip differential, V-8s only $79
Glass backlight, convertible $39
Tinted glass $30
Convenience Group, console required with Select-Aire $32
Fingertip speed control, V-8 and SelectShift required . . $74
Remote-control left door mirror $10
Select-Aire conditioner $360
Push-button AM radio $360
AM/FM stereo radio $61
Stereo-Sonic Tape System, AM radio required $181
Sport deck rear seat, 2+2 only $65
Full-width front seat, hardtop and 2+2 only, not available
 with console $32
Tilt-Away steering wheel $66
Center console, radio required $54
Interior Decor Group
 (in convertibles and models with full-width front seat) $110
 . . . . (in others without full-width front seat) $124
Two-tone hood paint $19
Accent paint stripe $14
Vinyl roof, hardtop. $74
Wheel covers, not available with GT or V-8 Sports Trim
 Group $34
Whitewall tires. $33

1968 MUSTANG PRODUCTION CHART

Model	Doors/Body/Seating	Factory Price	Shipping Weight	Prod. Total
01	2/hardtop/4	$2602	635	249,447
02	2/fastback/4	$2712	659	42,325
03	2/convertible/4	$2814	2745	25,376

NOTE: Total series output was 317,148 units. This figure included 9,009 Deluxe hardtops; 6,113 hardtops equipped with bench seats; 7,661 Deluxe fastbacks; 256 fastbacks equipped with bench seats; 853 Deluxe hardtops equipped with bench seats and 3,339 Deluxe convertibles.

1968 2+2 GT (FMC)

1968 2+2 GT (FMC)

**Top: 1968 hardtop California Special
Above Left: 1968 optional styled
steel wheel
Above Right: 1968 California Special
side scoop**

**1969 SportsRoof Mach 1
Owner: Gene Eaton**

1969

In 1969, Ford reached the peak of its performance years with an array of engines and speed packages the likes of which Detroit is unlikely to offer ever again. (Some, like Mustang tuner extraordinaire Carroll Shelby, even felt that there were too many Ford-badged choices in the marketplace and that the overlap was detrimental to the company's identity.) No less than nine V-8 powerplants were available during the 1969-70 period, including an "economy" 302-cid unit, the awesome 302-cid Boss motor, a 351-cid Windsor, a 351-cid Cleveland, a final-year 390-cid, a 428-cid Cobra Jet, a 428-cid Super Cobra Jet, a 429-cid in "wedge head" form, and the ground-pounding 429-cid Boss plant. Ford's stable during this period included the Mach 1, GT, Boss 302, Boss 429, Shelby GT-350 and Shelby GT-500—all high-performance models built from the same basic platform.

The Mustang's proliferation of models in 1969 was a very General Motors-like strategy and may have reflected the influence Semon "Bunkie" Knudsen had on the Ford lineup. Knudsen, who became president of Ford Motor Company after resigning as a General Motors executive vice president, gained notoriety for his 11th-hour transformation of the 1957 Pontiac from an "old maid's" car into a youth-oriented machine, which he accomplished in a matter of weeks.

Knudsen was hired on February 6, 1968. While he didn't have enough time to change long-range product development for model year 1969, it's just about certain he went to work on the marketing thrust immediately. At Ford, part of his Mustang marketing strategy involved hiring GM designer Larry Shinoda

and turning him loose to create what became the racetrack-inspired 1969 Boss 302. Because Knudsen was personally fond of the fastback body style, it became the basis for a series of hot-performing "buzz bombs."

With such a variety of big-block V-8s, it is no surprise that the new-for-1969 Mustang was also larger than ever to accommodate such powerplants. The new Mustang wheelbase remained the same as previous ponies at 108 inches, but overall length grew by 3.8 inches. The Mustang's profile was sleeker than ever, beginning with a windshield more steeply raked than the 1968 model. Quad round headlamps were used for the first (and only) time on a production Mustang in 1969. The outer lenses were deeply recessed into the fender openings, while the inboard units were set into the grille ends.

The indented scoop (or cove) that had visually "pinched" the Mustang's waist since its introduction was missing from the 1969 design; instead, a feature line ran from the tip of the front fender to just behind the rear door seam. On convertibles and coupes, a rear-facing, non-functional air vent sat just in front of the rear wheel opening; fastbacks featured a backwards C-shaped scoop. The SportsRoof (formerly known as 2+2) had a 0.9-inch lower roofline than earlier fastbacks, and it gained a small rear window that abutted the door glass.

With so many dress-up packages in the lineup for the fastback and convertible, it was appropriate that the coupe receive its own special designation for 1969 in the form of the Grandé. It offered a vinyl roof, plush interior, deluxe two-spoke steering wheel, color-keyed racing mirrors, full wheel-covers, electric clock, bright exterior body moldings, dual outside paint stripes, and luxury foam bucket seats—all for only $231 above the normal hardtop with comparable equipment.

All body styles could be ordered with the $147 GT Equipment Group (when teamed with specific options). GT equipment was not available in combination with Grandé coupes, six-cylinder engines, or the base 302-cid V-8. Because it competed against other Ford offerings that year, only 4,973 Mustang GTs were sold in 1969. The base GT engine was a 351-cid Windsor V-8 with 250 horsepower. Mustangs ordered with the GT package also got special handling equipment, lower body racing stripes, dual exhausts, pin-type hood lock latches, simulated hood scoop with integral turn signal indicators (shaker scoop with the 428CJ Ram Air V-8), three-speed manual transmission, four-wheel drum brakes, glass-belted white sidewall tires, and styled steel wheels with Argent Silver trim and GT hubcaps.

What would become Ford's most popularly ordered performance upgrade, the Mach 1, was introduced in 1969. Available only on the SportsRoof body, the Mach 1 came standard with a matte black hood, simulated hood scoop, and exposed NASCAR-style hood lock pins, which could be deleted. A spoiler cost extra. A reflective side stripe and rear stripes carried the model designation just behind the front wheel arches, and above the chrome pop-up gas cap. Chrome styled steel wheels and chrome exhausts tips (when optional four-barrel carburetors were ordered) were other bright touches. Also featured were dual color-keyed racing mirrors, and a handling suspension. Mach 1s also had the fanciest interior appointments, with high-back bucket seats;

black carpets; a Rim-Blow steering wheel; center console; clock; sound-deadening insulation; and teakwood-grained trim on the doors, dash and console. Base engine was a 351-cid two-barrel Windsor V-8. This was essentially a stroked 302-cid Ford V-8 with raised deck height, which created a great street performance engine. Options included the 351-cid 290-hp four-barrel V-8 and a 390-cid 320-hp V-8.

"Mustang Mach 1—holder of 295 land speed records," proclaimed the 1969 *Performance Buyer's Digest*. "This is the one that Mickey Thompson started with. From its wide-oval, belted tires to its wind tunnel-designed SportsRoof, the word is 'go.'" The copy pointed out that the production car had "the same wind-splitting sheetmetal as the specially modified Mach 1 that screamed around Bonneville clocking over 155, hour after hour, to break some 295 USAC speed and endurance records."

The awesome Cobra Jet 428-cid V-8 engine introduced midway through the '68 season once again made an appearance on the Mustang option list. It was available with either the GT or Mach 1 package in Cobra Jet (CJ-428) or Super Cobra

1969 convertible

1969 folding rear seat

1969 Deluxe Decor Group interior

**1969 hardtop Grandé
Owner: Sam Dean**

1969 hardtop Grandé

Jet (SCJ-428) form. The base Cobra Jet generated 335 hp at 5200 rpm and 440 lbs.-ft. of torque at 3400 rpm, while the SCJ was the same engine with Ram Air induction, a hardened steel cast crankshaft, special "LeMans" connecting rods and improved balancing for drag racing. It had the same advertised horsepower but was, in reality, more powerful. After one dragstrip test, *Hot Rod* called a CJ-equipped Mustang "the fastest running pure stock in the history of man."

A total of 81.5 percent of 1969 Mustangs came equipped with V-8s. The other 19.5 percent contained two six-cylinder options, including a new 250-cid six with 155 hp. Automatic transmission installations ran just over 71 percent, but four-speed manual gearboxes (wide- or close-ratio) were found in nearly 11 percent. Power brakes were added to 31.5 percent of production and 66 percent featured power steering.

DATA PLATE DECODING

The Vehicle Identification Number is stamped on an aluminum tab on the instrument panel, viewable through windshield. The warranty number was at the top left-hand corner of the warranty plate (mounted on the driver's door). The data on the upper row of codes (body code, color code, trim code, etc.) was a narrow, unfinished band that crossed the data plate, horizontally, nearly at its center.

VEHICLE WARRANTY NUMBER
MODEL YEAR

9 – 1969

ASSEMBLY PLANT

F – Dearborn, Michigan
R – San Jose, California
T – Metuchen, New Jersey

BODY SERIAL NUMBERS

01 – hardtop
02 – fastback
03 – convertible

ENGINE CODE

T – 200-cid 1-bbl. 6-cyl.
L – 250-cid 1-bbl. 6-cyl.
F – 302-cid 2-bbl. V-8
G – 302-cid 4-bbl. V-8 (Boss)
H – 351-cid 2-bbl. V-8
M – 351-cid 4-bbl. V-8
S – 390-cid 4-bbl. V-8
Q – 428-cid 4-bbl. V-8 (Cobra Jet)
R – 428-cid 4-bbl. V-8 (Super Cobra Jet)
Z – 429-cid 4-bbl. V-8 (Boss)

CONSECUTIVE UNIT NUMBER

Begins at 100001 at each factory

CODE NUMBERS
BODY CODE

63A – fastback
63B – fastback, luxury
63C – fastback, Mach 1
65A – hardtop coupe
65B – hardtop coupe, luxury
65C – hardtop, bench seats
65D – hardtop coupe, bench seats, luxury
65E – hardtop coupe, Grandé
76A – convertible
76B – convertible, luxury

PAINT CODE

A	Raven Black	S	Champagne Gold
B	Royal Maroon	T	Candyapple Red
C	Black Jade	W	Meadowlark Yellow
D	Acapulco Blue	Y	Indian Fire Red
E	Aztec Aqua	2	New Lime
F	Gulfstream Aqua	3	Calypso Coral
I	Lime Gold	4	Silver Jade
M	Wimbledon White	6	Pastel Gray
P	Winter Blue		

ASSEMBLY DATE CODE

The next group of symbols consisted of two numbers and a letter, which represent the assembly date code. The numbers give the day (i.e.: "01" = first day) and the letter designates month of year, following normal progression (i.e.: "A" = January; "B" = February, etc.), except that the letters "I" and "O" are skipped.

AXLE RATIO CODES*

1/J – 2.50:1	8/Q – 3.20:1
2/K – 2.75:1	9/R – 3.25:1
3/L – 2.79:1	A/S – 3.50:1
4/M – 2.80:1	B/T – 3.07:1
5/N – 2.83:1	C/U – 3.08:1
6/O – 3.00:1	
7/P – 3.10:1	

* left character indicates conventional axle/right character denotes limited-slip unit

TRANSMISSION CODE

1 – 3-speed manual	U – C-6 automatic
5 – 4-speed manual	W – C-4 automatic
6 – 4-speed manual	X – FMX automatic

1969 hardtop (JH)

1969 Boss 302 (JH)

ENGINES

200-cid 1-bbl. Inline Six
Valves . . . . overhead
Block . . . . cast iron
Displacement . . . . 200 cid
Bore and stroke . . . . 3.68 x 3.13 inches
Compression ratio 8.8:1
Brake hp . . . . 115 at 3800 rpm
Main bearings 7
Valve lifters . . . . hydraulic
Carburetor . . . . Motorcraft 1-bbl.
Code . . . . T

250-cid 1-bbl. Inline Six
Valves . . . . overhead
Block . . . . cast iron
Displacement . . . . 250 cid
Bore and stroke . . . . 3.68 x 3.91 inches
Compression ratio 9.0:1
Brake hp . . . . 155 at 4400 rpm
Main bearings 7
Valve lifters . . . . hydraulic
Carburetor . . . . Motorcraft 1-bbl.
Code L

302-cid 2-bbl. V-8
Valves . . . . overhead
Block . . . . cast iron
Displacement . . . . 302 cid
Bore and stroke . . . . 4.00 x 3.00 inches
Compression ratio 9.5:1
Brake hp . . . . 220 at 4600 rpm
Main bearings 5
Valve lifters . . . . hydraulic
Carburetor . . . . Motorcraft 2-bbl.
Code . . . . F

302-cid 4-bbl. Boss V-8
Valves . . . . overhead
Block . . . . cast iron
Displacement . . . . 302 cid
Bore and stroke . . . . 4.00 x 3.00 inches
Compression ratio 10.5:1
Brake hp . . . . 290 at 5000 rpm
Main bearings 5
Valve lifters . . . . mechanical
Carburetor . . . . Holley 4-bbl.
Code . . . . G

351-cid 2-bbl. V-8
Valves . . . . overhead

351-cid (continued)
Block . . . . cast iron
Displacement . . . . 351 cid
Bore and stroke . . . . 4.00 x 3.50 inches
Compression ratio 9.5:1
Brake hp . . . . 250 at 4600 rpm
Main bearings 5
Valve lifters . . . . hydraulic
Carburetor . . . . Motorcraft 2-bbl.
Code . . . . H

351-cid 4-bbl. V-8
Valves . . . . overhead
Block . . . . cast iron
Displacement . . . . 351 cid
Bore and stroke . . . . 4.00 x 3.50 inches
Compression ratio 10.7:1
Brake hp . . . . 290 at 4800 rpm
Main bearings 5
Valve lifters . . . . hydraulic
Carburetor . . . . Motorcraft 4-bbl.
Code . . . . M

390-cid 4-bbl. V-8
Valves . . . . overhead
Block . . . . cast iron
Displacement . . . . 390 cid
Bore and stroke . . . . 4.05 x 3.78 inches
Compression ratio 10.5:1
Brake hp . . . . 320 at 4600 rpm
Main bearings 5
Valve lifters . . . . hydraulic
Carburetor . . . . Holley 4-bbl.
Code . . . . S

428-cid 4-bbl. Cobra Jet V-8
Valves . . . . overhead
Block . . . . cast iron
Displacement . . . . 428 cid
Bore and stroke . . . . 4.13 x 3.98 inches
Compression ratio 10.6:1
Brake hp . . . . 335 at 5200 rpm
Main bearings 5
Valve lifters . . . . hydraulic
Carburetor . . . . Holley 4-bbl.
Code . . . . Q

428-cid 4-bbl. Super Cobra Jet V-8
Valves . . . . overhead
Block . . . . cast iron
Displacement . . . . 428 cid
Bore and stroke . . . . 4.13 x 3.98 inches

1969 MUSTANG PRODUCTION CHART

Model	Doors/Body/Seating	Factory Price	Shipping Weight	Prod. Total
01 (65A-D)	2/hardtop/4	$2618/2723	2690	127,954
01 (65E)	2/hardtop Grandé/4	$2849/2954	2981	22,182
02 (63A-B)	2/fastback/4	$2618/2723	2713	61,980
02 (63C)	2/fastback Mach 1/4	$3122	3175	72,458
03 (76A-B)	2/convertible/4	$2832/2937	2800	14,746

NOTE 1: Total series output was 299,824 units.
NOTE 2: Data above slash for six/below slash for V-8.
NOTE 3: Series output included 5,210 Deluxe hardtops; 4,131 hardtops equipped with bench seats; 5,958 Deluxe fastbacks; 504 Deluxe hardtops equipped with bench seats; and 3,439 Deluxe convertibles.

Compression ratio 10.5:1
Brake hp . . . . 360 at 5400 rpm
Main bearings 5
Valve lifters. . . . . hydraulic
Carburetor. . . . . Holley 4-bbl.
Code . . . . R

429-cid 4-bbl. Boss V-8

Valves . . . . overhead
Block . . . . cast iron
Displacement . . . . 429 cid
Bore and stroke. . . . . 4.36 x 3.59 inches
Compression ratio 11.3:1
Brake hp . . . . 370 at 5600 rpm
Main bearings 5
Valve lifters. . . . . hydraulic
Carburetor. . . . . Holley 4-bbl.
Code . . . . Z

CHASSIS

Wheelbase . . . . 108 inches
Overall length . . . . 187.4 inches
Tires. . . . . C78-14 four-ply tubeless blackwall
. . . . (E78-14 four-ply on small V-8-equipped models)
. . . . (F70-14 four-ply on large V-8-equipped models)
. . . . (F60-15 Polyglas tires on Boss models)

OPTION LIST

302 cid/220 hp two-barrel V-8, not available in Mach 1 $105
351 cid/250 hp two-barrel V-8, standard in Mach 1
. . . . (in other models) $163
351 cid/290 hp four-barrel V-8 . . . . (in Mach 1) $26
. . . . (in other models) $189
390 cid/320 hp four-barrel V-8 . . . . (in Mach 1) $100
. . . . (in other models) $158
428 cid/335 hp four-barrel V-8 . . . . (in Mach 1) $224
. . . . (in other models) $288
428-cid four-barrel Cobra Jet V-8 including Ram Air
. . . . (in Mach 1) $357
. . . . (in other models) $421
SelectShift Cruise-O-Matic transmission
. . . . (six-cylinder engines) $191
. . . . (302 and 351 V-8s) $201
. . . . (390 and 428 V-8s) $222
Four-speed manual . . . . (302 and 351 V-8s) $205
. . . . (390 and 428 V-8s) $254
Power disc brakes, not available with 200-cid inline six $65
Power steering. $95
Power top convertible $53
GT Equipment Group, not available on Grandé or with six-
cylinder or 302-cid V-8 . . . . $147

Tachometer, V-8s only $54
Handling suspension, not available on Grandé or with six-
cylinders and 428 V-8s $31
Competition suspension, standard on Mach 1 and GT; 428
V-8 required $31
Glass backlight, convertible $39
Limited slip differential, 250 inline six and 302 V-8 . . . $42
Traction-Lok differential, not available on sixes and
302 V-8s $64
Intermittent windshield wipers $17
High-back front bucket seats, not available in Grandé . $85
Color-keyed dual racing mirrors, standard in Mach 1 and
Grandé $19
Power ventilation, not available with Select-Aire $40
Electric clock, standard in Mach 1 and Grandé $16
Tinted windows and windshield $32
Speed control, V-8 and automatic transmission required. $74
Remote-control left door mirror. $13
Select-Aire conditioner, not available with 200 inline six or
428 V-8 w/four-speed. $380
Push-button AM radio $61
AM/FM stereo radio $181
Stereo-Sonic tape system, AM radio required. $134
Rear seat speaker, hardtop and Grandé $13
Rear seat deck, Sportsroof and Mach 1. . . . . $97
Full-width front seat, hardtop, not available with console
. . . . $32
Tilt-Away steering wheel $66
RimBlow Deluxe steering wheel $36
Console $54
Interior Decor Group, not available on Mach 1 and Grandé
. . . . $101
. . . . (with dual racing mirrors) $88
Deluxe Interior Decor Group, Sportsroof and convertible
. . . . $133
. . . . (with dual racing mirrors) $120
Deluxe seat belts with reminder light. $16
Vinyl roof, hardtop. $84
Wheel covers, not available on Mach 1, Mustang GT or
Grandé. . . . . . (included with exterior Decor Group) $21
Wire wheel covers, not available with Mach 1 and Mustang
GT, standard on Grandé
. . . . (with Exterior Decor Group) $58
. . . . (without Exterior Decor Group) $80
Exterior Decor Group, not available on Mach 1 and Grandé,
. . . . $32
Chrome styled steel wheels, standard on Mach 1; not avail-
able on Grandé or with 200 inline six $117
. . . . (with GT Equipment Group) $78
. . . . (with Exterior Decor Group) $95
Adjustable head restraints, not available on Mach 1 . . . $17

1969 convertible (FMC)

1969 SportsRoof (FMC)

Ford was delighted to give birth to a set of twins in 1969—the ready-to-race Boss 302 and 429 were both built around state-of-the-art, high-performance powerplants.

The Boss 302's V-8 was the ultimate evolution of the 260- and 289-cid Mustang V-8 introduced in 1965, with special cylinder heads that gave it a performance advantage over the previous small-block Mustangs. These "Cleveland" heads (so called because of their similarity to those used on the 351-cid engine made in Ford's Cleveland, Ohio, foundry) used canted intake and exhaust valves that permitted the fitting of bigger ports and valves and a straighter flowing fuel/air mixture that gave better volumetric efficiency.

Boss 302 intake valves measured a massive 2.23 inches in 1969, and exhaust valves were 1.71 inches—incredibly large for a production-type small-block engine. "Semi-hemi" combustion chambers were also different from those of the earlier small-blocks, with an advanced wedge design that resembled the shape of the chambers in the Ford 427 racing engine. The camshaft had 290 degrees of duration for both valves and a .290-inch lift. The crankshaft, balanced both statically and dynamically (with the rods and pistons in place), was made of forged steel to stand up to high rpms. It was anchored in place by five main bearings, of which the three center units have four-bolt caps. Forged steel connecting rods were used. Other features included a high-rise, aluminum intake manifold with a single 780-cfm four-barrel Holley carburetor; pop-up type pistons; a dual-point distributor; a high-pressure oil pump; lightweight, stamped rocker arms; screw-in rocker arm studs and pushrod guide plates (with specially hardened pushrods); an oil pan windage baffle and screw-in freeze plugs.

After considering the car's target audience, Ford wisely chose to install only manual transmissions (there were two to choose from) in the Boss 302, with a floor-mounted Hurst shifter handling shifting chores. Surprisingly, the wide-ratio four-speed was best suited with the 302 for street performance and dragstrip use. The close-ratio option was better utilized for road racing.

According to published reports at the time, the Boss 302 outclassed "most of the world's big-engined musclecars." The Boss 302 was Ford's answer to the Camaro Z28 on the Sports Car Club of America's Trans-American racing circuit and a worthy competitor on the showroom floor. Others reported a slightly modified Boss 302 engine would keep increasing power clear up to 8000 rpm, which suggests that some owners were bypassing the rpm limiter that kicked in around 5800 rpm and randomly cut spark to the cylinders to keep the revs under about 6150 rpm. Clearly, Ford's peak horsepower rating of 290 at 5800 rpm was conservative, although it was convenient for advertising, as the Camaro Z28 advertised that number.

Three axle ratios were offered: a standard 3.50 non-locking version, plus the Traction-Lok 3.50 and 3.91. There was also a No-Spin axle available with a 4.30 ratio built by Detroit Automotive. To prevent buildup of stress points in the axle shafts, Ford installed fully machined units with larger axle shaft splines, an extra-strength cast nodular iron center section, and larger wheel seals.

Because it would be called upon to keep the Boss stuck to corners on the racetrack, the front suspension received high-rate (350 inch-pounds) springs, heavy-duty direct-acting Gabriel shock absorbers, and a special steel stabilizer bar with specifically calibrated rubber mounts. The Hotchkiss type rear suspension had 150 inch-pounds leaf springs and it used a staggered shock absorber arrangement. The left shock absorber was bolted behind the axle and the right one was ahead of the axle. Wheel hop, bounce and the tendency of the tires to break tread were substantially controlled with this setup. Ford also added a rear stabilizer bar for improved cornering. This induced a little oversteer, but helped keep the rear end from swaying.

The Boss 302 brake system included discs in the front and power assist. Power steering was available as an option to help with the quick 16:1 ratio—especially desirable with the wide F60-15 tires. Final details on the Boss 302 package included black tail lamp bezels; a black chrome backlight molding; black headlamp castings; color-keyed, dual square mirrors; a black-finished hood, rear decklid and lower back panel; dual exhausts; hub caps with trim rings; black tape identification on the front fender and front

spoiler; a 45-ampere battery; and a Space-Saver spare tire.

From the driver's seat, the Boss was still basic Mustang in layout, with circular gauges, dash lights to monitor oil pressure and electrical systems, and a tachometer. Two very desirable Boss options were an adjustable rear deck lid spoiler and rear window SportSlats. To qualify as a production model by Trans-Am racing rules, Ford was required to produce a minimum of 1,000 Boss 302 Mustangs; the car's popularity racked up 1,934 sales in 1969.

The 302's bigger brother, the Boss 429, was born because Ford had still another engine it wanted to place into competition—this time on the NASCAR circuit. The decision was made to install the new-for-1969 429-cid semi-hemi big-block in the popular Mustang platform after predictions that it would be easier to sell 500 such models than a Torino-based supercar. Kar Kraft, an aftermarket firm in Brighton, Michigan, was contracted to build Boss 429s. Since the Mustang's engine compartment was not designed to house such a wide powerplant, the job required a big shoehorn and a lot of suspension changes and chassis modifications.

Body alterations included engine bay bracing, inner wheel well sheetmetal work, and flared wheel housings (to accommodate a widened track and the use of seven-inch Magnum 500 wheel rims). The hood received a huge, functional scoop, and a special spoiler underlined the front bumper. Power steering and brakes, a Traction-Lok axle with 3.91 gears, and the Boss 302's rear spoiler were also included. All Boss 429s had the fancy Decor Group interior option, high-back bucket seats, deluxe seat belts, wood-trimmed dash and console treatment and Visibility Group option. Automatic transmission and air conditioning were not available, but the $4,932 price tag included all of the above.

Horsepower for the Boss 429 was advertised as 375, although real ratings were rumored to be much higher. A total of 1,358 Boss 429s were constructed during the 1969 calendar year. This included 857 of the 1969 models made in early 1969 and 499 1970 models built late in the summer.

For 1970, the Boss 302 package continued with minor changes, including the stock Mustang's revised front and rear styling, new Grabber paint colors, and a "hockey stick" striping treatment with the name "Boss 302" above and on the "blade" on the upper front fender. Wide 15x7-inch steel wheels with hubcaps and trim rings were standard, while the shaker hood was an option. High-back bucket seats were added to the standard features list. Smaller diameter valves and a new crankshaft were used in the small-block performance V-8 and most Boss 302s used finned aluminum valve covers. A rear sway bar was added to the suspension and the front one was thickened.

In its January 1970 edition, *Hot Rod* reported that the new Boss was "definitely the best handling car Ford has ever built." *Motor Trend* called the Boss Mustang, "The word of our time. Good, only better, fuller, rounder and more intense," praise that put the car even above competitors GTO, Road Runner and Chevelle. Not surprisingly, the practical-thinking *Consumer Guide* labeled it "uncomfortable at any speed over anything but the smoothest surface."

Unfortunately for performance fans, the passing of the Boss 302 at the end of 1970 marked the end of the high-compression, high-revving Detroit musclecars.

1969 Boss 302 (PH)

1970 Mach 1
Owners: Mike and Lori Rayburn

1970

After launching such a massive range of Mustang performance and cosmetic packages in 1969, it's understandable that only subtle changes to the Mustang's front and rear were the most obvious differences between the 1969 and 1970 models. On all 1970 Mustangs, single headlamps located inside a wider grille opening were flanked by simulated air intakes and the tail lamp housing was slightly restyled. Gone were the side-mounted fake air intakes to the rear of the door. The front fender-mounted reflector grew larger for 1970 and became a vertical strip above the bumper line.

Mach 1s featured the new front end, taillights recessed in a flat panel with honeycomb trim between them and ribbed aluminum rocker panel moldings (with big Mach 1 call-outs). A black-striped hood with standard fake scoop replaced the 1969's matte-black hood. Optional hood clips from 1969 were replaced with new twist-in pins, and a shaker hood scoop was available with the 351 V-8. A redesigned steering wheel was the big interior change. A larger rear stripe, larger rear call-out, mag-type hubcaps, wide 14x7-inch wheels, and bright oval exhaust tips were also new. Black-painted styled wheels were a no-cost option.

The GT package disappeared after 1969, but the stylish, coupe-only Grandé package was available again in 1970. The Boss twins once again set the standard for high-performance Mustangs, though for their final year of production.

The 1970 Mustang was a gradual continuation of the 1969 editions designed before Bunkie Knudsen arrived at Ford. Interestingly, Knudsen would not be at Ford long enough to see the 1970 Mustangs introduced. Chairman Henry Ford II never explained his August 1969 firing of Knudsen, although it was believed Ford II wanted to move away from musclecars and motorsports, which Knudsen favored. Others guessed that Knudsen had too rapidly built up a power base in an operation that preferred family-centralized power and perhaps tried to overstep the limits of his power too often.

Three executives initially replace Knudsen: Lee Iacocca became executive vice president and president of North American Operations; Robert L. Stevenson held the same titles for International Operations; and Robert J. Hampson was executive vice president and president of Non-Automotive Operations. Within a year, Iacocca would become Ford's overall president.

With new competition from the Dodge Challenger, plus totally redesigned Barracudas, Camaros and Firebirds, the Mustang lost around 100,000 sales in 1970. A total of 190,727 1970 Mustangs were built. Ford ceased its official racing activities late in the 1970 calendar year. Before getting out of racing, Ford captured the 1970 Trans-Am title with the Mustang.

DATA PLATE DECODING

The Vehicle Identification Number is stamped on an aluminum tab on the instrument panel, viewable through windshield. A vehicle certification label replaced the warranty plate in 1970. While it still gives much of the same information as before, it is found on the body side of where the driver's door closes.

VEHICLE WARRANTY NUMBER MODEL YEAR

0 – 1970

ASSEMBLY PLANT

F – Dearborn, Michigan
R – San Jose, California
T – Metuchen, New Jersey

BODY SERIAL NUMBERS

01 – hardtop
02 – fastback
03 – convertible
04 – Grandé
05 – Mach 1

ENGINE CODE

T – 200-cid 1-bbl. 6-cyl.
L – 250-cid 1-bbl. 6-cyl.
F – 302-cid 2-bbl. V-8
G – 302-cid 4-bbl. V-8 (Boss)
H – 351-cid 2-bbl. V-8
M – 351-cid 4-bbl. V-8
Q – 428-cid 4-bbl. V-8 (Cobra Jet)
R – 428-cid 4-bbl. V-8 (Super Cobra Jet)
Z – 429-cid 4-bbl. V-8 (Boss)

CONSECUTIVE UNIT NUMBER

Begins at 100001 at each factory

CODE NUMBERS
BODY CODE

63A – fastback
63B – fastback, luxury
63C – fastback, Mach 1
65A – hardtop coupe
65B – hardtop coupe, luxury
65C – hardtop coupe, bench seats
65E – hardtop coupe, Grandé
76A – convertible
76B – convertible, luxury

PAINT CODE

A	Raven Black	S	Medium Gold
C	Dark Ivy Green Metallic		Metallic
D	Yellow	T	Red
G	Medium Lime Metallic	U	Grabber Orange
J	Grabber Blue	Z	Grabber Green
K	Bright Gold Metallic	1	Calypso Coral
M	Wimbledon White	2	Light Ivy Yellow
N	Pastel Blue	6	Silver Blue
Q	Medium Blue Metallic		

1970 optional sports slats

1970 Mach 1 interior door panel

Left: 1970 Mach 1 interior
Right 1970 inboard light, fake scoop

1970 Shaker hood scoop

1970 hardtop (JH)

ASSEMBLY DATE CODE

The next group of symbols consisted of two numbers and a letter, which represent the assembly date code. The numbers give the day (i.e.: "01" = first day) and the letter designates month of year, following normal progression (i.e.: "A" = January; "B" = February, etc.), except that the letters "I" and "O" are skipped.

AXLE RATIO CODES*

0 – 2.50:1	8 – 3.20:1
2/K – 2.75:1	9/R – 3.25:1
3 – 2.79:1	A/S – 3.50:1
4/M – 2.80:1	B – 3.07:1
5 – 2.83:1	C – 3.08:1
6/O – 3.00:1	NA/V – 3.91:1
7 – 3.10:1	NA/W – 4.30:1

* left character indicates conventional axle/right character denotes limited-slip unit

TRANSMISSION CODE

1 – 3-speed manual
5 – 4-speed manual
6 – 4-speed manual
U – C-6 automatic
W – C-4 automatic
X – FMX automatic

ENGINES

200-cid 1-bbl. Inline Six
Valves . . . . .overhead
Block . . . . .cast iron
Displacement . . . . .200 cid
Bore and stroke . . . . .3.68 x 3.13 inches
Compression ratio 8.8:1
Brake hp . . . . .115 at 3800 rpm
Main bearings 7
Valve lifters . . . . .hydraulic
Carburetor . . . . .Motorcraft 1-bbl.
Code . . . . .T

250-cid 1-bbl. Inline Six
Valves . . . . .overhead
Block . . . . .cast iron
Displacement . . . . .250 cid
Bore and stroke . . . . .3.68 x 3.91 inches
Compression ratio 9.0:1
Brake hp . . . . .155 at 4400 rpm
Main bearings 7

1970 SportsRoof (JH)

Valve lifters . . . . .hydraulic
Carburetor . . . . .Motorcraft 1-bbl.
Code L

302-cid 2-bbl. V-8
Valves . . . . .overhead
Block . . . . .cast iron
Displacement . . . . .302 cid
Bore and stroke . . . . .4.00 x 3.00 inches
Compression ratio 9.5:1
Brake hp . . . . .220 at 4600 rpm
Main bearings 5
Valve lifters . . . . .hydraulic
Carburetor . . . . .Motorcraft 2-bbl.
Code . . . . .F

302-cid 4-bbl. Boss V-8
Valves . . . . .overhead
Block . . . . .cast iron
Displacement . . . . .302 cid
Bore and stroke . . . . .4.00 x 3.00 inches
Compression ratio 10.6:1
Brake hp . . . . .290 at 5800 rpm
Main bearings 5
Valve lifters . . . . .mechanical
Carburetor . . . . .Holley 4-bbl.
Code . . . . .G

351-cid 2-bbl. V-8
Valves . . . . .overhead
Block . . . . .cast iron
Displacement . . . . .351 cid
Bore and stroke . . . . .4.00 x 3.50 inches
Compression ratio 9.5:1
Brake hp . . . . .250 at 4600 rpm
Main bearings 5
Valve lifters . . . . .hydraulic
Carburetor . . . . .Motorcraft 2-bbl.
Code . . . . .H

351-cid 4-bbl. V-8
Valves . . . . .overhead
Block . . . . .cast iron
Displacement . . . . .351 cid
Bore and stroke . . . . .4.00 x 3.50 inches
Compression ratio 11.0:1
Brake hp . . . . .300 at 5400 rpm
Main bearings 5
Valve lifters . . . . .hydraulic
Carburetor . . . . .Motorcraft 4-bbl.
Code . . . . .M

428-cid 4-bbl. Cobra Jet V-8
Valves . . . . .overhead
Block . . . . .cast iron
Displacement . . . . .428 cid
Bore and stroke . . . . .4.13 x 3.98 inches
Compression ratio 10.6:1
Brake hp . . . . .335 at 5400 rpm
Main bearings 5
Valve lifters . . . . .hydraulic
Carburetor . . . . .Holley 4-bbl.
Code . . . . .Q

428-cid 4-bbl. Super Cobra Jet V-8

Valves . . . . .overhead
Block . . . . .cast iron
Displacement . . . . .428 cid
Bore and stroke . . . . .4.13 x 3.98 inches
Compression ratio 10.5:1
Brake hp .360 at 5400 rpm
Main bearings 5
Valve lifters . . . . .hydraulic
Carburetor . . . . .Holley 4-bbl.
Code . . . . .R

429-cid 4-bbl. Boss V-8

Valves . . . . .overhead
Block . . . . .cast iron
Displacement . . . . .429 cid
Bore and stroke . . . . .4.36 x 3.59 inches
Compression ratio 11.3:1
Brake hp .375 at 5600 rpm
Main bearings 5
Valve lifters . . . . .mechanical
Carburetor . . . . .Holley 4-bbl.
Code . . . . .Z

CHASSIS

Wheelbase . . . . .108 inches
Overall length . . . . .187.4 inches
Tires . . . . .C78-14 four-ply tubeless blackwall
. . . . . (E78-14 four-ply on small V-8-equipped models)
. . . . . (F70-14 four-ply on large V-8-equipped models)
. . . . . (F60-15 Polyglas tires on Boss models)

OPTION LIST

351 cid/250 hp V-8 . . . .(in Mach 1) standard
. . . .(in other Mustangs) $45
351 cid/300 hp V-8 . . . .(in Mach 1) $48
. . . .(in other Mustangs) $93
428 cid/335 hp Cobra Jet V-8 engine with Ram Air
   induction . . . .(in Mach 1) $376
. . . . (in other Mustangs) $421
Cruise-O-Matic automatic transmission $222
Four-speed manual transmission $205
Power steering $95
Power front disc brakes $65
Limited slip differential $43
Styled steel wheels $58
Magnum 500 chrome wheels $129
AM radio $61
AM/FM stereo radio $214
AM/8-track stereo $134
Center console $54
Tilt steering wheel $45
Exterior Decor Group $78
Vinyl roof $84
. . . . (on Grandé) $26
Wheel covers $26
Rocker panel moldings $16

1970 MUSTANG PRODUCTION CHART

Model	Doors/Body/Seating	Factory Price	Shipping Weight	Prod. Total
01 (65A-D)	2/hardtop/4	$2721/2822	2721/2923	82,569
01 (65E)	2/hardtop Grandé/4	$2926/3028	2806/3008	13,581
02 (63A-B)	2/fastback/4	$2771/2872	2745/2947	45,934
02 (63C)	2/fastback Mach 1/4	$3271	3240	40,970
03 (76A-B)	2/convertible/4	$3025/3126	2831/3033	7,673

NOTE 1: Total series output was 190,727.

1970 hardtop (FMC)

1970 Boss 429   Owner: Aaron Scott

1970 Boss 429

1970 Boss 429

1970 Z-code Boss 429/4V V-8

1970 Decor Group seat

Above: 1971 Mach 1, 429 SCJ V-8
Owner: Miles DeCoste
Right: 1971 optional SportsRoof
spoiler

1971

The 1971 Mustangs were completely restyled—a design that to this day remains the largest ever for the marque. Styling left little doubt that the cars were Mustangs, but they were lower, wider, and heavier than any previous models. A full-width grille, incorporating the headlights within its opening, was used, and the Mustang corral was again seen in the center.

Still built around the winning proportions of the 1965 model, the cars now looked like more muscular (or fatter, depending on your perspective) distant cousins to the original design. In this evolutionary step, some new features were apparent, such as the flatter roof shape of the fastback models and the "tunnel backlight" (basically a recessed rear window) built into hardtop coupes.

The 1971 Mustangs had a slightly longer wheelbase (109 inches) and gained 2.1 inches of length over the 1970 model. They measured 189.5 inches bumper-to-bumper, 7.1 inches more than the original 1965 model. They were also 3.0 inches wider than the 1970 Mustang and 6.8 inches wider than the 1965 version. Weights were up an average of 500 pounds from the previous year.

With our turn-of-the-millennium sensibilities and hindsight, it's difficult to understand how a car company could justify making a model bigger and heavier with each passing year. Remember, though, that in 1971 Ford was still happily building cars and engines around the unkept promise of eternally inexpensive fuel.

Ford's desire was to evolve the Mustang into a platform capable of creating a high-performance supercar or a luxurious and spacious daily transportation for sporty young families. Big-block power was nothing new to the Mustang line—

the 390-cid V-8 was a performance option as early as 1967—but in 1969 it took an outside company and a big shoehorn to wrap a Mustang around the Boss 429 engine. Marketers and engineers apparently saw this as a weakness of the 1969-70 models and sought to rectify the situation with an engine compartment big enough to handle any powerplant in the Ford family. Another perceived positive was that the longer body gave designers more precious inches to create passenger seating that was more comfortable than the original ponycar.

Unfortunately, Ford's timing and instincts proved to be slightly off. When this "fourth-generation" Mustang was in the planning stages (roughly 1968-70), car companies and the American public were willing partners in a horsepower escalation that seemed to have no end. By the time the all-new 1971 hit the showrooms, high insurance premiums and increasing government safety and emissions regulations were putting the brakes on all that enthusiasm.

Model distinctions were very similar to the previous car: hardtop, SportsRoof and convertible. The Grandé, Mach 1, and Boss models were back, however, a new Boss 351 replaced the Boss 302 and Boss 429. Its 330-hp 351-cid Cleveland engine became the Mustang's small-block, high-performance V-8.

The corral protecting the chrome pony inside returned to the center of the grille on standard models. An optional grille deleted the corral, but offered amber auxiliary lights imbedded in the honeycomb-textured surface. On these models, the galloping horse was depicted on a small tri-bar emblem in the grille's center. A chrome bumper and chrome fender and hood moldings were standard, except on Mach 1s and Boss 351s.

Standard equipment for Mustangs included color-keyed nylon carpeting; floor-mounted shift lever; high-back bucket seats; steel door guard rails; DirectAire ventilation; concealed wipers with cowl air inlets; a mini-console with ash tray; arm rests; courtesy lights; a cigar lighter; a heater and defroster; an all-vinyl interior; a glove box; the 250-cid six; E78-14 fiberglass-belted black sidewall tires; and, on convertibles, a power top.

To that list the coupe-only Grandé added bright pedal pad surrounds; deluxe cloth high-back bucket seat trim; deluxe instrument panel trim; a deluxe two-spoke steering wheel; an electric clock; molded trim panels with integral pull handles and arm rests; a rear ash tray in the right quarter trim panel; dual accent paint stripes; color-keyed dual racing mirrors (left-hand mirror remote-controlled); rocker panel moldings; vinyl roof; full wheelcovers; and wheel lip moldings.

Mach 1s received the standard SportsRoof equipment, plus a color-keyed spoiler/bumper with color-keyed hood and front fender moldings. Also color-keyed were the dual racing mirrors, with the left-hand mirror featuring remote-control operation. Mach 1s came standard with the sport lamp grille; competition suspension; hubcaps and trim rings; a black, honeycomb-textured back panel appliqué; a pop-open gas cap; a deck lid paint stripe; black or argent silver lower body side finish with bright moldings at the upper edge; E70-14 whitewalls; and the base V-8. NASA-style hood scoops were optional at no extra charge.

The new car's heavier body would have been too much for the small 200-cid inline six-cylinder; in its place at the bottom of the powerplant list for 1971 was a slightly more powerful 250-cid six. A mild, 210-hp 302-cid engine was the standard V-8 for the line, with other small-block offerings including 240- and 285-hp versions of the 351-cid V-8, plus the Boss 351 powerplant.

Ford-loving performance buffs had watched in horror as the Mustang's family of 1969-70 tarmac terrors boiled down to only two real speed options in 1971. While the race-bred Boss 302 and 429 went the way of the dodo bird, a new Boss was born in 1971 that gave customers brief hope that high-performance wasn't dead at Ford. The Boss 351 was the car that most appealed to street performance buffs, and it was a better-balanced car than the big-block Fords. Similar in looks to the Mach 1, the Boss' standard equipment included all of the Mustang basics, plus a functional NASA-style hood with Black or Argent Silver full hood paint treatment, hood lock pins, and Ram Air engine decals. Also featured were racing mirrors; honeycombed grille; hubcaps and trim rings; black

1971 standard Mach 1 body-color bumper

**Left: 1971 standard wheels
Right: 1971 standard Mach 1 pop-up cap**

1971 lockdowns for Dual Ram Induction hood

1971 J-code 429/4V V-8

1971 optional Mach 1 Sports Interior

or argent silver body side tape stripes (these also became optional on Mach 1s late in the year); color-keyed hood and front fender moldings; Boss 351 nomenclature; dual exhausts; power front disc brakes; a Space-Saver spare tire; a competition suspension with staggered rear shocks; a 3.91:1 axle ratio with Traction-Lok differential; a functional black spoiler, shipped "knocked-down" inside the car for dealer installation; an 80-ampere battery; Ford's Instrumentation Group option; an electronic rpm-limiter; high-back bucket seats; a special cooling package; a wide-ratio four-speed manual transmission with Hurst shifter; the 351-cid H.O. (high-output) V-8 with 330 hp; and F60-15 belted blackwall tires. A chrome bumper was standard on Boss 351s, while the Mach 1-style color-keyed bumper was an option.

Ironically, after Ford built the biggest Mustang ever to hold its largest corporate engines, only one big-block was available in 1971—and only for half of the year! The new 429 Cobra Jet (429CJ) engine sold for $372 more than the cost of the base V-8. A 429 Cobra Jet Ram Air (429CJ-R) option was $436 above the base V-8. Both were rated at 370 hp. A 429 Super Cobra Jet with Dual Ram Air induction and a 375-hp rating was available for $531 over the base V-8.

Hydraulic valve lifters, four-bolt main caps, dress-up aluminum valve covers and a GM Quadrajet four-barrel carburetor were part of the 429CJ-R performance package. The 429SCJ-R featured mechanical lifters, adjustable rocker arms, a larger Holley four-barrel carburetor, and forged pistons.

Mustangs with the 429CJ-R engine came with a competition suspension; Mach 1 hood; 80-ampere battery; 55-ampere alternator; dual exhausts; extra-cooling package; bright engine dress-up kit with cast aluminum rocker covers and a 3.25:1 ratio, non-locking rear axle. It was not available with air conditioning combined with the Drag Pak option or with the Dual Ram induction option. A C-6 Cruise-O-Matic or close-ratio four-speed manual transmission was required, along with disc brakes. Power steering was required on air-conditioned cars. The 429SCJ engine required the Drag Pak option and a 3.91:1 or 4.11:1 high-ratio rear axle. This final-year big-block was available in all three body styles.

Contrary to legend the big-block Mustangs have generated, the 429 V-8 available this year was in no way related to the Boss engine of 1969-70, which was derived from Ford's "semi-hemi" NASCAR racing engine. They were actually 460-cid blocks from Thunderbirds and Lincolns destroked to 429 cubic inches and topped with "wedge" heads.

Comparing a 429 CJ Mach 1 to a Boss 351, *Sports Car Graphic* magazine declared the big-block car to be only marginally faster, with a zero-to-60 time of 6.3 seconds versus the Boss' 6.6. The 429 pulled the big pony through the quarter-mile in 14.6 seconds at 99.4 miles per hour, while the small-block managed 14.7 seconds and 96.2 miles per hour. Considering it was down 78 cubic inches, the Boss 351 performed quite well against the Mach 1.

The options list—always praised by Ford for its broad range—still gave Mustang buyers the ability to customize their purchases straight from the dealership. Wheel choices included the Magnum 500 chromed styled steel wheels that cost $120 for Mach 1s and Boss 351s, $129 for Grandés, and $155 for other Mustangs. This package included an F78-14 Space-Saver spare tire and required F60-15 raised white-letter tires and the competition suspension. A Dual Ram Air induction option was also offered for the Boss 351 at $65. It included appropriate Ram Air decals. A rear decklid spoiler was available for SportsRoof, Mach 1, and Boss 351 models for $32.

Buyers of the Boss 351 and convertible could order the Décor Group interior for $97; on other Mustangs the special seats and door panels were an extra $78. It included a choice of knitted vinyl or cloth and vinyl high-back bucket seats (knitted vinyl was required for convertibles); a rear ashtray; deluxe left- and right-hand black instrument panel appliqués; a deluxe two-spoke steering wheel; molded door trim panels on convertibles and Boss 351s; color-keyed racing mirrors (left-hand remote-control), if not standard and rocker panel and wheel lip moldings (except on the Boss 351).

As if its less-than-spectacular engine lineup didn't clue in the average enthusiast, it should be noted that Ford had officially pulled factory support out of motorsports the previous year. Considering that the government and insurance companies were slipping a noose around the neck of the high-performance automobile, history suggests this was a smart move.

Mustang production for 1971 continued to decline, dropping to 149,678. Of this total, about 1,250 were made with 429 Cobra Jet and Super Cobra Jet V-8s—the last big-block Mustangs ever built. Of all Mustangs built in the model year 1971, some 5.3 percent had four-speed manual transmissions; 5.6 percent had stereo eight-track tape players; 1.9 percent had power windows; and 29 percent had vinyl roofs.

J.B. Naughton was the chief executive officer of the Ford Division this year. This branch of the corporation was also known as Ford Marketing Corp.

DATA PLATE DECODING

The Vehicle Identification Number is stamped on an aluminum tab on the instrument panel, viewable through windshield. A vehicle certification label replaced the warranty plate in 1970. While it still gives much of the same information as before, it is found on the body side of where the driver's door closes.

1971 optional Mach 1 Sports Interior door panel

1971 optional Mach 1 Sports Interior seat

VEHICLE WARRANTY NUMBER
MODEL YEAR

1 – 1971

ASSEMBLY PLANT

F – Dearborn, Michigan
T – Metuchen, New Jersey

BODY SERIAL NUMBERS

01 – hardtop
02 – fastback
03 – convertible
04 – Grande
05 – Mach 1

ENGINE CODE

L – 250-cid 1-bbl. 6-cyl.
F – 302-cid 2-bbl. V-8
H – 351-cid 2-bbl. V-8
M – 351-cid 4-bbl. V-8 (through May 1971)
M – 351-cid 4-bbl. V-8 (Cobra Jet)
R – 351-cid 4-bbl. V-8 (Boss)
C – 429-cid 4-bbl. V-8 (Cobra Jet)
J – 429-cid 4-bbl. V-8 (Super Cobra Jet)

CONSECUTIVE UNIT NUMBER

Begins at 100001 at each factory

CODE NUMBERS
BODY CODE

63D – fastback
63R – fastback, Mach 1
65D – hardtop coupe
65F – hardtop coupe, Grande
76D – convertible

PAINT CODE

A	Raven Black	Z	Grabber Green Metallic
B	Maroon Metallic	P	Medium Green Metallic
C	Dark Ivy Green Metallic	V	Light Pewter Metallic
		Z	Grabber Green Metallic
D	Grabber Yellow	3	Bright Red
E	Medium Yellow Gold	5	Medium Brown Metallic
I	Grabber Lime	6	Silver Blue Metallic
J	Grabber Blue	8	Light Gold
M	Wimbledon White	SPEC	Gold Metallic
N	Pastel Blue	SPEC	Gold Glamour

ASSEMBLY DATE CODE

The next group of symbols consisted of two numbers and a letter, which represent the assembly date code. The numbers give the day (i.e.: "01" = first day) and the letter designates month of year, following normal progression (i.e.: "A" = January; "B" = February, etc.), except that the letters "I" and "O" are skipped.

AXLE RATIO CODES*

2/K – 2.75:1	A/S – 3.50:1
3 – 2.79:1	B – 3.07:1
4/M – 2.80:1	NA/V – 3.91:1
6/O – 3.00:1	NA/Y – 4.11:1
9/R – 3.25:1	

* left character indicates conventional axle/right character denotes limited-slip unit

TRANSMISSION CODE

1 – 3-speed manual
5 – 4-speed manual (2.78 final drive)
6 – 4-speed manual (2.32 close-ratio final drive)
U – C-6 automatic
W – C-4 automatic
X – FMX automatic

ENGINES

250-cid 1-bbl. Inline Six

Valves	overhead
Block	cast iron
Displacement	250 cid
Bore and stroke	3.68 x 3.91 inches
Compression ratio	9.0:1
Brake hp	145 at 4000 rpm
Main bearings	7
Valve lifters	hydraulic
Carburetor	Motorcraft 1-bbl.
Code	L

302-cid 2-bbl. V-8

Valves	overhead
Block	cast iron
Displacement	302 cid
Bore and stroke	4.00 x 3.00 inches
Compression ratio	9.0:1
Brake hp	210 at 4600 rpm
Main bearings	5
Valve lifters	hydraulic
Carburetor	Motorcraft 2-bbl.
Code	F

1971 optional Dual Ram Induction hood

1971 Boss 351 (JH)

351-cid 2-bbl. V-8

Valves . . . . .overhead
Block . . . . .cast iron
Displacement . . . . .351 cid
Bore and stroke . . . . .4.00 x 3.50 inches
Compression ratio 9.0:1
Brake hp . . . . .240 at 4600 rpm
Main bearings 5
Valve lifters . . . . .hydraulic
Carburetor . . . . .Motorcraft 2-bbl.
Code . . . . .H

351-cid 4-bbl. (Cobra Jet after May 1971) V-8

Valves . . . . .overhead
Block . . . . .cast iron
Displacement . . . . .351 cid
Bore and stroke . . . . .4.00 x 3.50 inches
Compression ratio 10.7:1
Brake hp .285 at 5400 rpm (through May 1971) 280 (after)
Main bearings 5
Valve lifters . . . . .hydraulic
Carburetor . . . . .Motorcraft 4-bbl.
Code . . . . .M

351-cid 4-bbl. Boss V-8

Valves . . . . .overhead
Block . . . . .cast iron
Displacement . . . . .351 cid
Bore and stroke . . . . .4.00 x 3.50 inches
Compression ratio 11.1:1
Brake hp . . . . .330 at 5400 rpm
Main bearings 5
Valve lifters . . . . .hydraulic
Carburetor .Holley 4-bbl.
Code . . . . .R

429-cid 4-bbl. Cobra Jet V-8

Valves . . . . .overhead
Block . . . . .cast iron
Displacement . . . . .429 cid
Bore and stroke . . . . .4.36 x 3.59 inches
Compression ratio 11.3:1
Brake hp . . . . .370 at 5400 rpm
Main bearings 5
Valve lifters . . . . .hydraulic
Carburetor .Holley 4-bbl.
Code C

429-cid 4-bbl. Super Cobra Jet V-8

Valves . . . . .overhead
Block . . . . .cast iron
Displacement . . . . .429 cid
Bore and stroke . . . . .4.36 x 3.59 inches
Compression ratio 11.5:1
Brake hp . . . . .375 at 5600 rpm
Main bearings 5
Valve lifters . . . . .mechanical
Carburetor .Holley 4-bbl.
Code . . . . .J

CHASSIS

Wheelbase . . . . .109 inches
Overall length . . . . .189.5 inches
Tires . . . . .E78-14 blackwall

OPTION LIST

351 cid/240 hp V-8 engine $45
351 cid/285 hp Cleveland V-8 engine $93
429 cid/370 hp Cobra Jet V-8 engine $372
Cruise-O-Matic automatic transmission . . . . . .$217-$238
Four-speed manual transmission $216
Power steering $115
Power front disc brakes $70
Limited-slip differential $48
Magnum 500 chrome wheels . . . .(Mach 1) $120
. . . .(Grandé) $129
. . . .(other models) $155
AM radio $66
AM/FM stereo radio $214
AM/8-track stereo $129
Center console $60
Electric rear window defogger $48
NASA-style hood scoops . . . . .no charge
Drag-Pac rear axle . . . .(3.91:1 ratio) $155
. . . .(4.11:1 ratio) $207
Vinyl roof $26
White sidewall tires $34

1971 hardtop (FMC)

	1971 MUSTANG PRODUCTION CHART			
Model	Doors/Body/Seating	Factory Price	Shipping Weight	Prod. Total
(65D)	2/hardtop/4	$2911/3006	2937/3026	65,696
02 (63D)	2/fastback/4	$2973/3068	2907/2993	23,956
03 (76D)	2/convertible/4	$3227/3322	3059/3145	6,121
04 (65F)	2/hardtop Grande/4	$3117/3212	2963/3049	17,406
05 (63R)	2/fastback Mach 1/4	$3268	3220	36,449

NOTE 1: Total series output was 149,678 units.
NOTE 2: Data above slash for six/below slash for V-8.
NOTE 3: Boss 351 output was 1,806 units at $4,124 base price per car. Shipping weight was 3,281 pounds.

1971 SportsRoof (PH)

1971 Grandé (PH)

1971 Mustang Boss 351 Fastback
(Old Cars Weekly)

1971 Mustang hardtop
(Richard Fuchs)

**1972 Sprint convertible
Owner: Ben Mandell**

1972

Comparing inches and pounds, the 1971-73 Mustang was more similar to today's full-size Taurus four-door sedan than it was the original 1965 pony car. Ford's advertising, however, described the somewhat heavy beast as a "sports compact."

The 1972 Mustang was a virtual twin to the previous model, with buyers having the choice of two distinct grille treatments depending on which boxes were checked on the options list. Bumpers could be either chromed or painted body color. Base models sported cursive "Mustang" lettering on the far right of the decklid overhang; the Mach 1 received a decal instead.

According to Ford's figuring, the Mustang lineup for 1972 included the hardtop, SportsRoof, convertible, Grandé and Mach 1—the Boss 351 did not return for a second year. ComfortWeave knitted vinyl upholstery, an instrument panel appliqué and molded door trim panels were standard in the convertibles.

Patriotic fervor swept through Ford in 1972 as the company released a series of red, white, and blue color schemes based on its Mustangs, Mavericks, and Pinto Runabouts. The "A" package, released midyear, was simply known as the Sprint Decor option. The bulk of the Mustang Sprint body was white with light medium-blue paint all around the lower perimeter. Two wide blue stripes decorated the hood. The lower back panel was also blue. A red pinstripe ran along the lower body, emphasizing the color break. The interior was also two-tone white and blue. Each Sprint included dual white racing mirrors, color-keyed seats and carpets, and white sidewall tires with color-keyed hubcaps and trim rings. A flag-like decal commemorating the 1972 Olympics was on the rear fender. A "B" Sprint package substituted mag-type

wheels, F60-15 raised white-letter tires and a competition suspension. Although Ford dealers were limited to fastbacks and hardtops when ordering the Sprint Decor option, it has been documented that 50 convertibles were built for use in the Washington, D.C., Cherry Day parade.

Not only was the 1972 a cosmetic twin to the 1971, but the list of features was just about identical. Standard equipment for all hardtops, SportsRoofs, and convertibles included concealed wipers; rocker panel and wheel lip moldings; a lower back panel appliqué with bright moldings; color-keyed dual racing mirrors; recessed exterior door handles; "bottle cap" hubcaps; DirectAire ventilation; a heater and defroster; high-back bucket seats; and bonded door trim panels with pull handles and arm rests (in hardtop and fastback form). All cars came standard with a mini-console; carpeting; courtesy lights; a deluxe two-spoke steering wheel with wood-tone insert; E78-14 bias-ply blackwall tires; a three-speed floor-mounted transmission; and the 250-cid six (rated at 98 SAE net horsepower).

If power windows were not ordered, the SportsRoof came with fixed rear quarter windows, and a tinted glass backlight was standard. Convertibles added a five-ply power-operated top; a color-keyed top boot; a tinted windshield; a glass backlight; a bright upper back panel molding; knit-vinyl seat trim; molded door handles; and black instrument panel appliqués.

To the standard equipment list the coupe-only Grandé added a vinyl roof with Grandé script; unique body side tape stripes; unique full wheelcovers; a trunk floor mat; Lambeth cloth and vinyl upholstery; bright pedal pads; deluxe instrument panel trim with black camera case; and wood-tone appliqués; a panel-mounted electric clock; and a rear ashtray.

All basic SportsRoof equipment was standard on the

Mach 1, plus a competition suspension; a choice of a hood with or without NASA-style scoop (with 302 V-8 only); a color-keyed front spoiler bumper; color-keyed hood and fender moldings; a black honeycomb grille with integral sports lamps; a black back panel appliqué; Black or Argent Silver lower body finish; front and rear valance panels; a rear tape stripe with Mach 1 decals; hubcaps and wheel trim rings; a 302-cid two-barrel V-8 (with 136 net horsepower); and E70-14 bias-ply belted white sidewall tires. The Mach 1 interior included knit-vinyl high-back bucket seats with accent stripes; an electric clock; triple instrument pod gauges; door trim panels with integral pull handles and armrests; deep-embossed carpet runners; the deluxe instrument panel with black appliqués and a wood-tone center section; and a rear seat ashtray. This could be added to other fastbacks at extra cost.

Three 351-cid V-8s of were optional in Mustangs—the regular two-barrel version, the regular four-barrel version, and the four-barrel H.O. option offering 168, 200, and 275 hp, respectively. (If all the 1972 engine output figures seem like a massive drop from 1971 horsepower ratings, it's because the new numbers were expressed in SAE net horsepower.)

The options list was smaller in 1972, the previous year's big-block 429 being the most obvious deletion. Some choices that appealed to enthusiast buyers included Color Glow paints ($34 extra); the instrumentation group with tachometer, trip odometer, and three-pod gauge cluster ($55 on Grandés and $70 on other Mustangs); front disc brakes ($62); AM/FM stereo ($191); Sport Deck rear seat for SportsRoofs which included a Space-Saver spare, folding rear seat, and load floor ($75); a Black or Argent Silver body side tape stripe for Mach 1s and Mustangs with Decor Group trim ($23); Magnum 500 chrome wheels ($107 to $138 not including the required competition suspension and F60-15 tires); Dual Ram induction ($58 with any 351 V-8 including a NASA hood with Black or Argent Silver two-tone paint, hood lock pins and Ram Air engine decals); and the Mach 1 Sports Interior package ($115 for standard SportsRoofs).

The Grandé attracted about 600 additional buyers and the convertible drew an additional 280-odd orders. All other models saw substantial drops and total output was just 125,093 units. Because of a sales decline that had been occurring for several years, the San Jose, California, plant

1972 Sprint convertible

1972 Sprint convertible

1972 interior

1972 Sprint commemorative decal

1972 Q-code 351/4V V-8

had stopped building Mustangs in 1971; the Metuchen, New Jersey, factory converted to Pinto production in 1972, leaving Dearborn as the country's sole provider of pony cars.

Of the cars sold in 1972, 27 percent had a four-speed manual transmission, 3.9 percent had Tilt-Telescope steering, 6.2 percent wore optional styled wheels, and 32.3 percent had vinyl tops.

There were no changes in top Ford management, although B.E. Bidwell would soon be elected vice-president and general manager of Ford Marketing Corp.

DATA PLATE DECODING

The Vehicle Identification Number is stamped on an aluminum tab on the instrument panel, viewable through windshield. A vehicle certification label replaced the warranty plate in '70. While it still gives much of the same information as before, it is found on the body side of where the driver's door closes.

VEHICLE WARRANTY NUMBER
MODEL YEAR

2 – 1972

ASSEMBLY PLANT

F – Dearborn, Michigan

BODY SERIAL NUMBERS

01 – hardtop
02 – fastback
03 – convertible
04 – Grande
05 – Mach 1

ENGINE CODE

L – 250-cid 1-bbl. 6-cyl.
F – 302-cid 2-bbl. V-8
H – 351-cid 2-bbl. V-8
Q – 351-cid 4-bbl. V-8 (CJ)
R – 351-cid 4-bbl. V-8 (HO)

CONSECUTIVE UNIT NUMBER

Begins at 100001 at each factory

CODE NUMBERS
BODY CODE

63D – fastback
63R – fastback, Mach 1
65D – hardtop coupe
65F – hardtop coupe, Grande
76D – convertible

PAINT CODE

2B – Bright Red
2J – Maroon
3B – Light Blue
3F – Grabber Blue
3J – Bright Blue Metallic
4C – Ivy Glow
4E – Bright Lime
4F – Medium Lime Metallic
4P – Medium Green Metallic
4Q – Dark Green Metallic
5A – Light Pewter Metallic
5H – Medium Brown Metallic
6C – Medium Yellow Gold
6E – Medium Bright Yellow
6F – Gold Glow
9A – White

ASSEMBLY DATE CODE

The next group of symbols consisted of two numbers and a letter, which represent the assembly date code. The numbers give the day (i.e.: "01" = first day) and the letter designates month of year, following normal progression (i.e.: "A" = January; "B" = February, etc.), except that the letters "I" and "O" are skipped.

AXLE RATIO CODES*

2/K – 2.75:1
3 – 2.79:1
4/M – 2.80:1
6/O – 3.00:1
9/R – 3.25:1
A/S – 3.50:1
B – 3.07:1
NA/V – 3.91:1
* left character indicates conventional axle/right character denotes limited-slip unit

TRANSMISSION CODE

1 – 3-speed manual
5 – 4-speed manual
E – 4-speed manual
U – C-6 automatic
W – C-4 automatic
X – FMX automatic

1972 Mach 1
Owner: Shane Bryant

1972 Mach 1

ENGINES

250-cid 1-bbl. Inline Six

Valves . . . . .overhead
Block . . . . .cast iron
Displacement . . . . .250 cid
Bore and stroke . . . . .3.68 x 3.91 inches
Compression ratio 8.0:1
Brake hp . . . . .98 at 3400 rpm
Main bearings 7
Valve lifters . . . . .hydraulic
Carburetor . . . . .Motorcraft 1-bbl.
Code L

302-cid 2-bbl. V-8

Valves . . . . .overhead
Block . . . . .cast iron
Displacement . . . . .302 cid
Bore and stroke . . . . .4.00 x 3.00 inches
Compression ratio 8.5:1
Brake hp . . . . .140 at 4000 rpm
Main bearings 5
Valve lifters . . . . .hydraulic
Carburetor . . . . .Motorcraft 2-bbl.
Code . . . . .F

351-cid 2-bbl. V-8

Valves . . . . .overhead
Block . . . . .cast iron
Displacement . . . . .351 cid
Bore and stroke . . . . .4.00 x 3.50 inches
Compression ratio 8.6:1
Brake hp 168
Main bearings 5
Valve lifters . . . . .hydraulic
Carburetor . . . . .Motorcraft 2-bbl.
Code . . . . .H

351-cid 4-bbl. Cobra Jet V-8

Valves . . . . .overhead
Block . . . . .cast iron
Displacement . . . . .351 cid
Bore and stroke . . . . .4.00 x 3.50 inches
Compression ratio 8.6:1
Brake hp 200
Main bearings 5
Valve lifters . . . . .hydraulic
Carburetor . . . . .Holley 4-bbl.
Code . . . . .Q

351-cid 4-bbl. HO V-8

Valves . . . . .overhead
Block . . . . .cast iron
Displacement . . . . .351 cid
Bore and stroke . . . . .4.00 x 3.50 inches
Compression ratio 8.6:1
Brake hp 275
Main bearings 5
Valve lifters . . . . .hydraulic
Carburetor . . . . .Holley 4-bbl.
Code . . . . .R

CHASSIS

Wheelbase . . . . .109 inches
Overall length . . . . .189.5 inches
Tires . . . . .E78-14 blackwall
(**Note:** Additional tire sizes are noted in text when used as standard equipment on specific models.)

OPTION LIST

351-cid/177-hp Cleveland V-8 . . . .$41
351-cid/266-hp Cleveland V-8 engine $115
351-cid/275-hp High-Output V-8 with four-barrel carbure-
 tion . . . .$841-$870
Cruise-O-Matic transmission $204
Four-speed manual transmission $193
Power steering $103
Power front disc brakes $62
Limited-slip differential $43
Magnum 500 chrome wheels . . . .$108-$139
Center console . . . .$53-$97
Vinyl roof $79
White sidewall tires $34

1972 optional Mach 1 Sports Interior

1972 MUSTANG PRODUCTION CHART

Model	Doors/Body/Seating	Factory Price	Shipping Weight	Prod. Total
01 (65D)	2/hardtop/4	$2729/2816	2941/3025	7,350
02 (63D)	2/fastback/4	$2786/2873	2909/2995	15,622
03 (76D)	2/convertible/4	$3015/3101	3061/3147	6,401
04 (65F)	2/hardtop Grande/4	$2915/3002	2965/3051	18,045
05 (63R)	2/fastback Mach 1/4	$3053	3046	27,675

NOTE 1: Total series output was 125,093 units.
NOTE 2: Data above slash for six/below slash for V-8.

1972 hardtop

1972 hardtop (FMC)

1972 Grandé (PH)

1972 hardtop (FMC)

1973 Grandé (JH)

In the early 1970s many changes took place in the American auto industry—some from market forces, some from government micromanaging—that sent the once-revered Mustang into a decade-long identity crisis. A visit to the Ford showroom in 1973, where it appeared to be business as usual, revealed a Mustang little changed from the previous two years. Ford announced early in the year that the "final" Mustang convertible would be built sometime during the year, with no plans to revive the body style in the foreseeable future. Car magazines busily fleshed out rumors and leaks from Ford about a new, downsized Mustang to be introduced as an early 1974 model.

The 1973 Mustang suffered from another weight and size increase, owing largely to a new impact-resistant front bumper that was required to meet federal safety regulations. While the color-keyed bumper extended the overall length of the Mustang by another four inches (to a whopping 194!), critics had to admit that the car's styling did not suffer from the mandatory device as much as other Ford products. A new crosshatch-design grille, featuring a floating pony badge at the center (or tri-bar emblem on sportier models) and an eggcrate-style insert with vertical parking lights in the outboard segments gave the 1973 model a mild facelift.

Standard equipment was about the same as in 1972. The list included a 250-cid six or 302-cid V-8; E78-14 bias-belted black sidewall tires; rocker panel and wheel lip moldings; a lower back panel appliqué with a bright molding; a chrome rectangular left-hand rearview mirror; all-vinyl upholstery

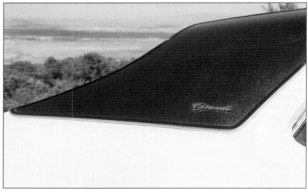

1973 Grandé vinyl top (JH)

and door trim; a front mini-console; color-keyed loop-pile carpeting; a deluxe two-spoke steering wheel with wood-tone insert; a cigarette lighter; a seatbelt reminder system and door courtesy lamps. SportsRoofs added a tinted back window and fixed rear quarter windows. Convertibles also had under-dash courtesy lamps, a power-operated convertible top, a color-keyed top boot, a glass backlight, ComfortWeave knit-vinyl seat trim and power front disc brakes.

Returning for its final year, the Grandé hardtop gave buyers color-keyed dual racing mirrors; a vinyl roof; body side tape striping; special wheelcovers; a trunk mat; Lambeth cloth and vinyl seat trim; molded door panels with integral arm rests; bright pedal pads; a deluxe instrument panel and an electric clock.

The Mach 1 took on a new body side stripe scheme that relocated the model name to just behind the door edge. Standard equipment for the Mach 1 included a 302-cid 136-hp V-8; competition suspension; choice of a NASA- or plain-style hood; E70-14 whitewall Wide-Oval tires; color-keyed dual racing mirrors; black grille; black back panel appliqué; hubcaps with wheel trim rings; tinted back window; all-vinyl upholstery and door trim; and high-back front bucket seats.

Some safety refinements were made to the instrument panel, primarily to eliminate protruding objects and glare. Larger brakes were used, too. New, flame-retardant interior fabrics were required. The emissions system also received some attention. Engine choices were virtually identical to 1972.

In its final year, the big Mustang saw a jump in sales, owing largely to Ford's news that 1973 would be its last year of convertible production (convertible sales doubled to more than 11,000). When it was all said and done, the count stood at 134,817 units for the model year.

DATA PLATE DECODING

The Vehicle Identification Number is stamped on an aluminum tab on the instrument panel, viewable through windshield. A vehicle certification label replaced the warranty plate in '70. While it still gives much of the same information as before, it is found on the body side of where the driver's door closes.

VEHICLE WARRANTY NUMBER
MODEL YEAR

3 – 1973

ASSEMBLY PLANT

F – Dearborn, Michigan

BODY SERIAL NUMBERS

01 – hardtop
02 – fastback
03 – convertible
04 – Grande
05 – Mach 1

ENGINE CODE

L – 250-cid 1-bbl. 6-cyl.
F – 302-cid 2-bbl. V-8
H – 351-cid 2-bbl. V-8
Q – 351-cid 4-bbl. V-8 (CJ)

CONSECUTIVE UNIT NUMBER

Begins at 100001 at each factory

CODE NUMBERS
BODY CODE

63D – fastback
63R – fastback, Mach 1
65D – hardtop coupe
65F – hardtop coupe, Grande
76D – convertible

PAINT CODE

2B – Bright Red
3B – Light Blue
3D – Medium Blue Metallic
3K – Blue Glow
4B – Bright Green Gold Metallic
4C – Ivy Glow
4N – Medium Aqua
4P – Medium Green Metallic
4Q – Dark Green Metallic
5H – Medium Brown Metallic
5M – Medium Copper Metallic
5T – Saddle Bronze Metallic
6C – Medium Yellow Gold
6E – Medium Bright Yellow
6F – Gold Glow
9A – Wimbledon White

ASSEMBLY DATE CODE

The next group of symbols consisted of two numbers and a letter, which represent the assembly date code. The numbers give the day (i.e.: "01" = first day) and the letter designates month of year, following normal progression (i.e.: "A" = January; "B" = February, etc.), except that the letters "I" and "O" are skipped.

1973 convertible (FMC)

AXLE RATIO CODES*

2/K – 2.75:1	9/R – 3.25:1
3/L – 2.79:1	A/S – 3.50:1
6/O – 3.00:1	G – 3.55:1
7 – 3.40:1	NA/V – 3.91:1

* left character indicates conventional axle/right character denotes limited-slip unit

TRANSMISSION CODE

1 – 3-speed manual
5 – 4-speed manual
E – 4-speed manual
U – C-6 automatic
W – C-4 automatic
X – FMX automatic

ENGINES

250-cid 1-bbl. Inline Six
Valves . . . . .overhead
Block . . . . .cast iron
Displacement . . . . .250 cid
Bore and stroke . . . . .3.68 x 3.91 inches
Compression ratio 8.0:1
Brake hp . . . . .98 at 3400 rpm
Main bearings 7
Valve lifters . . . . .hydraulic
Carburetor . . . . .Motorcraft 1-bbl.
Code L

302-cid 2-bbl. V-8
Valves . . . . .overhead
Block . . . . .cast iron
Displacement . . . . .302 cid
Bore and stroke . . . . .4.00 x 3.00 inches
Compression ratio 8.5:1
Brake hp . . . . .140 at 4000 rpm
Main bearings 5
Valve lifters . . . . .hydraulic
Carburetor . . . . .Motorcraft 2-bbl.
Code . . . . .F

351-cid 2-bbl. V-8
Valves . . . . .overhead
Block . . . . .cast iron
Displacement . . . . .351 cid

Bore and stroke . . . . .4.00 x 3.50 inches
Compression ratio 8.6:1
Brake hp . . . . .177 at 3800 rpm
Main bearings 5
Valve lifters . . . . .hydraulic
Carburetor . . . . .Motorcraft 2-bbl.
Code . . . . .H

351-cid 4-bbl. Cobra Jet V-8
Valves . . . . .overhead
Block . . . . .cast iron
Displacement . . . . .351 cid
Bore and stroke . . . . .4.00 x 3.50 inches
Compression ratio 8.6:1
Brake hp . . . . .248 at 5400 rpm
Main bearings 5
Valve lifters . . . . .hydraulic
Carburetor .Holley 4-bbl.
Code . . . . .Q

CHASSIS

Wheelbase . . . . .109 inches
Overall length . . . . .189.5 inches
Tires . . . . .E78-14 blackwall
(**Note:** Additional tire sizes are noted in text when used as standard equipment on specific models.)

OPTION LIST

302-cid two-barrel V-8 standard in Mach 1, in other models $87
351-cid two-barrel V-8 . . . .$128
351-cid four-barrel V-8 . . . . (including 55-amp alternator; heavy-duty 55-amp battery; special intake manifold; special valve springs and dampers; large-capacity 4300-D carburetor; 25-inch diameter dual exhaust outlets; modified camshaft and four-bolt main bearing caps. Requires Cruise-O-Matic 3.25:1 axle ratio or four-speed manual transmission, 3.50:1 axle combination, power front disc brakes and competition suspension) . . . $194
California emission testing $14
SelectShift Cruise-O-Matic transmission $204
Four-speed manual transmission with Hurst shifter, not available with six-cylinder $193
Power front disc brakes, standard on convertible; required with 351 V-8 . . . .$62
Power windows $113
Power steering, required with Tilt-Away steering wheel
. . . .$103
SelectAire conditioning, including extra cooling package . . (not available on six-cylinder with three-speed manual transmission) $368
Console . . . .(in Grande) $53
(in other models) $68
Convenience Group (including trunk light; glove compartment light; map light; underhood light; 'lights-on' warning buzzer; automatic seatback releases; under-dash courtesy lights . . . . .standard on convertible; parking brake warning light; and glove compartment lock . .$46
Electric rear window defroster, not available with convertible or six-cylinder $57
Tinted glass . . . .(convertible) $14
(others) $36

1973 Mach 1 (FMC)

Instrumentation Group, including tachometer, trip odometer and oil pressure, ammeter and temperature gauges; included with Mach 1 Sports Interior, not available on six-cylinders . . . . (in Grande without console) $55 in other models $71

Color-keyed dual racing mirrors, standard on Grande, Mach 1 . . . . $23

AM radio $59

AM/FM stereo radio $191

Sport deck rear seat Sportsroof, Mach 1 only $86

Deluxe three-spoke Rim-Blow steering wheel $35

Tilt-Away steering wheel, power steering required . . . $41

Deluxe leather-wrapped two-spoke steering wheel . . . $23

Stereo-Sonic Tape System, AM radio required $120

Intermittent windshield wipers $23

Optional axle ratios $12

Traction-Lok differential $43

Heavy-duty 70-amp hour battery (standard hardtop and convertible with 351 two-barrel in combination with Instrument Group or SelectAire) $14

Extra cooling package, standard with SelectAire, not available on six-cylinder $13

Dual Ram Induction, 351 two-barrel V-8, including functional NASA-type hood with black or argent two-tone paint, hood lock pins, Ram-Air engine decals $58

Rear deck spoiler, with Sportsroof or Mach 1 only $29

Competition suspension, including extra heavy-duty front and rear springs, extra heavy-duty front and rear shock absorbers, standard with Mach 1 and not available with six-cylinder $28

Deluxe seat and shoulder belts package, standard without shoulder belts in convertible $15

Deluxe Bumper Group including rear rubber bumper inserts and full-width horizontal strip $25

Rear bumper guards $14

Decor Group, including black or argent lower bodyside paint with bright upper edge moldings, unique grille with Sportslamps; trim rings with hubcaps (deletes rocker panel and wheel lip moldings with Decor Group) $51

Door edge guards, included with Protection Group . . . $6

Color-keyed front floor mats $13

Metallic Glow paint $35

Two-tone hood paint . . . . (for Mach 1) $18
. . . . (for other models) $34

Protection Group, including vinyl-insert bodyside moldings; spare tire lock; door edge guards; deletes bodyside tape stripe . . . . (on Grande) $23
. . . . (on other models) $36
(but not available on Mach 1 or Mustangs with Decor Group)

Vinyl roof on hardtops, including C-pillar tri-color ornament (standard on Grande) $80

Three-quarter vinyl roof for Sportsroofs only $52

Mach 1 Sports Interior, for Mach 1 and V-8 Sportsroof only, including knitted vinyl trim; high-back bucket seats with accent stripes; Instrumentation Group; door trim panels with integral pull handles and armrests; color-accented, deep-embossed carpet runners; Deluxe black instrument panel applique with wood-tone center section; bright pedal pads and rear seat ashtray $115

Black or argent bodyside stripes, with Decor Group only
. . . . $23

Trim rings with hubcaps, standard on Mach 1 and Mustangs with Decor Group
. . . . (for Grande) $8
. . . . (for other models) $31

Sports wheel covers on Grande $56
. . . . . . (on Mach 1 or Mustangs with Decor Group) $48
. . . . (on other models) $79

Forged aluminum wheels . . . . (on Grande) $119
. . . . (on Mach 1 or Mustangs with Decor Group) $111
. . . . (on other models) $142

OPTION POPULARITY

Automatic transmission .90.4%
Three-speed manual transmission 6.7%
Four-speed manual transmission 2.9%
Power steering 92.9%
Power brakes 77.9%
Tilt steering wheel 5.6%
Tinted glass 62.8%
Power windows 3.2%
Air conditioning 56.2%

1973 MUSTANG PRODUCTION CHART

Model	Doors/Body/Seating	Factory Price	Shipping Weight	Prod. Total
01 (65D)	2/hardtop/4	$2760/2847	2984/3076	51,430
02 (63D)	2/fastback/4	$2820/2907	2991/3083	10,820
03 (76D)	2/convertible/4	$3102/3189	3106/3198	11,853
04 (65F)	2/hardtop Grande/4	$2946/3033	2982/3074	25,274
05 (63R)	2/fastback Mach 1/4	$3088	3090	35,440

NOTE 1: Total series output was 134,817 units.
NOTE 2: Data above slash for six/below slash for V-8.

1974 Ghia (FMC)

1974

All eyes were on Ford Motor Co. August 28, 1973, for the launch of the most-anticipated automobile since the 1965 Mustang. The eyes belonged to Mustang enthusiasts, Ford stockholders, corporate planners, the automotive press, and the American buying public in general. Ford had spent more than two intense years in marketing clinics and in the design studios testing and building hundreds of different ideas to replace the bloated and aging 1971-73 Mustang. Thousands of factors were taken into account during the creation process—government-imposed emissions restrictions, rising insurance premiums for performance cars and a market that suddenly seemed smitten by small, sporty cars from Japan and Germany were three of the most dominant.

Ford had received steady criticism for turning first the Thunderbird, then the Mustang, into overweight, gas-guzzling images of their former selves, and its designers were charged with the task of turning a plodding Clydesdale back into a galloping pony. At the start of the project, the designers and engineers faced four major objectives. The all-new Mustang had to 1) offer high perceived value for the money, 2) be of a sensible size, 3) display a high level of engineering excellence and 4) be a stylish car. The design would be so much a departure from the 1973 model that Ford's public relations department suggested it be known as the "Mustang II."

The Mustang II powertrain lineup was entirely new. Gone were the big-block V-8s—in fact, there were no V-8s slated for duty in the new car—and in their place were metric-measured four-cylinder engines and German-built V-6s. The base engine was a 2.3-liter "Lima" four (named for its production plant in Ohio) that had a single overhead camshaft and power output comparable to Ford's heavier 200-cid inline six-cylinder. Like every other component

designed specifically for the Mustang II, the engine was subjected to intense research and development to insure that it met high noise, vibration, and harshness (NVH) standards. Service-free hydraulic valve-lash adjusters were unique for any overhead cam four-cylinder and made the engine especially attractive to the II's target market. Major emissions equipment was designed into the engine and not just attached later. Metric measurement meant that the Lima could share components with Ford products around the world. It delivered up to 23 miles per gallon, which was considered quite economical for an American car at that time.

The optional 2.8-liter V-6 was pirated from Ford of Germany's Mercury Capri—a popular, sporty little import car that many believed the Mustang II should have imitated more closely. It delivered 105 hp and in many cases mechanical headaches. Problems with engine valves, piston rings, and the cooling system were typical. Many buyers who spent $229 extra for this engine were sorry they had. In retrospect, exclusive use of a four-cylinder and V-6 was probably a mistake. With a V-8, sales would probably have gone even higher. By the time 1975 models bowed Ford had rectified this miscue.

The Mustang II was certainly shorter than its predecessor. Its 96.2-inch wheelbase was 11.8 inches less than that of the original Mustang and more than a foot down from the 1973 wheelbase. Far from a mistake was the decision to stay with long hood/short deck styling, a slightly protruding nose with a mostly oval-shaped grille, and single headlamps. Though changed more than ever before, the basic Mustang image was still preserved in the new car, although it had many modern touches.

Ford's marketers lost many nights of sleep over the decision to offer more than one body style based on the II platform. Despite a targa-topped, teaser show car known as the Sportiva II, at no point was consideration given to the creation of an open-air car, but debate still raged internally between the notchback and hatchback camps. At one point just 16 months before the start of production, the company had given the green light to a fastback-only II when potential customers in a San Francisco marketing clinic showed great enthusiasm for the notchback. (As it turned out, notchback sales would eclipse those of the hatchback, probably due to the hatchback's slight resemblance to its cheaper Pinto cousin.) What eventually emerged from the planning meetings was a lineup featuring a notchback coupe (often referred to as a "hardtop" and, in one press release, a "two-door sedan"), a 2+2 hatchback (also referred to as a "fastback" or "three-door"), an upscale Ghia coupe, and a performance-oriented, hatchback-based Mach 1.

Base prices for 1974 Mustang IIs ran from $3,081 to $3,621, although optional equipment and packages had many shoppers gasping to find stickers reading well over $4,500. Ford kept production costs to the bare minimum by using the same trick it employed for the original Mustang: spinning the new car off an existing model. In this case, the Pinto was the base vehicle, with which the Mustang II shared some components (although fewer than its detractors would claim). To Ford's credit, many of those components were upgraded and installed in such ways that their characteristics were in keeping with the more expensive Mustang.

Ford placed many unseen innovations into the Mustang II in hopes of delivering big-car luxury and ride in a small package. Interior noise was greatly reduced by melting rubber sheets into the floorpan during assembly—more rubber was used in the II for soundproofing than in many larger cars. Powertrain noises were addressed by the use of a larger-diameter driveshaft. A U-shaped, isolated subframe (known to Ford engineers as the "toilet seat") killed much road noise before it could get to the passenger compartment.

A Hotchkiss-type rear suspension and rack-and-pinion steering complemented the new Mustang's unitized body with front isolated mini-frame. The rear suspension consisted of longitudinal semi-elliptic leaf springs (four leaves), while the independent front suspension used ball joints, a stabilizer bar, and compression-type struts. Window sticker prices were up from those of the 1973 Mustangs on a model-for-model basis. For instance, the 1973 Mach 1 V-8 listed for $3,088 versus $3,621 for a 1974 Mach 1 with V-6. Economy didn't come cheap!

Mustang II styling represented a blending of the work of Ford's top stylists (like Eugene Bordinat, Al Mueller, L. David Ash, and Dick Nesbitt) with the ideas of Italian designers who worked at Ghia. Ford had acquired a controlling interest in that Italian firm in 1970, and it was Ghia that turned out a drivable Mustang II design exercise for Lee Iacocca in only two months' time.

Body design details included separate FORD block letters above the grille, facing upward; single round headlamps recessed into squarish housings; a front bumper that protruded forward in the center, matching the width of the grille; rub strips wrapped only slightly onto the bumper sides; door sheetmetal with a sculptured, depressed area that began near the back and extended for a short distance on the quarter panel, following the contour of the wheel opening; a curvaceous bodyside crease that ran below the door handle; B-pillars and conventional quarter windows on notchbacks; sharply tapered quarter windows that came to a point at the rear on hatchbacks; European-style tail lamps consisting of three side-by-side sections with a small back-up lens at the bottom of each center section and larger amber turn signal lenses; large FORD block letters on the panel between the tail lamps above the license plate

housing; one-piece fiberglass-reinforced front ends and color-keyed urethane-coated bumpers; wheel lip moldings; side marker lights with die-cast bezels; recessed door handles and slim high-luster exterior trim moldings.

Long-time Mustang features like a floor-mounted shifter (four-speed), bucket seats (low-back), vinyl upholstery, and carpeting were standard in Mustang IIs. Even full wheelcovers returned to the regular equipment list to emphasize the link to the past. A long equipment list now included such modern niceties as solid-state ignition, front disc brakes, a tachometer, steel-belted whitewalls, simulated burled walnut interior appliqués, and Euro-styled armrests. The 2+2 models also included a folding rear seat and styled wheels.

Ghia model upgrades included deluxe color-keyed seat belts and remote-controlled door mirrors; a Super Sound package; shag carpeting; wood-tone door panel accents; a digital clock; spoke-style wheelcovers; a super-soft color-coordinated vinyl roof covering; and a choice of super-soft vinyl or Westminster cloth interior trims. Mach 1s added the following to standard 2+2 equipment: 2.8-liter V-6; dual color-keyed remote-control mirrors; Wide-Oval steel-belted black sidewall radial tires; black lower body side paint; deck lid striping; and styled steel wheels with trim rings. About the hottest option available for 1974 Mustang IIs (except Ghias) was the Rallye package, which required the 2.8-liter V-6. It included a limited-slip differential; raised white-letter steel-belted tires; an extra-cooling package; a competition suspension; dual color-keyed; remote-control door mirrors; styled steel wheels; a Sport exhaust system; a digital clock; and a leather-wrapped steering wheel.

Compared to 134,817 units sold in 1973, the Mustang II's first-year sales of 385,993 proved that Lee Iacocca's "little jewel" had more than a little bit of the original Mustang's charm. Of course, it didn't hurt that like the 1965, the Mustang II enjoyed an 18-month introductory season. Despite sluggish initial sales, the 1974 Mustang II earned 4.75 percent of the industry's total output, a piece of the market not occupied by the Mustang since 1967.

Promoting the car as a luxury model backfired to a degree, but the II quickly found its real niche as an economy car, and IIs were shipped to dealers with fewer options. Viewed in this light, and considering the impact of the 1973 OPEC oil embargo, its timing was perfect. Ford advertised it as "the right car at the right time"—a slogan that proved more truthful than the company first thought. Customers were more attracted to the cheaper models, with the low-end hardtop and 2+2 accounting for 252,470 of all first-year Mustang IIs produced.

DATA PLATE DECODING

The Vehicle Identification Number is stamped on an aluminum tab on the instrument panel, viewable through windshield. A vehicle certification label is found on the body side of where the driver's door closes.

VEHICLE WARRANTY NUMBER
MODEL YEAR

4 – 1974

ASSEMBLY PLANT

F – Dearborn, Michigan
R – San Jose, California

BODY SERIAL NUMBERS

02 – coupe
03 – hatchback
04 – coupe, Ghia
05 – hatchback, Mach 1

ENGINE CODE

Y – 140-cid (2.3-liter) 2-bbl. SOHC 4-cyl.
Z – 171-cid (2.8-liter) 2-bbl. V-6

CONSECUTIVE UNIT NUMBER

Begins at 100001 at each factory

CODE NUMBERS
BODY CODE

60F – coupe
69F – hatchback
60H – coupe, Ghia
69R – hatchback, Mach 1

PAINT CODE

1G – Silver Metallic
2B – Bright Red
2M – Dark Red
3B – Light Blue
3N – Medium Bright Blue Metallic
4B – Bright Green Gold Metallic
4T – Green Glow
4W – Medium Lime Yellow
5J – Ginger Glow
5M – Medium Copper Metallic
5T – Saddle Bronze Metallic
5U – Tan Glow
6C – Medium Yellow Gold
9C – Pearl White

ENGINES
140-cid (2.3-liter) 2-bbl. Inline Four

Valves . . . . .overhead
Camshaft . . . . .single overhead
Block . . . . .cast iron
Displacement . . . . .140 cid/2.3 liters
Bore and stroke . . . . .3.78 x 3.13 inches
Compression ratio 8.4:1
SAE net hp . . . . .88 @ 5000 rpm
Torque . . . . .116@ 2600 rpm
Main bearings 5
Valve lifters . . . . .hydraulic
Carburetor . . . . .Motorcraft 2-bbl.
Code . . . . .Y

171-cid (2.8-liter) 2-bbl. V-6

Valves . . . . .overhead
Block . . . . .cast iron
Displacement . . . . .171 cid/2.8 liters
Bore and stroke . . . . .3.66 x 2.70 inches
Compression ratio 8.7:1
SAE net hp . . . . .105 @ 4600 rpm
Torque . . . . .140 @ 3200 rpm
Main bearings 4
Valve lifters . . . . .solid
Carburetor . . . . .Motorcraft 2-bbl.
Code . . . . .Z

CHASSIS

Wheelbase . . . . .96.2 inches
Overall length . . . . .175 inches
Height . . . .(coupe) 50.0 inches
. . . .(hatchback) 49.7 inches
Width 70.2
Front tread width . . . . .55.6 inches
Rear tread width . . . . .55.8 inches
Tires . . . . .B78-13 belted blackwall
. . . .(Ghia model) BR78-13

(**Note:** Additional tire sizes are noted in text when used as standard equipment on specific models.)

1974 base 2+2 (FMC)

TECHNICAL

Final drive ratio . . . . (four-cylinder, four-speed) 2.79:1
. . . . (four-cylinder, automatic) 3.18:1
. . . . (V-6) 3.00:1
Steering . . . . rack and pinion
Front suspension . . . .
   compression strut with lower trailing links, stabilizer
   bar and coil springs
Rear suspension . . . .
   Hotchkiss rigid axle w/semi-elliptic leaf springs (four
   leaves), anti-sway bar
Brakes . . . . (front) 9.3-inch disc
. . . . (rear) 9.0-inch drum
Ignition . . . . electronic
Body construction . . .unibody w/front isolated mini-frame
Fuel tank . . . . .13 gallons

OPTION LIST

2.8-liter (171 cid/105 hp) V-6, standard in Mach 1
. . . .(in other Mustang IIs) $299
SelectShift Cruise-O-Matic $212
Convenience Group includes: dual color-keyed remote
   control door mirrors; right visor vanity mirror; inside
   day/night mirror; parking brake boot and rear ashtray,
   on Mustangs with Luxury Interior Group $41
   (on Mach 1 or Mustangs with Rallye Package) $21
   (on other Mustangs) $57
Light Group includes: underhood, glovebox, map, ashtray
   and instrument panel courtesy lights, plus trunk or
   cargo area courtesy light and warning lamps for parking
   brake, "door ajar" and "headlamps-on" $44
Luxury Interior Group includes: super-soft vinyl upholstery; Deluxe door panels with large armrests and
   wood-tone accents; Deluxe rear quarter trim; 25-ounce
   cut-pile carpeting; sound package; parking brake boot;
   door courtesy lamps; rear ashtray; standard in Ghia, in
   other Mustangs $100
Maintenance Group includes: shop manual; spare bulbs;
   fire extinguisher; flares; warning flag; fuses; tire gauge;
   bungee cord; lube kit; trouble light; pliers; screwdriver
   and crescent wrench $44
Rallye Package (2.8-liter V-8 required; not available on
   Ghia) includes Traction-Lok differential; steel-belted
   raised white letter tires; extra-cooling package; competition suspension; dual color-keyed remote-control door
   mirrors; styled steel wheels; Sport exhaust system; digital clock and leather-wrapped steering wheel
   . . . . (on Mach 1) $150

. . . . (on 2+2) $284
. . . . (on others) $328
SelectAire conditioning $383
Anti-theft alarm system $75
Traction-Lok differential $45
Heavy-duty battery $14
Color-keyed Deluxe seat belts, standard in Ghia
. . . .(in others) $17
Front and rear bumper guards $37
Digital clock, standard in Ghia . . . .(in others) $36
Console $43
Electric rear window defroster $59
California emission equipment $19
Full tinted glass $37
Dual color-keyed door mirrors, standard in Ghia and
   Mach 1 . . . .(in others) $36
Rocker panel moldings $14
Vinyl-insert bodyside moldings $50
Glamour paint $36
Pin stripes $14
Power brakes $45
Power steering $106
Radios, AM $61
   (AM/FM monaural) $124
   (AM/FM stereo) $222
   (AM/FM stereo with tape player) $346
Competition suspension, including heavy-duty springs;
   adjustable shocks; rear anti-roll bar and 195/70 BWL
   BWL tires $37
Flip-out quarter windows, for 2+2 and Mach 1 hatchbacks
   only $29
Vinyl roof, hardtop only, standard on Ghia
   . . . . (on other models) $83
Fold-down rear seat $61
Super Sound Package, standard in Ghia . . .(in others) $22
Leather-wrapped steering wheel $30
Sunroof $149
Luggage compartment trim $28
Picardy velour cloth trim, Ghia $62
Wheel trim rings, standard on Ghia . . . . . .(on others) $32

1974 MUSTANG PRODUCTION CHART

Model	Doors/Body/Seating	Factory Price	Shipping Weight	Prod. Total
02 (60F)	2/coupe/4	$3081	2620	177,671
03 (69F)	3/hatchback/4	$3275	2699	74,799
04 (60H)	2/coupe Ghia/4	$3427	2866	89,477
05 (69R)	3/hatchback Mach 1/4	$3621	2778	44,046

NOTE 1: Total series output was 385,993 units.

During its five-year run, the Mustang II would see very few changes, but when the 1975 Mustang II lineup was introduced in September, 1974, it brought many modifications that went unnoticed by casual enthusiasts. A 302-cid (5.0-liter) V-8 returned to the Mustang II lineup after a one-year absence; its installation mandating most of the 1975 model's changes. A longer hood, repositioned radiator, new mounts for the plastic grille and new number two crossmember were necessary to shoehorn the V-8 into a car that had not been designed around such a large powerplant.

Mustang IIs with V-8s all came with a SelectShift automatic transmission, while V-6s were manually shifted. The standard 2.3-liter four came with both kinds of transmissions. Other changes for 1975 included a new steering wheel that retained two spokes, but with a slight re-design. There were no changes in standard equipment or in the ingredients of the Ghia or Mach 1 package. There was a new Ghia Silver Luxury Group package that cost $151. It included Silver Metallic paint; a silver Normande-grain half-vinyl roof; a stand-up hood ornament; Cranberry body striping; silver body side moldings; an all-Cranberry interior in Media velour cloth; and a color-keyed headliner, center console, and sun visors. All models came standard with steel-belted radial tires and solid state ignition.

The Rallye package was available again for 2+2s ($218) and Mach 1s ($168). Likewise, the 5.0-liter V-8 was $172 in Mach 1s and $199 in other models. This 122-hp two-barrel engine was often described as "thirsty," as it got only 13.7 to 15.9 miles per gallon. It could move the Mustang II along at 105 miles per hour, however, and sent it down the quarter-mile in 17.9 seconds at 77 miles per hour. V-8 equipped Mustang IIs came standard with the 3.5-gallon auxiliary fuel tank (optional on other models) that was introduced this year. The midyear introduction of an MPG package pushed Mustang performance to a new low, but the four-cylinder powerplant, when teamed with a 3.18:1 rear axle, produced a claimed 30-plus miles per gallon.

The long list of standard equipment continued from the car's introduction, including vinyl bucket seats; cut-pile carpeting on the floor and lower door; full instrumentation with tachometer, fuel, ammeter and temperature gauges; and simulated burled walnut woodtone accents on the instrument panel, shift handle and parking brake. After the V-8, probably the most exciting news for the II was the availability of a manually operated sunroof option.

The standard 2+2 fastback added a fold-down rear seat and styled steel wheels. The Ghia coupe had all base equipment plus Deluxe color-keyed seat belts; dual color-keyed, remote controlled outside rearview door mirrors; radial whitewalls; Super Sound package; shag carpeting; woodgrained door accent panels; digital clock; choice of Westminster cloth or super-soft vinyl trim; color-keyed vinyl roof; and spoke-style wheel covers. The Mach 1 fastback model had all equipment used on the 2+2 plus color-

keyed remote-control outside rearview door mirrors; steel-belted BR70-13 wide oval tires; black lower bodyside paint; specific rear deck lid striping; styled steel wheels with trim rings; and the 2.8-liter V-6 engine.

With a regular 12-month model year, Ford saw production of the 1975 Mustang II taper off to 188,575 cars or 2.88 percent of the industry total. This was still an improvement over the last of the big Mustangs and helped keep sales trending in the right direction from the marque's lowest point.

DATA PLATE DECODING

The Vehicle Identification Number is stamped on an aluminum tab on the instrument panel, viewable through windshield. A vehicle certification label is found on the body side of where the driver's door closes.

VEHICLE WARRANTY NUMBER
MODEL YEAR

5 – 1975

ASSEMBLY PLANT

F – Dearborn, Michigan
R – San Jose, California

BODY SERIAL NUMBERS

02 – coupe
03 – hatchback
04 – coupe, Ghia
05 – hatchback, Mach 1

ENGINE CODE

Y – 140-cid (2.3-liter) 2-bbl. SOHC 4-cyl.
Z – 171-cid (2.8-liter) 2-bbl. V-6
F – 302-cid (5.0-liter) 2-bbl. V-8

CONSECUTIVE UNIT NUMBER

Begins at 100001 at each factory

CODE NUMBERS
BODY CODE

60F – coupe
69F – hatchback
60H – coupe, Ghia
69R – hatchback, Mach 1

PAINT CODE

1C – Black
1G – Silver Metallic
2B – Bright Red
2M – Dark Red
3E – Bright Blue Metallic
3M – Silver Blue Glow
3Q – Pastel Blue
4T – Green Glow

4V – Dark Yellow Green Metallic
4Z – Light Green
5M – Medium Copper Metallic
5Q – Dark Brown Metallic
5U – Tan Glow
6E – Bright Yellow
9D – Polar White

ENGINES

140-cid (2.3-liter) 2-bbl. Inline Four

Valves . . . . overhead
Camshaft . . . . single overhead
Block . . . . cast iron
Displacement . . . . 140 cid/2.3 liters
Bore and stroke . . . . 3.78 x 3.13 inches
Compression ratio 8.4:1
SAE net hp 83
Main bearings 5
Valve lifters . . . . hydraulic
Carburetor . . . . Motorcraft 2-bbl.
Code . . . . Y

171-cid (2.8-liter) 2-bbl. V-6

Valves . . . . overhead
Block . . . . cast iron
Displacement . . . . 171 cid/2.8 liters
Bore and stroke . . . . 3.66 x 2.70 inches
Compression ratio 8.7:1
SAE net hp . . . . 97 @ 4400 rpm
Main bearings 4
Valve lifters . . . . solid
Carburetor . . . . Motorcraft 2-bbl.
Code . . . . Z

302-cid (5.0-liter) 2-bbl. V-8

Valves . . . . overhead
Block . . . . cast iron
Displacement . . . . 302 cid/5.0 liters
Bore and stroke . . . . 4.00 x 3.00 inches
Compression ratio 8.0:1
SAE net hp . . . . 122 @ 4000
Main bearings 5
Valve lifters . . . . hydraulic
Carburetor . . . . Motorcraft 2-bbl.
Code . . . . F

CHASSIS

Wheelbase . . . . 96.2 inches
Overall length . . . . 175 inches
Height . . . . (coupe) 50.0 inches
. . . . (hatchback) 49.7 inches
Width 70.2
Front tread width . . . . 55.6 inches
Rear tread width . . . . 55.8 inches

TECHNICAL

Final drive ratio . . . . (four-cylinder, four-speed) 2.79:1
. . . . (four-cylinder, automatic) 3.18:1
. . . . (V-6) 3.00:1
. . . . (V-8) 2.79:1
Steering . . . . rack and pinion

Front suspension . . . .
compression strut with lower trailing links,
bar and coil springs
Rear suspension . . . .
Hotchkiss rigid axle w/semi-elliptic leaf springs
(four leaves), anti-sway bar
Brakes . . . . (front) 9.3-inch disc
. . . . (rear) 9.0-inch drum
Ignition . . . . electronic
Body construction . . . unibody w/front isolated mini-frame
Fuel tank . . . . 13 gallons
. . . . . . (optional, standard on V-8 models) 16.5 gallons

OPTION LIST

Exterior Accent Group $151
Select-Aire conditioning $401
Anti-Theft alarm system $71

Deluxe color-keyed seat belts, standard Ghia
. . . . (in other models) $51
Front and rear bumper guards $31
Digital quartz electric clock $37
Console $63
Electric rear window defroster $59
California emissions equipment $41
Fuel monitor warning light $14
Deck lid luggage rack $43
Dual color-keyed outside rearview door mirrors, standard
Ghia/Mach 1 . . . . (on others) $36
Rocker panel moldings $14
Color-keyed vinyl insert type bodyside moldings $51
Power steering $111
Glass moon roof $422
Radio . . . . (AM) $63
. . . . (AM/FM) $124
. . . . (AM/FM stereo) $213
. . . . (same with 8-track) $333
Glamour paint $43
Vinyl roof for hardtop coupe, standard with Ghia,
on others $83
Fold-down rear seat, standard in fastbacks, on others . $61
Leather-wrapped steering wheel $30
Pin striping $18
Sun roof $195
Competition suspension, includes heavy-duty springs;
adjustable shock absorbers; rear anti-roll bar; and
195/70 blackwall (or White Line tires on Ghia or others
with Exterior Accent Group) $43
. . . . (on Mach 1) $25
. . . . (on others) $55
Velour cloth interior trim $63
Flip-out rear quarter windows on fastbacks $31
Four-speed manual transmission with floor shift . . standard
. . . . (Select-Shift Cruise-O-Matic) $227
171-cid/2.8-liter V-6 engine . . . . (in Mach 1) no charge
. . . . (in other models) $253
302-cid/5.0-liter V-8 engine . . . . (in Mach 1) $172
. . . . (in other models) $199
Traction-Lok differential $46
Heavy-duty battery $14
Extended range fuel tank $18

OPTION PACKAGES

Convenience Group, includes dual, color-keyed, remote-controlled outside rearview door mirrors; right-hand visor/vanity mirror; inside day/night mirror; parking brake boot; and rear ashtray
. . . . (with Luxury Interior Group) $48
. . . . (on Mach 1 or models with Rallye Package or Exterior Accent Group) $29
. . . . (on other models) $65

Light Group, includes underhood glovebox; ashtray; dashboard courtesy lights; plus map, "door ajar" and "headlamps-on" warning lights. $33

Security Lock Group, includes locking gas cap; inside hood release lock and spare tire lock. $14

Luxury Interior Group, includes Super-Soft vinyl seats; door trim with large armrests; Deluxe rear quarter trim; door courtesy lights; color-keyed seat belts; shag carpets; parking brake boot; rear ashtray and Super-Sound package. $100

Ghia Silver Luxury Group . ., for Ghia coupe only, includes Silver metallic paint; silver Nommande-grain half vinyl roof; stand-up hood ornament; Cranberry striping; Silver bodyside moldings; all-Cranberry interior in Media velour cloth; color-keyed sun visors and headliner, plus center console. $151

Maintenance Group, includes shop manual; bulbs; fire extinguisher; flares; warning flag; fuses; tire gauge; bungee cord; lube kit; trouble light; pliers; screwdriver; and crescent wrench. $45

Rallye Package, includes Traction-Lok differential; 195/70 raised white letter tires; extra-cooling package; bright exhaust tips; competition suspension package; dual color-keyed, remote-control outside rearview door mirrors; leather-wrapped steering wheel; and styled steel wheels with trim rings. . . . . (on Mach 1) $168
. . . . (on 2+2) $218
. . . . (on other models) $262

Protection Group, includes door edge guards; front floor mats; and license plate frames
. . . . (on Mach 1) $19
. . . . (on others) $27

\ 1975 MUSTANG PRODUCTION CHART				
Model	Doors/Body/Seating	Factory Price	Shipping Weight	Prod. Total
02 (60F)	2/coupe/4	$3529/3801	2660/2775	85,155
03 (69F)	3/hatchback/4	$3818/4090	2697/2812	30,038
04 (60H)	2/coupe Ghia/4	$3938/4210	2704/2819	52,320
05 (69R)	3/hatchback Mach 1/4	$4188	2879	21,062

NOTE 1: Total series output was 188,575 units.
NOTE 2: Data above slash for four-cylinder/below slash for V-6.

1976 Cobra II (FMC)

1976

Ford's desire to market the Mustang II as a car to make everyone happy produced some confusing and conflicting ad copy regarding the 1976. For example, an August, 1975, factory sales catalog entitled *The 1976 Fords* shows a picture of a Ghia notchback with the message, "MUSTANG II: Our small, sporty personal car." Interestingly, a headline on the descriptive copy across from the photo calls the Mustang II, "America's best-selling small luxury car." A few months later (October 1975), the company's 24-page *Free Wheelin'* sales booklet touted the Mustang II as an economy car.

With sales of 187,567 Mustang IIs in 1976, Iacocca's "little jewel" dominated the domestic subcompact sporty car market in its third year. Improvements in fuel economy at a time when the nation was still skittish about buying more gas guzzlers, and a few enhancements such as stalk-mounted windshield wiper controls (first seen mid-1975) kept the II on a path of slow but steady evolution. Another minor change when the 1976 model was introduced on Oct. 3, 1975, was that black bumper rub strips replaced the former horizontal stainless steel bumper inserts with white stripes on all models.

New options for 1976 included intermittent wipers; a four-speed manual transmission for the V-8 cars; sporty plaid trim on seating surfaces; expanded availability of Ghia luxury coupe colors; whitewall tires; a AM radio with stereo tape player; and two youthful appearance packages. The first new offering was the Stallion model. It included the standard notchback or 2+2 ingredients with the following changes: black grille and surround moldings; black moldings and wiper arms; bright lower body side moldings; Stallion decals; black-painted lower fenders, lower doors, lower quarter panels, lower front and rear bumpers, and rocker panels; and styled steel wheels.

The Stallion package (offered for Mustang MPGs, Pinto MPGs and Mavericks) was usually shown in black and silver and many books suggest this was the only choice of colors. However, The 1976 Fords catalog shows a 2+2 with the Stallion option in a Bright Yellow (6E) and Black (1C) two-tone combination. The *Free Wheelin'* booklet says Stallions came "with colorful paint masked by blackout body panels." It specifies colors of Silver Metallic, Bright Red, Bright Yellow, Polar White, and Silver Blue Glow (extra-cost) for the Maverick Stallion, suggesting that Mustang Stallions also came in these same five hues.

The big image-enhancer for 1976, however, was the Cobra II package—a hatchback-only model with the look, but not the performance, of a Shelby Mustang. "Cobra strikes again," said the *Free Wheelin'* catalog (which was a youth-oriented, 24-page color booklet and probably one of the sexiest pieces of factory literature Ford ever produced). "New Cobra II. Ford's Mustang II wrapped in an appearance package that does justice to the Cobra name. So striking, it's already a sales success." It was hard to believe from a piece of literature printed in October 1975, that the exciting-looking Cobra option was "already a sales success;" however, the Cobra II was on its way to reaching an approving audience, since the package was available on all 2+2s with any engine.

Jim Wangers, who generally receives credit for fathering the Pontiac GTO, was responsible for designing and installing the Cobra II-unique graphics and aerodynamic pieces at a small plant near the Dearborn Ford factory. His company, Motortown, would produce all Cobra IIs for 1976, but Ford took the popular package in-house for 1977 and 1978. The $325 option was definitely the model year's biggest Mustang news. Carroll Shelby even appeared in the sales catalog to promote the Cobra II.

As if to prove the new Cobra was primarily an appearance package, the car started with Mustang II MPG standard equipment like rack and pinion steering; front disc brakes; and the 2.3-liter four-cylinder, two-barrel engine (for added punch, the V-6 or V-8 could be added). Then the following special Cobra II equipment was added: bold racing stripes; a blacked-out grille; racing mirrors; rear quarter window louvers; a front air dam; a non-functional hood scoop; a rear deck lid spoiler; a brushed aluminum instrument panel and door panel appliques; Cobra insignias on the front fenders; styled steel wheels and BR70 steel-belted tires with raised white letters. The 1976 Cobra II came in white with blue stripes, blue with white stripes, or black with gold stripes.

The base models with the four-cylinder were all called MPGs. They had the same standard equipment as before. To improve economy, the Mustang II received a lower optional 2.79:1 axle ratio and an optional wide-ratio transmission. The printed standard equipment list looked longer, because body-color urethane bumpers, Ford Lifeguard Design safety features, and bright window moldings were specifically mentioned. Ghia upgrades were basically the same, although the stand-up hood ornament was no longer standard. It was part of the Luxury Group option. The Mach 1 (the official name "Mustang II Mach 1 2+2 3-door" sounded almost algebraic) also had the same add-ons as before. Strangely, since the V-6 was standard, the Mach 1 did not come as an MPG, although the Cobra did.

Playing off Henry Ford's famous "any color as long as it's black" statement about the Model T Ford, the 1976 sales booklet put colorful promotional emphasis on an "all-black Mustang II with blackout grille, wipers and window moldings and styled steel wheels," a "classic black Mustang II MPG 2+2 with bright grille, window moldings, and wheelcovers" and a "Red Mach 1." The three cars were photographed with eight young mechanics working on a street rod and a Mustang race car, with new Mustang IIs and a Cobra II parked nearby. The smaller Mustang II engines were robbed of some power in 1976, with the four going from 97 to 92 hp and the V-6 dropping from 105 to 103 hp. However, the V-8 got a substantial boost from 122 to 139 hp.

Model year production for 1976 stayed at just about the same level at 187,567 units. That was 2.31 percent of the auto industry's total domestic output. The small Mustang still seemed to be struggling to find its real identity. In addition to everything else it was trying to be, the new Cobra II was a musclecar "wannabe." In the long run, adding some real muscle was the key to a success that would come after the Mustang II era.

DATA PLATE DECODING

The Vehicle Identification Number is stamped on an aluminum tab on the instrument panel, viewable through windshield. A vehicle certification label is found on the body side of where the driver's door closes.

VEHICLE WARRANTY NUMBER
MODEL YEAR

6 – 1976

ASSEMBLY PLANT

F – Dearborn, Michigan
R – San Jose, California

BODY SERIAL NUMBERS

02 – coupe
03 – hatchback
04 – coupe, Ghia
05 – hatchback, Mach 1

ENGINE CODE

Y – 140-cid (2.3-liter) 2-bbl. SOHC 4-cyl.
Z – 171-cid (2.8-liter) 2-bbl. V-6
F – 302-cid (5.0-liter) 2-bbl. V-8

CONSECUTIVE UNIT NUMBER

Begins at 100001 at each factory

CODE NUMBERS
BODY CODE

60F – coupe
69F – hatchback
60H – coupe, Ghia
69R – hatchback, Mach 1

PAINT CODE

1C – Black
1G – Silver Metallic
2B – Bright Red
2M – Dark Red
3E – Bright Blue Metallic

1976 Stallion (FMC)

1976 Stallion (FMC)

3M – Silver Blue Glow
4T – Medium Ivy Bronze Metallic
4V – Dark Yellow Green Metallic
4Z – Light Green
5M – Medium Chestnut Metallic
5Q – Dark Brown Metallic
5U – Tan Glow
6E – Bright Yellow
9D – Polar White
Tu-Tone
6P/6V – Cream/Medium Gold Metallic
9D/2R – White/Bright Red
9D/3E – White/Bright Blue Metallic

ENGINES

140-cid (2.3-liter) 2-bbl. Inline Four

Valves . . . . overhead
Camshaft . . . . single overhead
Block . . . . cast iron
Displacement . . . . 140 cid/2.3 liters
Bore and stroke . . . . 3.78 x 3.13 inches
Compression ratio 9.0:1
Brake hp . . . . 92 @ 5000 rpm
Main bearings 5
Valve lifters . . . . hydraulic
Carburetor . . . . Holley-Weber 2-bbl.
Code . . . . Y

171-cid (2.8-liter) 2-bbl. V-6

Valves . . . . overhead
Block . . . . cast iron
Displacement . . . . 171 cid/2.8 liters
Bore and stroke . . . . 3.66 x 2.70 inches
Compression ratio 8.7:1
Brake hp . . . . 103 @ 4400 rpm
Main bearings 4
Valve lifters . . . . solid
Carburetor . . . . Holley-Weber 2-bbl.
Code . . . . Z

302-cid (5.0-liter) 2-bbl. V-8

Valves . . . . overhead
Block . . . . cast iron
Displacement . . . . 302 cid/5.0 liters
Bore and stroke . . . . 4.00 x 3.00 inches
Compression ratio 8.0:1
Brake hp . . . . 139 @ 3600 rpm
Main bearings 5

Valve lifters . . . . hydraulic
Carburetor . . . . Motorcraft 2-bbl.
Code . . . . F

CHASSIS

Wheelbase . . . . 96.2 inches
Overall length . . . . 175 inches
Height . . . . (coupe) 50.0 inches
. . . . (hatchback) 49.7 inches
Width 70.2
Front tread width . . . . 55.6 inches
Rear tread width . . . . 55.8 inches
Tires B78x13
. . . . (Ghia) BR78x13
. . . . (Mach 1) BR70x13

TECHNICAL

Final drive ratio . . . . (four-cylinder, four-speed) 2.79:1
. . . . (four-cylinder, automatic) 3.18:1
. . . . (V-6) 3.00:1
. . . . (V-8) 2.79:1
Steering . . . . rack and pinion
Front suspension . . . .
compression strut with lower trailing links, stabilizer bar
and coil springs
Rear suspension . . . .
Hotchkiss rigid axle w/semi-elliptic leaf springs (four
leaves), anti-sway bar
Brakes . . . . (front) 9.3-inch disc
. . . . (rear) 9.0-inch drum
Ignition . . . . electronic
Body construction . . . unibody w/front isolated mini-frame
Fuel tank . . . . 13 gallons
. . . . . . (optional, standard on V-8 models) 16.5 gallons

OPTION LIST

140-cid/2.3-liter four-cylinder
. . . . (credit from base V-6 price) $272
Cruise-O-Matic automatic transmission $239
Optional axle ratio $13
Traction-Lok differential $48
Power brakes $54
Power steering $117
Competition suspension . . . . $29-$191
Heavy-duty 53-amp battery $14
Extended-range fuel tank $24
Engine block heater $17
California emission system $49

1976 Ghia (FMC)

1976 Cobra II (FMC)

Cobra II package $325
Cobra II modification package $287
Rallye package . . . . (Mach 1) $163
. . . . (hardtop) $267-$399
Ghia luxury group. $177
Stallion option $72
Exterior accent group $169
Luxury interior group. $117
Convenience group $35
Light group . . . . $28-$41
Protection group . . . . $36-$43
Air conditioning. $420
Rear defroster, electric. $70
Tinted glass $46
Leather-wrapped steering wheel. $33
Electric clock. $17
Digital clock. $40
Fuel monitor warning light. $18
Anti-theft alarm $83
Security lock group $16
Dual-note horn $6
Color-keyed mirrors. $42
AM radio $71
. . . . (w/tape player) $192
AM/FM radio $128
AM/FM stereo radio $173
. . . . (w/tape player) $299
Exterior: Glass moonroof $470
Manual sunroof $230

Vinyl roof. $86
Half-vinyl roof . . . . (Ghia only) no charge
Glamour paint $54
Two-tone paint/tape $84
Pinstriping $27
Bumper guards, front/rear $34
color-keyed vinyl-insert bodyside molding $60
Rocker panel moldings. $19
Pivoting rear quarter windows $33
Decklid luggage rack $51
Console $71
Fold-down rear seat $72
Velour cloth trim $99
Color-keyed deluxe seatbelts $17
Cast aluminum spoke wheels . . . . $96-$182
Forged aluminum wheels. . . . . $96-$182
Styled steel wheels . . . . (base coupe, base hatchback) $51
. . . . (Ghia) no charge
Trim rings $35
B78 x 13 BSW $84
B78 x 13 WSW . . . . $33-$52
BR78 x 13 BSW $97
BR78 x 13 WSW . . . . $33-$130
BR70 x 13 RWL . . . . $30-$160
CR70 x 13 WSW . . . . $10-$169
195/70R13 WSW . . . . $22-$191
195/70R13 RWL . . . . $12-$203
195/70R13 wide WSW . . . . $5-$208

1976 MUSTANG PRODUCTION CHART

Model	Doors/Body/Seating	Factory Price	Shipping Weight	Prod. Total
02 (60F)	2/coupe/4	$3525/3791	2678/2756	78,508
03 (69F)	3/hatchback/4	$3781/4047	2706/2784	62,312
04 (60H)	2/coupe Ghia/4	$3859/4125	2729/2807	37,515
05 (69R)	3/hatchback Mach 1/4	$4209/4154	2822/NA	9,232

NOTE 1: Total series output was 187,567 units.
NOTE 2: Data above slash for four-cylinder/below slash for V-6 (on 60F, 69F and 60H).

1977 Mach 1 (JH)

1977

There were few significant changes in the Mustang II for 1977. Updates included new colors and a revision in the wood-tone interior trim appliqués that changed from a burled walnut appearance to a simulated pecan woodgrain. The four and the V-6 both lost a few more horsepower as emission upgrades continued to choke off engine performance. The V-8 retained its 139-hp rating. California models used a variable-venturi carburetor. Buyers in that state were also limited to four-cylinder Mustang IIs or V-8 cars with automatic transmissions.

A Sports Performance package consisted of the 5.0-liter two-barrel V-8, heavy-duty four-speed manual transmission, power steering, power brakes and radial-ply tires. Joining the option list were simulated wire wheel covers; painted cast aluminum spoke wheels; a flip-up removable sunroof; four-way manual bucket seats and high-altitude option. On the all-new twin-panel T-roof option (available only on hatchback models), a wide black band ran across the top (except with the Cobra II).

The basic notchback for 1977 carried the standard four-cylinder engine with Dura-Spark ignition; four-speed manual gearbox; front disc brakes; color-keyed urethane bumpers; low-back bucket seats with vinyl trim, B78 x 13 tires; and full wheel covers. Bright moldings highlighted the windshield, drip rail, belt, back window, and center pillar. Mustang II hatchbacks included a front spoiler at no extra cost (which could be deleted); along with a sport steering wheel; styled steel wheels; B78 x 13 bias-belted raised-white-letter or 195R/70 whitewall tires; blackout grille; and brushed aluminum instrument panel appliqués.

Ordering a Ghia notchback model added a half-vinyl roof, pinstripes, unique wheel covers, and bodyside moldings with color-keyed vinyl inserts. Ghia interiors could have Media Velour cloth with large armrests.

Stepping up another notch, the Mach 1 carried a standard 2.8-liter V-6 and sported a black paint treatment on lower bodyside and back panel. Also included were dual sport mirrors, a Mach 1 emblem, and raised-white-letter BR70 x 13 (or 195R/70) steel-belted radial tires on styled steel wheels with trim rings.

The Cobra II option package climbed more than $220 in price, to $535. The 1977 Cobra again came in white with blue racing stripes, blue with white stripes, or black with gold stripes, plus a choice of two new color combinations: white with color-keyed red accent stripes and white with green stripes.

Early-in-the-year Cobras had COBRA II lettering low on the doors; later cars had much larger lettering that ran higher up on the doors. Flat black greenhouse moldings, vertical-style quarter-window louvers (without the snake), and rear-window louvers also became standard. So was a narrow band of flat black along the upper doors. Cobra II equipment also included dual black sport mirrors; a rear-opening hood scoop; BR70 or 195/R70 x 13 RWL tires; and brushed aluminum door trim inserts. The package required extra-cost power brakes.

Other desirable options were the $422 Ghia Sports Group and the Rallye package. The latter was $88 on most cars, but only $43 for Mach 1s, Cobras, and cars with the Exterior Accent Group option. The Sports Group included black or tan paint with a black Odense grain or a Chamois Lugano grain vinyl roof. Other ingredients were body side moldings with matching vinyl inserts; a blacked out grille; a luggage rack with color-keyed leather hold-down straps and bright buckles; cast aluminum wheels with chamois-painted spokes; color-keyed interior appointments; plus a center console and a leather-wrapped steering wheel.

The late-arriving 2+2 Rallye Appearance Package replaced the Stallion option. It included dual gold accent stripes on hood and bodysides; flat black wiper arms, door handles, lock cylinders, and antenna; dual black sport mirrors; and Argent styled steel wheels with trim rings. A gold-color surround molding highlighted the black grille (which lost its horse emblem). Also included were gold tail lamp accent moldings and dual gold accent stripes in bumper rub strips. A black front spoiler was a no-cost option. Black and Polar White body colors were offered with the package. Inside were black or white vinyl seats with gold ribbed velour Touraine cloth inserts and gold welting, and gold accent moldings on door panels. As for real performance upgrades, the new Rallye package included dual racing mirrors, heavy-duty springs and cooling, adjustable shocks and rear stabilizer bar.

Model year production was 153,173 units, an 18.3 percent decrease from 1976. It represented 1.68 percent of the total industry output. Part of both declines was due to a United Auto Workers strike at Ford. Just over 25 percent of all 1977 Mustang IIs were ordered with V-8s, versus 17.6 percent in 1976.

DATA PLATE DECODING

The Vehicle Identification Number is stamped on an aluminum tab on the instrument panel, viewable through windshield. A vehicle certification label is found on the body side of where the driver's door closes.

VEHICLE WARRANTY NUMBER
MODEL YEAR

7 – 1977

ASSEMBLY PLANT

F – Dearborn, Michigan
R – San Jose, California

BODY SERIAL NUMBERS

02 – coupe
03 – hatchback
04 – coupe, Ghia
05 – hatchback, Mach 1

ENGINE CODE

Y – 140-cid (2.3-liter) 2-bbl. SOHC 4-cyl.
Z – 171-cid (2.8-liter) 2-bbl. V-6
F – 302-cid (5.0-liter) 2-bbl. V-8

CONSECUTIVE UNIT NUMBER

Begins at 100001 at each factory

CODE NUMBERS
BODY CODE

60F – coupe
69F – hatchback
60H – coupe, Ghia
69R – hatchback, Mach 1

PAINT CODE

1C – Black
2R – Bright Red
5Q – Dark Brown Metallic
6E – Bright Yellow
6P – Cream
6V – Golden Glow
7H – Bright Aqua Glow
7Q – Light Aqua Metallic
7S – Medium Emerald Glow
8G – Orange
8H – Tan
8K – Bright Saddle Metallic
9D – Polar White
Tu-Tone
6P/6V – Cream/Medium Gold Metallic
9D/2R – White/Bright Red
9D/7Q – White/Light Aqua Metallic

ENGINES

140-cid (2.3-liter) 2-bbl. Inline Four

Valves . . . . overhead
Camshaft . . . . single overhead
Block . . . . cast iron
Displacement . . . . 140 cid/2.3 liters
Bore and stroke . . . . 3.78 x 3.13 inches
Compression ratio 9.0:1
Brake hp . . . . 89 @ 4800 rpm
Main bearings 5
Valve lifters . . . . hydraulic
Carburetor . . . . Motorcraft 2-bbl.
Code . . . . Y

1977 Ghia (FMC)

1977 Cobra II (FMC)

171-cid (2.8-liter) 2-bbl. V-6

Valves . . . . overhead
Block . . . . cast iron
Displacement. . . . . 171 cid/2.8 liters
Bore and stroke. . . . . 3.66 x 2.70 inches
Compression ratio 8.7:1
Brake hp . . . . 93 @ 4200 rpm
Main bearings 4
Valve lifters . . . . solid
Carburetor. Motorcraft 2-bbl.
Code . . . . Z

302-cid (5.0-liter) 2-bbl. V-8

Valves . . . . overhead
Block . . . . cast iron
Displacement. . . . . 302 cid/5.0 liters
Bore and stroke. . . . . 4.00 x 3.00 inches
Compression ratio 8.4:1
Brake hp . . . . 139 @ 3600 rpm
Main bearings 5
Valve lifters. . . . . hydraulic
Carburetor. Motorcraft 2-bbl.
Code . . . . F

CHASSIS

Wheelbase . . . . 96.2 inches
Overall length . . . . 175 inches
Height. (coupe) 50.3 inches
. . . . (hatchback) 50.0 inches
Width 70.2
Front tread width. . . . . 55.6 inches
Rear tread width . . . . 55.8 inches
Tires B78x13
. . . . (Ghia) BR78x13
. . . . (Mach 1) BR70x13

TECHNICAL

Final drive ratio. . . . . (four-cylinder) 3.18:1
. . . . (V-6, V-8) 3.00:1
Steering. . . . . rack and pinion
Front suspension . . . .
compression strut with lower trailing links, stabilizer bar
and coil springs
Rear suspension . . . .
Hotchkiss rigid axle w/semi-elliptic leaf springs (four
leaves), anti-sway bar
Brakes . . . . (front) 9.3-inch disc
. . . . (rear) 9.0-inch drum
Ignition . . . . electronic
Body construction . . . unibody w/front isolated mini-frame
Fuel tank . . . . 13 gallons
. . . . . . (optional, standard on V-8 models) 16.5 gallons

OPTION LIST

140-cid/2.3-liter four-cylinder
. . . . (credit from base V-6 price) $289
170-cid/2.8-liter V-6. $289
302-cid/5.0-liter V-8. $230
Cruise-O-Matic transmission $253
Power brakes. $58
Power steering. $124
Heavy-duty battery $16
California emission system $52
High-altitude emissions $39
Cobra II package. $535
Sports performance package. . . . . $451-$607
. . . . (exc. Mach 1) $163
Rallye package . . . . $43-$88
Ghia sports group $422
Exterior accent group $216
Appearance decor group . . . . $96-$152
Luxury interior group $124

1977 Cobra II (FMC)

Convenience group . . . . $37-$71	Full vinyl roof $90
Light group . . . . $29-$43	Front spoiler . . . . no charge
Protection group . . . . $39-$46	Metallic glow paint $58
Air conditioning $446	Pinstriping $28
Rear defroster, electric $73	Color-keyed vinyl-insert bodyside moldings $64
Tinted glass $48	Rocker panel moldings $20
Leather-wrapped steering wheel . . . . $35-$49	Decklid luggage rack $54
Digital clock $42	Console $76
Dual sport mirrors $45	Four-way driver's seat $33
AM radio $76	Fold down rear seat $77
. . . . (w/tape player) $204	Media velour cloth trim $105
AM/FM radio $135	Color-keyed deluxe seatbelts $18
AM/FM stereo radio $184	Wire wheel covers . . . . $33-$86
. . . . (w/tape player) $317	Forged aluminum wheels . . . . $102-$193
T-top roof . . . . (Cobra II hatchback) $587	Lacy spoke aluminum wheels . . . . $102-$193
. . . . (Mach 1 hatchback) $629	. . . . (white) $153-$243
Flip-up open air roof $147	Styled steel wheels . . . . $37-$90
Manual sunroof $243	Trim rings $37

1977 MUSTANG PRODUCTION CHART

Model	Doors/Body/Seating	Factory Price	Shipping Weight	Prod. Total
02 (60F)	2/coupe/4	$3702/3984	2627/2750	67,783
03 (69F)	3/hatchback/4	$3901/4183	2672/2795	49,161
04 (60H)	2/coupe Ghia/4	$4119/4401	2667/2790	29,510
05 (69R)	3/hatchback Mach 1/4	$4332/4284	2785/NA	6,719

NOTE 1: Total series output was 153,173 units. Totals shown include 20,937 Mustangs produced as 1978 models but sold as 1977 models (9,826 notchbacks, 7,019 hatchbacks, 3,209 Ghias, and 883 Mach 1s) due to a problem with emissions regulations.
NOTE 2: Data above slash for four-cylinder/below slash for V-6 (on 60F, 69F and 60H).
NOTE 3: Data above slash for V-6/below slash for V-8 (on 69R).

1977 2+2 (FMC)

1978 King Cobra (JH)

1978

When introduced on Oct. 7, 1977, the 1978 Mustang II lineup was still reigning supreme over its competitors in the domestic sporty subcompact class. In its final year of production before the all-new "Fox" Mustang debuted, the II received very little in the way of improvements—the one notable exception being the "look at me" King Cobra package.

Powered by a 2.3-liter four with four-speed transmission, the standard Mustang II featured an electronic ignition system, front disc brakes, rack-and-pinion steering, a tachometer, and an ammeter among its extensive list of equipment. Separate rear seat cushions and new color choices, plus new designs in door trim, seat trim, and carpets were added to the list for 1978. Mechanical upgrades included a plastic cooling fan for the V-6 engine, an electronic voltage regulator (replacing the old electromechanical version) and optional variable-ratio power steering (first introduced on the Fairmont).

Dress-up packages continued to proliferate on the Mustang II's option list, however, as the Mustang's unique personality had always appealed to young buyers who liked cars loaded with extras. A Rallye Appearance package featured gold and flat black accents combined with complementary cloth seat inserts to accentuate its sporty 2+2 appeal. The simulated convertible T-Roof, with dual removable tinted glass panels, was now entering its first full model year as an option on the base and Mach 1 hatchbacks.

For the third year in a row, more power was robbed from the base four (now rated at 88 hp) and the optional V-6 (down to 90 hp). The V-8 was again credited with the same 139 hp. SelectShift Cruise-O-Matic transmission was $225 extra with V-8s or the King Cobra option and $263 in other models.

The Mach 1, a proven sales success, returned again. It included the 2.8-liter V-6, styled wheels and raised white-letter tires, plus black front and rear bumpers and lower body side paint. A brushed aluminum instrument panel appliqué and full instrumentation added to its youthful appeal.

Continuing as a fun-to-own, fun-to-drive car, the Cobra II carried on in the form introduced at mid-year in 1977. Tricolor tape stripes decorated bodysides and front spoiler, front bumper, hood, hood scoop, roof, decklid and rear spoiler. Huge "Cobra" block letters went on the center bodyside tape stripe and decklid spoiler, a Cobra decal appeared on the back spoiler, and a Cobra II snake emblem sat on the black grille. The package also included flat black greenhouse moldings, black quarter-window and backlight louvers, black rocker panels and dual racing mirrors, a narrow black band along upper doors, and a rear-opening hood scoop.

The new "Boss of the Mustang stable" is how Ford described its King Cobra. The package might be viewed as a regular Cobra and more of the same, with plenty of striping and lettering. The King did without the customary bodyside striping, but sported a unique tape treatment including a giant snake decal on the hood and pinstriping on the greenhouse, decklid, wheel lips, rocker panels, belt, over-the-roof area, and around the side windows. Up front was a tough-looking spoiler. The 302-cid (5.0-liter) V-8 was standard on the King, along with a four-speed transmission and power brakes and power steering. A "King Cobra" nameplate went on each door and the back spoiler and a "5.0L" badge appeared on the front hood scoop. The King Cobra also had rear quarter flares, a black grille and moldings, and color-keyed dual sport mirrors. Raised-white-letter tires rode lacy-spoke aluminum wheels with twin rings and a Cobra symbol on the hubs.

A Fashion Accessory Group, aimed at women, consisted

1978 King Cobra (FMC)

of a four-way adjustable driver's seat, striped cloth seat inserts, illuminated entry, lighted driver's vanity visor mirror, coin tray, and door pockets. It came in nine body colors.

Another "active lifestyle" Mustang II variant was the Ghia hardtop, especially appealing when fitted with the Sports Group package. It had a luxurious, color-coordinated interior and complementary exterior accents. This year's edition came with the black and Chamois color choices, or Dark Blue exterior paint. Also included was a blacked-out grille, color-coordinated moldings, pin stripes, leather-wrapped steering wheel, floor console, and vinyl seat trim.

Model year production leaped to 192,410 units in the Mustang II's final season. That represented 2.15 percent of all domestic auto output. V-8 engines were optionally installed in 17.9 percent of the Mustang IIs.

DATA PLATE DECODING

The Vehicle Identification Number is stamped on an aluminum tab on the instrument panel, viewable through windshield. A vehicle certification label is found on the body side of where the driver's door closes.

VEHICLE WARRANTY NUMBER
MODEL YEAR

8 – 1978

ASSEMBLY PLANT

F – Dearborn, Michigan
R – San Jose, California

BODY SERIAL NUMBERS

02 – coupe   04 – coupe, Ghia
03 – hatchback   05 – hatchback, Mach 1

ENGINE CODE

Y – 140-cid (2.3-liter) 2-bbl. SOHC 4-cyl.
Z – 171-cid (2.8-liter) 2-bbl. V-6
F – 302-cid (5.0-liter) 2-bbl. V-8

CONSECUTIVE UNIT NUMBER

Begins at 100001 at each factory

CODE NUMBERS

For automotive historians, the year 1978 is perhaps as significant to the evolution of the automobile as the invention of the assembly line. It was in that year that the government's corporate average fuel economy (CAFE) standards went into effect.

CAFE meant that each automobile manufacturer would be responsible for producing fuel-efficient automobiles—fuel-efficiency being defined as a specific miles per gallon rating as applied to the entire fleet. In other words, Ford's Mustang II Cobra II in V-8 trim only got about 17 mpg, which meant that for every Cobra II sold in 1978, Ford had to sell a car that averaged 19 mpg in order to achieve that year's randomly assigned 18-mpg goal. For 1979, the goal was 19 mpg; for 1980, 20 mpg; for 1981, 22 mpg—up to 1985, when 27.5 mpg was expected.

BODY CODE

60F – coupe
69F – hatchback
60H – coupe, Ghia
69R – hatchback, Mach 1

PAINT CODE

1C – Black
1G – Silver Metallic
2R – Bright Red
3A – Dark Midnight Blue
46 – Dark Jade Metallic
5M – Medium Chestnut Metallic
5Q – Dark Brown Metallic
6E – Bright Yellow
7H – Bright Aqua Glow
7Q – Aqua Metallic
7S – Medium Emerald Glow
8W – Chamois Glow
83 – Light Chamois
85 – Tangerine
9D – Polar White

Tu-Tone
1G/1C – Silver Metallic/Black
1G/2R – Silver Metallic/Bright Red
2R/1C – Bright Red/Black
2R/9D – Bright Red/White
46/9D – Dark Jade Metallic/White
6E/1C – Bright Yellow/Black
7H/9D – Bright Aqua Metallic/White
7Q/9D – Light Aqua Metallic/White
83/5M – Light Chamois/Medium Chestnut Metallic
85/9D – Tangerine/White
9D/1C – White/Black
9D/2R – White/Bright Red
9D/7Q – White/Light Aqua Metallic

ENGINES
140-cid (2.3-liter) 2-bbl. Inline Four

Valves . . . . overhead
Camshaft . . . . single overhead
Block . . . . cast iron
Displacement . . . . 140 cid/2.3 liters
Bore and stroke . . . . 3.78 x 3.13 inches
Compression ratio 9.0:1
Brake hp . . . . 88 @ 4800 rpm
Main bearings 5
Valve lifters . . . . hydraulic
Carburetor . . . . Motorcraft 2-bbl.
Code . . . . Y

171-cid (2.8-liter) 2-bbl. V-6

Valves . . . . overhead
Block . . . . cast iron
Displacement . . . . 171 cid/2.8 liters
Bore and stroke . . . . 3.66 x 2.70 inches
Compression ratio 8.7:1
Brake hp . . . . 90 @ 4200 rpm
Main bearings 4
Valve lifters . . . . solid
Carburetor . . . . Motorcraft 2-bbl.
Code . . . . Z

302-cid (5.0-liter) 2-bbl. V-8

Valves . . . . overhead
Block . . . . cast iron
Displacement . . . . 302 cid/5.0 liters
Bore and stroke . . . . 4.00 x 3.00 inches
Compression ratio 8.4:1
Brake hp . . . . 139 @ 3600 rpm
Main bearings 5
Valve lifters . . . . hydraulic
Carburetor . . . . Motorcraft 2-bbl.
Code . . . . F

CHASSIS

Wheelbase . . . . 96.2 inches
Overall length . . . . 175 inches
Height . . . . (coupe) 50.3 inches
. . . . (hatchback) 50.0 inches
Width 70.2
Front tread width . . . . 55.6 inches
Rear tread width . . . . 55.8 inches
Tires B78x13
. . . . (Ghia) BR78x13
. . . . (Mach 1) BR70x13

TECHNICAL

Final drive ratio . . . . (four-cylinder) 3.18:1
. . . . (V-6, four-speed) 3.00:1
. . . . (V-6, automatic) 3.40:1
. . . . (V-8) 2.79:1
Steering . . . . rack and pinion
Front suspension . . . .
    compression strut with lower trailing links, stabilizer bar
    and coil springs
Rear suspension . . . .
    Hotchkiss rigid axle w/semi-elliptic leaf springs (four
    leaves), anti-sway bar
Brakes . . . . (front) 9.3-inch disc
. . . . (rear) 9.0-inch drum
Ignition . . . . electronic
Body construction . . . unibody w/front isolated mini-frame
Fuel tank . . . . 13 gallons
. . . . . (optional, standard on V-8 models) 16.5 gallons

OPTION LIST

140-cid/2.3-liter four-cylinder
. . . . (credit from base V-6 price) $213
170-cid/2.8-liter V-6 . . . . $213
302-cid/5.0-liter V-8 . . . . $361
. . . . (exc. Mach 1) $148
Cruise-O-Matic transmission . . . . (with V-8) $225
. . . . (with other engines) $263
Power brakes $64
Power steering $131
Engine block heater $12
California emission system $69
High-altitude emissions . . . . no charge
Cobra II package, hatchback only . . . . $677-$700
King Cobra package, hatchback only $1253
Fashion accessory package, coupe only $207
Rallye package . . . . $43-$93
Rallye appearance package $163
Ghia sports group $361

Exterior accent group: pinstripes, wide bodyside moldings,
    dual remote sport mirrors, and whitewalls on styled
    wheels . . . . $163-$245
Appearance decor group: lower body two-tone, pinstripes,
    styled wheels, brushed aluminum dash appliqué
    . . . . $128-$167
Luxury interior group . . . . $149-$155
Convenience group: interval wipers, vanity and
    day/night mirrors, and pivoting rear quarter windows on
    hatchback . . . . $34-$81
Light group . . . . $40-$52
Appearance protection group . . . . $24-$36
Air conditioning $459
Rear defroster, electric $77
Tinted glass $53
Leather-wrapped steering wheel . . . . $34-$49
Digital clock $43
Trunk light $4
Color-keyed driver's sport mirror $16
Dual sport mirrors $49
Day/night mirror $7
AM radio $72
. . . . (w/tape player) $192
AM/FM radio $120
AM/FM stereo radio $161
. . . . (w/8 track or cassette tape player) $229
T-Roof "convertible" option . . . . $587-$629
Flip-up open air roof $167
Full vinyl roof $99
Front spoiler $8
Metallic glow paint $40
Pinstriping $30
Color-keyed bodyside moldings $66
Rocker panel moldings $22
Bumper guards, front and rear $37
Lower bodyside protection $30
Console $75
Four-way driver's seat $33
Fold-down rear seat $90
Wilshire cloth trim $100
Ashton cloth/vinyl trim $12
Color-keyed deluxe seatbelts $18
Wire wheel covers . . . . $12-$90
Forged aluminum wheels . . . . $173-$252
. . . . (white) $187-$265
Lacy spoke aluminum wheels . . . . $173-$252
. . . . (white) $187-$265
Styled steel wheels . . . . $59-$78
Trim rings $39

1978 MUSTANG PRODUCTION CHART

Model	Doors/Body/Seating	Factory Price	Shipping Weight	Prod. Total
02 (60F)	2/coupe/4	$3555/3768	2608/2705	81,304
03 (69F)	3/hatchback/4	$3798/4011	2654/2751	68,408
04 (60H)	2/coupe Ghia/4	$3972/4185	2646/2743	34,730
05 (69R)	3/hatchback Mach 1/4	$4253/4401	2733/NA	7,968

NOTE 1: Total series output was 192,410 units. Totals shown do not include 20,937 Mustangs produced as 1978 models, but sold as 1977 models.
NOTE 2: Data above slash for four-cylinder/below slash for V-6 (on 60F, 69F and 60H).
NOTE 3: Data above slash for V-6/below slash for V-8 (on 69R).

**1979 Pace Car Replica
Owner: Daniel Carpenter***

1979

Although the little Mustang II enjoyed sales success when compared to the American auto industry as a whole, it gave enthusiasts little to be excited about. Concerns that the replacement, due as a 1979 model, might not be any more thrilling to drive led to rumors that the Mustang name might be relegated to an options package on a less-sporty Ford product. With the introduction of the all-new, practically sized and smartly styled Mustang, Ford announced to the world that America's favorite pony car was facing a bright and, literally, turbocharged future.

As is its habit, Ford built the new Mustang around a platform it would share with more humble cars. Deep down under the new pony's distinctive sheet metal was Ford Fairmont and Mercury Zephyr DNA in the form of the "Fox" unit-body platform. Nearly 75 years after the Wright brothers showed off a working definition of the term "aerodynamics" at Kitty Hawk, Detroit came to understand that incorporating basic principles of aviation science into passenger car design could pay off in big ways. A car shaped like a barn door requires an enormous amount of horsepower and precious fossil fuels to push through the air at 60 miles an hour; however, a vehicle designed more like a drop of water can cheat the wind.

With engine-management technology still quite primitive, the best way to get good mileage from a car was to reduce the drag the wind created as it met a body panel at

*Carpenter, whose Concord, N.C., collection of late-model Mustangs is limited to cars with fewer than 500 miles, displays his vehicles as they came from the Ford factory prior to dealer prepping. This never-driven 1979 Pace Car Replica is not wearing its front bumper/spoiler because Ford shipped the units in padded, protective boxes in the rear of each car so as to prevent damage to the low-slung plastic.

speed. In production trim, the fifth-generation pony car set a milestone for Ford by registering a slippery 0.44 coefficient of drag for the fastback and 0.46 for the notchback. (Just four years later, the Thunderbird would surpass the Mustang by 20 percent in the wind tunnel when its curvy surface turned in a 0.35.)

The new model's diet of advanced plastics, aluminum, high-strength/low-alloy steel, thinner but stronger glass, and slimmer passenger compartment components made it 200 pounds lighter than the previous year's smaller Mustang II. Fastback and notchback both registered in the 2,600-pound range. Specs for the new pony included a 100.4-inch wheelbase, an overall length of 179.1 inches and a body width of 69.1 inches. Interior space was increased by more than 20 percent.

Soft urethane bumpers and an additional four inches in overall length further removed the Fox-based pony from the Mustang II. The aerodynamic wedge design featured a sloping front and hood, and sculptured roofline. A lowered window line gave the Mustang large glass area for improved visibility. As in the prior version, two-door notchback and three-door hatchback bodies were offered in base and Ghia levels.

The new hatchback did not have the sharply angled fastback shape of the former Mustang. The notchback two-door did look more like a sedan than its predecessor, though enthusiasts still tend to view it as a coupe (especially since a convertible would appear on that body a few years later).

Both body styles had sail-shaped quarter windows that were wider at the base, but the hatchback's were much narrower at the top, almost triangle-shaped. Both models had a

1979 Pace Car Replica

1979 Pace Car interior

1979 Pace Car grille

1979 Pace Car hood graphics, scoop

1979 Pace Car fender decal

1979 Pace Car seats

1979 TR metric-sized wheel

set of tall louver-like ribs formed in a tapered panel on the "C" pillar and angled to match the quarter window's rear edge, but the hatchback had one more of them. Staggered, recessed quad rectangular headlamps replaced the former single round units. The outer units sat a little farther back than the inner pair. The new black crosshatch grille (with 10 x 5-hole pattern) angled forward at the base and no longer held a Mustang badge. It did have FORD lettering at the driver's side. Rectangular amber parking/signal lamps were mounted in the bumper, just below the outboard headlamps. Narrow amber front side marker lenses followed the angle of front fender tips. Well below the front bumper was an air scoop with five holes. On the hood, above the grille, was a round tri-color Mustang emblem. A "2.8" or "5.0" badge on the front fenders, at the cowl ahead of the door, denoted a V-6 or V-8 engine under the hood. Tail lamps were wider than before, now wrapping around each quarter panel.

Most customers attracted to the fresh new design were able to ignore the fact that the powerplants, the 88-horsepower, 2.3-liter four-cylinder; 2.8-liter V-6; and 5.0-liter V-8 were essentially Mustang II carryovers. (The V-6 was produced initially, until a supply problem forced Ford to substitute its ancient 200-cid inline six-cylinder.)

Accompanying the forward-look sheet metal was the engine of the future—at least as far as Ford marketers were concerned at the time—an optional turbocharged version of the 2.3-liter four rated at 131 hp. According to Ford, the blown four offered "V-8 performance without sacrificing fuel economy" with company test results indicating the Mustang turbo could zip from zero to 55 miles an hour in just over 8 seconds (a little quicker than a V-8).

An innovative serpentine belt was used to drive engine accessories and is a component that continues in Mustangs and most other passenger cars to this day. Mustang's new front suspension system used a hydraulic shock strut to replace the conventional upper arm. In the rear was a new four-bar link-and-coil system, replacing the old Hotchkiss design that relied on leafsprings.

Unlike the Mustang II era, performance packages actually contributed to the car's thrill-behind-the-wheel quotient. Two such packages were offered in 1979. The basic handling suspension with 14-inch radial tires included different spring rates and shock valving, stiffer bushings in the front

suspension and upper arm in the rear, plus a special rear stabilizer bar. The second level package came with a Michelin TRX tire option, featuring ultra-low aspect ratio tires introduced on Ford's European Granada. The TRX's 15.35-inch (390mm) size demanded special metric wheels. That package also included unique shock valving, increased spring rates, and wider front and rear stabilizer bars.

All 1979 Mustangs had dashboards with full instruments, including tachometer, trip odometer, and gauges for fuel, oil pressure, alternator, and temperature. Interiors were also blessed with bucket seats, simulated woodgrain instrument panel appliqué, and stalk-mounted controls (to activate horn, headlamp dimmer and wiper/washer). Standard equipment for the chassis included rack-and-pinion steering, manual front disc brakes, and a front stabilizer bar. Also standard were vinyl door trim with carpeted lower panel, squeeze-open lockable glovebox, day/night mirror, lighter, black remote driver's mirror, and full wheel covers. Fastbacks had black rocker panel moldings, full wraparound body side moldings with dual accent stripe insert, and semi-styled wheels with black sport hub covers and trim rings. Quite a few options joined the list this year, including a sport-tuned exhaust, cruise control, tilt steering, leather seat trim, and interval windshield wipers.

Ghia Mustangs wore many color-keyed components including dual remote-control mirrors, quarter louvers, and body side molding inserts. Ghias also had turbine-style wheel covers, BR78 x 14-inch radial tires, pinstripes, body-color window frames, a "Ghia" badge on the decklid or hatch, low-back bucket seats with European-type headrests, and convenience pockets in color-keyed door panels. Interiors came in six leather colors and five of soft cloth.

The costly ($1173) Cobra package included a 2.3-liter turbocharged four, turbo hood scoop with "Turbo" nameplate, 190/65R x 390 TRX tires on metric forged aluminum wheels, and a special suspension. Cobras had blacked-out greenhouse trim, black lower bodyside tape treatment, and wraparound bodyside moldings with dual color-keyed inserts. Also included on the Cobra were color-keyed grille and quarter louvers, dual sport mirrors, black bumper rub strips with dual color-keyed inserts, an 8000-rpm tachometer, engine-turned instrument cluster panel, sport-tuned exhaust, and bright tailpipe extension. Rocker panel moldings were deleted on Cobras; optional hood graphics cost $78 extra.

If the second-generation Mustang lacked some of the pizzazz of the original pony car, the "new breed" third-

1979 F-code 5.0-liter/2V V-8

generation edition offered a chance to boost the marque's image. Ready for the 1980s, the Mustang offered a pleasing blend of American and European design. Of many styling proposals, the final one came from a team led by Jack Telnack of the Light Truck and Car Design Group.

New Mustang prices ranged from $4,071 to $5,097, a point Ford advertised as "still sticker-priced to help you bring one home in two-door or three-door models." A V-8 powered hatchback was selected to pace the 63rd annual Indianapolis 500 on May 27, 1979, and replicas were available through Ford dealerships. 1979 Mustangs were manufactured in two factories. The Dearborn plant produced 269,000 and a little more than 100,000 were turned out in a San Jose, California, factory.

Before the new Mustang was launched, Ford announced sales projections of 330,000 units or 16.5 percent of its 1979 plan. Considering the sluggishness in the auto market at the time, it did a great job breaking that goal with model year production of 369,936 units for a 4.02 percent industry share. Customers must have liked the new version, as the Mustang leaped from No. 22 to seventh in the sales race for 1979. Four-cylinders were ordered in 54.4 percent of 1979 Mustangs, while 31.3 percent had V-6s (or the late-year inline-sixes) and only 14.3 percent had V-8s.

One month after the new Mustang's press preview in 1978, Henry Ford II fired Lee Iacocca. Iacocca moved on to a troubled Chrysler, taking along some hand-picked executives to engineer his famous turnaround of the company. Phillip Caldwell became second in command under board chairman Henry Ford II, where he held titles of vice chairman and president.

DATA PLATE DECODING

The Vehicle Identification Number is stamped on an aluminum tab on the instrument panel, viewable through windshield. A vehicle certification label is found on the body side of where the driver's door closes.

VEHICLE WARRANTY NUMBER
MODEL YEAR

9 – 1979

ASSEMBLY PLANT

F – Dearborn, Michigan
R – San Jose, California

BODY SERIAL NUMBERS

02 – coupe
03 – hatchback
04 – coupe, Ghia
05 – hatchback, Ghia

ENGINE CODE

Y – 140-cid (2.3-liter) 2-bbl. SOHC 4-cyl.
W – 140-cid (2.3-liter) 2-bbl. SOHC 4-cyl. turbocharged
Z – 171-cid (2.8-liter) 2-bbl. V-6
T – 200-cid (3.3-liter) 1-bbl. 6-cyl.
    (replaced code Z engine mid-year)
F – 302-cid (5.0-liter) 2-bbl. V-8

CONSECUTIVE UNIT NUMBER

Begins at 100001 at each factory

CODE NUMBERS
BODY CODE

66B – coupe
61R – hatchback
66H – coupe, Ghia
61H – hatchback, Ghia

PAINT CODE

1C – Black
1G – Silver Metallic
1P – Medium Grey Metallic
2H – Red Glow
2P – Bright Red
3F – Light Medium Blue
3H – Medium Blue Glow
3J – Bright Blue
46 – Dark Jade Metallic
5M – Medium Chestnut Metallic
5W – Medium Vaquero Gold
64 – Bright Yellow
83 – Light Chamois
85 – Tangerine
9D – Polar White
Tu-Tone
?/1C – All/Black
1G/1C – Silver Metallic/Black
1G/2R – Silver Metallic/Medium Grey Metallic
3F/3J – Light Medium Blue/Bright Blue

1979 Sport Option hatchback (FMC)

1979 hatchback (FMC)

ENGINES

140-cid (2.3-liter) 2-bbl. Inline Four
Valves . . . . overhead
Camshaft . . . . single overhead
Block . . . . cast iron
Displacement . . . . 140 cid/2.3 liters
Bore and stroke . . . . 3.78 x 3.13 inches
Compression ratio 9.0:1
Brake hp . . . . 88 @ 4800 rpm
Main bearings 5
Valve lifters . . . . hydraulic
Carburetor . . . . Motorcraft 2-bbl.
Code . . . . Y

140-cid (2.3-liter) 2-bbl. Inline Four Turbo
Valves . . . . overhead
Camshaft . . . . single overhead
Block . . . . cast iron
Displacement . . . . 140 cid/2.3 liters
Bore and stroke . . . . 3.78 x 3.13 inches
Compression ratio 9.0:1
Brake hp . . . . 131 @ 4800 rpm
Main bearings 5
Valve lifters . . . . hydraulic
Carburetor . . . . Holley 2-bbl.
Code . . . . W

171-cid (2.8-liter) 2-bbl. V-6
Valves . . . . overhead
Block . . . . cast iron
Displacement . . . . 171 cid/2.8 liters
Bore and stroke . . . . 3.66 x 2.70 inches
Compression ratio 8.7:1
Brake hp . . . . 109 @ 4800 rpm
Main bearings 4
Valve lifters . . . . solid
Carburetor . . . . Ford 2-bbl.
Code . . . . Z

200-cid (3.3-liter) 1-bbl. Inline Six
Valves . . . . overhead
Block . . . . cast iron
Displacement . . . . 200 cid
Bore and stroke . . . . 3.68 x 3.13 inches
Compression ratio 8.6:1
Brake hp . . . . 85 @ 4000 rpm

Main bearings 7
Valve lifters . . . . hydraulic
Carburetor . . . . Holley 1-bbl.
Code . . . . T

302-cid (5.0-liter) 2-bbl. V-8
Valves . . . . overhead
Block . . . . cast iron
Displacement . . . . 302 cid/5.0 liters
Bore and stroke . . . . 4.00 x 3.00 inches
Compression ratio 8.4:1
Brake hp . . . . 140 @ 3600 rpm
Main bearings 5
Valve lifters . . . . hydraulic
Carburetor . . . . Motorcraft 2-bbl.
Code . . . . F

CHASSIS
Wheelbase . . . . 100.4 inches
Overall length . . . . 179.1 inches
Height . . . . 51.8 inches
Width . . . . 69.1 inches
Front tread width . . . . 56.6 inches
Rear tread width . . . . 57.0 inches
Tires B78x13
. . . . (Ghia) BR78x14

TECHNICAL
Final drive ratio . . . . (four-cylinder, V-6) 3.08:1
. . . . (four-cylinder turbo) 3.45:1
. . . . (V-8, automatic) 2.47:1
Steering . . . . rack and pinion
Front suspension . . . .
    modified MacPherson hydraulic shock struts with coil
    springs and stabilizer bar
Rear suspension . . . .
    four-bar link and coil spring system, anti-sway bar
    (with V-8)
Brakes . . . . (front) 9.3-inch disc
. . . . (front, V-8) 10.4-inch disc
. . . . (rear) 9.0-inch drum
Ignition . . . . electronic
Body construction . . . unibody w/front isolated mini-frame
Fuel tank . . . . 11.5 gallons
. . . . (V-6, V-8) 12.5 gallons

1979 notchback (FMC)

1979 notchback (FMC)

OPTION LIST

Turbocharged 140-cid four-cylinder	$542
170-cid V-6 (later 200-cid six)	$273
302-cid V-8	$514
Sport-tuned exhaust	$34
Automatic transmission	$307
Power brakes	$70
Variable-ratio power steering	$141
Handling suspension	$33
Engine block heater	$13
Heavy-duty battery	$18
California emission system	$76
High-altitude emissions	$33
Cobra package	$1173
Cobra hood graphics	$78
Sport option	$175
Exterior accent group	$72
Interior accent group	$108-$120
Light group	$25-$37
Protection group	$33-$36
Power lock group	$99

Air conditioning	$484
Rear defroster, electric	$84
Fingertip speed control	$104-$116
Tinted glass	$59
(windshield only)	$25
Leather-wrapped steering wheel	$41-$53
Tilt steering wheel	$69-$81
Interval wipers	$35
Rear wiper/washer	$63
Trunk light	$5
Driver's remote mirror	$18
Dual remote mirrors	$52
AM radio	$72
(w/digital clock)	$119
(w/tape player)	$192
AM/FM radio	$120
AM/FM stereo radio	$176
(w/8 track or cassette tape player)	$243
Premium sound system	$67
Dual rear speakers	$42
Radio flexibility option	$90

1979 Pace Car Replica
Owner: Richard Pollard

1979 Mustang coupe (OCW)

1979 Pace Car Replica (OCW)

Flip-up open-air roof $199
Full vinyl roof $102
Metallic glow paint $41
Lower two-tone paint $78
Bodyside/decklid pinstripes $30
Wide bodyside moldings $66
Narrow vinyl-insert bodyside moldings $39
Rocker panel moldings $24
Mud/stone deflectors $23
Lower bodyside protection $30
Console $140
Four-way driver's seat $35
Cloth seat trim $20
Ghia cloth seat trim $42
Accent cloth seat trim $29
Leather seat trim $282
Front floor mats $18

Color-keyed deluxe seatbelts $20
Wheels and Tires: Wire wheel covers . . . . $60-$99
Turbine wheel covers . . . . $10-$39
Forged metric aluminum wheels . . . . $259-$298
Cast aluminum wheels . . . . $251-$289
Styled steel wheels w/trim rings . . . . $55-$94
B78 x 13 WSW $43
C78 x 13 BSW $25
. . . . (WSW) $69
B78 x 14 WSW $66
C78 x 14 BSW $48
BR78 x 14 BSW $124
. . . . (WSW) $43-$167
CR78 x 14 WSW . . . . $69-$192
. . . . (RWL) $86-$209
TRX 190/65R 390 Michelin BSW . . . . $117-$241
Tire Note: Lower prices are for Mustang Ghia.

Model	Doors/Body/Seating	Factory Price	Shipping Weight	Prod. Total
1979 MUSTANG PRODUCTION CHART				
02 (66B)	2/coupe/4	$4071/4344	2431/2511	156,666
03 (61R)	3/hatchback/4	$4436/4709	2451/2531	120,535
04 (66H)	2/coupe Ghia/4	$4642/4915	2539/2619	56,351
05 (61H)	3/hatchback Ghia/4	$4824/5097	2548/2628	36,384

NOTE 3: Data above slash for V-6/below slash for V-8 (on 69R).

1979 notchback (FMC)

1980 notchback (FMC)

1980

Ford made very few modifications to the Fox-bodied Mustang in its sophomore year. The base four-cylinder engine enjoyed a 23 percent fuel economy improvement, and there were only minor changes to the turbocharged version. The 200-cid straight six remained on the lineup after replacing the 2.8-liter V-6 at the end of 1979.

For the second time since it was introduced in 1968 (the first being the Mustang II's introductory year), the venerable 302-cid (5.0-liter) V-8 was dropped. In its place Ford put a de-bored 255-cid (4.2-liter) V-8 in an attempt to increase gas mileage for the fleet. While it probably helped Ford reach its CAFE goals for the year, its 117 hp was 14 less than the lighter turbocharged four-cylinder. Both the non-turbocharged 2.3-liter four and inline six could have a four-speed manual gearbox (overdrive fourth with the six), while all engines could be ordered with automatics.

As could be expected, appearance of the modern, resized Mustang changed little. The sporty Cobra model received a specific front/rear aerodynamic treatment to further distinguish it from cheaper models. As such, the package went up in price to $1,482. Cobra's slat-style three-hole grille, hood scoop (with simulated rear opening), front air dam (with built-in foglamps) and rear spoiler were restyled with the 1979 Indy Pace Car replica in mind. The tape treatment was also revised, and all Cobras came standard with TRX suspension. Features included black lower Tu-Tone treatment;

special bodyside and quarter window taping; dual black sport mirrors; sport-tuned exhaust with bright tailpipe extension; black bumper rub strips; 190/65R-390 TRX tires on forged metric aluminum wheels; engine-turned instrument cluster panel with Cobra medallion; bodyside molding with dual color-keyed accent stripes; 8000-rpm tachometer; and the turbocharged engine. "Cobra" lettering appeared on quarter windows.

Base and Ghia models were offered again in notchback or hatchback form. Base notchbacks had black bumper rub strips; hatchback bumpers wore dual argent stripe inserts. Hatchbacks also had full wraparound, wide black bodyside moldings with dual argent inserts. Both models carried high-back vinyl bucket seats. Notchback rear pillar louvers were color-keyed, while the hatchback's were black. Ghia added low-back bucket seats with Euro-style headrests, a roof assist handle, color-keyed window frames, dual remote mirrors, pin striping, 14-inch tires, turbine wheel covers and "Ghia" insignia on decklid or hatch.

All models now rode on high-pressure P-metric radial tires and benefited from halogen headlamps. Maintenance-free batteries were standard, and radios gained a Travelers' Advisory Band. Semi-metallic front disc brake pads were included with optional engines. A new Carriage Roof option for the notchback model was supposed to resemble a convertible, even though the car had a solid "B" pillar. It used diamond-grain vinyl. Other new options included a roof luggage rack, cargo area cover (hatchback), liftback window louvers, and Recaro adjustable seatback bucket seats with improved thigh support. Inside door handles were relocated to the upper door.

After more than a decade spent avoiding factory involvement in motorsports, Ford renewed its interest in 1980. The initials of the International Motor Sports Association were used on a concept car called the Mustang IMSA. Powered by a hopped-up version of the turbo four, the IMSA wore fat Pirelli tires and a lot of competition-like flares, spoilers and air dams. Ford envisioned a return to the glory days of the 1960s, when its parts branch created a tidy profit center merchandising bolt-on performance hardware to enthusiasts.

Englishman Michael Kranefuss, Ford's European competition director, was brought to Dearborn to organize a Special Vehicle Operations (SVO) group. The purpose of the SVO team was threefold. First, it would help interested race drivers build up competition versions of the new Mustang. Second was the creation of a series of specialty "image" cars to generate interest in GT sports car racing. Third on the list was to help conceive/create kits of bolt-on parts that could be purchased by average Mustang owners to modify their street cars for road-and-track use in IMSA or SCCA events.

The McLaren Mustang was introduced with lots of fanfare later in the year, including a cover on *Motor Trend* and articles in many buff books. The $25,000 car looked like the IMSA Mustang concept vehicle, with many extensive body modifications and many special accessories like Euro-style BBS alloy wheels. The power plant was a 175-hp version of the turbocharged four "tweaked" by McLaren Engines. Only 250 units were made.

Model year production of 1980 Mustangs peaked at 271,322 cars. Of that total, 67.6 percent had fours and 29.7 had six-cylinders. Increasing gas prices were partly responsible for the fact that only 2.7 percent of Mustang buyers specified the new 4.2-liter V-8.

For 1980, the Mustang maintained just about the same share of total automobile business, with a 4.01 percent market share, but the market shrunk by two million units.

DATA PLATE DECODING

The Vehicle Identification Number is stamped on an aluminum tab on the instrument panel, viewable through windshield. A vehicle certification label is found on the body side of where the driver's door closes.

VEHICLE WARRANTY NUMBER
MODEL YEAR

0 – 1980

ASSEMBLY PLANT

F – Dearborn, Michigan
R – San Jose, California

BODY SERIAL NUMBERS

02 – coupe
03 – hatchback
04 – coupe, Ghia
05 – hatchback, Ghia

ENGINE CODE

A – 140-cid (2.3-liter) 2-bbl. SOHC 4-cyl.
W – 140-cid (2.3-liter) 2-bbl. SOHC 4-cyl. turbocharged
B – 200-cid (3.3-liter) 1-bbl. 6-cyl.
D – 255-cid (4.2-liter) 2-bbl. V-8

CONSECUTIVE UNIT NUMBER

Begins at 100001 at each factory

CODE NUMBERS
BODY CODE

66B – coupe
61R – hatchback
66H – coupe, Ghia
61H – hatchback, Ghia

PAINT CODE

1C – Black
1G – Silver Metallic
1P – Medium Grey Metallic
2G – Bright Bittersweet
3F – Light Medium Blue
3H – Medium Blue Glow
3J – Bright Blue
5T – Bright Caramel
6N – Bright Yellow
8A – Dark Chamois Metallic
8D – Bittersweet Glow
8N – Dark Cordovan Metallic
8W – Chamois Glow
9D – Polar White
27 – Bright Red
Tu-Tone
1G/1P – Silver Metallic/Medium Grey Metallic
1G/8N – Silver Metallic/Dark Cordovan Metallic
2G/8N – Bright Bittersweet/Dark Cordovan Metallic
3F/3J – Light Medium Blue/Bright Blue
8A/8W – Dark Chamois Metallic/Chamois Glow
8N/8D – Dark Cordovan Metallic/Bittersweet Glow
8W/8A – Chamois Glow/Dark Chamois Metallic
8D/8N – Bittersweet Glow/Dark Cordovan Metallic
9D/6N – Polar White/Bright Yellow
9D/8D – Polar White/Bittersweet Glow

ENGINES

140-cid (2.3-liter) 2-bbl. Inline Four

Valves . . . . overhead
Camshaft . . . . single overhead
Block . . . . cast iron
Displacement . . . . 140 cid/2.3 liters
Bore and stroke . . . . 3.78 x 3.13 inches
Compression ratio 9.0:1
Brake hp . . . . 88 @ 4600 rpm
Main bearings 5
Valve lifters . . . . hydraulic
Carburetor . . . . Motorcraft 2-bbl.
Code . . . . A

140-cid (2.3-liter) 2-bbl. Inline Four Turbo

Valves . . . . overhead
Camshaft . . . . single overhead
Block . . . . cast iron
Displacement . . . . 140 cid/2.3 liters
Bore and stroke . . . . 3.78 x 3.13 inches
Compression ratio 9.0:1
Brake hp . . . . 150 @ 4800 rpm
Main bearings 5
Valve lifters . . . . hydraulic
Carburetor . . . . Holley 2-bbl.
Code . . . . W

200-cid (3.3-liter) 1-bbl. Inline Six

Valves . . . . overhead
Block . . . . cast iron
Displacement . . . . 200 cid
Bore and stroke . . . . 3.68 x 3.13 inches
Compression ratio 8.6:1
Brake hp . . . . 91 @ 4000 rpm
Main bearings 7
Valve lifters . . . . hydraulic
Carburetor . . . . Holley 1-bbl.
Code . . . . B

255-cid (4.6-liter) 2-bbl. V-8

Valves . . . . overhead
Block . . . . cast iron
Displacement . . . . 255 cid/4.6 liters
Bore and stroke . . . . 3.68 x 3.00 inches
Compression ratio 8.8:1
Brake hp . . . . 119 @ 3800 rpm
Main bearings 5
Valve lifters . . . . hydraulic
Carburetor . . . . Motorcraft 2-bbl.
Code . . . . D

CHASSIS

Wheelbase . . . . 100.4 inches
Overall length . . . . 179.1 inches
Height . . . . 51.8 inches
Width . . . . 69.1 inches
Front tread width . . . . 56.6 inches
Rear tread width . . . . 57.0 inches
Tires P185/80R-13
. . . . (Ghia) P175/75R-14

TECHNICAL

Final drive ratio . . . . (four-cylinder, V-6) 3.08:1
. . . . (four-cylinder turbo) 3.45:1
. . . . (V-8, automatic) 2.26:1
Steering . . . . rack and pinion
Front suspension . . . .
    modified MacPherson hydraulic shock struts with coil
    springs and stabilizer bar
Rear suspension . . . .
    four-bar link and coil spring system, anti-sway bar
    (with V-8)
Brakes . . . . (front) 9.3-inch disc
. . . . (front, V-8) 10.4-inch disc
. . . . (rear) 9.0-inch drum
Ignition . . . . electronic
Body construction . . . unibody w/front isolated mini-frame
Fuel tank . . . . 11.5 gallons
. . . . (V-8) 12.5 gallons

OPTION LIST

Turbocharged 140-cid four-cylinder $481
200-cid six $219
255-cid V-8 . . . . $338
. . . . (Cobra package) $144 credit
Sport-tuned exhaust . . . . (V-8 only) $38
Automatic transmission $340
Optional axle ratio $18
Power brakes $78
Power steering $160

Handling suspension $35
Engine block heater $15
Heavy-duty battery $20
California emission system $253
High-altitude emissions $36
Cobra package $1482
Cobra hood graphics $88
Sport option (black rocker/belt moldings and door/window
    frames, full wraparound bodyside molding with dual
    argent stripe insert, sport wheel trim rings and steering
    wheel) . . . . $168-$186
Exterior accent group $63
Interior accent group . . . . $120-$134
Light group $41
Appearance protection group . . . . $38-$41
Power lock group $113
Air conditioning $583
Rear defroster, electric $96
Fingertip speed control . . . . $116-$129
Tinted glass $65
. . . . (windshield only) $29
Leather-wrapped steering wheel . . . . $44-$56
Tilt steering wheel . . . . $78-$90
Interval wipers $39
Rear wiper/washer $79
Trunk light $5
Driver's remote mirror $19
Dual remote mirrors $58
AM radio $93
AM/FM radio $145
AM/FM stereo radio $183
. . . . (w/8 track tape player) $259
. . . . (w/cassette player) $271
Premium sound system $94
Dual rear speakers $38
Radio flexibility option $63
Flip-up open-air roof . . . . $204-$219
Carriage roof $625
Full vinyl roof $118
Metallic glow paint $46
Lower two-tone paint $88
Bodyside/decklid pinstripes $34
Accent tape stripes . . . . $19-$53
Hood scoop $31
Liftgate louvers $141
Narrow vinyl-insert bodyside moldings $43
. . . . (wide) $74
Rocker panel moldings $30
Roof luggage rack $86
Mud/stone deflectors $25
Lower bodyside protection $34
Console $166
Four-way driver's seat $38
Recaro high-back bucket seats $531
Cloth/vinyl bucket seats . . . . $21-$46
Vinyl low-back bucket seats . . . . no charge
Accent cloth/vinyl seat trim $30
Leather low-back bucket seats $345
Cargo area cover $44
Front floor mats $19
Color-keyed seatbelts $23
Wire wheel covers . . . . $79-$121
Turbine wheel covers . . . . $10-$43

Forged metric aluminum wheels . . . . $313-$355
Cast aluminum wheels . . . . $279-$321
Styled steel wheels w/trim rings . . . . $61-$104
P185/80R-13 WSW $50
P175/75R-14 BSW $25

. . . . (WSW) $50-$75
P185/75R-14 BSW . . . . $25-$49
. . . . (WSW) $75-$100
. . . . (RWL) $92-$117
TRX 190/65 390 BSW . . . . $125-$250

1980 MUSTANG PRODUCTION CHART

Model	Doors/Body/Seating	Factory Price	Shipping Weight	Prod. Total
02 (66B)	2/coupe/4	$4884/5103	2497/2532	128,893
03 (61R)	3/hatchback/4	$5194/5413	2531/2566	98,497
04 (66H)	2/coupe Ghia/4	$5369/5588	2565/2600	23,647
05 (61H)	3/hatchback Ghia/4	$5512/5731	2588/2623	20,285

NOTE 1: Total series output was 271,322 units.
NOTE 2: Figures to left of slash are for four-cylinder engine, to right of slash for six-cylinder. A V-8 engine cost $119 more than the six.

1981 Cobra (FMC)

1981

For Mustang's third season on the Fox platform, few changes were evident.

The same limited array of powertrains continued to be available, with three optional engines and seven optional transmissions. The turbocharged four-cylinder was dropped for reliability reasons, although sales literature of the period suggests it was still being produced.

A five-speed manual overdrive gearbox was offered for the first time in 1981—initially on four-cylinder models—for an extra $152. Its fifth gear was an overdrive ratio, but the lower four did not offer close-ratio gearing. Some critics found fault with the five-speed's shift pattern, which put fifth gear right next to fourth. A Traction-Lok rear axle was available as an option starting in 1981.

Also joining the option list was a T-Roof with twin removable tinted glass panels, offered on either the two-door notchback or three-door hatchback. The new T-Roof met all federal body structure regulations, as a result of body modifications that included the use of H-shaped reinforcements.

Other new options included reclining bucket seats (either high- or low-back), power windows and remote right convex mirror. An optional console included a graphic display module that contained a digital clock measuring elapsed time and warnings for low fuel or washer fluid level as well as inoperative lights.

Cobra equipment, now a $1,588 package, was similar to 1979-80, including 190/65R-390 TRX tires on forged metric aluminum wheel, an 8000-rpm tachometer, lower two-tone paint, "Cobra" tape treatment, hood scoop, sport-tuned

exhaust, dual black sport mirrors, black bumper rub strips, bodyside moldings with dual accent stripes. and black greenhouse moldings. The Cobra had a built-in front spoiler, black quarter-window louvers, model-unique medallion on dash and door trim and a handling suspension. Taping could be deleted from the Cobra package, if desired, knocking $65 off the price, but the bold hood decal cost $90 extra.

1981 would be the final year for the Cobra option; it would be replaced the next season with the GT. The Cobra name would make a very impressive return in 1993 on a special Mustang produced by Ford's Special Vehicle Team.

Mustang prices rose sharply this year, as did those of other Ford products, with stickers ranging from $6,171 (base coupe) to $6,942 (Ghia hatchback). Production dropped off to 182,552 Mustangs, all produced in Dearborn, which lowered the marque's share of industry sales to 2.73 percent. Four-cylinders were most popular, with a 62 percent installation rate, while V-8 sales improved slightly to 3.3 percent.

DATA PLATE DECODING

A new-for-1981 17-character Vehicle Identification Number is stamped on an aluminum tab on the instrument panel, viewable through windshield. A vehicle certification label is found on the body side of where the driver's door closes.

VEHICLE WARRANTY NUMBER MANUFACTURER ID

1FA – Ford Motor Co.

RESTRAINT SYSTEM

B – active belts

VEHICLE CLASSIFICATION

P – passenger car

BODY SERIAL NUMBERS

10/14 – coupe
15 – hatchback

12 – coupe, Ghia
13 – hatchback, Ghia

ENGINE CODE

A – 140-cid (2.3-liter) 2-bbl. SOHC 4-cyl.
B – 200-cid (3.3-liter) 1-bbl. 6-cyl.
D – 255-cid (4.2-liter) 2-bbl. V-8

CHECK DIGIT

for internal use

MODEL YEAR

B – 1981

ASSEMBLY PLANT

F – Dearborn, Michigan

CONSECUTIVE UNIT NUMBER

Begins at 100001 at each factory

CODE NUMBERS
BODY CODE

66B – coupe
61R – hatchback
66H – coupe, Ghia
61H – hatchback, Ghia

PAINT CODE

1C – Black
1G – Light Pewter Metallic
2G – Bright Bittersweet
3H – Medium Blue Glow
3J – Midnight Blue Metallic
5Q – Dark Brown Metallic
6N – Bright Yellow
8D – Bittersweet Glow
8N – Dark Cordovan Metallic
9D – Polar White
17 – Medium Pewter Metallic
24 – Red
27 – Bright Red
86 – Pastel Chamois

1981 notchback, T-tops (FMC)

Tu-Tone
1T/1C – Light Pewter Metallic/Black
17/1C – Medium Pewter Metallic/Black
2G/1C – Bright Bittersweet/Black
24/1C – Red/Black
27/1C – Bright Red/Black
6N/1C – Bright Yellow/Black
8D/1C – Bittersweet Glow/Black
8N/1C – Dark Cordovan Metallic/Black
86/1C – Pastel Chamois/Black
9D/1C – Polar White/Black
17/1T – Medium Pewter Metallic/Light Pewter Metallic
24/9D – Red/Polar White
9D/8D – Polar White/Bittersweet Glow

ENGINES

140-cid (2.3-liter) 2-bbl. Inline Four

Valves . . . . overhead
Camshaft . . . . single overhead
Block . . . . cast iron
Displacement . . . . 140 cid/2.3 liters
Bore and stroke . . . . 3.78 x 3.13 inches
Compression ratio 9.0:1
Brake hp . . . . 88 @ 4600 rpm
Main bearings 5
Valve lifters . . . . hydraulic
Carburetor . . . . Motorcraft 2-bbl.
Code . . . . A

200-cid (3.3-liter) 1-bbl. Inline Six

Valves . . . . overhead
Block . . . . cast iron
Displacement . . . . 200 cid
Bore and stroke . . . . 3.68 x 3.13 inches
Compression ratio 8.6:1
Brake hp . . . . 94 @ 4000 rpm
Main bearings 7
Valve lifters . . . . hydraulic
Carburetor . . . . Holley 1-bbl.
Code . . . . B

255-cid (4.6-liter) 2-bbl. V-8

Valves . . . . overhead
Block . . . . cast iron
Displacement . . . . 255 cid/4.6 liters
Bore and stroke . . . . 3.68 x 3.00 inches
Compression ratio 8.2:1
Brake hp . . . . 115 @ 3400 rpm
Main bearings 5
Valve lifters . . . . hydraulic
Carburetor . . . . Motorcraft 2-bbl.
Code . . . . D

CHASSIS

Wheelbase . . . . 100.4 inches
Overall length . . . . 179.1 inches
Height . . . . 51.8 inches
Width . . . . 69.1 inches
Front tread width . . . . 56.6 inches
Rear tread width . . . . 57.0 inches
Tires P185/80R-13
. . . . (Ghia) P175/75R-14

TECHNICAL

Final drive ratio. . . . . (four-cylinder) 3.08:1
. . . . (V-6, four-speed) 3.45:1
. . . . V-6, automatic) 2.73:1
. . . . (V-8) 2.26:1
Steering. . . . . rack and pinion
Front suspension . . . .
    modified MacPherson hydraulic shock struts with coil
    springs and stabilizer bar
Rear suspension . . . .
    four-bar link and coil spring system, anti-sway bar
    (with V-8)
Brakes . . . . (front) 9.3-inch disc
. . . . (front, V-8) 10.4-inch disc
. . . . (rear) 9.0-inch drum
Ignition . . . . electronic
Body construction . . . unibody w/front isolated mini-frame
Fuel tank. . . . . 12.5 gallons

OPTION LIST

200-cid six $213
255-cid V-8 . . . . $263
. . . . (Cobra package) $346 credit
Sport-tuned exhaust . . . . (V-8 only) $38
Five-speed manual transmission. $152
Automatic transmission $349
Traction-Lok differential $63
Optional axle ratio. $20
Power brakes $76
Power steering $163
Handling suspension $43
Engine block heater $16
Heavy-duty battery $20
California emission system $46
High-altitude emissions $38
Cobra package. $1588
. . . . (tape delete) $65 credit
Cobra hood graphics $90
Sport option. . . . . $52-$72
Interior accent group . . . . $126-$139
Light group $43
Appearance protection group $41
Power lock group . . . . $93-$120
Air conditioning. $560
Rear defroster, electric. $107
Fingertip speed control $132

Power windows $140
Tinted glass $76
. . . . (windshield only) $29
Leather-wrapped steering wheel . . . . $49-$61
Tilt steering wheel. $80-$93
Interval wipers $41
Rear wiper/washer $85
Trunk light. $6
Driver's remote mirror $20
Dual remote mirrors $56
AM/FM radio $51
AM/FM stereo radio $88
. . . . (w/8 track tape player) $162
. . . . (w/cassette player) $174
Premium sound system $91
Dual rear speakers $37
Radio flexibility option $61
AM radio delete . . . . $61 credit
T-Roof $874
Flip-up open-air roof . . . . $213-$228
Carriage roof $644
Full vinyl roof $115
Metallic glow paint $48
Two-tone paint . . . . $121-$155
Lower two-tone paint $90
Pinstriping $34
Accent tape stripes $54
Hood scoop $32
Liftgate louvers $145
Rocker panel moldings. $30
Roof luggage rack $90
Mud/stone deflectors $26
Lower bodyside protection. $37
Console $168
Recaro high-back bucket seats $732
Cloth/vinyl bucket seats . . . . $22-$48
Accent cloth/vinyl seat trim. $30
Leather low-back bucket seats $359
Cargo area cover . . . . (hatchback) $45
Front floor mats . . . . $18-$20
Color-keyed seatbelts $23
Wire wheel covers . . . . $77-$118
Turbine wheel covers . . . . $10-$41
Forged metric aluminum wheels $340
Cast aluminum wheels. $305
Styled steel wheels w/trim rings . . . . $60-$101

1981 MUSTANG PRODUCTION CHART

Model	Doors/Body/Seating	Factory Price	Shipping Weight	Prod. Total
10 (66B)	2/coupe/4	$6171/6384	2524/2551	77,458
15 (61R)	3/hatchback/4	$6408/6621	2544/2571	77,399
12 (66H)	2/coupe Ghia/4	$6645/6858	2558/2585	13,422
13 (61H)	3/hatchback Ghia/4	$6729/6942	2593/2620	14,273

NOTE 1: Total series output was 182,552 units.
NOTE 2: Figures to left of slash are for four-cylinder engine, to right of slash for six-cylinder engine. A V-8 engine was priced $50 higher than the six.

1982 GT (FMC)

1982

"The Boss is Back!" declared Ford ads. The biggest news of the year was indeed the return of the 302-cid (5.0-liter) V-8 to the Mustang lineup. The 5.0-liter powerplant, when teamed with a two-barrel carburetor, low-restriction air cleaner and four-speed transmission, is most often associated with the new GT model, although it could be installed in the entire Mustang line. It generated 157 hp and recorded the fastest zero-to-60 mph time of any American car at the time—some magazines reported times in the low seven-second range!

Available in hatchback form only, the $8,308 GT came equipped with the top-grade TRX suspension, front and rear spoilers, fog lamps, blackout treatment, console, luxury seat trim, and other bits of sportiness. All other Mustang engines were carryovers from 1981, including the unloved 4.2-liter V-8. Even though that de-bored V-8 made 40 hp less than the new 5.0-liter, it was offered in the GT as a $57 credit option.

Other engines in the Mustang lineup included the standard 2.3-liter four and 200-cid inline six-cylinder. A lockup torque converter (all three gears) was included on automatics with the inline six or small V-8 engine. A high-altitude emissions system was available with all engines. All Ford engines were painted light gray beginning with the 1982 model year. Appearance changed little for 1981, but model designations were revised throughout the line. The new models included L, GL and GLX, as well as the GT.

Mustang L was the new base model, with full wheel covers, full wraparound body side moldings, and an AM radio. New standard equipment included seatbelts with tension relievers; a remote-control left-hand mirror; new flash-to-pass headlamp feature; and new screw-on gas cap tethered to the filler neck. Fourteen-inch wheels with P-metric (P175/75R-14) steel-belted radial tires were made standard

on the 1982 Mustang, as well as a larger gas tank (up from 12.5 to 15.4 gallons). Four-cylinder Mustangs with air conditioning gained an electro-drive cooling fan. Radios had dual front speakers plus wiring for two more.

The GT package added P185/75R-14 blackwall steel-belted radials on cast aluminum wheels, a handling suspension, dual black remote mirrors, and built-in fog lamps. Styling features included body-colored front fascia with integral spoiler and air dam, three-slot grille, color-keyed rear spoiler, and body-color cowl grille. "GT" identification appeared on the liftgate. Body-color headlamp frames replaced the black doors on other models. Black body side moldings had a black plastic insert and aluminum end caps. Equipment included a Traction-Lok differential, power brakes and steering, and a console with digital clock and diagnostic warning module. Blackout treatment continued on interior components. An optional TR performance package could enhance the handling qualities of all Mustang models. It included Michelin TRX tires on forged metric aluminum wheels and a handling suspension with rear stabilizer bar.

With Mustang sales declining by almost one-third, only 130,418 Mustangs were produced in 1982; however, an important swing in the market was taking place that would mean good news to the accountants at Ford. Due to lower gas prices, high-performance cars were becoming very marketable. The Mustang 5.0-liter GT was well positioned to capitalize on this trend; in fact, in its first year, V-8 installations rose to 25.5 percent of all Mustangs—about five times more than the number sold in 1981. That was far above a goal of 20,000 to 25,000 V-8s that Ford had set at the start of the 1982 selling season.

DATA PLATE DECODING

A 17-character Vehicle Identification Number is stamped on an aluminum tab on the instrument panel, viewable through windshield. A vehicle certification label is found on the body side of where the driver's door closes.

VEHICLE WARRANTY NUMBER MANUFACTURER ID

1FA – Ford Motor Co.

RESTRAINT SYSTEM

B – active belts

VEHICLE CLASSIFICATION

P – passenger car

BODY SERIAL NUMBERS

10 – coupe, L/GL
16 – hatchback, GL/GT
12 – coupe, GLX
13 – hatchback, GLX

ENGINE CODE

A – 140-cid (2.3-liter) 2-bbl. SOHC 4-cyl.
B – 200-cid (3.3-liter) 1-bbl. 6-cyl.
D – 255-cid (4.2-liter) 2-bbl. V-8
F – 302-cid (5.0-liter) 2-bbl. V-8

CHECK DIGIT

for internal use

MODEL YEAR

C – 1982

ASSEMBLY PLANT

F – Dearborn, Michigan

CONSECUTIVE UNIT NUMBER

Begins at 100001 at each factory

CODE NUMBERS
BODY CODE

66B – coupe
61B – hatchback
66H – coupe, GLX
61H – hatchback, GLX

PAINT CODE

1C – Black
1G – Silver Metallic
1P – Medium Grey Metallic

3D – Dark Blue Glow
3H – Medium Blue Glow
6Y – Medium Vanilla
6Z – Pastel Vanilla
8D – Bittersweet Glow
8N – Dark Cordovan Metallic
9D – Polar White
17 – Medium Pewter Metallic
24 – Red
27 – Bright Red
61 – Medium Yellow
Tu-Tone
1G/1C – Silver Metallic/Black
1P/1C – Medium Grey Metallic/Black
1P/1G – Medium Grey Metallic/Silver Metallic
3D/1C – Dark Blue Metallic/Black
3D/3H – Dark Blue Metallic/Medium Blue Glow
3H/1C – Medium Blue Glow/Black
6Y/1C – Medium Vanilla/Black
6Z/1C – Pastel Vanilla/Black
6Y/6Z – Medium Vanilla/Pastel Vanilla
8D/1C – Bittersweet Glow/Black
8N/1C – Dark Cordovan Metallic/Black
8N/8D – Dark Cordovan Metallic/Bittersweet Glow
9D/1C – Polar White/Black
24/1C – Red/Black
27/1C – Bright Red/Black
61/1C – Medium Yellow/Black

ENGINES

140-cid (2.3-liter) 2-bbl. Inline Four

Valves . . . . overhead
Camshaft . . . . single overhead
Block . . . . cast iron
Displacement . . . . 140 cid/2.3 liters
Bore and stroke . . . . 3.78 x 3.13 inches
Compression ratio 9.0:1
Brake hp . . . . 86 @ 4600 rpm
Main bearings 5
Valve lifters . . . . hydraulic
Carburetor . . . . Motorcraft 2-bbl.
Code . . . . A

200-cid (3.3-liter) 1-bbl. Inline Six

Valves . . . . overhead
Block . . . . cast iron

1982 GT (JH)

1982 GT interior (JH)

Displacement . . . . 200 cid
Bore and stroke . . . . 3.68 x 3.13 inches
Compression ratio 8.6:1
Brake hp . . . . 87 @ 3800 rpm
Main bearings 7
Valve lifters . . . . hydraulic
Carburetor . . . . Holley 1-bbl.
Code . . . . B

255-cid (4.6-liter) 2-bbl. V-8

Valves . . . . overhead
Block . . . . cast iron
Displacement . . . . 255 cid/4.6 liters
Bore and stroke . . . . 3.68 x 3.00 inches
Compression ratio 8.2:1
Brake hp . . . . 120 @ 3400 rpm
Main bearings 5
Valve lifters . . . . hydraulic
Carburetor . . . . Motorcraft 2-bbl.
Code . . . . D

302-cid (5.0-liter) 2-bbl. V-8

Valves . . . . overhead
Block . . . . cast iron
Displacement . . . . 302 cid/5.0 liters
Bore and stroke . . . . 4.00 x 3.00 inches
Compression ratio 8.3:1
Brake hp . . . . 157 @ 4200 rpm
Main bearings 5
Valve lifters . . . . hydraulic
Carburetor . . . . Motorcraft 2-bbl.
Code . . . . F

CHASSIS

Wheelbase . . . . 100.4 inches
Overall length . . . . 179.1 inches
Height . . . . 51.4 inches
Width . . . . 69.1 inches
Front tread width . . . . 56.6 inches
Rear tread width . . . . 57.0 inches
Tires P175/75R-14
. . . . (GT) P185/75R-14

TECHNICAL

Final drive ratio 2.73:1

. . . . (four-cylinder, five-speed) 3.45:1
. . . . (four-cylinder, automatic) 3.08:1
. . . . (302 V-8, four-speed) 3.08:1
Steering . . . . rack and pinion
Front suspension
    modified MacPherson hydraulic shock struts with coil
    springs and stabilizer bar
Rear suspension
    four-bar link and coil spring system, anti-sway bar
    (with V-8)
Brakes . . . . (front) 9.3-inch disc
. . . . (front, V-8) 10.4-inch disc
. . . . (rear) 9.0-inch drum
Ignition . . . . electronic
Body construction . . . unibody w/front isolated mini-frame
Fuel tank . . . . 15.4 gallons

OPTION LIST

200-cid six $213
255-cid V-8 . . . . $263
. . . . (w/GT) $57 credit
302-cid V-8 . . . . $452
. . . . (w/TR performance package) $402
Five-speed manual transmission $196
Automatic transmission $411
Traction-Lok differential $76
Optional axle ratio . . . . no charge
Power brakes $93
Power steering $190
TR performance suspension package . . . . $533-$583
. . . . (GT) $105
Handling suspension $50
Engine block heater $17
Heavy-duty battery $24
California emission system $46
High-altitude emissions . . . . no charge
Light group $49
Appearance protection group $48
Power lock group $139
Air conditioning $676
Rear defroster, electric $124
Fingertip speed control $155
Power windows $165
Tinted glass $88
. . . . (windshield only) $32

1982 MUSTANG PRODUCTION CHART

Model	Doors/Body/Seating	Factory Price	Shipping Weight	Prod. Total
10 (66B)	2/coupe L/4	$6345/7062	2511/2635	Note 3
10 (66B)	2/coupe GL/4	$6844/7468	2528/2652	45,316
16 (61B)	3/hatchback GL/4	$6979/7390	2565/2689	69,348
12 (66H)	2/coupe GLX/4	$6980/7604	2543/2667	5,828
13 (61H)	3/hatchback GLX/4	$7101/7725	2579/2703	9,926
16 (61B)	3/hatchback V-8 GT/4	$8308	2629	Note 4

NOTE 1: Total series output was 130,418 units.
NOTE 2: Figures to left of slash are for four-cylinder engine, to right of slash for six-cylinder engine. A V-8 engine was priced $50 higher than the six. (The higher amount includes the cost of an automatic transmission.) A 255 cid V-8 engine was priced $70 higher than the six; a 302 V-8 was $189 higher.
NOTE 3: Production of L model is included in GL total.
NOTE 4: Ford figures include GT production in GL hatchback total above. Other industry sources report a total of 23,447 GT models produced.

Leather-wrapped steering wheel. $55
Tilt steering wheel $95
Interval wipers. $48
Rear wiper/washer $101
Trunk light. $7
Remote right mirror. $41
AM/FM radio $76
AM/FM stereo radio $106
. . . . (w/8-track or cassette player) $184
Premium sound system $105
Dual rear speakers. $39
AM radio delete . . . . $61 credit
T-Roof $1021
Flip-up open-air roof $276
Carriage roof $734
Full vinyl roof $137
Metallic glow paint. $54
Two-tone paint . . . . $138-$177
Lower two-tone paint. $104

Accent tape stripes $62
Hood scoop $38
Liftgate louvers $165
Black rocker panel moldings $33
Lower bodyside protection. $41
Console $191
Recaro high-back bucket seats. $834
Cloth/vinyl seats . . . . $23-$51
Leather low-back bucket seats $409
Cargo area cover $51
Front floor mats, carpeted $22
Wire wheel covers. . . . . $91-$141
Cast aluminum wheels . . . . $348-$398
Styled steel wheels w/trim rings . . . . $72-$122
P175/75R-14 WSW. $66
P185/75R-14 BSW $30
. . . . (WSW) $66-$96
. . . . (RWL) $85-$116

1983 GT (JH)

1983

The biggest news of the year was the return of the convertible body style to the Mustang family. A midyear introduction available only in top-line GLX trim, it came complete with an electric top, a real glass rear window, and room for four. Advertising boasted, "It also comes complete with the wind in your hair and a pounding in your heart. And that makes it a Mustang." More than 20,000 sold in that abbreviated first year at a base price of $9,449 each.

Reluctant to commit wholesale to the untested topless car market, Ford subcontracted the ragtop conversion to Cars & Concepts of Brighton, Michigan. C&C received steel-topped notchbacks directly from the Ford factory. Convertibles could be ordered with any of the powertrains, except for the four-cylinder/automatic transmission combo.

A more aerodynamic facelift made the 1983 Mustang look like a new car from the front, but it was largely a carryover model—underneath was the slightly improved Fox chassis introduced in 1979. All Mustangs had a new angled-forward front end and new front fascia, with deeply recessed headlamp housings. A narrower grille design tapered inward slightly at the base, with a Ford oval in its center. Rectangular parking lamps stood at bumper level, as before, below the outboard headlamps. Tail lamps continued the wraparound design, but in restyled form.

Engine choices were improved for 1983. The base 2.3-liter four-cylinder was upgraded with a more efficient one-barrel carburetor and long-reach sparkplugs. The antique inline six-cylinder was replaced this year by a modern "Essex" 3.8-liter V-6 that cranked out 105 hp (versus the inline unit's 87 hp) and 181 lbs.-ft. of torque (versus 158 lbs.-ft.) with a two-barrel carburetor.

Another return to the Mustang lineup was the unlamented and un-missed turbocharger option that had been dropped at the end of model year 1980. While Ford's first attempt at a blown pony had been a simple mating of the stock 2.3-liter four to a high-pressure, high-tech device that produced more customer complaints than it did horsepower, the 1983 powerplant showed some real engineering savvy. Ford's development work promised a turbocharged platform with more power, better reliability, and greater operating efficiency. Perhaps the greatest improvements were the elimination of the carburetor for Bosch port electronic fuel injection and the re-positioning of the turbo so it sat upstream of the induction system instead of downstream. The hyperaspirated four also benefited from forged-aluminum pistons, valves made from high-tech alloys, a lighter flywheel and an oil cooler. With an 8.0:1 compression ratio the new fastback and convertible Turbo GTs produced 145 hp and 180 lbs.-ft. of torque on premium unleaded gas.

While the blown four got the attention of tech-heads everywhere who predicted a day when all performance cars would be turbocharged, it was the normally aspirated 5.0-liter H.O. V-8 that brought the real ammunition to Ford's escalating horsepower war with General Motors. The 5.0 received a new four-barrel carburetor (the first such combo on a Mustang since 1970), an aluminum intake manifold, a high-flow air cleaner, and valvetrain mods. The changes bumped the Mustang's advertised horsepower to 175.

A new manual five-speed gearbox, optional with the four, had Ford's U-shaped shift motion between fourth and fifth gear. A Borg-Warner T5 close-ratio five-speed arrived later for the GT's high-output 5.0-liter V-8, hooked to a 3.27:1 final drive. An upshift indicator light option (with manual transmission) was available, to show the most fuel-efficient shift points.

When sitting side by side in the showroom, the Turbo GT did not fare so well against its V-8 brother. Interestingly, the turbo cost about $250 more than the 5.0, yet couldn't be ordered in its first year with an automatic transmission or air conditioning. Measuring happiness with a stopwatch, the turbocharged car took just less than 10 seconds to reach 60 mph from a standstill (by some published reports), whereas the

GT could rip off the same speed test in just over six seconds. Needless to say, customers scratched their heads, repeated the age-old mantra "There's no substitute for cubic inches," then ordered the cheaper, faster V-8 GT. Only 483 Turbo GTs were built in 1983. The turbo four sold in much higher numbers in the new Thunderbird Turbo Coupe, a larger car than the Mustang that, interestingly, had no V-8 option.

Why was Ford so insistent on pushing turbocharging to a reluctant public? Ford was probably the only American automaker at the time that remembered how quickly the Arab oil embargo had turned profits into losses; it simply didn't want to get caught in the middle of another fuel shortage without efficient platforms.

All Mustang tires increased by at least one size for 1983, while the optional handling suspension got thicker antisway bars plus springs and shocks tuned for sportier driving. The package became available without the formerly mandatory Michelin TRX tires.

Joining the option list were: cloth sport performance lowback bucket seats; turbine wheel covers; restyled wire wheel covers; convex right hand mirror; new special two-tone paint and tape treatment; and TRX tires and wheels without the TR performance suspension. Several options were deleted, including the rear wiper/washer, dual rear speakers, carriage roof, liftgate louvers, accent tape stripe and Recaro seats.

Standard equipment on the L (base) Mustang included black bumper rub strips; halogen headlamps; three-speed heater/defroster; woodtone instrument panel appliqué; quarter-window louvers; black remote left mirror; AM radio and four-spoke steering wheel with woodgrain insert. Also standard: four-speed manual gearbox; full wheel covers; argent accent striping; cigarette lighter; and high-back reclining bucket seats with vinyl upholstery. Mustang GL added black rocker panel; door and window frame moldings; dual accent bodyside pinstripes; a black sport steering wheel; lower-carpeted door trim panels; right visor vanity mirror and low-back bucket seats. Mustang GLX came with dual bright remote-control mirrors; woodgrain-insert four-spoke steering wheel; bright rocker panel moldings; map pockets in the driver's door trim panel and a light group. The GLX convertible included power brakes; tinted glass; dual black remote-control mirrors; black rocker moldings; and automatic transmission. Mustang GT carried a standard Traction-Lok rear axle; power brakes and steering; black grille; rear spoiler; black hood scoop; handling suspension and five-speed manual gearbox. GT models could have Michelin TRX tires on cast aluminum wheels and

a console with digital clock and diagnostic module, but no dual accent body side pinstriping. Black frames around the windshield, window, and doors completed the GT's appearance.

Model year production for 1983 came to 120,873 Mustangs. Only 25.7 percent had a turbocharged or normally aspirated four-cylinder engine, as the V-8 zoomed to 30.3 percent popularity. The rest had V-6s. Automatic transmissions were installed in 56 percent, while 24.2 percent had four-speeds and 19.8 had five-speeds.

DATA PLATE DECODING

A 17-character Vehicle Identification Number is stamped on an aluminum tab on the instrument panel, viewable through windshield. A vehicle certification label is found on the body side of where the driver's door closes.

VEHICLE WARRANTY NUMBER MANUFACTURER ID

1FA – Ford Motor Co.

RESTRAINT SYSTEM

B – active belts

VEHICLE CLASSIFICATION

P – passenger car

BODY SERIAL NUMBERS

26 – coupe
27 – convertible
28 – hatchback

ENGINE CODE

A – 140-cid (2.3-liter) 1-bbl. SOHC 4-cyl.
T – 140-cid (2.3-liter) EFI SOHC 4-cyl. turbocharged
3 – 232-cid (3.8-liter) 2-bbl. V-6
F – 302-cid (5.0-liter) 4-bbl. V-8 HO

CHECK DIGIT

for internal use

MODEL YEAR

D – 1983

ASSEMBLY PLANT

F – Dearborn, Michigan

1983 5.0 liter convertible (OCW)

CONSECUTIVE UNIT NUMBER

Begins at 100001 at each factory

CODE NUMBERS
BODY CODE

66B – coupe, convertible
61B – hatchback

PAINT CODE

1C – Black
1G – Silver Metallic
2G – Bright Bittersweet
3D – Dark Academy Blue Metallic
3L – Midnight Blue Metallic
5U – Dark Walnut Metallic
8Q – Light Desert Tan
9D – Polar White
9N – Desert Tan Glow
24 – Red
27 – Bright Red
38 – Light Academy Blue Glow
61 – Medium Yellow

ENGINES

140-cid (2.3-liter) 1-bbl. Inline Four

Valves . . . . overhead
Camshaft . . . . single overhead
Block . . . . cast iron
Displacement . . . . 140 cid/2.3 liters
Bore and stroke . . . . 3.78 x 3.13 inches
Compression ratio 9.0:1
Brake hp . . . . 90 @ 4600 rpm
Main bearings 5
Valve lifters . . . . hydraulic
Carburetor . . . . Carter 1-bbl.
Code . . . . A

140-cid (2.3-liter) EFI Inline Four Turbo

Valves . . . . overhead
Camshaft . . . . single overhead
Block . . . . cast iron
Displacement . . . . 140 cid/2.3 liters
Bore and stroke . . . . 3.78 x 3.13 inches
Compression ratio 8.0:1

Brake hp . . . . 145 @ 5000 rpm
Main bearings 5
Valve lifters . . . . hydraulic
Induction . . . . electronic fuel injection
Code . . . . T

232-cid (3.8-liter) 2-bbl. V-6

Valves . . . . overhead
Block/heads . . . . cast iron/aluminum
Displacement . . . . 232 cid
Bore and stroke . . . . 3.80 x 3.40 inches
Compression ratio 8.7:1
Brake hp . . . . 105 @ 4000 rpm
Main bearings 4
Valve lifters . . . . hydraulic
Carburetor . . . . Motorcraft 2-bbl
Code 3

302-cid (5.0-liter) 2-bbl. V-8 HO

Valves . . . . overhead
Block . . . . cast iron
Displacement . . . . 302 cid/5.0 liters
Bore and stroke . . . . 4.00 x 3.00 inches
Compression ratio 8.3:1
Brake hp . . . . 175 @ 4000 rpm
Main bearings 5
Valve lifters . . . . hydraulic
Carburetor . . . . Holley 4-bbl.
Code . . . . F

CHASSIS

Wheelbase . . . . 100.4 inches
Overall length . . . . 179.1 inches
Height . . . . 51.9 inches
Width . . . . 69.1 inches
Front tread width . . . . 56.6 inches
Rear tread width . . . . 57.0 inches
Tires P185/75R-14
(GT) P205/70R-14 or P220/55R390 TRX

TECHNICAL

Final drive ratio . . . . (four-speed) 3.08:1
. . . . (five-speed) 3.45:1
. . . . (automatic) 3.08:1 or 2.73:1

1983 MUSTANG PRODUCTION CHART

Model	Body	Doors/Body/Seating	Factory Price	Shipping Weight	Prod. Total
26	66B	2/coupe L/4	$6727/7036	2532/2621	Note 1
26/60C	66B	2/coupe GL/4	$7264/7573	2549/2638	Note 1
28/60C	61B	3/hatchback GL/4	$7439/7748	2584/2673	Note 1
26/602	66B	2/coupe GLX/4	$7398/7707	2552/2641	Note 1
28/602	61B	3/hatchback GLX/4	$7557/7866	2587/2676	Note 1
27/602	66B	2/convertible V-6 GLX/4	$9449	2759	Note 1
28/932	61B	3/hatchback V-8 GT/4	$9328	2891	Note 1
27/932	66B	2/convertible V-8 GT/4	$13,479	N/A	Note 1
28/932	61B	3/hatchback Turbo GT/4	$9714	N/A	Note 1

NOTE 1: Ford reports total production of 33,201 two-doors, 64,234 hatchbacks, and 23,438 convertibles. Total series output was 120,873 units.
NOTE 2: Figures to left of slash are for four-cylinder engine, to right of slash for V-6. A 4-bbl. 302-cid V-8 engine cost $1,044 more than the V-6 ($595 more on the GLX convertible). The price of the GLX convertible jumped sharply after the model year began, to $12,467.

Steering. . . . . rack and pinion
Front suspension . . . .
   modified MacPherson hydraulic shock struts with coil
   springs and stabilizer bar
Rear suspension . . . .
   four-bar link and coil spring system, anti-sway bar (with
   V-8)
Brakes . . . . (front) 9.3-inch disc
. . . . (front, V-8) 10.4-inch disc
. . . . (rear) 9.0-inch drum
Ignition . . . . electronic
Body construction . . . unibody w/front isolated mini-frame
Fuel tank. . . . . 15.4 gallons

OPTION LIST

232-cid V-6 . . . . $309
302-cid V-8 . . . . $1343
. . . . (convertible) $595
Five-speed manual transmission. $124
Automatic transmission $439
Traction-Lok differential $95
Optional axle ratio . . . . no charge
Power brakes $93
Power steering. $202
Handling suspension $252
Engine block heater. $17
Heavy-duty battery $26
California emission system $76
High-altitude emissions . . . . no charge
Sport performance package $196
Light group $55
Appearance protection group. $60
Power lock group $160
Air conditioning. $724

Rear defroster, electric. $135
Fingertip speed control $170
Power windows $180
Tinted glass $105
. . . . (windshield only) $38
Leather-wrapped steering wheel. $59
Tilt steering wheel $105
Interval wipers. $49
Remote right mirror. $44
AM/FM radio $82
AM/FM stereo radio $109
. . . . (w/8-track or cassette player) $199
Premium sound system $117
AM radio delete . . . . $61 credit
T-Roof $1055
Flip-up open-air roof $310
Metallic glow paint. $54
Two-tone paint . . . . $150-$189
Liftgate louvers. . . . . (hatchback) $171
Rocker panel moldings. $33
Lower bodyside protection. $41
Console $191
Cloth/vinyl seats . . . . $29-$57
Leather low back bucket seats $415
Front floor mats, carpeted $22
Wire wheel covers . . . . $98-$148
Turbine wheel covers . . . . no charge
Cast aluminum wheels . . . . $354-$404
Styled steel wheels w/trim rings . . . . $78-$128
P185/75R-14 WSW. $72
P195/75R-14 WSW. $108
P205/75R-14 BSW $224
TRX P220/55R390 BSW . . . . $327-$551

1983 GLX convertible (FMC)

1984 20th Anniversary model (JH)

1984

1984 was a special year in many ways. Only a few years earlier, Mustang II performance buyers lived with a choice of a single engine available in identically prepared cars—their only real differences boiling down to how much tape was applied to the car from the factory. In 1984, a driving enthusiast could walk into a Ford dealership and drive home with a grin on his face in one of an array of high-performance machines—a happy situation that reminded some of the vast offerings enjoyed in the 1969 Mustang model line.

At the top of the wish list, the GT came standard with increased power from the 5.0-liter H.O. V-8 (now rated at 175 hp in four-barrel form) and a Borg-Warner T-5 five-speed manual transmission. In addition to a striped hood and GT decals, the GT sported a functional front air dam. Integral fog lamps were added to cars produced in early 1984 and thereafter. Automatic overdrive transmission was a new option.

A new, less powerful, version of the 302-cid V-8 joined the 1984 lineup, producing 165 hp with a throttle body electronic fuel injection (EFI) system. It was installed in Mustangs ordered with either the three-speed automatic or four-speed automatic unit with overdrive. A higher-output version of the four-barrel V-8, producing 205 hp, was announced for December arrival but delayed until the 1985 model year (when it would produce 210 hp).

Once again, the Turbo GT model combined the efficiency of a 2.3-liter, overhead cam four-cylinder engine with the response of electronic fuel-injection and the on-demand power of turbocharging. By the end of the 1984 model year, only 3,000 Turbo GT hatchbacks and 600 convertibles had been sold for the entire 1983-84 run, leaving Ford no choice but to cancel the unusual model.

Fresh temptation for performance-minded Mustangers came in the form of the new SVO, introduced midyear. Developed by Ford's Special Vehicle Operations department, the SVO raised the bar on turbo technology with an air-to-air intercooler on its 2.3-liter turbocharged, fuel-injected four-cylinder engine—a package that produced 175 hp with improved low-end grunt. The SVO package included a Borg-Warner T-5 five-speed manual gearbox with Hurst linkage, four-wheel disc brakes, performance suspension with adjustable Koni gas-filled shocks, P225/50VR-16 Goodyear NCT tires on cast aluminum 16 x 7-inch wheels, and a functional hood scoop.

The SVO could, according to Ford, hit 134 miles per hour and get to 60 from a standstill in just 7.5 seconds. Inside were multi-adjustable articulated leather bucket seats. SVO's shock absorbers and struts had three settings: cross-country (for front and rear); GT (front only); and competition (front and rear). Four-wheel disc brakes were standard.

The SVO had a much different front than the standard Mustang, with a grille-less fascia and integrated fog lamps. Just a single slot sat below the hood panel, which contained a Ford oval. Large single rectangular headlamps were deeply recessed and flanked by large wraparound lenses. A polycarbonate, dual-wing rear spoiler was meant to increase downforce on the car at speed, while rear-wheel "spats" directed airflow around the wheel wells.

SVO's price tag was more than double that of a base Mustang four-cylinder. Offered in hatchback form only, SVO was available in Black, Silver Metallic, Dark Charcoal Metallic or Red Metallic. Interiors were all Charcoal. Only six major options were available for SVO because it had so much standard equipment: air conditioning; power windows; power door locks; cassette player; flip-up sunroof; and leather seat trim. Standard SVO equipment included an 8000-rpm tachometer; quick-ratio power steering; Traction-Lok rear axle; leather-wrapped steering wheel; shift knob and brake handle; unique instrument panel appliqués; narrow body side moldings; and unique

C-pillar and tail lamp treatments. A premium/regular fuel switch calibrated the ignition instantly. Revised pedal positioning allowed "heel and toe" downshifting, and a footrest for the left foot improved the driver's position during hard cornering.

Ford's Special Vehicle Operations Department was formed in 1981 to supervise the company's renewed involvement in motorsports (among other duties) and to develop special limited-edition high-performance vehicles. Its special turbo Mustang was the first of those offered as a production model. *Motor Trend* called the SVO "the best-driving street Mustang the factory has ever produced." *Road & Track* claimed the SVO "outruns the Datsun 280ZX, out-handles the Ferrari 308 and Porsche 944 ... and it's affordable." Its hefty price tag meant the SVO was targeted toward more affluent, car-conscious consumers.

Another special model for 1984 commemorated the Mustang's 20th anniversary. All 5260 units were produced around the GT package, whether ordered with the turbo four or V-8. Available only in Oxford White with Canyon Red interiors, the cars were further distinguished by articulated sports seats, rocker panel tape treatment that read "G.T. 350" and various emblems and medallions that harkened back to the '60s model. Unfortunately, no one at Ford got permission from Carroll Shelby, who owned all rights to the name. Shelby, who was working at the time with Mustang "father" Lee Iacocca at Chrysler, sued Ford over the incident.

Standard models looked the same as in 1983. Throughout the line were new steering wheels with center horn, new instrument panel appliqués and split folding rear seats. Mustang instrument panels had red lighting this year.

The series lineup was simplified for 1984. GL and GLX models of 1983 were gone, replaced by a single LX series. A convertible was offered again this year, in both LX and GT form. The GT series displayed a new front air dam, with road lamps available. For 1984, the base model was the Mustang L, offering a high level of equipment at a relatively low cost, including the 2.3-liter overhead cam four with a four-speed manual transmission, an upshift indicator light to help motorists save fuel and a starter interlock that prevented drivers with manual transmissions from engaging the car's starter without depressing the clutch pedal.

Mustang buyers could now get the base L in hatchback form as well as notchback. Convertible lovers could enjoy droptops in LX form (where the V-6 was now standard), as V-8 GTs or Turbo GTs. With the start of the 1984 model year, Ford began producing the convertible on its own assembly line.

Throttle-body electronic fuel injection was added to the 3.8-liter V-6, which increased the horsepower to 120 and pounds-feet of torque to 205. Only the SelectShift automatic transmission could be mated to the '84 V-6.

All Mustangs, starting in 1984, came equipped with Ford's new EEC-IV (electronic engine control system, fourth generation), that monitored engine functions while optimizing performance.

As American car makers began building performance into their products again, tire technology accelerated as well, with the Mustang getting the newest shoes as quickly as anyone. GT rubber was upgraded to a 130-mph V-rating for 1984, and the unusually sized TRX wheel/tire combo was dropped at the end of the year.

141,480 Mustangs of all flavors were produced in 1984.

DATA PLATE DECODING

A 17-character Vehicle Identification Number is stamped on an aluminum tab on the instrument panel, viewable through windshield. A vehicle certification label is found on the body side of where the driver's door closes.

VEHICLE WARRANTY NUMBER MANUFACTURER ID

1FA – Ford Motor Co.

RESTRAINT SYSTEM

B – active belts

VEHICLE CLASSIFICATION

P – passenger car

BODY SERIAL NUMBERS

26 – coupe
27 – convertible
28 – hatchback

ENGINE CODE

A – 140-cid (2.3-liter) 1-bbl. SOHC 4-cyl.
T – 140-cid (2.3-liter) EFI SOHC 4-cyl. Turbocharged (Turbo GT)
W – 140-cid (2.3-liter) EFI SOHC 4-cyl. Turbocharged (SVO)
3 – 232-cid (3.8-liter) EFI V-6
F – 302-cid (5.0-liter) EFI V-8
M – 302-cid (5.0-liter) 4-bbl. V-8 HO

CHECK DIGIT

for internal use

MODEL YEAR

E – 1984

ASSEMBLY PLANT

F – Dearborn, Michigan

CONSECUTIVE UNIT NUMBER

Begins at 100001 at each factory

CODE NUMBERS
BODY CODE

66B – coupe, convertible
61B – hatchback

1984 M-code 5.0-liter/4V V-8 (JH)

PAINT CODE

- 1C – Black
- 1E – Silver Metallic
- 2B – Medium Canyon Red Glow
- 5C – Dark Academy Blue Metallic
- 8Q – Light Desert Tan
- 9C – Bright Copper Glow
- 9J – Desert Tan Glow
- 9L – Oxford White
- 9W – Dark Charcoal Metallic
- 27 – Bright Canyon Red
- 35 – Light Academy Blue Glow

ENGINES

140-cid (2.3-liter) 1-bbl. Inline Four

Valves	overhead
Camshaft	single overhead
Block	cast iron
Displacement	140 cid/2.3 liters
Bore and stroke	3.78 x 3.13 inches
Compression ratio	9.0:1
Brake hp	88 @ 4000 rpm
Main bearings	5
Valve lifters	hydraulic
Carburetor	Carter 1-bbl.
Code	A

140-cid (2.3-liter) EFI Inline Four Turbo GT

Valves	overhead
Camshaft	single overhead
Block	cast iron
Displacement	140 cid/2.3 liters
Bore and stroke	3.78 x 3.13 inches
Compression ratio	8.0:1
Brake hp	145 @ 4600 rpm
Main bearings	5
Valve lifters	hydraulic
Induction	electronic fuel injection
Code	T

140-cid (2.3-liter) EFI Inline Four SVO

Valves	overhead
Camshaft	single overhead
Block	cast iron
Displacement	140 cid/2.3 liters
Bore and stroke	3.78 x 3.13 inches
Compression ratio	8.0:1
Brake hp	175 @ 4400 rpm
Main bearings	5
Valve lifters	hydraulic
Induction	electronic fuel injection
Code	W

232-cid (3.8-liter) EFI V-6

Valves	overhead
Block/heads	cast iron/aluminum
Displacement	232 cid
Bore and stroke	3.80 x 3.40 inches
Compression ratio	8.7:1
Brake hp	120 @ 3600 rpm
Main bearings	4
Valve lifters	hydraulic
Induction	electronic fuel injection
Code	3

302-cid (5.0-liter) EFI V-8

Valves	overhead
Block	cast iron
Displacement	302 cid/5.0 liters
Bore and stroke	4.00 x 3.00 inches
Compression ratio	8.3:1
Brake hp	165 @ 3800 rpm
Main bearings	5
Valve lifters	hydraulic
Induction	electronic fuel injection
Code	F

302-cid (5.0-liter) 4-bbl. V-8 HO

Valves	overhead
Block	cast iron
Displacement	302 cid/5.0 liters
Bore and stroke	4.00 x 3.00 inches
Compression ratio	8.3:1
Brake hp	175 @ 4000 rpm
Main bearings	5
Valve lifters	hydraulic
Carburetor	Holley 4-bbl.
Code	M

CHASSIS

Wheelbase	100.5 inches
Overall length	179.1 inches
	(SVO) 181 inches

1984 MUSTANG PRODUCTION CHART

Model	Body	Doors/Body/Seating	Factory Price	Shipping Weight	Prod. Total
26	66B	2/coupe L/4	$7098/7507	2538/2646	Note 1
28	61B	3/hatchback L/4	$7269/7678	2584/2692	Note 1
26/602	66B	2/coupe LX/4	$7290/7699	2559/2667	Note 1
28/602	61B	3/hatchback LX/4	$7496/7905	2605/2713	Note 1
27/602	66B	2/convertible V-6 LX/4	$11,849	2873	Note 1
28/932	61B	3/hatchback GT/4	$9762/9578	2753/2899	Note 1
27/932	66B	2/convertible GT/4	$13,245/13,051	2921/3043	Note 1
28/932	61B	3/hatchback SVO/4	$15,596	2881	Note 1

NOTE 1: Ford reports total production of 37,680 two-doors, 86,200 hatchbacks and 17,600 convertibles. Total series output was 141,480 units.
NOTE 2: For Ls and LXs figures to left of slash are for four-cylinder engine, to right of slash for V-6. A 302-cid V-8 engine cost $1,165 more than the V-6 ($318 more on the LX convertible).
NOTE 3: For GTs figures to left of slash are for turbocharged four, to right for V-8.

Height . . . . 51.9 inches
Width. . . . . 69.1 inches
Front tread width. . . . . 56.6 inches
. . . . (SVO) 57.8 inches
Rear tread width . . . . 57.0 inches
. . . . (SVO) 58.3 inches
Tires P185/75R-14
. . . . (GT) P205/70R-14

TECHNICAL

Final drive ratio . . . . (four-speed) 3.08:1
. . . . (five-speed) 3.27:1
. . . . (V-6) 3.08:1
. . . . (V-8, five-speed) 3.08:1
. . . . (V-8, three-speed automatic) 2.73:1
. . . . (V-8, four-speed automatic) 3.27:1
. . . . (turbo) 3.45:1
Steering. . . . . rack and pinion
Front suspension . . . .
    modified MacPherson hydraulic shock struts with coil
    springs and stabilizer bar
    (SVO) adds gas-pressurized adjustable shocks
Rear suspension . . . .
    four-bar link and coil spring system, anti-sway bar (with
    SVO and GT Turbo)
Brakes . . . . (front) disc
. . . . (rear) drum
. . . . (rear SVO) disc
Ignition . . . . electronic
Body construction . . . unibody w/front isolated mini-frame
Fuel tank. . . . . 15.4 gallons

OPTION LIST

232-cid V-6 . . . . $409
302-cid V-8 package $1574
. . . . (LX convertible) $727
Five-speed manual transmission . . . . no charge
Three-speed automatic transmission $439
Four-speed overdrive automatic transmission $551
Traction-Lok differential $95
Optional axle ratio . . . . no charge
Power brakes $93
Power steering $202
Handling suspension $252
. . . . (w/VIP package) $50
Engine block heater $18
Heavy-duty battery $27

California emission system $99
High-altitude option . . . . no charge
SVO competition preparation package
. . . . (delete air cond., power locks, AM/FM/cassette and
                    power windows) $1253 credit
VIP package for L/LX with AM/FM stereo or tilt wheel . $93
. . . . (both) $196
VIP package for GT $110
20th anniversary VIP package . . . . (GT) $25-$144
Light/convenience group . . . . $55-$88
Power lock group $177
Air conditioning. $743
Rear defroster, electric. $140
Fingertip speed control $176
Power windows $198
Tinted glass $110
Tilt steering wheel $110
Interval wipers. $50
Remote right mirror. $46
    AM/FM stereo radio $109
. . . . (w/cassette player) $222
. . . . (SVO or w/VIP package) $113
Premium sound system $151
AM radio delete . . . . $39 credit
T-Roof $1074
. . . . (w/VIP package) $760
Flip-up open-air roof $315
Metallic glow paint. $54
L/LX . . . . $150-$189
Lower two-tone paint. $116
Liftgate louvers. . . . . (hatchback) $171
Rocker panel moldings. $39
Lower bodyside protection. $41
Console $191
Articulated sport seats $196
    High-back vinyl bucket seats . . . . (L) $29
. . . . (low-back, LX/GT) $29
Leather bucket seats $189
Front floor mats, carpeted $22
Wire wheel covers $98
Cast aluminum wheels $354
Styled steel wheels w/trim rings $78
P185/75R-14 WSW $72
P195/75R-14 WSW $108
P205/75R-14 BSW $224
TRX P220/55R390 BSW . . . . $327-$551
. . . . (GT) $27 credit

1984 SVO (FMC)

1985 GT (PH)

1985

The Mustang's theme for 1985 might very well have been "More power!" as its high-performance powerplants got even hotter. The GT's 5.0-liter H.O. V-8 benefited from the combination of old-fashioned hot rod tricks and new technology, enjoying a power boost to 210 hp through the use of low-friction roller tappets and a high-performance camshaft. Stainless steel headers replaced "high-flow" cast-iron manifolds, with twin pipes purging the hot exhaust gases through individual catalytic converters. What had been lost horsepower was regained through the use of a new accessory drive system that reduced the air conditioner compressor, power steering pump, and alternator to half speed.

The fuel-injected version of the 5.0 (still only available with automatic transmission) produced 165 hp. 1985 marked the final year a four-barrel carburetor would appear on the 5.0-liter H.O. powerplant before Ford followed the industry trend to fuel injection across the board. GT upgrades for 1985 included a T-5 transmission with shorter gear throws, a quad-shock system in the rear, a larger rear stabilizer bar, and Goodyear Eagle P225/60VR-15 "Gatorback" unidirectional tires mounted on new alloy wheels.

SVO engineers were no doubt pleased when their self-named Mustang model was revised midyear with a new look (primarily flush-mounted headlamps) and an impressive 205 hp. Once again, hot rod met high-tech under the hood with a higher-performance cam, higher-flow exhaust system, reconfigured turbocharger, larger injectors, and greater boost accounting for the increase. Race driver Jackie Stewart, a Ford consultant, promoted "The New Turbo Math" in an advertisement for the SVO. He said "Proven in race cars, the intercooled turbo is now in the Mustang SVO, the only American production car to have

this kind of turbo. Ford is in the forefront of this new turbo technology." The price of the all-out sports car dropped slightly, to $14,521, but sales also fell to 1,954 units.

As a final sign that the public was just not ready to pay a premium for a turbocharged four-cylinder when a perfectly good V-8 put out more power, it is interesting to note that Ford made one more attempt to sell its Turbo GT model in 1985 before retiring the idea permanently.

The base L series was dropped, making LX the bottom-level Mustang. Standard LX equipment now included power brakes and steering; remote-control right-side mirror; dual-note horn; interval windshield wipers; and an AM/FM stereo radio. As before, both notchback and hatchback bodies were offered. New standard interior features included a console; low-back bucket seats (on LX); articulated sport seats (on GT); luxury door trim panels; and covered visor mirrors. The convertible's quarter trim panels were revised to accommodate a refined seatbelt system. Mechanical radio faces switched to a contemporary flat design. All Mustangs had larger tires this year, with added urethane lower body side protection. A new electronic AM/FM stereo radio with cassette player was added to the options list. Both the 3.8-liter V-6 and 5.0-liter V-8 had a new oil warning light.

All 1985 Mustangs wore a new front-end look with a four-hole integral air dam below the bumper, flanked by low rectangular parking lamps. GTs also sported integral fog lamps. A grille similar to the one on the SVO—essentially one wide slot with angled sides in a sloping front panel—appeared on all Mustangs displaying a Ford oval. Tail lamps were full-width (except for the license plate opening), with backup lenses at the upper portion of each inner section. A Ford script oval stood above the right tail lamp. Most Mustang exterior trim and accents switched from black to a softer charcoal shade. All models had new charcoal front and rear bumper rub strips and body side moldings. Also new were a charcoal hood paint/tape treatment, a revised decklid decal, and GT nomenclature (where applicable) molded into the body side strip.

Robert L. Rewey took over as vice president and general manager of Ford Division in 1985. He enjoyed a great first year at the helm, as the company's sales increased the third year in a row.

At the start of the model run, Ford made a forecast of 128,000 Mustang sales. In reality, 156,514 units were produced. They accounted for an even two percent of total industry output. Records showed that 31.7 percent of all 1985 Mustangs were V-8s and that 7.4 percent of those were fuel-injected. Fours were used in 55.5 percent, with 1.3 percent of those having turbochargers. Another 12.7 percent had the throttle-body-injected V-6.

DATA PLATE DECODING

A 17-character Vehicle Identification Number is stamped on an aluminum tab on the instrument panel, viewable through windshield. A vehicle certification label is found on the body side of where the driver's door closes.

VEHICLE WARRANTY NUMBER
MANUFACTURER ID

1FA – Ford Motor Co.

RESTRAINT SYSTEM

B – active belts

VEHICLE CLASSIFICATION

P – passenger car

BODY SERIAL NUMBERS

26 – coupe
27 – convertible
28 – hatchback

ENGINE CODE

A – 140-cid (2.3-liter) 1-bbl. SOHC 4-cyl.
W – 140-cid (2.3-liter) EFI SOHC 4-cyl. Turbocharged (SVO)
3 – 232-cid (3.8-liter) EFI V-6
M – 302-cid (5.0-liter) EFI V-8, automatic
M – 302-cid (5.0-liter) 4-bbl. V-8 HO, five-speed

CHECK DIGIT

for internal use

MODEL YEAR

F – 1985

ASSEMBLY PLANT

F – Dearborn, Michigan

CONSECUTIVE UNIT NUMBER

Begins at 100001 at each factory

CODE NUMBERS
BODY CODE

66B – coupe, convertible
61B – hatchback

PAINT CODE

1B– Medium Charcoal
1C – Black

1Q – Silver
1U – Oxford Grey
2C – Canyon Red
2R – Jalapena Red
3M – Pastel Regatta Blue
3Y – Medium Regatta Blue
8L – Sand Beige
8Y – Dark Sable
9L – Oxford White

ENGINES

140-cid (2.3-liter) 2-bbl. Inline Four
Valves . . . . overhead
Camshaft . . . . single overhead
Block . . . . cast iron
Displacement . . . . 140 cid/2.3 liters
Bore and stroke . . . . 3.78 x 3.13 inches
Compression ratio 9.0:1
Brake hp . . . . 88 @ 4000 rpm
Main bearings 5
Valve lifters . . . . hydraulic
Carburetor . . . . Carter 1-bbl.
Code . . . . A

140-cid (2.3-liter) EFI Inline Four SVO
Valves . . . . overhead
Camshaft . . . . single overhead
Block . . . . cast iron
Displacement . . . . 140 cid/2.3 liters
Bore and stroke . . . . 3.78 x 3.13 inches
Compression ratio 8.0:1
Brake hp . . . . 205 @ 5000 rpm
Main bearings 5
Valve lifters . . . . hydraulic
Induction . . . . electronic fuel injection
Code . . . . W

232-cid (3.8-liter) EFI V-6
Valves . . . . overhead
Block/heads . . . . cast iron/aluminum
Displacement . . . . 232 cid
Bore and stroke . . . . 3.80 x 3.40 inches
Compression ratio 8.7:1
Brake hp . . . . 120 @ 3600 rpm
Main bearings 4
Valve lifters . . . . hydraulic
Induction . . . . electronic fuel injection
Code 3

302-cid (5.0-liter) EFI V-8, automatic transmission models
Valves . . . . overhead
Block . . . . cast iron
Displacement . . . . 302 cid/5.0 liters
Bore and stroke . . . . 4.00 x 3.00 inches
Compression ratio 8.3:1
Brake hp . . . . 165 @ 4200 rpm
Main bearings 5
Valve lifters . . . . hydraulic
Induction . . . . electronic fuel injection
Code . . . . M

302-cid (5.0-liter) 4-bbl. V-8 HO, manual transmission models

Valves . . . . overhead
Block . . . . cast iron
Displacement . . . . 302 cid/5.0 liters
Bore and stroke . . . . 4.00 x 3.00 inches
Compression ratio 8.3:1
Brake hp . . . . 210 @ 4400 rpm
Main bearings 5
Valve lifters . . . . hydraulic
Carburetor . . . . Holley 4-bbl.
Code . . . . M

CHASSIS

Wheelbase . . . . 100.5 inches
Overall length . . . . 179.3 inches
. . . . (SVO) 180.8 inches
Height . . . . 52.1 inches
Width . . . . 69.1 inches
Front tread width . . . . 56.6 inches
. . . . (SVO) 57.8 inches
Rear tread width . . . . 57.0 inches
. . . . (SVO) 58.3 inches
Tires P195/75R-14
. . . . (GT) P225/60R-15
. . . . (SVO) P225/50VR-16

TECHNICAL

Final drive ratio . . . . (four-speed) 3.08:1
. . . . (automatic) 3.27:1
. . . . (V-6) 2.73:1
. . . . (V-8, five-speed) 3.08:1
. . . . (V-8, four-speed automatic) 3.27:1
. . . . (turbo) 3.45:1
Steering . . . . rack and pinion, power assisted
Front suspension . . . .
   modified MacPherson hydraulic shock struts with coil
   springs and stabilizer bar
   (SVO) adds gas-pressurized adjustable shocks
Rear suspension . . . .
   four-bar link and coil spring system, anti-sway bar
   (with SVO and GT)
Brakes . . . . (front) disc
. . . . (rear) drum
. . . . (rear SVO) disc
Ignition . . . . electronic
Body construction . . . unibody w/front isolated mini-frame
Fuel tank . . . . 15.4 gallons

OPTION LIST

232-cid V-6 . . . . (LX) $439
302-cid V-8 package $1000
. . . . (LX convertible) $152
Five-speed manual transmission . . . . (LX) $124
Three-speed automatic transmission . . . . (LX) $439
Four-speed overdrive automatic transmission . . (LX) $676
. . . . (GT) $551
Traction-Lok differential $95
Optional axle ratio . . . . NC
Handling suspension . . . . (LX) $258
Engine block heater $18
Heavy-duty battery $27
California emission system $99
High-altitude option . . . . no charge
SVO competition preparation package
   . . . . (delete air cond., power locks, AM/FM/cassette and
                           power windows) $1417 credit
Light/convenience group $55
Power lock group . . . . $177-$210
Air conditioning $743
Rear defroster, electric $140
Fingertip speed control $176
Power windows $198
. . . . (convertible) $272
Tinted glass $110
Tilt steering wheel . . . . (LX) $110
AM/FM stereo radio w/cassette player . . . . . . (LX/GT) $148
Electronic AM/FM stereo w/cassette . . . . (LX/GT) $300
Premium sound system . . . . (LX/GT) $138
Radio delete . . . . $148 credit
T-Roof . . . . (hatchback) $1074
Flip-up open-air roof . . . . (hatchback) $315
Lower two-tone paint $116
Single wing spoiler . . . . (SVO) no charge
Console $191
Low-back vinyl bucket seats . . . . (LX) $29
Leather sport performance bucket seats (LX convertible) $780
. . . . (GT convertible) $415
. . . . (SVO) $189
Wire wheel covers . . . . (LX) $98
Styled steel wheels $178
P205/75R-14 WSW $109
P205/70VR-14 BSW $238
P225/60VR-15 SBR BSW $665

1985 MUSTANG PRODUCTION CHART

Model	Body	Doors/Body/Seating	Factory Price	Shipping Weight	Prod. Total
26/602	66B	2/coupe LX/4	$6885/8017	2559/2667	Note 1
28/602	61B	3/hatchback LX/4	$7345/8477	2605/2713	Note 1
27/602	66B	2/convertible V-6 LX/4	$11,985	2873	Note 1
28/932	61B	3/hatchback GT/4	$9885	2899	Note 1
27/932	66B	2/convertible GT/4	$13,585	3043	Note 1
28/939	61B	3/hatchback SVO/4	$14,521	2881	Note 1

NOTE 1: Ford reports total production of 56,781 coupes, 84,623 hatchbacks, and 15,110 convertibles. Total series output was 156,514 units.

NOTE 2: For LX coupe and hatchback figures to left of slash are for four-cylinder engine, to right of slash for V-6 (including the price of the required automatic transmission). A 302-cid H.O. V-8 engine cost $561 more than the V-6 ($152 more on the LX convertible).

**1986 SVO
Owner: Robert Tunney**

1986

The Mustang's 1986 model lineup was the same as 1985: LX two-door sedan or hatchback (and convertible), GT hatchback and convertible, and SVO. Gone was the four-barrel 5.0-liter H.O. and taking its place was the sequential port fuel injected 5.0-liter H.O. rated at 200 hp and 285 lbs.-ft. of torque. In addition to the new induction system, the H.O. benefited from redesigned heads, an improved water pump and a stronger block design. The new V-8 was standard in the GT and an option for the LX. All Mustang V-8 models with five-speed manual transmissions also received an upshift indicator light to tell drivers when to shift for maximum fuel economy.

The new V-8 could be hooked to a five-speed manual (overdrive) transmission or automatic overdrive. The GT included a special suspension, Goodyear Eagle VR performance tires, quick-ratio power steering, and articulated front sport seats. For 1986, the wide grey GT hood stripe could be deleted on request of the customer. The LX came standard with full body side striping, power brakes and steering, and extras such as interval wipers, luxury sound package, and an AM/FM stereo radio (which could be deleted for credit).

The throttle-body-injected V-6 with 120 hp was standard in LX ragtops and optional in other models. Base engine remained the 2.3-liter four, which was mated to a five-speed manual transmission or optional automatic.

The Mustang's appearance was essentially the same as in the previous year. The sloping center front-end panel held a Ford oval at the top, and a wide single opening below. The quad rectangular headlamps were deeply recessed. Parking lamps stood far down on the front end. Side marker lenses were angled to match the front fender tips. Tail lamps were distinctly split into upper and lower sections by a full-width divider bar. "Mustang" lettering sat above the left tail lamp, a Ford oval above the right.

Turbine wheel covers switched from bright/argent to bright/black. The Mustang's rear axle was upgraded to 8.8 inches with the standard 2.73:1 axle ratio or optional 3.08:1 (cars with automatic transmissions were equipped with 3.27:1 rear gears), for use with the 5.0-liter V-8. Viscous engine mounts were added on the 3.8-liter V-6 and the V-8, as had been used on the turbo four starting in mid-year 1985. Ford boosted its anti-corrosion warranty, added sound-deadening material, and adopted a single-key lock system.

A third, high-mounted brake lamp was a new safety feature made mandatory for 1986. The two-door LX notchback had the device added to the package tray; GT and SVO were modified to take it on the spoilers. Hatchback LX models added a spoiler to house that brake lamp, while LX and GT convertibles installed a luggage rack with integrated brake lamp.

Preferred Equipment Packages included such items as air conditioning, styled wheels and Premium Sound System. In 1986, the SVO, still equipped with its 205-hp turbo four, continued with a higher-again $15,272 price tag. It sold a slightly higher total of 3,382 units (bringing its three-year total to 9,844), but 1986 would be its last year of production.

Overall Mustang production was up for 1986. Way up! For the model year, 244,410 were made. This was a 2.84 market share, up almost a full percent!

DATA PLATE DECODING

A 17-character Vehicle Identification Number is stamped on an aluminum tab on the instrument panel, viewable through windshield. A vehicle certification label is found on the body side of where the driver's door closes.

VEHICLE WARRANTY NUMBER
MANUFACTURER ID

1FA – Ford Motor Co.

RESTRAINT SYSTEM

B – active belts

VEHICLE CLASSIFICATION

P – passenger car

BODY SERIAL NUMBERS

26 – coupe
27 – convertible
28 – hatchback

ENGINE CODE

A – 140-cid (2.3-liter) 1-bbl. SOHC 4-cyl.
W – 140-cid (2.3-liter) EFI SOHC 4-cyl. Turbocharged (SVO)
3 – 232-cid (3.8-liter) EFI V-6
M – 302-cid (5.0-liter) EFI V-8 HO

CHECK DIGIT

for internal use

MODEL YEAR

G – 1986

ASSEMBLY PLANT

F – Dearborn, Michigan

CONSECUTIVE UNIT NUMBER

Begins at 100001 at each factory

CODE NUMBERS
BODY CODE

66B – coupe, convertible
61B – hatchback

PAINT CODE

1B– Dark Grey Metallic
1C – Black
2A – Bright Red
9L – Oxford White

ENGINES

140-cid (2.3-liter) 2-bbl. Inline Four

Valves . . . . overhead
Camshaft . . . . single overhead
Block . . . . cast iron
Displacement . . . . 140 cid/2.3 liters
Bore and stroke . . . . 3.78 x 3.13 inches
Compression ratio 9.5:1
Brake hp . . . . 88 @ 4200 rpm
Main bearings 5
Valve lifters . . . . hydraulic
Carburetor . . . . Carter 1-bbl.
Code . . . . A

140-cid (2.3-liter) EFI Inline Four SVO

Valves . . . . overhead
Camshaft . . . . single overhead
Block . . . . cast iron
Displacement . . . . 140 cid/2.3 liters
Bore and stroke . . . . 3.78 x 3.13 inches
Compression ratio 8.0:1
Brake hp . . . . 205 @ 5000 rpm
Main bearings 5
Valve lifters . . . . hydraulic
Induction . . . . electronic fuel injection
Code . . . . W

232-cid (3.8-liter) EFI V-6

Valves . . . . overhead
Block/heads . . . . cast iron/aluminum
Displacement . . . . 232 cid
Bore and stroke . . . . 3.80 x 3.40 inches
Compression ratio 8.7:1
Brake hp . . . . 120 @ 3600 rpm
Main bearings 4
Valve lifters . . . . hydraulic
Induction . . . . electronic fuel injection
Code 3

1986 SVO front clip

1986 W-code 2.3-liter/EFI turbocharged four-cylinder

302-cid (5.0-liter) EFI V-8 HO

Valves . . . . overhead
Block . . . . cast iron
Displacement. . . . . 302 cid/5.0 liters
Bore and stroke. . . . . 4.00 x 3.00 inches
Compression ratio 9.2:1
Brake hp . . . . 200 @ 4400 rpm
Main bearings 5
Valve lifters. . . . . hydraulic
Induction . . . . electronic fuel injection
Code. . . . . M

CHASSIS

Wheelbase . . . . 100.5 inches
Overall length . . . . 179.3 inches
. . . . (SVO) 180.8 inches
Height . . . . 52.1 inches
. . . . (convertible) 51.9 inches
Width. . . . . 69.1 inches
Front tread width. . . . . 56.6 inches
. . . . (SVO) 57.8 inches
Rear tread width . . . . 57.0 inches
. . . . (SVO) 58.3 inches
Tires P195/75R-14
. . . . (GT) P225/60R-15
. . . . (SVO) P225/50VR-16

TECHNICAL

Final drive ratio. . . . . (four-speed) 3.08:1
. . . . (automatic) 3.27:1
. . . . (V-6) 2.73:1
. . . . (V-8, five-speed) 2.73:1
. . . . (V-8, four-speed automatic) 3.27:1
. . . . (turbo) 3.73:1
Steering . . . . rack and pinion, power assisted
Front suspension . . . .
modified MacPherson hydraulic shock struts with
coil springs and stabilizer bar
. . . . (SVO) adds gas-pressurized adjustable shocks
Rear suspension . . . .
four-bar link and coil spring system, anti-sway bar
(with SVO and GT)
Brakes . . . . (front) disc
. . . . (rear) drum
. . . . (rear SVO) disc
Ignition . . . . electronic
Body construction . . . unibody w/front isolated mini-frame
Fuel tank. 15.4 gallons

OPTION LIST

232-cid V-6 . . . . (LX) $454
302-cid V-8 package $1120
. . . . (LX convertible) $106
Five-speed manual transmission . . . . (LX) $124
Three-speed automatic transmission
. . . . (LX, standard on convertible) $510
Four-speed overdrive automatic transmission . . (LX) $746
. . . . (GT) $622
Engine block heater $18
Heavy-duty battery $27

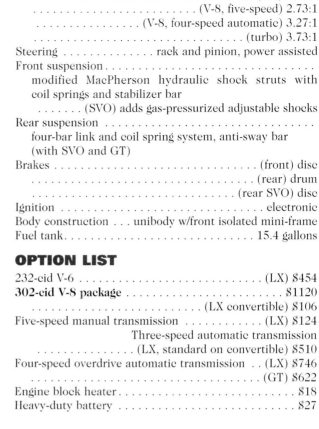

1986 SVO wheels

1986 SVO "spats"

1986 SVO dashboard

1986 SVO leather seats

California emission system. $102
High-altitude option . . . . no charge
SVO competition preparation package
. . . . (equipment deleted) $1451 credit
Light/convenience group $55
Power lock group . . . . $182-$215
Air conditioning. $762
Rear defroster, electric. $145
Fingertip speed control $176
Power windows $207
. . . . (convertible) $282
Tinted glass $115
Tilt steering wheel . . . . (LX) $115
AM/FM stereo radio w/cassette player. . . . . . (LX/GT) $148
Electronic seek/scan AM/FM stereo w/cassette
. . . . (LX/GT) $300

Premium sound system $138
Radio delete. . . . . $148 credit
T-Roof . . . . (hatchback) $1100
Flip-up open-air roof . . . . (hatchback) $315
Lower charcoal accent paint $116
Single wing spoiler. . . . . (SVO) no charge
Console w/clock and systems monitor $191
Vinyl bucket seats . . . . (LX) $29
Articulated leather sport bucket seats
. . . . (LX convertible) $807
. . . . (GT convertible) $429
Leather seat upholstery. . . . . (SVO) $189
Wire wheel covers . . . . (LX) $98
Styled steel wheels. $178
P205/75R-14 WSW. $109
P225/60VR-15 on cast aluminum wheels $665

1986 MUSTANG PRODUCTION CHART

Model	Doors/Body/Seating	Factory Price	Shipping Weight	Prod. Total
26 (66B)	2/coupe LX/4	$7189/8153	2601/2722	Note 1
28 (61B)	3/hatchback LX/4	$7744/8708	2661/2782	Note 1
27 (66B)	2/convertible V-6 LX/4	$12,821	2908	Note 1
28 (61B)	3/hatchback GT/4	$10,691	2976	Note 1
27 (66B)	2/convertible GT/4	$14,523	3103	Note 1
28 (61B)	3/hatchback SVO/4	$15,272	3028	Note 1

NOTE 1: Ford reports production of 84,774 coupes, 22,946 convertibles, and 117,690 hatchbacks. Total production is 224,410 units.
NOTE 2: For LX coupe and hatchback figures to left of slash are for four-cylinder engine, to right of slash for V-6 (including the price of the required automatic transmission). The 302-cid H.O. V-8 engine cost $1,120 more than the four ($106 more on the LX convertible).

1986 LX notchback (FMC)

1986 GT
Owner: Daniel Carpenter*

1986 GT spoiler

1986 T-tops

1986 tail lamp

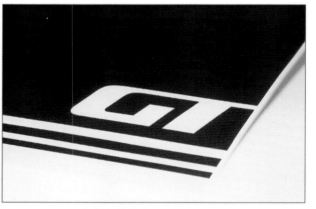

1986 GT hood decal

*Carpenter, whose Concord, N.C., collection of late-model Mustangs is limited to cars with fewer than 500 miles, displays his vehicles as they came from the Ford factory prior to dealer prepping. This never-driven 1986 GT still retains all factory markings, tags, stickers and identifying decals.

1986 GT

1986 GT

1986 headlights

1986 GT stow area

1986 GT interior

1986 M-code 5.0-liter/EFI V-8

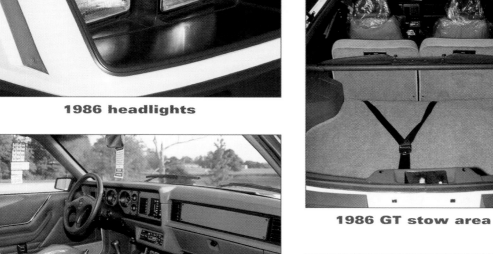

1986 GT wheel

1987 GT (FMC)

1987

Ford's Fox-bodied pony car received a fresh look for 1987 with the first significant restyling since its debut in 1979. No one outside of Ford Motor Company could predict at the time that the new look would endure with very little change for the next seven years!

Perhaps the most important aspect of the Mustang's life in 1987 is that Ford was considering replacing it with a Japanese-designed front-driver. Earlier in the 1980s, corporate planners had developed a project named "SN8" (Ford-speak for sporty, North American project no. 8) to replace the Mustang's rear-drive Fox platform with a small, high-tech, European-style chassis. This scheme was not approved but another plan was soon hatched to have Japanese partner Mazda develop a similar platform that would be shared between the two companies and built in a plant in Flat Rock, Michigan.

It might seem counter-productive for a company to kill off a successful, legendary product that's selling in high numbers, but automakers must think anywhere from three to eight years down the road and consider all economic, political, and market possibilities. Ford was concerned about getting caught in the middle of another fuel crisis with showrooms full of thirsty V-8 performance cars; otherwise, it would not have spent so many development and marketing dollars on the 1979-86 turbocharged models. Chrysler earned its financial salvation by selling millions of bog-slow four-cylinder K-cars in the early 1980s, whereas Ford went from red ink to billions of dollars in cash reserves by creating an exciting, but balanced, product line anchored by its top-selling Taurus.

Plans for a "next-generation" Mustang could be executed for many millions of dollars less if Mazda's innovative engineering and production were utilized. Mazda stood to benefit from the deal by further aligning itself with an American corporate giant and perhaps escape the brunt of threatened import taxes and tariffs.

The public, when informed through several well-placed magazine articles, quickly clued Ford in on how it felt about keeping the Mustang alive, rear-wheel drive and all-American. Ford, to its credit, quickly changed tack and gave the front-drive Japanese-engineered car a "Probe" name-plate on its introduction as a 1989 model. It is interesting to note that Ford never reported losing Mustang sales to the Probe or vice versa—apparently, there weren't a lot customers who saw the choices as similar. Mazda's version of the shared platform was the MX-6.

The attractive 1987 revamp included new front and rear body fascias, aero headlamps and a prominent lower feature line accented with heavy moldings. The wind tunnel loved the car, with a base hatchback registering a 0.36 drag coefficient (compared to the 1979 model's 0.44), and the bulky GT three-door turning out a 0.38. Other changes inside the Mustang were a redesigned instrument panel that created a roomier passenger compartment, pod-mounted headlamp switches, and a center console.

The new Mustang retained a 100.5-inch wheelbase and 179-inch overall length. It was 68.3 inches wide and about 52 inches high (depending on body style) with a track of 56.6 inches in the front and 57 inches in the rear. Weights for various models ranged from 2,724 pounds (base coupe) to 3,214 pounds (GT convertible), roughly a 100-pound increase model-to-model over 1986 specs.

The standard engine in the base LX model notchbacks, hatchbacks and convertibles was the ubiquitous 2.3-liter four, improved for 1987 with a new multi-port fuel-injection system. Its output was up slightly to 90 hp and 130 lbs.-ft.

of torque. Optional in LX models and standard in GTs was a 225-hp 5.0-liter V-8. Its 25-hp gain was the result of a return to a pre-1986 cylinder head design. The V-6 and turbocharged four from 1986 were no longer offered. The SVO was gone, but the LX coupe with the 5.0-liter H.O. V-8 seemed nearly as exciting to speed freaks on a budget.

Also gone were the myriad choices of powerplant and model combinations. Both 1987 Mustang engines came with either a five-speed manual transmission or an optional automatic overdrive transmission. Other technical features included vented disc brakes in front, rear drum brakes and a modified MacPherson strut front suspension with coil springs. The rear suspension featured a live axle with links and coil springs.

The lengthy standard equipment list for the LX model also included a maintenance-free battery; a coolant recovery system; electronic ignition and engine controls; a three-speed heater/defroster; an inside hood release; a dual-note horn; a high-mount rear brake lamp; a 6,000-rpm tachometer; P105/75R-14 black sidewall tires; two-speed electric windshield wipers; blacked-out radio antenna, door handles, door lock bezels and front and rear bumper strips; body-color front lower fender extensions; dual halogen headlamps; dual remote-control mirrors; a body-color rear spoiler; full, single pinstripes; full wheelcovers; color-keyed carpeting; a cigarette lighter; a center console; inside door trim panels; a trip odometer, voltmeter, temperature gauge, fuel gauge and oil pressure gauge; a day/night rearview mirror; twin visor mirrors; an electronic AM/FM stereo radio with four speakers and an integral digital clock; color-keyed seatbelts; cloth seat trim; a two-spoke steering wheel; and dual sunvisors.

In addition to, or instead of, these features, three-door hatchbacks had tinted glass, a cargo area cover and a lockable glove box. Convertibles also had tinted glass, a retractable power cloth top, power vent windows, roll-down rear quarter windows, a rear luggage rack, and a top dust cover.

Mustang GTs added alert lights; a Traction-Lok axle; a sport-tuned exhaust system sporting dual outlets; a remote-control fuel-filler door; nitrogen gas shocks; a luxury sound package; front and rear stabilizer bars; power steering; a tilt steering wheel; Quadra-Shock rear suspension; a 7000-rpm tachometer; P225/60VR-15 black sidewall tires; a body-color front lower fascia with air scoop fender extensions; cast aluminum wheels; a driver's footrest; a front air dam; a scooped hood; body skirting; and wider, louver-slotted tail lamps.

Getting lots of attention was the convertible, priced at under $13,000, in LX form, or under $16,000, with GT equipment. About one out of every eight 1987 Mustangs built (a total of 20,328 cars) were reported to be ragtops. So successful was the convertible that Ford would no longer offer the once-popular T-top option after 1987 (except for a few early 1988 models).

Total model year production was 159,145 units for 1987, noticeably down from 1986, and industry analysts were ready to write off the Mustang as an "old" rear-drive car that had had its day. Mustang sales were only beginning to take off again, which would disprove the predictions of an early demise. Since the Mustang's major development and tooling costs had already been absorbed, it wound up generating extremely good profits. Ford would maintain it, without any really major alterations, all the way through the end of model year 1993.

DATA PLATE DECODING

A 17-character Vehicle Identification Number is stamped on an aluminum tab on the instrument panel, viewable through windshield. A vehicle certification label is found on the body side of where the driver's door closes.

VEHICLE WARRANTY NUMBER MANUFACTURER ID

1FA – Ford Motor Co.

RESTRAINT SYSTEM

B – active belts

VEHICLE CLASSIFICATION

P – passenger car

BODY SERIAL NUMBERS

40 – coupe, LX
41 – hatchback, LX
42 – hatchback, GT
44 – convertible, LX
45 – convertible, GT

ENGINE CODE

A – 140-cid (2.3-liter) EFI SOHC 4-cyl.
M – 302-cid (5.0-liter) EFI V-8 HO

CHECK DIGIT

for internal use

MODEL YEAR

H – 1987

ASSEMBLY PLANT

F – Dearborn, Michigan

CONSECUTIVE UNIT NUMBER

Begins at 100001 at each factory

CODE NUMBERS
BODY CODE

66B – coupe, convertible
61B – hatchback

1987 LX notchback with 5.0-liter V-8 (PH)

PAINT CODE

1C – Black
1K – Light Grey
2D – Scarlet Red
3R – Medium Shadow Blue Metallic
4E – Dark Sage
4M – Dark Slate Metallic
5H – Dark Clove Metallic
7H – Bright Regatta Blue Metallic
7N – Dark Shadow Blue Metallic
8L – Sand Beige
9L – Oxford White
9R – Dark Grey Metallic
66 – Medium Yellow

ENGINES

140-cid (2.3-liter) EFI Inline Four

Valves . . . . overhead
Camshaft . . . . single overhead
Block . . . . cast iron
Displacement . . . . 140 cid/2.3 liters
Bore and stroke . . . . 3.78 x 3.13 inches
Compression ratio 9.5:1
Brake hp . . . . 90 @ 3800 rpm
Main bearings 5
Valve lifters . . . . hydraulic
Induction . . . . electronic fuel injection
Code . . . . A

302-cid (5.0-liter) EFI V-8 HO

Valves . . . . overhead
Block . . . . cast iron
Displacement . . . . 302 cid/5.0 liters
Bore and stroke . . . . 4.00 x 3.00 inches
Compression ratio 9.2:1
Brake hp . . . . 225 @ 4000 rpm
Main bearings 5
Valve lifters . . . . hydraulic
Induction . . . . electronic fuel injection
Code . . . . M

CHASSIS

Wheelbase . . . . 100.5 inches
Overall length . . . . 179.6 inches
Height . . . . 52.1 inches
. . . . (convertible) 51.9 inches
Width . . . . 68.3 inches
Front tread width . . . . 56.6 inches
Rear tread width . . . . 57.0 inches
Tires P195/75R-14
. . . . (GT) P225/60VR-16

TECHNICAL

Steering . . . . rack and pinion, power assisted
Front suspension . . . .
  modified MacPherson hydraulic shock struts with coil
  springs and stabilizer bar
. . . . (GT) adds gas-pressurized shocks
Rear suspension . . . .
. . . . . four-bar link and coil spring system, anti-sway bar
  (with GT)
Brakes . . . . (front) disc
. . . . (rear) drum
Ignition . . . . electronic
Body construction . . . unibody w/front isolated mini-frame
Fuel tank . . . . 15.4 gallons

OPTION LIST

5.0-liter V-8 package
. . . . (LX) $1885
Four-speed overdrive automatic transmission $515
Climate Control Group . (air conditioning, heavy-duty bat-
tery, rear defogger, tinted glass)
. . . . (LX coupe w/four) $1005
. . . . (LX coupe w/V-8) $978
. . . . (LX convertible w/four) $740
. . . . (LX coupe w/V-8) $713
. . . . (GT hatchback) $858
. . . . (GT convertible) $713
  Air conditioning $788
Heavy-duty battery $27
Rear defogger $145
Tinted glass $120
Climate Control Group
(w/Premium Sound instead of rear defogger)
. . . . (LX coupe w/four) $1028
. . . . (LX coupe w/V-8) $1001
. . . . (LX convertible w/four) $908
. . . . (LX convertible w/V-8, GT) $881
Climate Control Group
(w/Custom Equipment Group and Premium Sound
instead of rear defogger)
. . . . (LX coupes w/four) $860
. . . . (LX coupes w/V-8) $833
. . . . (LX convertible w/four) $740
. . . . (LX convertible w/V-8, GT) $713
Custom Equipment Group (Graphic Equalizer, dual power
mirrors, lighted visor mirrors, tilt steering column,
power windows)
. . . . (LX coupe) $624
. . . . (LX convertible) $538
. . . . (GT hatchback) $500

1987 MUSTANG PRODUCTION CHART

Model	Doors/Body/Seating	Factory Price	Shipping Weight	Prod. Total
40 (66B)	2/coupe LX/4	$8043/9928	2724/3000	Note 1
41 (61B)	3/hatchback LX/4	$8474/10,359	2782/3058	Note 1
44 (66B)	2/convertible LX/4	$12,840/14,725	2921/3197	Note 1
42 (61B)	3/hatchback GT/4	$11,835	3080	Note 1
45 (66B)	2/convertible GT/4	$15,724	3214	Note 1

NOTE 1: Ford reports total production of 43,257 coupes, 32,074 convertibles and 94,441 hatchbacks. Total production is 159,145 units.
NOTE 2: For LX figures to left of slash are for four-cylinder engine, to right of slash for V-8.

.... (GT convertible) $414
Graphic Equalizer $218
Dual power mirrors $60
Lighted visor mirrors $100
Tilt steering column .... (LX) $124
Power windows .... (coupe) $222
.... (convertible) $296

Power Lock Group ....
    (remote fuel filler & decklid/hatch releases, AM/FM radio
    w/cassette, speed control, styled road wheels)
    .... (LX w/V-8) $735
    .... (GT) $519
    .... (LX) $244
    .... (GT) $206
AM/FM Stereo Radio w/cassette $137
Speed control $176

Styled road wheels .... (LX) $178
Bodyside molding insert stripe $49
AM/FM Stereo delete .... $206 credit
Flip-up/open-air sunroof $355
T-Roof .... (LX) $1737
    .... (LX w/Climate Control Group) $1667
    .... (LX w/Special Value Group) $1543
    .... (LX w/Custom Equipment Group) $1505
    .... (GT) $1608
    .... (GT w/Special Value Group) $1401
    .... (GT w/Custom Equipment Group) $1341
Premium Sound System $168
Wire wheel covers .... (LX) $98
Leather articulated sport seats ..... (LX convertible) $780
    .... (GT convertible) $415

1988 GT convertible (FMC)

1988

1988 was the second of many years Ford would bring the Mustang to market virtually unchanged from its 1987 restyling. With such a successful package, who could blame them?

The same three body styles were again offered in LX trim, with a pair of GTs (not offered in coupe form) also available. Prices jumped around $700 per closed model and around $1,100 for ragtops. The cars ranged from $8,726 up to $16,610. This was the year of a boom for the Mustang, as model year output zoomed to 211,225 cars.

The same two engine choices remained: the basic 2.3-liter four-cylinder or the pavement-pounding 5.0-liter H.O. V-8. The latter was often compared to 1988's flock of "high-tech" powerplants and regarded as old-fashioned. As *Motor Trend* writer Tony Swan said, "Ironically, the best all-out performer in the Ford power ladder is another yestertech 5.0-liter pushrod V-8, the one that's almost as venerable as those employed by GM." A stronger battery became standard equipment on LX models.

DATA PLATE DECODING

A 17-character Vehicle Identification Number is stamped on an aluminum tab on the instrument panel, viewable through windshield. A vehicle certification label is found on the body side of where the driver's door closes.

VEHICLE WARRANTY NUMBER
MANUFACTURER ID

1FA – Ford Motor Co.

RESTRAINT SYSTEM

B – active belts

VEHICLE CLASSIFICATION

P – passenger car

BODY SERIAL NUMBERS

40 – coupe, LX
41 – hatchback, LX
42 – hatchback, GT
44 – convertible, LX
45 – convertible, GT

ENGINE CODE

A – 140-cid (2.3-liter) EFI SOHC 4-cyl.
M – 302-cid (5.0-liter) EFI V-8 HO

CHECK DIGIT

for internal use

MODEL YEAR

J – 1988

ASSEMBLY PLANT

F – Dearborn, Michigan

CONSECUTIVE UNIT NUMBER

Begins at 100001 at each factory

CODE NUMBERS
BODY CODE

66B – coupe, convertible
61B – hatchback

PAINT CODE

1C – Black
1D – Dark Grey Metallic
1K – Light Grey
2H – Cabernet Red
2I – Bright Red
3R – Medium Shadow Blue Metallic
6V – Almond
7H – Bright Regatta Blue Metallic
7N – Dark Shadow Blue Metallic
9L – Oxford White
66 – Tropical Yellow

ENGINES

140-cid (2.3-liter) EFI Inline Four

Valves . . . . overhead
Camshaft . . . . single overhead
Block . . . . cast iron
Displacement . . . . 140 cid/2.3 liters
Bore and stroke . . . . 3.78 x 3.13 inches
Compression ratio 9.5:1
Brake hp . . . . 90 @ 3800 rpm
Main bearings 5
Valve lifters . . . . hydraulic
Induction . . . . electronic fuel injection
Code . . . . A

302-cid (5.0-liter) EFI V-8 HO

Valves . . . . overhead
Block . . . . cast iron
Displacement . . . . 302 cid/5.0 liters
Bore and stroke . . . . 4.00 x 3.00 inches
Compression ratio 9.2:1
Brake hp . . . . 225 @ 4200 rpm
Main bearings 5
Valve lifters . . . . hydraulic
Induction . . . . electronic fuel injection
Code . . . . M

CHASSIS

Wheelbase . . . . 100.5 inches
Overall length . . . . 179.6 inches
Height . . . . 52.1 inches
. . . . (convertible) 51.9 inches
Width . . . . 69.1 inches
Front tread width . . . . 56.6 inches
Rear tread width . . . . 57.0 inches
Tires P195/75R-14
. . . . (GT) P225/60VR-16

TECHNICAL

Steering . . . . rack and pinion, power assisted
Front suspension . . . .
. . . . . modified MacPherson hydraulic shock struts with
coil springs and stabilizer bar
. . . . (GT) adds gas-pressurized shocks
Rear suspension . . . .
four-bar link and coil spring system, anti-sway bar (with
GT)
Brakes . . . . (front) disc
. . . . (rear) drum
Ignition . . . . electronic
Body construction . . . unibody w/front isolated mini-frame
Fuel tank . . . . 15.4 gallons

OPTION LIST

5.0-liter V-8 package . . . . (LX) $1885
Four-speed overdrive automatic transmission $515
Preferred Equipment Package
. . . . (LX coupe, hatchback w/four) no charge
. . . . (LX coupe, hatchback w/V-8) $615
. . . . (LX convertible w/four) no charge
. . . . (LX convertible w/V-8) $555
. . . . (GT hatchback) $615
. . . . (GT convertible) $555
Manual control air conditioning $788
Power side windows $222

1988 LX convertible with 5.0-liter V-8 (FMC)

Tilt steering wheel $124
Dual illuminated visor mirrors $100
Custom Equipment Group . . . . (LX) $1034
. . . . (LX convertible) $934
. . . . (GT) $910
. . . . (GT convertible) $810
Bodyside molding insert stripe $49
Rear window defroster $145
Graphic equalizer $218
Power Lock Group $237
Dual electric remote mirrors $60
AM/FM radio w/cassette $137
Flip-up open-air roof $355
T-Roof . . . . (LX) $1800
. . . . (w/Preferred Equipment Package) $1505
. . . . (w/Custom Equipment Group) $1459
. . . . (w/Custom Equipment Group & Preferred
Equipment Package) $1163
. . . . (GT) $1659
. . . . (w/Preferred Equipment Package)

. . . . $1363
. . . . (w/Custom Equipment Group) $1437
. . . . (w/Custom Equipment Group & Preferred
Equipment Packages) $1141
Premium sound system $168
Speed control $182
Wire style wheel covers $178
Styled road wheels $178
Front License Plate Bracket . . . . no charge
Engine block heater $18
California emission system $99
High altitude emissions system . . . . no charge
Lower titanium accent treatment exterior paint
. . . . (GT) no charge
Leather articulated sport seats
. . . . (LX convertible) $780
. . . . (GT convertible) $415
Vinyl seat trim $37
P195/75R-14 WSW Tires $82

1988 MUSTANG PRODUCTION CHART

Model	Doors/Body/Seating	Factory Price	Shipping Weight	Prod. Total
40 (66B)	2/coupe LX/4	$8726/10,611	2751/3037	Note 1
41 (61B)	3/hatchback LX/4	$9221/11,106	2818/3105	Note 1
44 (66B)	2/convertible LX/4	$13,702/15,587	2953/3209	Note 1
42 (61B)	3/hatchback GT/4	$12,745	3193	Note 1
45 (66B)	2/convertible GT/4	$16,610	3341	Note 1

NOTE 1: A total of 211,225 Mustangs were produced for the U.S. market (53,221 coupes, 125,930 hatchbacks, and 32,074 convertibles).
NOTE 2: For LX figures to left of slash are for four-cylinder engine, to right of slash for V-8.

1988 LX notchback (FMC)

**1989 GT
Owner: Daniel Carpenter***

1989

1989 will probably always be remembered by Mustang enthusiasts as the year Ford "forgot" the car's 25th birthday. As hard as it is to believe, when the Mustang went into its silver anniversary year, the parent company did not issue a commemorative model, although magazines, fans, and performance authorities as revered as Jack Roush and Steve Saleen made some very strong suggestions that it do so.

One rumor at the time had Roush building an anniversary GT with a 351-cid V-8, twin turbos, and 400 horsepower—an awesome package that never materialized in showrooms, although a prototype was photographed. California-based Mustang tuner Saleen was set to debut his limited run of 160 300-hp SSC hatchbacks on the car's anniversary, but again Ford declined to give official status.

When commenting on the lack of a traditional anniversary model, Ford public relations suggested that the birthday would not occur on April 17, 1989 (25 years to the day since the Mustang's introduction), but on reaching the 1990 model year. Considering that Ford released its 20th anniversary car in 1984, this is a difficult argument. It is more likely that a combination of two factors account for the oversight.

When the 1984 car was produced wearing "G.T. 350" stripes, Carroll Shelby, the creator of that legendary model, sued Ford for using the name without permission. Ford could

*Carpenter, whose Concord, N.C., collection of late-model Mustangs is limited to cars with fewer than 500 miles, displays his vehicles as they came from the Ford factory prior to dealer prepping. This 1989 GT has only traveled 400 miles in its life.

have been cautious, therefore, due to the effect of its last attempt to mark the Mustang's anniversary. The more accepted explanation lies in Ford's intent to kill off the traditional rear-drive Mustang shortly after the 1989 model year.

Appearing late in the model year were 3,600 1990 5.0-liter LX convertibles decked out in Emerald Green with white interiors and tiny badges indicating the 25th anniversary. Except for the missed birthday, 1989 is remarkable for the Mustang only in that the six-millionth unit was built that year. Prices climbed again and each model gained a small amount of weight, but the engine and technical features stayed about the same.

The base Mustang LX was fun to drive with its responsive 2.3-liter four-cylinder engine, a five-speed manual transmission, power front disc brakes, modified MacPherson strut suspension, 20.0:1-ratio rack-and-pinion power steering, styled road wheels, and P195/75R-14 black sidewall steel-belted radial tires. Comfortable interiors with cloth reclining seats were standard. The three-model line had list prices from $9,050 to $17,512, and with the optional Special Value Group buyers got power locks, dual electric mirrors, an electronic AM/FM stereo with a cassette tape player, and more.

The GT hatchback ($13,272) and convertible ($17,512) added such niceties as aero body upgrades, the 225-hp 5.0-liter H.O. V-8, a five-speed manual transmission with

1989 GT wheel

overdrive fifth gear, 14.7:1 ratio power rack-and-pinion steering, a taut handling suspension system, and P225/60VR-15 unidirectional Goodyear Eagle tires on 15-inch diameter 16-spoke cast aluminum wheels.

The GT suspension was really a piece of high-tech work, with gas-pressurized hydraulic struts, variable-rate coil springs, and a stabilizer bar up front. The rear also featured variable-rate coils plus a Quadra-shock setup with vertically-mounted gas-pressurized shock absorbers, horizontally-mounted, freon-filled axle dampers, and a fat stabilizer bar. A new LX 5.0-L Sport series combined the entry-level model, 5.0-liter V-8 and the GT's multi-adjustable seats. Prices started at $11,410 for the coupe and reached $17,001 for the convertible.

From the time production started on Aug. 31, 1988, to when it ended on September 5, 1989 (later than usual) the factory at Dearborn cranked out 46 of the new Mustangs every hour. Model year output fell just slightly to 209,769 cars. A most revealing statistic was that 51.4 percent of all Mustangs built carried V-8 engines. The extreme popularity of the 5.0-liter H.O. Mustang had obviously given the marque a new lease on life, primarily based on its reputation and appeal as a high-performance car.

DATA PLATE DECODING

A 17-character Vehicle Identification Number is stamped on an aluminum tab on the instrument panel, viewable through windshield. A vehicle certification label is found on the body side of where the driver's door closes.

VEHICLE WARRANTY NUMBER MANUFACTURER ID

1FA – Ford Motor Co.

RESTRAINT SYSTEM

B – active belts

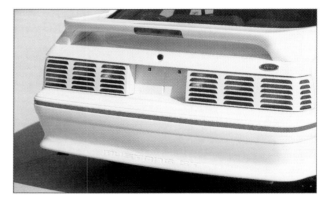

1989 GT tail lamp louvers

1989 GT headlamp and driving light

1989 M-code 5.0-liter/EFI V-8

1989 25th Anniversary badge

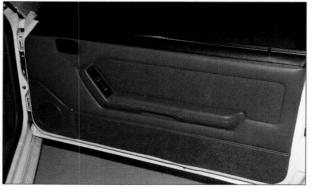

1989 GT door panel

VEHICLE CLASSIFICATION

P – passenger car

BODY SERIAL NUMBERS

40 – coupe, LX
41 – hatchback, LX
42 – hatchback, GT
44 – convertible, LX
45 – convertible, GT

ENGINE CODE

A – 140-cid (2.3-liter) EFI SOHC 4-cyl.
M – 302-cid (5.0-liter) EFI V-8 HO

CHECK DIGIT

for internal use

MODEL YEAR

K – 1989

ASSEMBLY PLANT

F – Dearborn, Michigan

CONSECUTIVE UNIT NUMBER

Begins at 100001 at each factory

CODE NUMBERS
BODY CODE

66B – coupe, convertible
61B – hatchback

PAINT CODE

1C – Black
1D – Dark Grey Metallic
1K – Light Grey
2H – Cabernet Red
2I – Bright Red
3R – Medium Shadow Blue Metallic
6V – Almond
7H – Bright Regatta Blue Metallic
7N – Dark Shadow Blue Metallic
9L – Oxford White
66 – Tropical Yellow

ENGINES

140-cid (2.3-liter) EFI Inline Four
Valves . . . . overhead
Camshaft . . . . single overhead
Block . . . . cast iron
Displacement. . . . . 140 cid/2.3 liters
Bore and stroke. . . . . 3.78 x 3.13 inches
Compression ratio 9.5:1
Brake hp . . . . 90 @ 3800 rpm
Main bearings 5
Valve lifters . . . . hydraulic
Induction . . . . electronic fuel injection
Code . . . . A

302-cid (5.0-liter) EFI V-8 HO
Valves . . . . overhead
Block . . . . cast iron
Displacement. . . . . 302 cid/5.0 liters
Bore and stroke. . . . . 4.00 x 3.00 inches
Compression ratio 9.2:1
Brake hp . . . . 225 @ 4200 rpm
Main bearings 5
Valve lifters . . . . hydraulic
Induction . . . . electronic fuel injection
Code . . . . M

CHASSIS

Wheelbase . . . . 100.5 inches
Overall length . . . . 179.6 inches
Height . . . . 52.1 inches
. . . . (convertible) 51.9 inches
Width. . . . . 69.1 inches
Front tread width. . . . . 56.6 inches
Rear tread width . . . . 57.0 inches
Tires P195/75R-14
. . . . (LX 5.0L Sport, GT) P225/60VR-16

TECHNICAL

Steering . . . . rack and pinion, power assisted
Front suspension
    modified MacPherson hydraulic shock struts with
    coil springs and stabilizer bar
    (GT) adds gas-pressurized shocks
Rear suspension . . . .
    four-bar link and coil spring system, anti-sway bar (with
    GT)
Brakes . . . . (front) disc
. . . . (rear) drum
Ignition . . . . electronic
Body construction . . . unibody w/front isolated mini-frame
Fuel tank. . . . . 15.4 gallons

1989 MUSTANG PRODUCTION CHART

Model	Doors/Body/Seating	Factory Price	Shipping Weight	Prod. Total
40 (66B)	2/coupe LX/4	$9050/11,410	2754/3045	Note 1
41 (61B)	3/hatchback LX/4	$9556/12,265	2819/3110	Note 1
44 (66B)	2/convertible LX/4	$14,140/17,001	2966/3257	Note 1
42 (61B)	3/hatchback GT/4	$13,272	3194	Note 1
45 (66B)	2/convertible GT/4	$17,512	3333	Note 1

NOTE 1: A total of 209,769 Mustangs were produced for the U.S. market (50,560 coupes, 116,965 hatchbacks, and 42,244 convertibles).
NOTE 2: For LX figures to left of slash are for four-cylinder engine, to right of slash for V-8.

OPTION LIST

Four-speed overdrive automatic transmission $515
Preferred Equipment Packages
LX w/four – Special Value Group, Power Lock Group, dual electric remote mirrors, AM/FM radio w/cassette player & clock, speed control, styled road wheels, power side windows .... (LX sedan or hatchback) no charge .... (LX convertible) no charge
LX V-8 Sport GT – Special Value Group, Power Lock Group, dual electric remote mirrors, AM/FM radio w/cassette player & clock, speed control, styled road wheels, power side windows, Custom Equipment Group, air conditioning, dual illuminated visor mirrors, tilt wheel, Premium Sound System .... (coupe or hatchback) $1006 .... (convertible) $487

Group Options Custom Equipment Groupdual illuminated visor mirrors, tilt wheel, Premium Sound System
.... (LX coupe or hatchback, four-cylinder) $1180
.... (LX convertible, four-cylinder) $1080
Bodyside molding insert stripe $61
Rear window defroster $150
Flip-up open-air roof $355
Wire style wheel covers $193
California emissions system $100
High-altitude emissions system . no chargeLower Titanium Accent Treatment Ext. Paint, GT .... no charge
Leather articulated sport seats..... (LX convertible) $855
(LX V-8 Sport convertible or GT convertible) $489
Vinyl seat trim $37
Front license plate bracket .... no charge
P195/75R-14 WSW Tires $82

1989 LX convertible (FMC)

**1990 LX notchback with 5.0-liter V-8
Owner: Jimmy Morrison/Morrison
Motor Co.**

1990

Federal regulations gave the Mustang its most important new equipment for 1990 in the form of a driver's side air bag and standard rear shoulder belts. Because of the steering wheel-mounted air bag, a tilt steering column was no longer available. Door panels now held map pockets, probably to make up for the now-missing console-mounted armrest.

Sedans, hatchbacks, and ragtops again came in LX and LX 5.0-liter series, with the hatchback and convertible available as GTs. The LX 5.0-liter models had the same beefy suspension and tires as the GT, while the GT package added spoilers and an air dam.

The base three-model line had list prices from $9,638 to $18,303. Standard equipment included the 2.3-liter four with electronic fuel-injection; power front disc brakes; five-speed manual overdrive transmission; P195/75R-14 black sidewall tires; sport bucket seats and a tachometer; plus all the other regular Mustang features. This year, the LX gained the 14.7:1 steering of last year's GT and new 14x5-inch stamped steel wheels with turbine wheelcovers.

The LX 2.3-liter also continued its tradition of affordability, by offering Special Value Packages all its own, which included power locks, dual electric remote-controlled mirrors, power side windows, a premium sound system and speed control (worth $835) for no extra charge. Convertible buyers got the same package free, but it was only a $328 "value" for them, as some of these ingredients were standard on ragtops.

The LX 5.0 Sport models came in three body styles, with prices starting at $12,107 for the coupe and reaching

$17,681 for the convertible. The LX 5.0L came with the heftier suspension and bigger tires from the GT, but without the GT's spoilers and air dams.

The GT hatchback ($13,929) and convertible ($18,303) again added aero body upgrades and a long list of additional goodies. There were 3,600 "25th Anniversary" 5.0-liter LX convertibles produced in Emerald Green with white interiors, 16-spoke wheels from the GT, and commemorative badges. Clearcoat paint was now optional, as was leather interior trim for the V-8 hatchbacks.

The Mustang tradition was recognized in sales literature. It included passages such as, "Mustang, the first pony car, brought affordable sporty car performance and styling to every street and highway in America. And what it did best 25 years ago, it still does the best today." The factory built 128,189 of the 1990 Mustangs, making it the fifth most popular compact car sold in America despite a nearly 50 percent drop from the previous year.

DATA PLATE DECODING

A 17-character Vehicle Identification Number is stamped on an aluminum tab on the instrument panel, viewable through windshield. A vehicle certification label is found on the body side of where the driver's door closes.

VEHICLE WARRANTY NUMBER MANUFACTURER ID

1FA – Ford Motor Co.

RESTRAINT SYSTEM

C – air bags, active belts

VEHICLE CLASSIFICATION

P – passenger car

BODY SERIAL NUMBERS

40 – coupe, LX
41 – hatchback, LX
42 – hatchback, GT
44 – convertible, LX
45 – convertible, GT

ENGINE CODE

A – 140-cid (2.3-liter) EFI SOHC 4-cyl.
M – 302-cid (5.0-liter) EFI V-8 HO

CHECK DIGIT

for internal use

MODEL YEAR

L – 1990

ASSEMBLY PLANT

F – Dearborn, Michigan

CONSECUTIVE UNIT NUMBER

Begins at 100001 at each factory

CODE NUMBERS
BODY CODE

66B – coupe, convertible
61B – hatchback

1990 rear passenger three-point restraint

PAINT CODE

AG – Bright Yellow
EH – Cabernet Red
EL – Wild Strawberry
EP – Bright Red
MA – Crystal Blue
MK – Twilight Blue
YC – Black
YF – Deep Emerald Green*
YF – Light Titanium
YO – Oxford White
YU – Deep Titanium
*LX 5.0L convertible special color

ENGINES

140-cid (2.3-liter) EFI Inline Four

Valves . . . . overhead
Camshaft . . . . single overhead
Block . . . . cast iron
Displacement . . . . 140 cid/2.3 liters
Bore and stroke . . . . 3.78 x 3.13 inches
Compression ratio 9.0:1
Brake hp . . . . 88 @ 4000 rpm
Main bearings 5
Valve lifters . . . . hydraulic
Induction . . . . electronic fuel injection
Code . . . . A

302-cid (5.0-liter) EFI V-8 HO

Valves . . . . overhead
Block . . . . cast iron
Displacement . . . . 302 cid/5.0 liters
Bore and stroke . . . . 4.00 x 3.00 inches
Compression ratio 9.0:1
Brake hp . . . . 225 @ 4200 rpm
Main bearings 5
Valve lifters . . . . hydraulic
Induction . . . . electronic fuel injection
Code . . . . M

CHASSIS

Wheelbase . . . . 100.5 inches
Overall length . . . . 179.6 inches
Height . . . . 52.1 inches
. . . . (convertible) 51.9 inches
Width . . . . 69.1 inches

1990 LX 25th Anniversary convertible (FMC)

Front tread width . . . . 56.6 inches
Rear tread width . . . . 57.0 inches
Tires P195/75R-14
. . . . (LX 5.0L Sport, GT) P225/60VR-16

TECHNICAL

Steering . . . . rack and pinion, power assisted
Front suspension . . . .
    modified MacPherson hydraulic shock struts with coil
    springs and stabilizer bar
    . . . . (GT) adds gas-pressurized shocks
Rear suspension . . . .
    four-bar link and coil spring system, anti-sway bar
    (with GT)
Brakes . . . . (front) disc
. . . . (rear) drum
Ignition . . . . electronic
Body construction . . . unibody w/front isolated mini-frame
Fuel tank . . . . 15.4 gallons

OPTION LIST

Four-speed overdrive automatic transmission $539
Preferred Equipment Packages
LX w/four – Special Value Group, Power Lock Group, dual
    electric remote mirrors, AM/FM radio w/cassette player
    & clock, speed control, styled road wheels, power side
    windows . . . . (LX sedan or hatchback) no charge
    . . . . (LX convertible) no charge

LX V-8 Sport GT – Special Value Group, Power Lock
    Group, dual electric remote mirrors, AM/FM radio w/cas-
    sette player & clock, speed control, styled road wheels,
    power side windows, Custom Equipment Group, air con-
    ditioning, dual illuminated visor mirrors, tilt wheel,
    Premium Sound System
    . . . . (coupe or hatchback) $1003
    . . . . (convertible) $496
Group Options Custom Equipment Groupdual illuminated
    visor mirrors, tilt wheel, Premium Sound System
    . . . . (LX coupe or hatchback, four-cylinder) $907
    . . . . (LX convertible, four-cylinder) $807
Rear window defroster $150
Flip-up open-air roof $355
Wire style wheel covers $193
Premium Sound System (6 premium speakers, 4-channel
    amplifier, 80 watts) $168
California emission system $100
High-altitude emissions . . . . no charge
Clearcoat exterior paint $91
Lower Titanium accent treatment . . . . (GT) $159
Leather seating surfaces on articulated sport seats . . . $489
Vinyl seat trim $37
Front license plate bracket . . . . no charge
Engine block heater $20
P195/75R-14 WSW Tires $82

1990 MUSTANG PRODUCTION CHART

Model	Doors/Body/Seating	Factory Price	Shipping Weight	Prod. Total
40 (66B)	2/coupe LX/4	$9638/12,107	2634/2715	Note 1
41 (61B)	3/hatchback LX/4	$10,144/12,950	2634/2715	Note 1
44 (66B)	2/convertible LX/4	$14,495/17,681	2871/2952	Note 1
42 (61B)	3/hatchback GT/4	$13,929	3065	Note 1
45 (66B)	2/convertible GT/4	$18,303	3213	Note 1

NOTE 1: A total of 128,189 Mustangs were produced (22,503 coupes, 78,728 hatchbacks, and 26,958 convertibles).
NOTE 2: Figures to left of slash are for LX four-cylinder, to right of slash for LX 5.0L Sport V-8.

1990 GT (FMC)

1991 LX convertible (JH)

1991

1991 saw the base Mustang cross the $10,000 mark for the first time, thanks to a 2.9 to 3.3 percent sticker price increase. It is worth noting, however, that V-8 convertibles could be had for less than $20,000. The base coupe, hatchback, and convertible line had list prices from $10,157 to $16,222. Standard equipment included the overhead cam 2.3-liter four with electronic multi-point fuel injection, power front disc brakes (rear drums), five-speed manual overdrive transmission, and P195/75R-14 black sidewall all-season LX tires.

The four-cylinder received a bump in power for 1991 from 88 hp to 105 hp through a new head design that incorporated two sparkplugs per cylinder. The four-cylinder received a 21/28 (city/highway miles per gallon) EPA rating with the five-speed and 22/30 with automatic. For the unchanged multi-point fuel-injected V-8, the figures were 18/25 with a five-speed and 17/24 with the automatic. These figures reflect the standard rear axle ratios.

The base LX 5.0-liter models offered three body styles, with prices starting at $13,270 and climbing to $19,242. The GT hatchback ($15,034) and convertible ($19,864) also suffered from the price increases. Both GT and LX 5.0-liter models received new, upsized 16-inch five-spoke aluminum wheels. New P225/55ZR-16 all-season performance tires were made standard on LX 5.0-liter and optional on GT. The new convertible top design looked crisper and fit lower in the well for a smoother profile when down.

Interior changes added new cloth seat materials on the 2.3-liter LX models. Other improvements included vinyl door trim panel inserts added to power window-equipped units and an articulated sport seat standard on the LX 5.0-

1991 GT (FMC)

liter sedan. Options added for 1991 included cargo tie down net, front floor mats, graphic equalizer, 15-inch cast aluminum wheels with P205/65R-15 BSW tires (2.3-liter LX), and 14-inch styled road wheels.

Mustang production for model year 1991 totaled 98,737 units, a 1.7 percent share of the overall market (down from 2.1 percent the previous season). For 1991, 63 percent of all Mustangs, a total of 62,204 cars, had V-8s under their hoods and 36,533 had four-cylinder powerplants.

DATA PLATE DECODING

A 17-character Vehicle Identification Number is stamped on an aluminum tab on the instrument panel, viewable through windshield. A vehicle certification label is found on the body side of where the driver's door closes.

VEHICLE WARRANTY NUMBER MANUFACTURER ID

1FA – Ford Motor Co.

RESTRAINT SYSTEM

C – air bags, active belts

VEHICLE CLASSIFICATION

P – passenger car

BODY SERIAL NUMBERS

40 – coupe, LX
41 – hatchback, LX
42 – hatchback, GT
44 – convertible, LX
45 – convertible, GT

ENGINE CODE

S – 140-cid (2.3-liter) EFI SOHC 4-cyl.
E – 302-cid (5.0-liter) EFI V-8 HO

CHECK DIGIT

for internal use

MODEL YEAR

M – 1991

ASSEMBLY PLANT

F – Dearborn, Michigan

CONSECUTIVE UNIT NUMBER

Begins at 100001 at each factory

CODE NUMBERS
BODY CODE

66B – coupe, convertible
61B – hatchback

PAINT CODE

EL – Wild Strawberry
EM – Medium Red
EP – Bright Red
MA – Light Crystal Blue
MK – Twilight Blue
YD – Black
YF – Deep Emerald Green
YG – Medium Titanium
YO – Oxford White
YX – Titanium Frost

ENGINES

140-cid (2.3-liter) EFI Inline Four

Valves	overhead
Camshaft	single overhead
Block	cast iron
Displacement	140 cid/2.3 liters
Bore and stroke	3.78 x 3.13 inches
Compression ratio	9.5:1
Brake hp	105 @ 4600 rpm
Main bearings	5
Valve lifters	hydraulic
Induction	electronic fuel injection
Sparkplugs	2 per cylinder
Code	S

302-cid (5.0-liter) EFI V-8 HO

Valves	overhead
Block	cast iron
Displacement	302 cid/5.0 liters
Bore and stroke	4.00 x 3.00 inches
Compression ratio	9.0:1
Brake hp	225 @ 4200 rpm
Main bearings	5
Valve lifters	hydraulic
Induction	electronic fuel injection
Code	E

CHASSIS

Wheelbase	100.5 inches
Overall length	179.6 inches
Height	52.1 inches
	(convertible) 51.9 inches
Width	69.1 inches
Front tread width	56.6 inches
Rear tread width	57.0 inches
Tires	P195/75R-14
	(LX 5.0L, GT) P225/55ZR-16

1991 GT convertible (PH)

TECHNICAL

Steering . . . . rack and pinion, power assisted
Front suspension . . . .
    modified MacPherson hydraulic shock struts with coil
    springs and stabilizer bar
    . . . . (GT) adds gas-pressurized shocks
Rear suspension . . . .
    four-bar link and coil spring system, anti-sway bar (with
    GT)
Brakes . . . . (front) disc
    . . . . (rear) drum
Ignition . . . . electronic
Body construction . . . unibody w/front isolated mini-frame
Fuel tank . . . . 15.4 gallons

OPTION LIST

Four-speed automatic overdrive transmission $595
Power Equipment Group including dual electric remote con-
trol mirrors, power side windows, Power Lock Group,
cargo tie-down net, front floor mats, speed control, AM/FM
Radio w/cassette player & clock, styled road wheels
. . . . (LX coupe and hatchback) $222
. . . . (LX convertible) $207
same as above, except for styled road wheels, plus Premium
Sound System, Custom Equipment Group, manual con-
trol air conditioning, dual illuminated visor mirrors
. . . . (LX 5.0L coupe and hatchback) $1314

. . . . (LX 5.0L convertible) $749
. . . . (GT hatchback) $1314
. . . . (GT convertible) $749
California emission system. $100
Vinyl low-back seats . . . . (LX) $37
Leather seating surfaces articulated sport seats
. . . . (LX 5.0L and GT) $489
Cargo tie-down net $66
Custom Equipment Group (LX coupe and hatchback) $917
Rear window defroster. (not available on convertible) $160
Floormats, front. $33
Graphic equalizer including Premium Sound $139
Clearcoat paint $91
Power Equipment Group . . (standard on convertible) $565
Premium Sound System. $168
AM/FM stereo radio w/cassette $155
Roof, flip-up open air . . . . (hatchback only) $355
Speed control. $210
Titanium lower bodyside accent treatment (GT only) $159
Wire wheel covers. . . . . (LX only) no charge
. . . . (other models) $193
Cast aluminum wheels w/P205/65R-15 BSW Tires
. . . . (LX only) $167
. . . . (other models) $360
Styled road wheels. . . . . (LX only) $193
Engine block heater. $20

1991 MUSTANG PRODUCTION CHART				
Model	Doors/Body/Seating	Factory Price	Shipping Weight	Prod. Total
40 (66B)	2/coupe LX/4	$10,157/13,270	2759/3037	Note 1
41 (61B)	3/hatchback LX/4	$10,663/14,055	2824/3102	Note 1
44 (66B)	2/convertible LX/4	$16,222/19,242	2960/3238	Note 1
42 (61B)	3/hatchback GT/4	$15,034	3191	Note 1
45 (66B)	2/convertible GT/4	$19,864	3327	Note 1

NOTE 1: A total of 98,737 Mustangs were produced (19,447 coupes, 57,777 hatchbacks, and 21,513 convertibles).
NOTE 2: Ford produced 24,428 GTs and 27,880 5.0L LXs.
NOTE 3: Figures to left of slash are for LX four-cylinder, to right of slash for LX 5.0L V-8.

1991 GT (FMC)

1992 LX convertible (FMC)

1992

With a major redesign already expected by dealers and customers for 1994, it's no surprise the Mustang continued for 1992 with precious few changes or that it reached its lowest sales level in the marque's history. As inflation continued to take its toll on the auto industry, the GT convertible had the dubious honor of being the first Mustang with a suggested retail price eclipsing $20,000, at $20,199. Base hardtops, hatchbacks, and convertibles ran from $10,215 to $16,899.

Standard equipment included the overhead cam 2.3-liter four with electronic fuel-injection, power front disc brakes (rear drums), five-speed manual overdrive transmission, and P195/75R-14 black sidewall all-season tires. All three body styles again came with LX or LX 5.0-liter series, with the hatchback and convertible available in GT trim. The base LX 5.0-liter Mustangs were priced from $13,422 to $19,644. The GT hatchback cost $15,243.

The 1992 Mustang received several body enhancements including color-keyed bodyside molding, bumper strips, a four-way power driver's seat option, and two new colors, Bimini Blue and Calypso Green. When all was said and done, the 1992 Mustang had a 79,280-unit model year, making it the fifth most popular compact car in the United States. Production was split almost evenly between four-cylinder models (36,307 made) and V-8s (36,893 built).

DATA PLATE DECODING

A 17-character Vehicle Identification Number is stamped on an aluminum tab on the instrument panel, viewable through windshield. A vehicle certification label is found on the body side of where the driver's door closes.

VEHICLE WARRANTY NUMBER MANUFACTURER ID

1FA – Ford Motor Co.

RESTRAINT SYSTEM

C – air bags, active belts

VEHICLE CLASSIFICATION

P – passenger car

BODY SERIAL NUMBERS

40 – coupe, LX
41 – hatchback, LX
42 – hatchback, GT
44 – convertible, LX
45 – convertible, GT

ENGINE CODE

S – 140-cid (2.3-liter) EFI SOHC 4-cyl.
E – 302-cid (5.0-liter) EFI V-8 HO

CHECK DIGIT

for internal use

MODEL YEAR

N – 1992

ASSEMBLY PLANT

F – Dearborn, Michigan

CONSECUTIVE UNIT NUMBER

Begins at 100001 at each factory

CODE NUMBERS
BODY CODE

66B – coupe, convertible
61B – hatchback

PAINT CODE

EL – Wild Strawberry
EM – Medium Red
EP – Bright Red
K3 – Bimini Blue
MA – Light Crystal Blue
MK – Twilight Blue
MM – Ultra Blue
PA – Deep Emerald Green
UA – Black
YG – Medium Titanium
YO – Oxford White
YX – Titanium Frost

ENGINES

140-cid (2.3-liter) EFI Inline Four

Valves . . . . overhead
Camshaft . . . . single overhead
Block . . . . cast iron
Displacement . . . . 140 cid/2.3 liters
Bore and stroke . . . . 3.78 x 3.13 inches
Compression ratio 9.5:1
Brake hp . . . . 105 @ 4600 rpm
Main bearings 5
Valve lifters . . . . hydraulic
Induction . . . . electronic fuel injection
Sparkplugs . . . . 2 per cylinder
Code . . . . S

302-cid (5.0-liter) EFI V-8 HO

Valves . . . . overhead
Block . . . . cast iron
Displacement . . . . 302 cid/5.0 liters
Bore and stroke . . . . 4.00 x 3.00 inches
Compression ratio 9.0:1
Brake hp . . . . 225 @ 4200 rpm
Main bearings 5
Valve lifters . . . . hydraulic
Induction . . . . electronic fuel injection
Code . . . . E

CHASSIS

Wheelbase . . . . 100.5 inches
Overall length . . . . 179.6 inches
Height . . . . 52.1 inches
. . . . (convertible) 51.9 inches
Width . . . . 69.1 inches
Front tread width . . . . 56.6 inches
Rear tread width . . . . 57.0 inches
Tires P195/75R-14
. . . . (LX 5.0L, GT) P225/55ZR-16

TECHNICAL

Steering . . . . rack and pinion, power assisted
Front suspension . . . .
. . . . . modified MacPherson hydraulic shock struts with coil
springs and stabilizer bar
. . . . (GT) adds gas-pressurized shocks
Rear suspension . . . .
four-bar link and coil spring system, anti-sway bar (with
GT)
Brakes . . . . (front) disc
. . . . (rear) drum
Ignition . . . . electronic
Body construction . . . unibody w/front isolated mini-frame
Fuel tank . . . . 15.4 gallons

OPTION LIST

Four-speed automatic overdrive transmission $595
Power Equipment Group including dual electric remote
control mirrors, power side windows, Power Lock
Group, cargo tie-down net, front floor mats, speed con-
trol, AM/FM Radio w/cassette player & clock, styled road
wheels
. . . . (LX coupe and hatchback) $276
. . . . (LX convertible) $122
same as above, except for styled road wheels, plus Premium
Sound System, Custom Equipment Group, manual con-
trol air conditioning, dual illuminated visor mirrors
. . . . (LX 5.0L coupe and hatchback) $551
. . . . (LX 5.0L convertible) no charge
. . . . (GT hatchback) $1367
. . . . (GT convertible) $763
California emission system $100
Vinyl low-back seats . . . . (LX) $76
Leather seating surfaces articulated sport seats
. . . . (LX 5.0L and GT) $523
Manual air conditioning $817
Convenience Group including cargo tie-down net, front
floor mats $99
Rear window defroster. (not available on convertible) $170
Premium Sound System including 6 premium speakers,
4-channel amplifier $168
Premium Sound System w/graphic equalizer $307
Clearcoat paint $91
Titanium lower bodyside accent treatment . . . . (GT) $159
Power Equipment Group including power door locks,
power decklid/liftgate, dual electric remote control
mirrors, power side windows $604
AM/FM stereo radio w/cassette $155
Flip-up open-air roof . . . . (fastback only) $355
4-way power driver's seat $183
Speed control $224
Cast aluminum wheels w/P205/65R-15 SBR BSW Tires
. . . . (LX convertible) $208
. . . . (LX coupe and hatchback) $401
Styled road wheels . . . . (LX only) $193
Engine block heater $20

1992 MUSTANG PRODUCTION CHART

Model	Doors/Body/Seating	Factory Price	Shipping Weight	Prod. Total
40 (66B)	2/coupe LX/4	$10,215/13,422	2775/3010	Note 1
41 (61B)	3/hatchback LX/4	$10,721/14,207	2834/3069	Note 1
44 (66B)	2/convertible LX/4	$16,899/19,644	2996/3231	Note 1
42 (61B)	3/hatchback GT/4	$15,243	3144	Note 1
45 (66B)	2/convertible GT/4	$20,199	3365	Note 1

NOTE 1: A total of 79,280 Mustangs were produced (15,717 coupes, 40,093 hatchbacks, and 23,470 convertibles).
NOTE 2: Ford produced 20,445 GTs and 19,131 5.0L LXs.
NOTE 3: Figures to left of slash are for LX four-cylinder, to right of slash for LX 5.0L V-8.

1992 LX convertible with 5.0-liter V-8 (FMC)

1992 LX convertible with 5.0-liter V-8 (FMC)

**1993 LX convertible with 5.0-liter V-8
Owner: Daniel Carpenter***

1993

The 14-year-old Fox-chassis Mustang went into 1993 (its final year) with only small changes made to distinguish it from the previous year. It came in LX, LX 5.0-liter, and GT form. Ford made one interesting change to the Mustang for 1993 that downgraded the 5.0-liter V-8 to 205 hp from the previously advertised 225 hp. There were no actual modifications made to the V-8; Ford made the change on paper only.

Base LX models, equipped with the 2.3-liter four-cylinder engine, stickered for $10,719 for the sedan, $11,224 for the hatchback, and $17,548 for the convertible. Standard LX equipment included a driver's side air bag; a heavy-duty 75-ampere alternator; a heavy-duty 58-ampere battery; power brakes with front discs and rear drums; color-keyed front and rear bumper rub strips; full carpeting; a digital clock; a center console with armrest; the 2.3-liter four-cylinder engine; a fuel cap tether; tinted glass; a color-keyed cloth headliner; dual horns; luxury sound insulation; dome, cargo area, underhood, ashtray, and glove box lamps; dual, manual remote-controlled rearview mirrors; dual covered visor mirrors; color-keyed body side moldings; an AM/FM radio with electronic tuning and four speakers; reclining low-back bucket seats; a front stabilizer bar; power steering; body side paint stripes; a tachometer; a five-speed manual

transmission; a trip odometer; cloth upholstery; a headlight warning chime; finned wheelcovers; intermittent windshield wipers; and P195/75R-14 steel-belted radial all-season black sidewall tires.

Hatchbacks came standard with a carpeted cargo area; a pivoting map lamp; a split-back, fold-down rear seat; and a rear spoiler. Convertibles also came with a power top; a top cover; a glass back window; power side windows; dual, powered, outside rearview mirrors; a trunk luggage rack; and a Lock Group including power door locks, a deck lid release and a fuel filler door release. They did not have a color-keyed cloth headliner.

LX 5.0-liter models were priced at $13,926 for the sedan, $14,710 for the hatchback, and $20,293 for the convertible. Standard extras for cars in this series (plus or instead of the basic equipment listing) included the 5.0-liter H.O. V-8 with electronic fuel-injection; Traction-Lok differential; a dual, sport-tuned exhaust system; articulated Sport seats with power lumbar support; constant-ratio power steering; a leather-wrapped steering wheel; a sport-type suspension package; cloth/vinyl upholstery; diagnostic warning lights; cast aluminum wheels; and P225/55ZR-16 black sidewall all-season steel-belted radial tires. All models included a higher wattage radio with an easy-to-read display. New options included a compact disc player and an electronic premium cassette radio.

---

*Carpenter, whose Concord, N.C., collection of late-model Mustangs is limited to cars with fewer than 500 miles, displays his vehicles as they came from the Ford factory prior to dealer prepping. This 1993 is one of Carpenter's "daily drivers," and registers 4,000 miles.

The GT hatchback ($15,747) and convertible ($20,848) also had a front air dam; fog lights; color-keyed, flared rocker panel moldings; no body side paint stripes; and performance tires of the same size as LX 5.0-liter models.

The aging Mustang lineup received a limited edition Cobra model in 1993 to go along with its LX and GT series. This specialty model, produced by Ford's in-house Special Vehicle Team (SVT), featured a "tweaked" 230-hp version of the GT's 5.0-liter V-8, five-speed manual transmission, 17-inch aluminum wheels, rear spoiler, and ground-effects trim. SVT sold 4,993 of the "street" Cobras and 107 race-ready "R" models. (See the Cobra section in this book for more details.)

Mustang production amounted to 114,228 units for model year 1993, an increase due in part to the fact that the figures included examples of the all-new 1994 model, which entered production in the fall of 1993 and gained immediate popularity.

DATA PLATE DECODING

A 17-character Vehicle Identification Number is stamped on an aluminum tab on the instrument panel, viewable through windshield. A vehicle certification label is found on the body side of where the driver's door closes.

VEHICLE WARRANTY NUMBER
MANUFACTURER ID

1FA – Ford Motor Co.

RESTRAINT SYSTEM

C – air bags, active belts

VEHICLE CLASSIFICATION

P – passenger car

BODY SERIAL NUMBERS

40 – coupe, LX
41 – hatchback, LX
42 – hatchback, GT
44 – convertible, LX
45 – convertible, GT

ENGINE CODE

S – 140-cid (2.3-liter) EFI SOHC 4-cyl.
E – 302-cid (5.0-liter) EFI V-8 HO
D – 302-cid (5.0-liter) EFI V-8 Cobra

CHECK DIGIT

for internal use

MODEL YEAR

P – 1993

ASSEMBLY PLANT

F – Dearborn, Michigan

1993 LX convertible with 5.0-liter V-8

1993 interior

1993 chrome wheel   **1993 controls**   **1993 E-code 5.0-liter/EFI V-8**

CONSECUTIVE UNIT NUMBER

Begins at 100001 at each factory

CODE NUMBERS
BODY CODE

66B – coupe, convertible
61B – hatchback

PAINT CODE

EG – Electric Red
EP – Bright Red
KF – Bright Blue
LA – Royal Blue
PD – Reef Blue
PM – Bright Calypso Green
WB – Vibrant Red
YC – Black
YN – Silver

ENGINES

140-cid (2.3-liter) EFI Inline Four

Valves . . . . overhead
Camshaft . . . . single overhead
Block . . . . cast iron
Displacement . . . . 140 cid/2.3 liters
Bore and stroke . . . . 3.78 x 3.13 inches
Compression ratio 9.5:1
Brake hp . . . . 105 @ 4600 rpm
Main bearings 5
Valve lifters . . . . hydraulic
Induction . . . . electronic fuel injection
Sparkplugs . . . . 2 per cylinder
Code . . . . S

302-cid (5.0-liter) EFI V-8 HO

Valves . . . . overhead
Block . . . . cast iron
Displacement . . . . 302 cid/5.0 liters
Bore and stroke . . . . 4.00 x 3.00 inches
Compression ratio 9.0:1
Brake hp . . . . 205 @ 4200 rpm
Main bearings 5
Valve lifters . . . . hydraulic
Induction . . . . electronic fuel injection
Code . . . . E

302-cid (5.0-liter) EFI V-8 Cobra

Valves . . . . overhead
Block . . . . cast iron
Displacement . . . . 302 cid/5.0 liters
Bore and stroke . . . . 4.00 x 3.00 inches
Compression ratio 9.0:1
Brake hp . . . . 235 @ 4600 rpm
Main bearings 5
Valve lifters . . . . hydraulic
Induction . . . . electronic fuel injection
Code . . . . D

CHASSIS

Wheelbase . . . . 100.5 inches
Overall length . . . . 179.6 inches
Height . . . . 52.1 inches
. . . . (convertible) 51.9 inches
Width . . . . 69.1 inches
Front tread width . . . . 56.6 inches
Rear tread width . . . . 57.0 inches
Tires P195/75R-14
. . . . (LX 5.0L, GT) P225/55ZR-16

TECHNICAL

Steering . . . . rack and pinion, power assisted
Front suspension
    modified MacPherson hydraulic shock struts with coil
    springs and stabilizer bar
    . . . . (GT) adds gas-pressurized shocks
Rear suspension . . . .
    four-bar link and coil spring system, anti-sway bar
    (with GT)
Brakes . . . . (front) disc
. . . . (rear) drum
Ignition . . . . electronic
Body construction . . . unibody w/front isolated mini-frame
Fuel tank . . . . 15.4 gallons

OPTION LIST

Four-speed automatic overdrive transmission $595
Power Equipment Group including dual electric remote
    control mirrors, power side windows, Power Lock
    Group, cargo tie-down net, front floor mats, speed con-
    trol, AM/FM Radio w/cassette player & clock, styled road
    wheels

1993 MUSTANG PRODUCTION CHART

Model	Doors/Body/Seating	Factory Price	Shipping Weight	Prod. Total
40 (66B)	2/coupe LX/4	$10,719/13,926	2751/3035	Note 1
41 (61B)	3/hatchback LX/4	$11,224/14,710	2812/3096	Note 1
44 (66B)	2/convertible LX/4	$17,548/20293	2973/3259	Note 1
42 (61B)	3/hatchback GT/4	$15,747	3144	Note 1
45 (66B)	2/convertible GT/4	$20,848	3365	Note 1

NOTE 1: A total of 114,228 Mustangs were produced (24,851 coupes, 62,077 hatchbacks and 27,300 convertibles).

NOTE 2: Ford produced 26,101 GTs and 22,902 5.0L LXs.

NOTE 3: Figure for hatchbacks includes 4,993 SVT Cobras and 107 SVT Cobra R models. See Cobra section in this book for more information.

NOTE 4: Figures to left of slash are for LX four-cylinder, to right of slash for LX 5.0L V-8.

.... (LX coupe and hatchback) $276
.... (LX convertible) $306
same as above, except for styled road wheels, plus Premium Sound System, Custom Equipment Group, manual control air conditioning, dual illuminated visor mirrors
.... (LX 5.0L coupe and hatchback) $567
.... (LX 5.0L convertible) no charge
.... (GT hatchback) $1383
.... (GT convertible) $779
California emission system..................... $100
Leather seating surfaces articulated sport seats
.... (LX 5.0L and GT) $523
Manual air conditioning....................... $817
Convenience Group including cargo tie-down net, front floor mats $99
Rear window defroster. (not available on convertible) $170

Engine block heater......................... $20
Dual illuminated visor mirrors $100
Clearcoat paint $91
Titanium lower bodyside accent treatment (GT only) $159
Power Equipment Group including dual electric remote control mirrors and power side windows........ $604
Flip-up open-air roof .... (fastback only) $355
4-way power driver's seat...................... $183
Speed control............................. $224
Cast aluminum wheels w/P205/65R-15 SBR BSW Tires
.... (LX convertible) $208
.... (LX coupe and hatchback) $401
Styled road wheels.................... (LX only) $193
AM/FM stereo radio w/CD player $629
AM/FM stereo radio w/cassette, auto reverse and Premium Sound $339

1993 LX convertible with 5.0-liter V-8 (FMC)

1993 GT (FMC)

1993 LX convertible with 5.0-liter V-8
Owner: Jimmy Morrison/Morrison Motor Co.

1993 LX convertible with 5.0-liter V-8

1993 LX convertible luggage rack

1993 LX convertible with 5.0-liter V-8

1994 GT coupe (JH)

1994

It doesn't take an automotive historian to figure that the 30th anniversary of a much-beloved American icon like the Mustang should be met with corporate-sponsored enthusiasm and at least one special model. In 1994, Ford's timing couldn't have been better. After minimal acknowledgment of the 25th anniversary, company planners managed to coordinate the introduction of the first truly new Mustang in 15 years with the marque's 30th birthday. Introduced on Oct. 15, 1993, as a 1994 model, the new Mustang was essentially a high-tech updating of the 1979 Fox chassis.

"Team Mustang," a group of Ford employees dedicated to the new car's concept and design, set up camp in an old Montgomery Ward warehouse south of Dearborn late in 1990. They were on a tight budget and even tighter schedule to meet aggressive goals for ride, handling, steering, powertrain performance, brakes, climate control, comfort, and noise/vibration/harshness (NVH). After surveying Mustang owners and collectors, the team recognized the need for a car that would not be seen as a clone of European or Japanese vehicles. At a time when cars from Germany and Japan were considered the standard-bearers for sophistication and quality, Ford was happy to continue producing a traditional American-designed/engineered/built package.

While the project was referred to as "SN-95" (sporty, North American market, concept no. 95), the platform on which the new car was designed was known as the Fox-4—an acknowledgement that the 1994 was still, deep down, a Fox. It should be noted, however, that of the SN-95's 1,850 parts, 1,330 were new. Ford's visual aid for this point was a

stripped chassis on a rotisserie that displayed areas in white (carryovers, mostly simple floorpans and non-structural bracketry), red (all new components), green (GT-specific such as upper strut tower brace) and yellow (convertible-only pieces such as the anti-resonant mass vibration damper and underbody X-brace).

Because chassis stiffness had always been a weakness of the 1979-93 generation (especially when the unplanned convertible came along), engineering goals for rigidity on the new platform were set quite high. The new convertible improved by 80 percent in the area of chassis torsion and 40 percent in bending, while the coupe saw upgrades of 44 percent in torsion and 56 percent in bending.

New techniques were used to achieve stiffness in the coupe, including bonding the windshield and backlight to their frames with a rigid urethane adhesive and by enlarging certain box sections as the rocker panels and roof rails. On the GT V-8 models, the structure was further improved with the addition of a bolt-in brace tying the front strut towers and cowl/firewall together—a trick Mustang modifiers had been using since the mid-1980s to get less flex out of the car under extreme cornering applications.

Mustang II marketers 20 years earlier tried to eliminate either the hatchback or coupe body style from the line, in hopes of reducing production costs and were thwarted by clinics showing a 50/50 split in customer preference. For 1994, Ford managed to kill off the hatchback by styling its coupe in such a way that it appealed to the fastback crowd, but had the tightness and quiet interior of a coupe.

Even the open-air convertible benefited from a thicker gauge of metal in the rocker panels (from 0.8 to 2.3 mm) as well as other stress-bearing panels. To insure a quiet topless ride, a 25-pound tuned mass damper was installed inside the right front fender well. Not wanting to chase after federal regulations a few years down the road, Ford's engineers designed the 1994 around upcoming side-impact specifications that involved ramming the side of the car with a 3,000-pound test sled traveling at 33 mph.

Ford designers made sure that the Mustang's new appearance would thrill some, appeal to others, but offend no one. Viewed from the front, the new pony resembled several models from the past, without really copying any of them directly. Aerodynamic headlights sat on either side of a curved grille cavity that, when combined with the smooth bumper cover and integrated air dam, provided a pleasant, smiling face.

Sticking with the time-honored tradition of a long hood and short deck, designers somewhat re-interpreted these as the sloping, air-cheating hood no longer gave the impression of hiding an extremely large engine. Modern production techniques did a better job of creating a coupe with a gently radiused top—the curvy, almost dome-like top really complemented the rounder body. Three-element taillights (lying horizontal on the 1994, unlike the 1965's vertical units) recalled some of the Mustang's early heritage and contributed to the impression of great body width when viewed from directly behind. A classic twin-cockpit theme ran throughout the new interior.

The 1994 Mustang measured 2.4 inches longer (181.5 inches bumper-to-bumper) than the first Fox car. Wheelbase increased between the two models by 0.9 inches to a total of 101.3. The most striking dimension change was in the width, wherein the 1994 was a muscular 71.9 inches compared to the slab-sided 1979's 69.1 inches. The 1994 Mustang's roofline was 1.4 inches higher than the 1979 at 52.9 inches.

Powerplants were upgraded slightly, with the four-cylinder dropped from the line in 1994. The same torquey 3.8-liter 145-hp V-6 that was already doing duty in Ford's Taurus, Thunderbird, and Lincoln Continental replaced the four and increased horsepower by 38%. The legendary 5.0-liter H.O. V-8 was boosted to 215 hp at 4200 rpm for 1994,

courtesy of a low-profile intake manifold (to fit under the more steeply raked hood) and pistons cast in hypereutectic aluminum alloy. (Mustangers were not expecting much more development of the 5.0 engine as Ford had already announced it would be replaced in 1997 with a version of the company's "modular" motor.) Both engines were available with standard five-speed manual or optional four-speed automatic transmissions.

Buyers of the base V-6 cars received 15-inch steel wheels with plastic covers and 205/65-15 all-season black sidewall Goodyear Eagle GA tires. As an option, those tires could be mounted on three-spoke, 15-inch alloy wheels. Standard GT wheels were five-spoke, 16-inch rims wearing 225/55-16 Firestone Firehawk rubber. An optional upgrade for the GT was a set of three-spoke 17-inchers shod with 245/45-17 Goodyear Eagle GTs.

Four-wheel disc brakes were applied to factory Mustangs for the first time in 1994 on both base and GT cars. This piece of standard equipment had been long in coming as far as Mustang fans were concerned. ABS was an extra-cost option.

Advertising played heavily on the fact that the 30-year heritage was alive and strong in the new design. "It is what it was," said the slogan used to advertise the car. The body sides were even scooped out to resemble the "coves" of the original ponycar. "This car will appeal to younger and older buyers alike," Ford Division general manager Ross H. Roberts said, adding, "There was no 'typical' Mustang buyer back in 1964 when the original came out (and) we're counting on rekindling that fervor."

The 1994 Mustang offered two models in each of two car lines: the base coupe was priced at $13,355 and its convertible counterpart retailed for $20,150. Standard equipment included front and rear body-colored fascias with Mustang nomenclature; Mustang emblem fender badges; aerodynamic halogen headlamps; wraparound tail lamps featuring three horizontal elements; dual, electric, remote-control mirrors

1994 GT convertible (JH)

(convex mirror on right-hand side); color-keyed rocker panel moldings; driver and passenger air bags; a front ashtray; three-point "active" seat belts; 16-ounce carpeting; a cigarette lighter; a digital quartz clock; a stand-alone console with armrest, storage bin, cup-holder and CD/cassette storage; a driver's side foot rest; a glove box; full-instrumentation (including tachometer and low-fluid lamp); an extensive Light Group assortment; dual visor mirrors with covers; reclining cloth bucket seats with cloth head restraints and four-way power driver's seat; split-back fold-down rear seat (not in convertibles); leather-wrapped shift knob and parking brake lever with automatic transmission; stalk-mounted controls; tilt steering with center horn-blow; soft, flow-through vinyl door trim panels with full armrests and cloth or vinyl inserts; a color-keyed headliner (including convertibles); color-keyed cloth sun visors; heavy-duty electrical components; power, side window de-misters; electronic engine control (EEC-V) system; stainless steel exhaust system; 15.4-gallon fuel tank with tethered cap; full tinted glass; Power Vent ventilation system; dual-note horn; a Power Lock Group option; a tunnel-mounted parking brake; an ETR stereo sound system with four 24-watt speakers; constant-ratio, power rack-and-pinion steering; modified MacPherson front suspension with stabilizer bar, links and coil springs; gas-pressurized front struts and rear shock absorbers; a mini-spare and interval-type windshield wipers.

Convertibles also had a power retractable soft top with a hard convertible top boot, illuminated visor mirrors, power deck lid release, power door locks and power side windows. The 1994 was Ford's first post-1973 Mustang convertible to be built as a topless car on the factory assembly line; earlier ragtops started life as coupes and had their roofs removed. A glass backlight was standard, with a built-in defroster costing extra. Convertible tops came in black, white or saddle.

The automotive trend toward bright, vibrant colors was not lost on Ford's planners. The 1994 Mustang could be ordered in one of 11 eye-catching hues, including Canary Yellow (GT only), Vibrant Red (GT only), Rio Red, Laser Red, Iris, Bright Blue, Deep Forest Green, Teal, Black, Opal Frost, and Crystal White. Interiors were available in five colors: Bright Red, Saddle, Opal Grey, Black and White (convertible only).

In addition to (or in place of) standard equipment, the GT coupe ($17,270) and convertible ($21,960) had front and rear fascias with GT nomenclature and black finish on the lower rear end; Mustang GT fender badges; fog lamps; a single-wing rear spoiler; 16x7.5-inch wide five-spoke cast aluminum wheels with locks; a 150-mph speedometer; GT bucket seats with cloth trim, cloth head restraints, adjustable cushions, power lumbar support, and a four-way power driver's seat; a leather-wrapped steering wheel; a Traction-Lok rear axle; handling brace to stiffen the engine compartment ("similar to those utilized by Ford NASCAR teams," said the brochure); stainless steel dual exhaust system; GT suspension package with variable-rate coil springs, unique-calibrated gas struts and shocks, and Quadra-shock rear suspension with strut lever brace and illuminated visor mirrors with hard covers.

One option that will be of particular interest to collectors is the short-lived removable hardtop offered to convertible buyers. Supply problems and the high cost of the option killed the company's enthusiasm and only 499 were delivered—all on the pricier SVT Cobras, and not until the 1995 model year.

The 1994 Mustang was also the first Ford to offer a dealer-installed mini-disc sound system, as well as a new Mach 460 system that used eight speakers to put out 460 peak watts of sound. The all-new Mustang readily won *Motor Trend* magazine's "Car of the Year" award, and it became the Indianapolis 500 pace car for the third time since 1964.

When the model year closed, sales of the new Mustang were respectable, with a total run of 123,198 units. That number included 42,883 base coupes (listing at $13,355 each), 18,333 base convertibles ($20,150), 30,592 GT coupes ($17,270), 25,381 GT convertibles ($21,950), 5,009 Cobra coupes ($21,300) and 10,000 Cobra convertibles ($25,605).

DATA PLATE DECODING

A 17-character Vehicle Identification Number is stamped on an aluminum tab on the instrument panel, viewable through windshield. A vehicle certification label is found on the body side of where the driver's door closes.

VEHICLE WARRANTY NUMBER MANUFACTURER ID

1FA – Ford Motor Co.

RESTRAINT SYSTEM

L – air bags, active belts

1994 GT coupe (PH)

1994 convertible (PH)

VEHICLE CLASSIFICATION

P – passenger car

BODY SERIAL NUMBERS

40 – coupe
42 – coupe, GT
44 – convertible
45 – convertible, GT

ENGINE CODE

4 – 232-cid (3.8-liter) EFI V-6
E – 302-cid (5.0-liter) EFI V-8
D – 302-cid (5.0-liter) EFI V-8 Cobra

CHECK DIGIT

for internal use

MODEL YEAR

R – 1994

ASSEMBLY PLANT

F – Dearborn, Michigan

CONSECUTIVE UNIT NUMBER

Begins at 100001 at each factory.

CODE NUMBERS
PAINT CODE

BZ – Canary Yellow*
E8 – Rio Red
E9 – Laser Red
ES – Vibrant Red*
GC – Iris
KF – Bright Blue
NA – Deep Forest Green
RD – Teal
UA – Black
WJ – Opal Frost
ZF – Crystal White
*GT only

ENGINES

232-cid (3.8-liter) EFI V-6

Valves . . . . overhead
Block . . . . cast iron
Displacement. 232 cid/3.8 liters
Bore and stroke. . . . . 3.80 x 3.40 inches
Compression ratio 9.0:1
Brake hp . . . . 145 @ 4000 rpm
Main bearings 4
Valve lifters. . . . . hydraulic
Induction . . . . electronic fuel injection
Code 4

302-cid (5.0-liter) EFI V-8

Valves . . . . overhead
Block . . . . cast iron
Displacement. 302 cid/5.0 liters
Bore and stroke. . . . . 4.00 x 3.00 inches
Compression ratio 9.0:1
Brake hp . . . . 215 @ 4200 rpm
Main bearings 5
Valve lifters. . . . . hydraulic
Induction . . . . electronic fuel injection
Code . . . . E

302-cid (5.0-liter) EFI V-8 Cobra

Valves . . . . overhead
Block . . . . cast iron
Displacement. 302 cid/5.0 liters
Bore and stroke. . . . . 4.00 x 3.00 inches
Compression ratio 9.0:1
Brake hp . . . . 240 @ 4800 rpm
Main bearings 5
Valve lifters. . . . . hydraulic
Induction . . . . electronic fuel injection
Code 0

CHASSIS

Wheelbase . . . . 101.3 inches
Overall length . . . . 181.5 inches
Height . . . . 52.9 inches
. . . . (convertible) 52.8 inches
Width. . . . . 71.8 inches
Front tread width. . . . . 60.6 inches
Rear tread width . . . . 59.1 inches
Tires P205/65R-15
. . . . (GT) P225/55ZR-16
. . . . (Cobra) P225/45ZR-17

TECHNICAL

Steering . . . . rack and pinion, power assisted
Front suspension . . . .
  modified MacPherson gas-pressurized shock struts with
  coil springs and stabilizer bar
Rear suspension . . . .
  four-bar link and coil spring system, gas shocks
Brakes . . . . (front) disc
. . . . (rear) disc
Ignition . . . . electronic
Body construction . . . unibody w/front isolated mini-frame
Fuel tank. . . . . 15.4 gallons

OPTION LIST

Four-speed automatic overdrive transmission (not available
  on Cobra). $790

1994 MUSTANG PRODUCTION CHART

Model	Doors/Body/Seating	Factory Price	Shipping Weight	Prod. Total
40	2/coupe/4	$13,355	3055	42,883
44	2/convertible/4	$20,150	3193	18,333
42	2/coupe GT/4	$17,270	3258	30,592
45	2/convertible GT/4	$21,960	3414	25,381

NOTE 1: A total of 123,198 Mustangs were produced, including 5,009 SVT Cobra coupes and 1,000 convertibles. See Cobra section in this book for more information.

Mustang 241A includes air conditioning and AM/FM stereo radio w/cassette. $565

Mustang 243A includes air conditioning, power side windows, power door locks, power decklid release, speed control, dual illuminated visor mirrors, 15-inch aluminum wheels, AM/FM stereo radio w/cassette and Premium Sound, remote keyless illuminated entry and cargo net. $1825
. . . . (convertible) $1415

(GT) includes air conditioning, speed control, dual illuminated visor mirrors, 15-inch aluminum wheels and AM/FM stereo radio w/cassette and Premium Sound
. . . . $1405
. . . . (GT convertible) $1405

Cobra coupe 250A includes air conditioning, rear window defroster, front floor mats and speed control $1185

Cobra convertible 250P includes air conditioning, rear window defroster, front floor mats, speed control, remote keyless illuminated entry, CD player and Mach 460 stereo system $2835

California emission system $95

15-inch aluminum wheels
. . . . (not available GT or Cobra) $265

17-inch aluminum wheels . . . . (GT only) $380

Leather sport bucket seats . . . . (convertible) $500
. . . . (GT) $500
. . . . (Cobra coupe) $500

Manual air conditioning $780

Anti-lock braking system . . . . . . (standard on Cobra) $565
Anti-theft system $235
Convertible hardtop. $1545
Rear window defroster $160
Front floor mats $30
Engine block heater. . . . . (not available on Cobra) $20
Bodyside moldings $50
AM/FM stereo radio w/cassette and Premium Sound . . . . .
. (standard Cobra, not available w/Mustang coupe) $165
Mach 460 AM/FM stereo radio w/cassette, seek & scan, 60-watt equalizer, upgraded speakers and amplifiers and CD changer. $375
CD player . . . . (not available w/Mustang coupe) $475

1994 GT wheel

1994 GT interior, Mach 460 stereo

1994 GT door panel

1994 GT interior

1994 Mach 460 speaker

1995 GT coupe
Owner: Jimmy Morrison/Morrison Motor Co.

1995

For 1995, as in generations past, the Mustang's sophomore year with a successful new design is usually remarkable in that only the mildest of changes are made. As far as the Mustang faithful were concerned, 1995 was significant as the final year for the venerable 5.0-liter V-8 that had served the Mustang well since its introduction in 1968 (with interruptions in 1974, 1980 and 1981). Not always the fastest people to accept changes to their pony car, purists were cautiously awaiting the Five-Oh's replacement—a 4.6-liter, overhead cam version of Ford's new "modular" family.

Perhaps to cater to 5.0-liter fans on a budget, Ford offered a GTS model that was essentially a GT without the sports seats, rear spoiler, and fog lamps. It did include the GT's standard 16-inch, five-spoke alloy wheels. The base Mustang continued to be offered with the 3.8-liter V-6. A power driver's seat moved from the standard equipment list to the options list. The only change in color choices was the departure of Iris and the introduction of Sapphire Blue. Interior and convertible top colors remained unchanged. Ford's removable hardtop option for the convertible was quietly dropped from all sales literature by the time the 1995 Mustangs were introduced.

Prices across the board were only increased slightly in 1995. The base coupe listed for $14,330; the base convertible, $20,795; the GTS coupe, $16,910; the GT coupe, $17,905; the GT convertible, $22,595; the Cobra coupe, $21,300; and the Cobra convertible topped the pile at $25,605. Sales were up in the second year of the new design, with a total of 185,986 units sold. That number included 137,722 coupes and 48,264 convertibles.

DATA PLATE DECODING

A 17-character Vehicle Identification Number is stamped on an aluminum tab on the instrument panel, viewable through windshield. A vehicle certification label is found on the body side of where the driver's door closes.

VEHICLE WARRANTY NUMBER MANUFACTURER ID

1FA – Ford Motor Co.

RESTRAINT SYSTEM

L – air bags, active belts

VEHICLE CLASSIFICATION

P – passenger car

BODY SERIAL NUMBERS

40 – coupe	44 – convertible
42 – coupe, GT	45 – convertible, GT

ENGINE CODE

4 – 232-cid (3.8-liter) EFI V-6
E – 302-cid (5.0-liter) EFI V-8
D – 302-cid (5.0-liter) EFI V-8 Cobra
C – 351-cid (5.8-liter) EFI V-8 Cobra R

CHECK DIGIT

for internal use

MODEL YEAR

S – 1995

ASSEMBLY PLANT

F – Dearborn, Michigan

CONSECUTIVE UNIT NUMBER

Begins at 100001 at each factory

CODE NUMBERS
PAINT CODE

BZ – Canary Yellow*
E8 – Rio Red
E9 – Laser Red
ES – Vibrant Red
JA – Sapphire Blue*
KF – Bright Blue
NA – Deep Forest Green
RD – Teal
UA – Black
WJ – Opal Frost
ZR – Crystal White
*GT/GTS only

ENGINES

232-cid (3.8-liter) EFI V-6

Valves . . . . overhead
Block . . . . cast iron
Displacement. . . . . 232 cid/3.8 liters
Bore and stroke. . . . . 3.80 x 3.40 inches
Compression ratio 9.0:1
Brake hp . . . . 145 @ 4000 rpm
Main bearings 4
Valve lifters. . . . . hydraulic
Induction . . . . electronic fuel injection
Code 4

302-cid (5.0-liter) EFI V-8

Valves . . . . overhead
Block . . . . cast iron
Displacement. . . . . 302 cid/5.0 liters
Bore and stroke. . . . . 4.00 x 3.00 inches
Compression ratio 9.0:1
Brake hp . . . . 215 @ 4200 rpm
Main bearings 5
Valve lifters. . . . . hydraulic
Induction . . . . electronic fuel injection
Code . . . . E

302-cid (5.0-liter) EFI V-8 Cobra

Valves . . . . overhead
Block . . . . cast iron
Displacement. . . . . 302 cid/5.0 liters
Bore and stroke. . . . . 4.00 x 3.00 inches
Compression ratio 9.0:1
Brake hp . . . . 240 @ 4800 rpm
Main bearings 5
Valve lifters. . . . . hydraulic
Induction . . . . electronic fuel injection
Code 0

CHASSIS

Wheelbase . . . . 101.3 inches
Overall length . . . . 181.5 inches
Height . . . . 53.0 inches

1995 GT coupe

```
                        . . . . . . . . . . . . . . . . . (convertible) 52.8 inches
Width. . . . . . . . . . . . . . . . . . . . . . . . 71.8 inches
Front tread width. . . . . . . . . . . . . . . . . 60.6 inches
Rear tread width . . . . . . . . . . . . . . . . . . 59.1 inches
Tires . . . . . . . . . . . . . . . . . . . . . . . . . . P205/65R-15
                        . . . . . . . . . . . . . . . . (GT) P225/55ZR-16
                        . . . . . . . . . . . . . . (Cobra) P225/45ZR-17
```

TECHNICAL

```
Steering . . . . . . . . . . . . . rack and pinion, power assisted
Front suspension. . . . . . . . . . . . . . . . . . . . . . . . . . . . . .
    modified MacPherson gas-pressurized shock struts with
    coil springs and stabilizer bar
Rear suspension . . . . . . . . . . . . . . . . . . . . . . . . . . . . . .
    four-bar link and coil spring system, gas shocks
Brakes . . . . . . . . . . . . . . . . . . . . . . . . . . . (front) disc
         . . . . . . . . . . . . . . . . . . . . . . . . . . (rear) disc
Ignition . . . . . . . . . . . . . . . . . . . . . . . . . . electronic
Body construction . . . unibody w/front isolated mini-frame
Fuel tank. . . . . . . . . . . . . . . . . . . . . . 15.4 gallons
```

OPTION LIST

Four-speed automatic overdrive transmission
. . . . (not available on Cobra) $815

Mustang 214A includes air conditioning, AM/FM stereo radio w/cassettes. $565

Mustang Cpe 243A includes air conditioning, power driver's seat, power side windows, power door locks, power decklid release, dual illuminated visor mirrors, speed control, AM/FM stereo radio w/cassette and Premium Sound, 15-inch aluminum wheels, remote eyless illuminated entry and cargo net $2030

1995 GT coupe

Mustang Conv 243C includes air conditioning, dual illuminated visor mirrors, speed control, AM/FM stereo radio w/cassette and Premium Sound, 15-inch aluminum wheels, remote keyless illuminated entry and cargo net $1625

GTS 248A includes air conditioning and AM/FM stereo radio w/cassette. $640

GT 249A includes air conditioning, power driver's seat, dual illuminated visor mirrors, speed control, AM/FM stereo radio w/cassette and Premium Sound and 15-inch aluminum wheels $1615

Cobra Cpe 250A includes air conditioning, rear window defroster, front floor mats and speed control $1260

Cobra Conv 250C air conditioning, rear window defroster, front floor mats, speed control, remote keyless illuminated entry, AM/FM stereo Mach 460 radio w/cassette, CD player and sport leather bucket seats $2755

```
California emission system . . . . . . . . . . . . . . . . . . . $95
15-inch aluminum wheels . . . . . . . . . . . (base only) $265
17-inch aluminum wheels . . . . . . . . . . . (GT only) $380
Sport leather bucket seats. . . . . . . (base convertible) $500
        . . . . . . . . . . . . . . . . . . . . . . (GT and Cobra) $500
Power driver's seat. . . . . . . . (not available on Cobra) $175
Manual air conditioning . . . . . . . . . . . . . . . . . . . $855
Anti-lock braking system . . . . . . . . (standard Cobra) $565
Anti-theft system . . . . . . . . . . . . . . . . . . . . . . . $145
Optional axle ratio . . . . . . . . . . . . . (GTS and GT) $45
Convertible hardtop . . . . . . . . . . . . . . . . . . . . . $1825
Electric rear window defroster . . . . . . . . . . . . . . $160
Front floor mats . . . . . . . . . . . . . . . . . . . . . . . . $30
Bodyside moldings . . . . . . . . . . . . . . (base and GT) $50
Speed control. . . . . . . . . . . . . . . . . . . . . . . . . . $215
CD player. . . . . . . . . . . . . . (not available on GTS) $375
AM/FM stereo radio w/cassette . . . . . (base and GTS) $165
AM/FM stereo Mach 460 Radio w/cassette . . . (Cobra) $375
        . . . . . . . . . . . . . . . . . . . . . . . . (base and GT) $670
AM/FM stereo radio w/CD player and Premium Sound
        . . . . . . . . . . . . . . . . . . . . . . . . . . . (Cobra) $140)
        . . . . . . . . . . . . . . . . . . . . . (base, GTS and GT) $435
Mach 460 sound system (GTS and Cobra convertible) $375
Engine block heater . . . . . . . (not available on Cobra) $20
```

Model	Doors/Body/Seating	Factory Price	Shipping Weight	Prod. Total
\multicolumn{5}{c}{**1995 MUSTANG PRODUCTION CHART**}				

Model	Doors/Body/Seating	Factory Price	Shipping Weight	Prod. Total
40	2/coupe/4	$13,355	3055	42,883
40	2/coupe/4	$14,330	3077	Note 1
44	2/convertible/4	$20,795	3257	Note 1
42	2/coupe GT/4	$17,905	3280	Note 1
45	2/convertible GT/4	$22,595	3451	Note 1
42	2/coupe GTS/4	$16,910	3246	Note 1

NOTE 1: A total of 185,986 Mustangs were produced, including 137,722 coupes, 48,264 convertibles, 4,005 SVT Cobra coupes, 1,003 Cobra convertibles and 250 R models. See Cobra section in this book for more information.

1996 GT coupe (FMC)

1996

Cosmetic changes to the Mustang were minimal for 1996. The three-element tail lamps were now oriented vertically, and the combination of clear lenses and complex reflectors was the first such setup on an American car. A new five-spoke, 17-inch wheel became optional on the GT, and the grille received a background screen to conceal the radiator.

The eyes of the Mustang world were focused under the hood of the GT in 1996. For reasons pertaining to its customer base, federal regulations, and corporate culture, Ford dropped the legendary 5.0-liter V-8 with the 1995 model and debuted the 4.6-liter, single-overhead cam (SOHC) "modular" engine in 1996. Measuring 31 cubic inches less than its predecessor (281 vs. 302), the 4.6-liter came to market with the exact same horsepower and torque ratings as the 1995—215 and 285, respectively. Although many were skeptical of the new, high-tech powerplant, the overhead camshaft allowed the V-8 to produce its power right up to a 6000-rpm redline, besting the pushrod 5.0 by 1500 rpms.

The 4.6-liter was not exactly experimental when it first saw Mustang duty. It was part of a family of modular engines Ford developed from a common platform. By this system, certain components are interchangeable across a line of powerplants, despite differences in displacement and number of cylinders. The first modular Ford appeared in the 1991 Lincoln Town Car, then became standard in the 1992 Crown Victoria/Mercury Marquis twins.

What excited enthusiasts the most about the new powerplant was Ford considered it a foundation for many improvements to come. The operating efficiency gained by the elimination of pushrods meant that more horsepower would be forthcoming. The Mustang's two valves per cylinder were now actuated directly by the overhead camshaft. Less reciprocal weight means greater power transfer.

Just as important from a consumer standpoint was the issue of the new V-8's reliability. Ford engineers assured buyers that the 4.6 liter's unique cylinder head bolt design and spacing meant cylinder and block distortion under stress were no longer factors in a high-performance application. Also, Ford's patented oil cooling system, which has no external oil or coolant lines but uses returning water from the radiator, was considered a real contributor to long engine life.

New technologies were incorporated into the modular motor's design, with lightweight pistons and connecting rods and a composite (plastic) intake manifold that increased runner length without taking up as much room as previous alloy versions. The alternator, air-conditioning compressor, and power steering pump were all directly mounted to the block, reducing underhood clutter. Platinum-tipped spark plugs and the accessory drive belt were rated for 100,000 miles before replacement. A new distributorless electronic ignition and second-generation onboard diagnostic program (OBD II) were further refines to the engine's management systems.

Partly due to the overhead camshafts, the 4.6 was slightly taller than the 5.0, which meant that accommodations had to be made underhood. An ingenious brake pump design that could fit into much smaller spaces than before builds its boost through the power steering pump. The crossmember that supports both engine and front suspension components had to be reconfigured to accommodate the different engine shape. Steering gear and suspension arms were lowered.

A power increase was even applied to the base V-6, taking it to 150 hp. At the same time, a stiffer block from the Thunderbird Super Coupe was adopted into the Mustang line.

Ford replaced its Borg-Warner-designed T-5 five-speed manual transmission and four-speed automatic with a beefier T-45 and a 4R70W automatic. The 4R70W is regulated more heavily by computers than the old automatic overdrive, and it is the first performance automatic from Ford in many years.

The GT received larger stabilizer bars, along with retuned shocks, progressive rate springs, and different bushings. Additional standard equipment on the base model included: AM/FM ETR stereo radio (four speakers); four-wheel power disc brakes; cloth reclining bucket and split folding rear seats; carpeting; console; dual remote mirrors; dual air bags; side glass defoggers; tinted glass; power steering; tilt wheel; oil pressure, tach, temp, and volt gauges; digital clock; trip odometer; front and rear stabilizer bars; front MacPherson struts; visor mirrors; "headlights on" warning tone; intermittent wipers; rocker panel moldings and courtesy lights.

Four new colors were available: Moonlight Blue, Deep Violet, Pacific Green, and Bright Tangerine (GT application only). In an effort to keep Mustangs in the hands of the people who paid for them, Ford applied its Passive Anti-Theft System (PATS) to all 1996 GT and Cobra models. PATS-equipped cars cannot be hotwired due to a specially coded ignition key and switch.

In 1996, a base coupe cost $15,180 (with 61,187 units produced), with the convertible coming in at $21,060 (15,246 made). The sporty GT ran $17,610 (31,624 made) with standard equipment and $23,495 (17,917 made) as a droptop. The high-profile Cobra coupe, at $24,810, sold 7,496 copies; the convertible, at $27,580, sold 2,510 examples.

DATA PLATE DECODING

A 17-character Vehicle Identification Number is stamped on an aluminum tab on the instrument panel, viewable through windshield. A vehicle certification label is found on the body side of where the driver's door closes.

VEHICLE WARRANTY NUMBER
MANUFACTURER ID

1FA – Ford Motor Co.

RESTRAINT SYSTEM

L – air bags, active belts

VEHICLE CLASSIFICATION

P – passenger car

BODY SERIAL NUMBERS

40 – coupe   45 – convertible, GT
42 – coupe, GT   47 – coupe, Cobra
44 – convertible   46 – convertible, Cobra

ENGINE CODE

4 – 232-cid (3.8-liter) EFI V-6
W – 281-cid (4.6-liter) EFI SOHC V-8
V – 281-cid (4.6-liter) EFI DOHC V-8 Cobra

CHECK DIGIT

for internal use

MODEL YEAR

T – 1996

ASSEMBLY PLANT

F – Dearborn, Michigan

CONSECUTIVE UNIT NUMBER

Begins at 100001 at each factory

CODE NUMBERS
PAINT CODE

CM – Bright Tangerine   NA – Deep Forest Green
E8 – Rio Red   PS – Pacific Green
E9 – Laser Red   UA – Black
JU – Deep Violet   WJ – Opal Frost
KM – Moonlight Blue   ZR – Crystal White
LF – Mystic*   *SVT Cobra only

ENGINES

232-cid (3.8-liter) EFI V-6
Valves . . . . overhead
Block . . . . cast iron
Displacement . . . . 232 cid/3.8 liters
Bore and stroke . . . . 3.80 x 3.40 inches
Compression ratio 9.0:1
Brake hp . . . . 150 @ 4000 rpm
Main bearings 4
Valve lifters . . . . hydraulic
Induction . . . . electronic fuel injection
Code 4

281-cid (4.6-liter) EFI SOHC V-8
Valves . . . . overhead
Camshaft . . . . single overhead cam
Block . . . . cast iron
Displacement . . . . 281 cid/4.6 liters
Bore and stroke . . . . 3.60 x 3.60 inches
Compression ratio 9.0:1
Brake hp . . . . 215 @ 4400 rpm
Valve lifters . . . . hydraulic
Induction . . . . electronic fuel injection
Code . . . . W

281-cid (4.6-liter) EFI DOHC V-8 Cobra
Valves . . . . overhead
Camshaft . . . . double overhead cam
Block . . . . aluminum
Displacement . . . . 281 cid/4.6 liters

1996 MUSTANG PRODUCTION CHART

Model	Doors/Body/Seating	Factory Price	Shipping Weight	Prod. Total
40	2/coupe/4	$15,180	3057	61,187
44	2/convertible/4	$21,060	3269	15,246
42	2/coupe GT/4	$17,610	3279	31,624
45	2/convertible GT/4	$23,495	3468	17,917

NOTE 1: A total of 135,620 Mustangs were produced, including 7,496 SVT Cobra coupes and 2,510 Cobra convertibles. See Cobra section in this book for more information.

Bore and stroke.................... 3.60 x 3.60 inches
Compression ratio .... 9.85:1Brake hp
.... 305 @ 5800 rpm
Valve lifters.......................... hydraulic
Induction .... electronic fuel injection
Code V

CHASSIS

Wheelbase .... 101.3 inches
Overall length .... 181.5 inches
.... (Cobra) 182.5 inches
Height .... 53.2 inches
.... (convertible) 53.4 inches
Width........................... 71.8 inches
Front tread width.................... 60.6 inches
Rear tread width .... 59.1 inches
Tires P205/65R-15
.... (GT) P225/55ZR-16
.... (Cobra) P245/45ZR-17

TECHNICAL

Steering .... rack and pinion, power assisted
Front suspension
   modified MacPherson gas-pressurized shock struts with
   coil springs and stabilizer bar
Rear suspension
   four-bar link and coil spring system, gas shocks
Brakes .... (front) disc
.... (rear) disc
Ignition .... electronic
Body construction ... unibody w/front isolated mini-frame
Fuel tank........................... 15.4 gallons

OPTION LIST

Four-speed automatic overdrive transmission
.... (not available onCobra) $815
(Mustang 241A) includes manual air conditioning and
   AM/FM stereo radio w/cassette $670
(Mustang 243A) includes air conditioning, dual illuminated
   visor mirrors, remote keyless entry, power driver's seat,
   power side windows, power door locks, power decklid
   release, speed control, 15-inch aluminum wheels and
   AM/FM stereo radio w/cassette and Premium Sound

.... (coupe) $2020
.... (convertible) $1590
(GT 248A) includes air conditioning and AM/FM stereo
   radio w/cassette..................... $670
(GT coupe 249A) includes anti-lock brakes, foglamps, GT
   sport seats, leather-wrapped steering wheel, rear spoiler,
   dual illuminated visor mirrors, air conditioning, power
   driver's seat, power windows, power door locks, power
   decklid release, speed control, cast aluminum wheels
   and AM/FM stereo radio w/cassette and Premium Sound
.... $2845
(GT convertible 249C) includes anti-lock brakes, air conditioning, speed control, cast aluminum wheels, power dri-
   ver's seat and AM/FM stereo radio w/cassette and
   Premium Sound $1650
(Cobra 250A) includes CD player, Mach 460 radio, anti-
   theft system and leather seats $1335
California emission system..................... $100
Air conditioning............................ $895
Anti-theft system $145
Optional axle ratio................. (GT only) $200
Anti-lock braking system ...... (standard on Cobra) $570
Electric rear window defroster.. (standard on Cobra) $170
Floor mats................. (standard on Cobra) $30
Engine block heater....... (not available on Cobra) $20
Remote keyless illuminated entry system
.... (standard on Cobra) $270
Dual illuminated visor mirrors $95
Bodyside moldings.......................... $60
AM/FM stereo radio w/cassette and Premium Sound.. $165
AM/FM stereo radio w/cassette and Premium Sound.. $295
Mach 460 AM/FM stereo radio w/cassette, seek and scan,
60-watt equalizer and CD changer $690
CD player $295
Power driver's seat.......... (standard on Cobra) $175
Leather sport bucket seats .... (convertible) $500
.... (GT) $500
Speed control .... (standard on Cobra) $215
Spoiler................................. $195
15-inch aluminum wheels .... (base model only) $265
17-inch aluminum wheels and P245/45ZR-17 BSW Tires
.... $400

1996 GT (JH)

1997 convertible (FMC)

1997

Ford rested on its Mustang laurels in 1997, having pulled off a minor miracle with the 4.6-liter's introduction the year before. Base model standard equipment included: five-speed manual transmission; PATS anti-theft system; AM/FM ETR stereo radio (four speakers); power front and rear disc brakes; cloth reclining bucket and split folding rear seats; cloth and vinyl door trim panels; carpeting; console w/armrest; dual power remote mirrors; dual air bags; side glass defoggers; tinted glass; power steering; tilt wheel; oil pressure, tach, temp and volt gauges; digital clock; trip odometer; front stabilizer bar; front MacPherson struts; 15-inch steel wheels with covers and P205/65R15 BSW tires; dual visor vanity mirrors; "headlights-on" warning tone; intermittent wipers; rocker panel moldings; courtesy lights; and trunk light.

New 17-inch rims with dark gray metallic centers became optional on the GT. A slight change in the upper grille opening allowed more air to the new cooling system. All automatic transmission-equipped cars received thicker shifters.

After a peak in 1995, the new Mustang design had its second straight year of decreased sales at 108,344. For 1997, Ford produced 56,812 base coupes (at a price of $15,880), 11,606 base convertibles ($21,280), 18,464 GT coupes ($18,525), 11,413 GT convertibles ($24,510), 6,961 Cobra coupes ($25,335), and 3,088 Cobra convertibles ($28,135).

DATA PLATE DECODING

A 17-character Vehicle Identification Number is stamped on an aluminum tab on the instrument panel, viewable through windshield. A vehicle certification label is found on the body side of where the driver's door closes.

VEHICLE WARRANTY NUMBER MANUFACTURER ID

1FA – Ford Motor Co.

RESTRAINT SYSTEM

L – air bags, active belts

VEHICLE CLASSIFICATION

P – passenger car

BODY SERIAL NUMBERS

40 – coupe
42 – coupe, GT
44 – convertible
45 – convertible, GT
47 – coupe, Cobra
46 – convertible, Cobra

ENGINE CODE

4 – 232-cid (3.8-liter) EFI V-6
W – 281-cid (4.6-liter) EFI SOHC V-8
V – 281-cid (4.6-liter) EFI DOHC V-8 Cobra

CHECK DIGIT

for internal use

MODEL YEAR

V – 1997

ASSEMBLY PLANT

F – Dearborn, Michigan

CONSECUTIVE UNIT NUMBER

Begins at 100001 at each factory

CODE NUMBERS
PAINT CODE

AZ – Aztec Gold
BG – Autumn Orange
E8 – Rio Red
E9 – Laser Red
JU – Deep Violet
KM – Moonlight Blue
NA – Deep Forest Green
PS – Pacific Green
UA – Black
ZR – Crystal White

ENGINES

232-cid (3.8-liter) EFI V-6

Valves . . . . overhead
Block . . . . cast iron
Displacement. . . . . 232 cid/3.8 liters
Bore and stroke. . . . . 3.80 x 3.40 inches
Compression ratio 9.0:1
Brake hp . . . . 150 @ 4000 rpm
Main bearings 4
Valve lifters. hydraulic
Induction . . . . electronic fuel injection
Code 4

281-cid (4.6-liter) EFI SOHC V-8

Valves . . . . overhead
Camshaft . . . . single overhead cam
Block . . . . cast iron
Displacement. . . . . 281 cid/4.6 liters
Bore and stroke. . . . . 3.60 x 3.60 inches
Compression ratio 9.0:1
Brake hp . . . . 215 @ 5000 rpm
Valve lifters. hydraulic
Induction . . . . electronic fuel injection
Code. . . . . W

281-cid (4.6-liter) EFI DOHC V-8 Cobra

Valves . . . . overhead
Camshaft . . . . double overhead cam
Block . . . . aluminum

Displacement. . . . . 281 cid/4.6 liters
Bore and stroke. . . . . 3.60 x 3.60 inches
Compression ratio 9.85:1
Brake hp . . . . 305 @ 5800 rpm
Valve lifters. hydraulic
Induction . . . . electronic fuel injection
Code V

CHASSIS

Wheelbase . . . . 101.3 inches
Overall length . . . . 181.5 inches
. . . . (Cobra) 182.5 inches
Height . . . . 53.2 inches
. . . . (convertible) 53.4 inches
Width. . . . . 71.8 inches
Front tread width. . . . . 60.5 inches
Rear tread width . . . . 59.2 inches
Tires P205/65TR-15
. . . . (GT) P225/55ZR-16
. . . . (Cobra) P245/45ZR-17

TECHNICAL

Steering . . . . rack and pinion, power assisted
Front suspension . . . .
    modified MacPherson gas-pressurized shock struts with
    coil springs and stabilizer bar
Rear suspension . . . .
    . . . . . . four-bar link and coil spring system, gas shocks
Brakes . . . . (front) disc
. . . . (rear) disc
Ignition . . . . electronic
Body construction . . . unibody w/front isolated mini-frame
Fuel tank. . . . . 15.4 gallons

OPTION LIST

Four-speed automatic overdrive transmission (not available
    on Cobra) $815
(Mustang 241A) includes air conditioning and AM/FM
    stereo radio w/cassette $615
(Mustang 243A) includes air conditioning, dual illuminated
    visor mirrors, remote keyless illuminated entry, power
    driver's seat, power side windows, power door locks,
    power decklid release, speed control, AM/FM stereo
    radio w/cassette and Premium Sound and 15-inch alu-
    minum wheels . . . . (coupe) $2115
    . . . . (convertible) $1615
(GT 248A) includes air conditioning and AM/FM stereo
    radio w/cassette. $670
(GT 249A) includes air conditioning, power driver's seat,
    power side windows, power door locks, power decklid
    release, speed control, AM/FM stereo radio w/cassette
    and Premium Sound and 15-inch aluminum wheels

1997 MUSTANG PRODUCTION CHART

Model	Doors/Body/Seating	Factory Price	Shipping Weight	Prod. Total
40	2/coupe/4	$15,880	3084	56,812
44	2/convertible/4	$21,280	3264	11,606
42	2/coupe GT/4	$18,525	3288	18,464
45	2/convertible GT/4	$24,510	3422	11,413

NOTE 1: A total of 108,344 Mustangs were produced, including 6,961 SVT Cobra coupes and 3,088 Cobra convertibles. See Cobra section in this book for more information.

. . . . (coupe) $2940
. . . . (convertible) $1685
(Cobra 250A) includes CD player, Mach 460 radio, anti-theft system and leather seats $1335
California emission system. $170
  Cast aluminum wheels w/P205/65TR-15 BSW Tires
. . . . (base model only) $265
Polished aluminum wheels w/P245/45ZR-17 BSW Tires
. . . . $500
Leather sport bucket seats . . . . (base model) $500
. . . . (GT) $500
Power driver's seat. $210
Air conditioning. $895
Sport Appearance Group includes rear decklid spoiler, 15-inch aluminum wheels, leather-wrapped steering wheel, lower bodyside accent stripe $345

Anti-lock braking system
. . . . (standard GT convertible and Cobra) $570
Anti-theft system $145
Optional axle ratio . . . . (not available on base) $200
Electric rear window defroster $190
Dual illuminated visor mirrors $95
Front floor mats. $30
Rear decklid spoiler . . . . . (standard GT convertible) $195
Remote keyless illuminated entry system . (GT only) $270
Speed control . . . . (GT only) $215
CD player $295
AM/FM stereo radio w/cassette $165
AM/FM stereo radio w/cassette and Premium Sound. . $295
Mach 460 AM/FM stereo radio w/cassette $690
Engine block heater. $20

1998 convertible

1998

Base, GT, and Cobra available in coupe and convertible body styles again comprised the Mustang lineup for 1998. The 3.8-liter V-6 (base Mustangs) and 4.6-liter V-8 (GT and Cobra models) were again the engines used, with the GT's powerplant gaining 10 hp from 215 to 225 hp.

Two new option packages were introduced to this carry-over model: a GT Sport Group that included the 17-inch aluminum wheels; hood and wraparound fender stripes; leather-wrapped shift knob and engine oil cooler; and the V-6 Sport Appearance Group that gave the buyer 16-inch cast-aluminum wheels, rear spoiler, leather-wrapped steering wheel, and a lower bodyside accent stripe.

Improvements to the Mustang for 1998 included polished aluminum wheels and a premium sound system with cassette and CD capability added as standard equipment on the base coupe and convertible. Other items added as standard equipment included air conditioning, power windows, power door locks, power decklid release, and remote keyless illuminated entry. In addition, the GT received a sound system upgrade, spoiler, and sport seats. The instrument panel-mounted clock pod was removed, with the clock function now falling to the radio display. The power receptacle was relocated inside the console storage box. Ford's SecuriLock anti-theft system was standard on the Mustang.

Mustangs equipped with the four-speed automatic transmission qualified as Low Emission Vehicles (LEV) in four states that posted tighter emissions standards: California, New York, Massachusetts, and Connecticut. 1998 produced a big spike in production, with 175,522 going to new homes. The total included 99,801 base coupes (at $15,970 list price), 21,254 base convertibles ($20,470), 28,789 GT coupes ($19,970), 17,024 GT convertibles ($23,970), 5,174 Cobra coupes ($25,710), and 3,480 Cobra convertibles ($28,510).

DATA PLATE DECODING

A 17-character Vehicle Identification Number is stamped on an aluminum tab on the instrument panel, viewable through windshield. A vehicle certification label is found on the body side of where the driver's door closes.

VEHICLE WARRANTY NUMBER MANUFACTURER ID

1FA – Ford Motor Co.

RESTRAINT SYSTEM

L – air bags, active belts

VEHICLE CLASSIFICATION

P – passenger car

BODY SERIAL NUMBERS

40 – coupe
42 – coupe, GT
44 – convertible
45 – convertible, GT
47 – coupe, Cobra
46 – convertible, Cobra

ENGINE CODE

4 – 232-cid (3.8-liter) EFI V-6
W – 281-cid (4.6-liter) EFI SOHC V-8
V – 281-cid (4.6-liter) EFI DOHC V-8 Cobra

CHECK DIGIT

for internal use

MODEL YEAR

W – 1998

ASSEMBLY PLANT

F – Dearborn, Michigan

CONSECUTIVE UNIT NUMBER

Begins at 100001 at each factory

CODE NUMBERS
PAINT CODE

BG – Autumn Orange
BZ – Chrome Yellow
ES – Performance Red
E8 – Rio Red
E9 – Laser Red
FU – Dark Green Satin
K6 – Atlantic Blue
K7 – Bright Atlantic Blue
PS – Pacific Green
UA – Black
YN -- Silver
ZR – Crystal White

ENGINES

232-cid (3.8-liter) EFI V-6

Valves . . . . overhead
Block . . . . cast iron
Displacement . . . . 232 cid/3.8 liters
Bore and stroke . . . . 3.80 x 3.40 inches
Compression ratio 9.0:1
Brake hp . . . . 150 @ 4000 rpm
Main bearings 4
Valve lifters . . . . hydraulic

Induction . . . . electronic fuel injection
Code 4

281-cid (4.6-liter) EFI SOHC V-8

Valves . . . . overhead
Camshaft . . . . single overhead cam
Block . . . . cast iron
Displacement . . . . 281 cid/4.6 liters
Bore and stroke . . . . 3.60 x 3.60 inches
Compression ratio 9.0:1
Brake hp . . . . 225 @ 4750 rpm
Valve lifters . . . . hydraulic
Induction . . . . electronic fuel injection
Code . . . . W

281-cid (4.6-liter) EFI DOHC V-8 Cobra

Valves . . . . overhead
Camshaft . . . . double overhead cam
Block . . . . aluminum
Displacement . . . . 281 cid/4.6 liters
Bore and stroke . . . . 3.60 x 3.60 inches
Compression ratio 9.85:1
Brake hp . . . . 305 @ 5800 rpm
Valve lifters . . . . hydraulic
Induction . . . . electronic fuel injection
Code V

CHASSIS

Wheelbase . . . . 101.3 inches
Overall length . . . . 181.5 inches
. . . . (Cobra) 182.5 inches
Height . . . . 53.2 inches
. . . . (convertible) 53.4 inches
Width . . . . 71.8 inches
Front tread width . . . . 60.5 inches
Rear tread width . . . . 59.2 inches
Tires P205/65TR-15
(GT) P225/55HR-16
(Cobra) P245/45ZR-17

TECHNICAL

Steering . . . . rack and pinion, power assisted
Front suspension
modified MacPherson gas-pressurized shock struts with coil springs and stabilizer bar
Rear suspension
. . . . . . four-bar link and coil spring system, gas shocks
Brakes . . . . (front) disc
. . . . (rear) disc
Ignition . . . . electronic
Body construction . . . unibody w/front isolated mini-frame
Fuel tank . . . . 15.4 gallons

1998 MUSTANG PRODUCTION CHART

Model	Doors/Body/Seating	Factory Price	Shipping Weight	Prod. Total
40	2/coupe/4	$15,970	3065	99,801
44	2/convertible/4	$20,470	3210	21,254
42	2/coupe GT/4	$19,970	3227	28,789
45	2/convertible GT/4	$23,970	3400	17,024

NOTE 1: A total of 175,522 Mustangs were produced, including 5,174 SVT Cobra coupes and 3,480 Cobra convertibles. See Cobra section in this book for more information.

OPTION LIST

Four-speed automatic overdrive transmission
. . . . (not available on Cobra) $815
Anti-theft system $145
Optional axle ratio. . . . . (GT only) $200
Anti-lock braking system $500
Convenience Group including front floor mats, rear window defroster, speed control and power driver's seat (seat is standard on GT) . . . . (base) $495
. . . . (GT) $295
GT Sport Group includes 17-inch 5-spoke aluminum wheels, hood stripe and wraparound fender stripes, leather-wrapped shift knob and engine oil cooler. . $595
V6 Sport Appearance Group includes 16-inch cast aluminum wheels, rear spoiler, leather-wrapped steering wheel, lower bodyside accent stripe
. . . . (base model only) $345

Electric rear window defroster $190
Dual illuminated visor mirrors
. . . . (standard on convertible) $95
Engine block heater $20
Color-keyed bodyside molding $60
Air conditioning. $895
Mach 460 AM/FM stereo radio w/cassette and CD changer compatibility. $395
Rear spoiler . . . . (standard on GT) $195
California emission system. $170
Leather bucket seats . . . . (base and GT only) $500
17-inch aluminum wheels w/P245/45ZR-17 BSW Tires
. . . . (GT only) $500

1998 convertible

1998 4-code 3.8-liter/EFI V-6

1998 convertible

1998 convertible
Owner: Jimmy Morrison/Morrison Motor Co.

1998 convertible interior

1998 gauges

1998 interior

1998 wheel

**1999 GT convertible
Owner: Jimmy Morrison/Morrison
Motor Co.**

1999

Remembering how badly it had been criticized in the press for "forgetting" the Mustang's 25th anniversary, Ford gave fans of the marque a year-long surprise party in 1999. All Mustangs (whether powered by the V-6 or V-8) wore beautiful wreath-design emblems on their front fenders that featured a solid ring encircling the classic running horse and tri-color bar.

Not content to merely spruce up a six-year-old design with fender jewelry, Ford's designers went on to give the line a much-appreciated facelift and tummy tuck, while prescribing some steroid therapy. The smooth, mostly feminine, curves of the 1994-98 Mustang were replaced with strong creases and straight lines. The sides of the car took on a more vertical angle, and the tallest scoop ever to grace a Mustang was installed just behind the door. This "pumping up" of the previous design reminded many Mustang fans of the changes that had given the original 1965 a body-builder look in 1967.

On GT models, the hood grew a simulated recessed scoop that recalled the air-grabber the 1968 sported when it received its first 428-cid V-8. GT exhaust tips also were enlarged slightly, from 2.75 inches to 3 inches. Up front, the Mustang's headlights took on a sinister appearance. Taillights received the same treatment as the rest of the car, going from soft and rounded to hard and harsh. Looking for ways to reduce weight at every turn, designers created a new decklid made from a sheet-molded compound.

While the exterior improvements were enough to bring new customers, there were refinements in areas that couldn't be seen so easily, such as the revised floorpan sealing and foam-packed rocker panels—both of which reduced road noise. Engineers reduced a troublesome "mid-car shake" on the convertible models through the use of subframe connectors and gained a tiny bit of rear suspension travel on all models by raising the drive tunnel 1.5 inches.

As the Mustang drew nearer to the end of the century, it received new technology provided in the form of an optional all-speed Traction Control System (TCS), a $230 option that worked in harmony with the also-optional (on base models) ABS to reduce tire spin in slippery conditions. Taller Mustangers no doubt appreciated the extra inch of travel built into the driver's seat for 1999. Thanks to a higher-lift camshaft, coil-on-plug ignition, bigger valves and a revised intake manifold, the V-8 Mustang received its biggest power increase since 1987. The GT's 4.6-liter was boosted to 260 hp, and the base, 3.8-liter V-6 jumped to 190 hp.

To commemorate the 35th anniversary in grand style, Ford produced a limited run of 5,000 Limited Edition models that stickered for $2,695 above the cost of a GT. Features included a special, raised hood scoop (at the end of a wide black stripe); rear deck wing; stand-out side scoops, black honeycomb decklid appliqué; body-color rocker moldings; Midnight Black GT leather interior with silver leather inserts; special floor mats with 35th anniversary script; and special aluminum shift knob (five-speeds only). Exterior colors were limited to Black, Silver, Crystal White and Performance Red. Mustangers did not realize it at the time, but the Limited Edition incorporated many of the cosmetic upgrades that would become standard with the 2001 model.

The heavily facelifted 1999 model, despite positive reviews from the motor press, saw a decline in sales from the previous year, at 133,637 total. The base coupe sold 73,180 units (at $16,470 apiece); the base convertible, 19,299 ($21,070); the GT coupe, 19,634 ($20,870); the GT convertible, 13,699 ($24,870); the Cobra coupe, 4,040 ($27,470) and the Cobra convertible, 4,055 ($31,470).

DATA PLATE DECODING

A 17-character Vehicle Identification Number is stamped on an aluminum tab on the instrument panel, viewable through windshield. A vehicle certification label is found on the body side of where the driver's door closes.

VEHICLE WARRANTY NUMBER
MANUFACTURER ID

1FA – Ford Motor Co.

RESTRAINT SYSTEM

L – air bags, active belts

VEHICLE CLASSIFICATION

P – passenger car

BODY SERIAL NUMBERS

40 – coupe
42 – coupe, GT
44 – convertible
45 – convertible, GT
47 – coupe, Cobra
46 – convertible, Cobra

ENGINE CODE

4 – 232-cid (3.8-liter) EFI V-6
X – 281-cid (4.6-liter) EFI SOHC V-8
V – 281-cid (4.6-liter) EFI DOHC V-8 Cobra

CHECK DIGIT

for internal use

MODEL YEAR

X – 1999

ASSEMBLY PLANT

F – Dearborn, Michigan

CONSECUTIVE UNIT NUMBER

Begins at 100001 at each factory

CODE NUMBERS
PAINT CODE

BZ – Chrome Yellow
ES – Performance Red
E8 – Rio Red
E9 – Laser Red
FU – Dark Green Satin
K6 – Atlantic Blue
K7 – Bright Atlantic Blue
SW – Electric Green
UA – Black
YN – Silver
ZR – Crystal White

ENGINES

232-cid (3.8-liter) EFI V-6

Valves . . . . overhead
Block . . . . cast iron
Displacement . . . . 232 cid/3.8 liters
Compression ratio 9.36:1
Bore and stroke . . . . 3.80 x 3.40 inches
Brake hp . . . . 190 @ 5250 rpm
Main bearings 4
Valve lifters . . . . hydraulic
Induction . . . . electronic fuel injection
Code 4

281-cid (4.6-liter) EFI SOHC V-8

Valves . . . . overhead
Camshaft . . . . single overhead cam
Block . . . . cast iron
Displacement . . . . 281 cid/4.6 liters
Compression ratio 9.0:1
Bore and stroke . . . . 3.60 x 3.60 inches
Brake hp . . . . 260 @ 5250 rpm
Valve lifters . . . . hydraulic
Induction . . . . electronic fuel injection
Code X

281-cid (4.6-liter) EFI DOHC V-8 Cobra

Valves . . . . overhead
Camshaft . . . . double overhead cam
Block . . . . aluminum
Displacement . . . . 281 cid/4.6 liters
Bore and stroke . . . . 3.60 x 3.60 inches

1999 MUSTANG PRODUCTION CHART

Model	Doors/Body/Seating	Factory Price	Shipping Weight	Prod. Total
40	2/coupe/4	$16,470	3069	73,180
44	2/convertible/4	$21,070	3211	19,299
42	2/coupe GT/4	$20,870	3273	19,634
45	2/convertible GT/4	$24,870	3429	13,699

NOTE 1: A total of 133,637 Mustangs were produced, including 4,040 SVT Cobra coupes and 4,055 Cobra convertibles. See Cobra section in this book for more information.

Compression ratio 9.85:1
Brake hp . . . . 320 @ 6000
Valve lifters . . . . hydraulic
Induction . . . . electronic fuel injection
Code V

CHASSIS

Wheelbase . . . . 101.3 inches
Overall length . . . . 183.5 inches
Height . . . . 53.2 inches
Width . . . . 73.1 inches
Front tread width . . . . 59.9 inches
Rear tread width . . . . 59.9 inches

TECHNICAL

Steering . . . . rack and pinion, power assisted
Front suspension . . . .
   modified MacPherson gas-pressurized shock struts with
   coil springs and stabilizer bar
Rear suspension . . . .
   . . . . . four-bar link and coil spring system, gas shocks
Brakes . . . . (front) disc
 . . . . (rear) disc
Ignition . . . . electronic
Body construction . . . unibody w/front isolated mini-frame
Fuel tank . . . . 15.4 gallons

OPTION LIST

Four-speed automatic overdrive transmission
. . . . (not available on Cobra) $815

Anti-lock braking system $500
Convenience Group including front floor mats, rear window
   defroster, speed control and power driver's seat
. . . . $550
GT Sport Group includes 17-inch 5-spoke aluminum
   wheels, hood stripe and wraparound fender stripes,
   leather-wrapped shift knob and engine oil cooler. . $595
V6 Sport Appearance Group includes 15-inch cast aluminum wheels, rear spoiler, leather-wrapped steering
   wheel, lower bodyside accent stripe
   . . . . (base model only) $310
35th Anniversary Limited Edition Package includes 17-
   inch 5-spoke aluminum wheels, black applique on hood,
   side scoops, rocker panel moldings, rear spoiler, taillamp
   applique, black and silver leather seats, silver door trim
   inserts, silver and black floor mats with 35th
   Anniversary logo and aluminum shifter knob
   . . . . (GT only) $2,695
Electric rear window defroster $190
Dual illuminated visor mirrors
. . . . (standard on convertible) $95
Color-keyed bodyside molding $60
Mach 460 AM/FM stereo radio w/cassette and CD changer
   compatibility $395
Rear spoiler . . . . (standard on GT) $195
California emission system . . . . no charge
Leather bucket seats . . . . (base and GT only) $500
17-inch aluminum wheels w/P245/45ZR-17 BSW Tires
. . . . (GT only) $500

Above: 1999 GT convertible (FMC)
Inset: 1999 anniversary fender emblem (FMC)

1999 GT convertible

1999 GT wheel

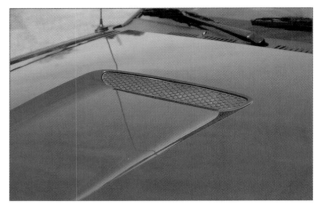

1999 GT hood scoop

1999 GT side vent

1999 spoiler

1999 GT convertible interior

1999 X-code 4.6-liter/EFI SOHC V-8

1999 35th Anniversary convertible (FMC)

1999 35th Anniversary convertible (FMC)

1999 4-code 3.8-liter/EFI V-6 (FMC)

1999 headlamp assembly (FMC)

**2000 coupe
Owner: Larry Vandeventer**

2000

Three new colors, Sunburst Gold, Performance Red, and Amazon Gold, replaced Chrome Yellow, Rio Red, and Dark Green Satin. That was about it for the obvious changes to the 2000 Mustang.

Two new safety features were added: child seat tether anchor brackets were attached to the rear seating areas of all Mustangs, and an interior decklid release with glow-in-the-dark illumination became standard equipment after news reports of carjacking victims being locked in the trucks of their cars.

The base coupe listed for $16,520; the base convertible, $21,370; the GT coupe, $21,015; and the GT convertible, $25,270.

DATA PLATE DECODING

A 17-character Vehicle Identification Number is stamped on an aluminum tab on the instrument panel, viewable through windshield. A vehicle certification label is found on the body side of where the driver's door closes.

VEHICLE WARRANTY NUMBER MANUFACTURER ID

1FA – Ford Motor Co.

RESTRAINT SYSTEM

L – air bags, active belts

VEHICLE CLASSIFICATION

P – passenger car

BODY SERIAL NUMBERS

40 – coupe
42 – coupe, GT
44 – convertible
45 – convertible, GT
47 – coupe, Cobra
46 – convertible, Cobra

ENGINE CODE

4 – 232-cid (3.8-liter) EFI V-6
X – 281-cid (4.6-liter) EFI SOHC V-8
H – 330-cid (5.4-liter) EFI DOHC V-8 Cobra R

CHECK DIGIT

for internal use

MODEL YEAR

Y – 2000

ASSEMBLY PLANT

F – Dearborn, Michigan

CONSECUTIVE UNIT NUMBER

Begins at 100001 at each factory

CODE NUMBERS
PAINT CODE

BP – Sunburst Gold
ES – Performance Red
E9 – Laser Red
K6 – Atlantic Blue
K7 – Bright Atlantic Blue
SU – Amazon Green
SW – Electric Green
UA – Black
YN – Silver
ZR – Crystal White

ENGINES

232-cid (3.8-liter) EFI V-6

Valves	overhead
Block	cast iron
Displacement	232 cid/3.8 liters
Compression ratio	9.36:1
Bore and stroke	3.80 x 3.40 inches
Brake hp	190 @ 5250 rpm
Main bearings	4
Valve lifters	hydraulic
Induction	electronic fuel injection
Code	4

281-cid (4.6-liter) EFI SOHC V-8

Valves	overhead
Camshaft	single overhead cam
Block	cast iron
Displacement	281 cid/4.6 liters
Compression ratio	9.0:1
Bore and stroke	3.60 x 3.60 inches
Brake hp	260 @ 5250 rpm
Valve lifters	hydraulic
Induction	electronic fuel injection
Code	W

330-cid (5.4-liter) EFI DOHC V-8 Cobra R

Valves	overhead
Camshaft	double overhead cam
Block/heads	cast iron/aluminum
Displacement	330 cid/5.4 liters
Bore and stroke	90.2 x 105.8 mm
Compression ratio	9.60:1
Brake hp	385 @ 6250
Valve lifters	hydraulic
Induction	electronic fuel injection
Code	H

CHASSIS

Wheelbase	101.3 inches
Overall length	183.2 inches
Height	(coupe) 53.1 inches
	(convertible) 53.2 inches
Width	73.1 inches
Front tread width	60.4 inches
Rear tread width	60.6 inches

TECHNICAL

Steering	rack and pinion, power assisted
Front suspension	modified MacPherson gas-pressurized shock struts with coil springs and stabilizer bar
Rear suspension	four-bar link and coil spring system, gas shocks
Brakes	(front) disc
	(rear) disc
Ignition	electronic
Body construction	unibody w/front isolated mini-frame
Fuel tank	15.7 gallons

OPTION LIST

Four-speed automatic overdrive transmission (not available on Cobra) $815
Anti-lock braking system $500
Traction control system $230
Convenience Group including front floor mats, rear window defroster, speed control and power driver's seat $550
V6 Sport Appearance Group includes 15-inch cast aluminum wheels, rear spoiler, leather-wrapped steering wheel, lower bodyside accent stripe (base model only) $310
Electric rear window defroster $190
Engine block heater $20
Dual illuminated visor mirrors (standard on convertible) $95
Mach 460 AM/FM stereo radio w/cassette and CD changer compatibility $395
Rear spoiler (standard on GT) $195
California emission system no charge
Leather bucket seats (base and GT only) $500
17-inch aluminum wheels w/P245/45ZR-17 BSW Tires (GT only) $500

2000 MUSTANG PRODUCTION CHART

Model	Doors/Body/Seating	Factory Price	Shipping Weight	Prod. Total
40	2/coupe/4	$16,520	3064	Note 1
44	2/convertible/4	$21,370	3203	Note 1
42	2/coupe GT/4	$21,015	3227	Note 1
45	2/convertible GT/4	$25,270	3375	Note 1

NOTE 1: Numbers were unavailable at the time of printing.

2000 coupe

2000 wheel

2000 coupe

2000 coupe, fold-down rear seat

2000 door panel

2000 GT (FMC)

2000 GT (FMC)

2001 GT convertible
Owners: Richard and Julie Canter

2001

The Mustang became even more of a 1960s musclecar throwback with the 2001 model when the pumped-up body gained a tall (though non-functional) hood scoop, side scoops, a revised spoiler and black-out trim around the headlights. Seventeen-inch wheels similar to the aftermarket American Racing Torq-Thrust rims seen on many Shelbys and other musclecars in the late 1960s became optional for the GT.

Through careful juggling of its equipment list, Ford managed to reduce the number of order combinations from the previous year's 2,600 to approximately 50 for 2001. Standard, Deluxe, and Premium Equipment Groups became the only offered option packages.

For the base coupe, the Standard Equipment Group included 15-inch painted alloy wheels; P205/65R15 all-season tires; electronic ignition; multi-port fuel injection; four-wheel disc brakes; stereo CD/radio/cassette; air conditioning; driver and passenger airbag; split fold-down rear seat; and SecuriLock Passive Anti-Theft System.

Base or GT model Deluxe Equipment Group included a rear spoiler; power driver's seat; leather-wrapped steering wheel (GT only); cloth front sport bucket seats (GT coupe/convertible); speed control and 17-inch painted aluminum wheels (GT only). These options could be added to the Deluxe package: automatic transmission; anti-lock brake system with Traction Control (requires automatic on coupe; standard on GT); Sport Appearance Group (V-6 only); Mach 460 in-dash six-disc CD changer and AM/FM

radio; leather-trimmed front bucket seats (V-6 convertible only); and leather-trimmed front Sport bucket seats (GT convertible only).

Ordering the Premium Equipment Group gave the Mustang buyer an automatic transmission (optional on convertibles); 16-inch bright alloy wheels; P225/55R-16 all-season tires; Mach 460 in-dash six-disc CD changer and AM/FM radio; leather-wrapped steering wheel; anti-lock brake system with Traction Control; leather-trimmed front sport bucket seats (GT only); and 17-inch five-spoke premium alloy wheels (GT only). Leather-trimmed front buckets seats, standard on convertibles, could also be added optionally.

All models came standard with a rear window defroster, while the "smoker's package" and block heater became dealer-installed accessories. A new six-disc CD changer became optional with the Mach 460 sound system.

Never one to shy away from a limited-production "special" model, Ford brought to showrooms in 2001 a version of its 2000 Bullitt show car. Based on the 1968 fastback driven by Steve McQueen in the gritty detective drama Bullitt, the coupe-only model featured exterior enhancements that visually and emotionally connect it to the famous chase scene. Modifications to the Bullitt Mustang included unique side scoops, 17-inch American Racing aluminum wheels, a lowered suspension, modified C-pillars, and quarter panel molding that set the car apart from a stock GT. Rocker panel moldings enhanced the lowered appearance. A bold, brushed aluminum fuel filler door was prominently placed on the quarter panel. Special Bullitt badging and polished-rolled tailpipe tips further distinguished the car. The Bullitt Mustang was available in Dark Highland Green, True Blue, and Black.

Providing 270 hp was a mildly modified 4.6-liter, with a twin 57mm-bore throttle body, cast aluminum intake manifold, and high-flow mufflers. Re-valved Tokico struts and shocks, unique stabilizer bars (front and rear), frame rail connectors, and 13-inch Brembo front rotors and performance calipers made up a unique suspension for this special Mustang model. Each of the 5,000-plus cars came with a unique serialized ID label.

The Bullitt package listed for $3,695 above the cost of a GT for 2001. The Mustang base coupe for 2001 listed for $16,995; the base convertible, $22,410; the GT coupe, $22,630; and the GT convertible, $28,035.

DATA PLATE DECODING

A 17-character Vehicle Identification Number is stamped on an aluminum tab on the instrument panel, viewable through windshield. A vehicle certification label is found on the body side of where the driver's door closes.

VEHICLE WARRANTY NUMBER
MANUFACTURER ID

1FA – Ford Motor Co.

RESTRAINT SYSTEM

F – air bags, active belts

VEHICLE CLASSIFICATION

P – passenger car

BODY SERIAL NUMBERS

40 – coupe
42 – coupe, GT
44 – convertible
45 – convertible, GT
47 – coupe, Cobra
46 – convertible, Cobra

ENGINE CODE

4 – 232-cid (3.8-liter) EFI V-6
X – 281-cid (4.6-liter) EFI SOHC V-8
X – 281-cid (4.6-liter) EFI SOHC V-8 Bullitt
V – 281-cid (4.6-liter) EFI DOHC V-8 Cobra

CHECK DIGIT

for internal use

MODEL YEAR

1 – 2001

ASSEMBLY PLANT

F – Dearborn, Michigan

CONSECUTIVE UNIT NUMBER

Begins at 100001 at each factory

CODE NUMBERS
PAINT CODE

B7 – Zinc Yellow
ES – Performance Red
E9 – Laser Red
L2 – True Blue
PY – Bullitt Green
SU – Amazon Green
SW – Electric Green
TK – Mineral Gray
UA – Black
YN – Silver
Z1 – Oxford White

ENGINES

232-cid (3.8-liter) EFI V-6
Valves . . . . overhead
Block . . . . cast iron
Displacement. . . . . 232 cid/3.8 liters
Compression ratio 9.36:1
Bore and stroke. . . . . 3.80 x 3.40 inches
Brake hp . . . . 190 @ 5250 rpm
Main bearings 4
Valve lifters. . . . . hydraulic
Induction . . . . electronic fuel injection
Code 4

2001 MUSTANG PRODUCTION CHART

Model	Doors/Body/Seating	Factory Price	Shipping Weight	Prod. Total
40/100A	2/coupe/4	$16,995	3064	Note 1
40/110A	2/deluxe coupe/4	$17,560	3066	Note 1
44/150A	2/deluxe convertible/4	$22,410	3208	Note 1
40/120A	2/premium coupe/4	$18,790	3066	Note 1
44/160A	2/premium convertible/4	$24,975	3208	Note 1
42/130A	2/deluxe coupe GT/4	$22,630	3241	Note 1
45/170A	2/deluxe convertible GT/4	$26,885	3379	Note 1
42/140A	2/premium coupe GT/4	$23,780	3241	Note 1
45/180A	2/premium convertible GT/4	$28,035	3379	Note 1
42/135A	2/Bullitt coupe/4	$26,320	3241	Note 2

NOTE 1: Numbers were unavailable at the time of printing.
NOTE 2: Approximately 5,000 Bullitt coupes were planned for 2001.

281-cid (4.6-liter) EFI SOHC V-8

Valves . . . . overhead
Camshaft . . . . single overhead cam
Block . . . . cast iron
Displacement. . . . . 281 cid/4.6 liters
Compression ratio 9.0:1
Bore and stroke. . . . . 3.60 x 3.60 inches
Brake hp . . . . 260 @ 5250 rpm
Valve lifters . . . . hydraulic
Induction . . . . electronic fuel injection
Code X

281-cid (4.6-liter) EFI SOHC V-8 Bullitt

Valves . . . . overhead
Camshaft . . . . single overhead cam
Block . . . . cast iron
Displacement. . . . . 281 cid/4.6 liters
Compression ratio 9.0:1
Bore and stroke. . . . . 3.60 x 3.60 inches
Brake hp 270
Valve lifters . . . . hydraulic
Induction . . . . electronic fuel injection
Code X

281-cid (4.6-liter) EFI DOHC V-8 Cobra

Valves . . . . overhead
Camshaft . . . . double overhead cam
Block . . . . aluminum
Displacement. . . . . 281 cid/4.6 liters
Bore and stroke. . . . . 3.60 x 3.60 inches
Compression ratio 9.85:1
Brake hp . . . . 320 @ 6000
Valve lifters . . . . hydraulic
Induction . . . . electronic fuel injection
Code V

CHASSIS

Wheelbase . . . . 101.3 inches
Overall length . . . . 183.2 inches
Height . . . . (coupe) 53.1 inches
. . . . (convertible) 53.2 inches
Width. . . . . 73.1 inches
Front tread width. . . . . 60.2 inches
Rear tread width . . . . 60.6 inches

TECHNICAL

Steering . . . . rack and pinion, power assisted
Front suspension . . . .
modified MacPherson gas-pressurized shock struts with coil
springs and stabilizer bar
Rear suspension . . . .
. . . . . four-bar link and coil spring system, gas shocks
Brakes . . . . (front) disc
. . . . (rear) disc
Ignition . . . . electronic
Body construction . . . unibody w/front isolated mini-frame
Fuel tank. . . . . 15.7 gallons

OPTION LIST

Four-speed automatic overdrive transmission (not available
on Bullitt or Cobra). $815
Anti-lock braking system, includes traction control
. . . (standard on base premium, GT and Cobra models)
$730
Traction control system $230
Convenience Group including front floor mats, rear window
defroster, speed control and power driver's seat . . (standard all models except standard V-6 coupe) $550
V6 Sport Appearance Group includes 15-inch cast aluminum wheels, rear spoiler, leather-wrapped steering
wheel, lower bodyside accent stripe
. . . . (base model only) $250
Engine block heater. $20
Bullitt Package includes 270-hp 4.6-liter V-8, unique stabilizer bars, unique performance brake calipers, unique
side scoops, unique rocker moldings, unique C-pillar and
glass, brushed aluminum fuel filler door, "Bullitt" badging, unique leather-surfaced seat trim, unique "Heritage"
instrument cluster, unique brushed aluminum accents,
underhood clearcoat paint (UA Black or PY Green),
charcoal interior and serialized special edition identification . . . . (available Bullitt coupe only) $3,695
Dual illuminated visor mirrors
. . . . (standard on convertible) $95
Mach 460 AM/FM stereo radio w/cassette and in-dash
6-disc CD changer . . . . . . (standard on base premium,
GT premium, Bullitt and Cobra) $550
Rear spoiler
. (standard on base deluxe coupe, basepremium GT) $195
California emission system . . . . no charge
Leather bucket seats . . . . . (base premium coupe and base
deluxe convertible only) $500
17-inch aluminum wheels w/P245/45ZR-17 BSW Tires
. . . . (GT only) $500

2001 GT convertible

2001 GT side vent

2001 GT badge

2001 GT hood scoop

2001 GT wheel

2001 GT convertible interior

2001 X-code 4.6-liter/EFI SOHC V-8

2001 Bullitt coupe (FMC)

2001 Bullitt gauges (FMC)

2001 Bullitt fuel filler door (FMC)

2001 Bullitt shifter (FMC)

2001 coupe (FMC)

2001 coupe (FMC)

**1965 Shelby GT-350
Owner: Lee Mathias**

1965 Shelby

Carroll Shelby and his high-performance Cobras and Mustangs cut a wide path through the automotive world of the 1960s. His GT-350s and GT-500s probably did more for the sporty image of Ford's Mustang than did all the clever advertising campaigns combined. His cars are more valuable today than they were in the 1965-67 period, when the tiny Shelby American company was still in operation at 6501 West Imperial Highway, behind Los Angeles International Airport. Why the cars should be more in demand now makes an interesting story; one outdone only by the highlights of the cars themselves. In short, it was quite a ride for the Texas chicken farmer who had to retire from racing due to a bad heart after winning the 1959 LeMans!

After running into the "not invented here" syndrome at Chevrolet, Shelby convinced Ford in 1962 to work with him on a limited-production run of cars that would combine the company's 260-cid V-8 with a lightweight British roadster chassis and body. Henry Ford II's eagerness to create a stable of world class racecars and stand on the same European podiums as Enzo Ferrari's drivers made the project an easy sell for the smooth-talking Texan.

Shelby introduced the first roadster prototype at the 1962 New York Auto Show billed as the "260" Cobra (the snake part of the name having appeared to Shelby in a dream, legend has it). Subsequent versions were the fast "289" and the fantastically fast "427" types. Although only about 1,000 Cobras were made up through the mid-1960s, they were so startling that

even now, nearly 40 years later, the Cobra name universally translates as "ultimate, unparalleled performance!"

In 1964 Shelby's Cobras came within six points of catching Ferrari for the World GT Championship, so it was not surprising that the California-based modifier was tapped to breathe some life into Ford's new Mustang. What Shelby put together was a pony that could strike like a snake.

Shelby American began production of the GT-350 (a name created when Shelby asked how many feet were between the main assembly line and the engine room) in December of 1964. By arrangement with Ford, Shelby received an allotment of Wimbledon White fastbacks directly from the San Jose, California, factory with black interiors and the 289-cid/271-horsepower K-code V-8. The first batch was 110 units because that was more than the 100 Shelby needed to get his cars approved for production by the Sports Car Club of America (SCCA).

Running the first year's production of GT-350s all in white was done more for practicality than for the sake of style. In order to operate as efficiently as possible, it was decided to stick to one color so the Ford and Shelby assembly lines could be better coordinated; white was the obvious color choice since it was assumed that many GT-350s would find their way to racetracks and be painted to suit the owner's taste.

One of the legendary stories concerning Shelby and his Mustangs tells that the company was fast approaching the

Jan. 1, 1965, deadline to get SCCA's approval of the minimum 100 cars. Never one to shy away from a challenge, Shelby took the 110 stock white Mustang fastbacks that were waiting to be converted to GT-350s and parked them in his ready-to-ship lot when the sanctioning body inspectors visited.

Converting the cars to GT-350s followed an ancient racing formula: remove anything from the car that didn't directly make it faster. This meant that many stock Mustang parts were either deleted at the Ford factory or pulled at Shelby American, including hoods, rear seats, exhaust systems, and the decorative grille bars.

While Shelby American was run with the precision and resourcefulness of a race team, many factors, including budget considerations, supplier issues, and time constraints made for "running changes" throughout the Shelby-Mustang's life. For example, the 16-inch wood-rimmed, three-spoke steering wheel on early Shelbys was found to rub against some drivers' thighs and was replaced by a 15-inch unit. Once that change was in place, Shelby's English supplier for the steering wheel (the same craftsmen who produced similar pieces for the Cobra) began randomly changing little style elements from batch to batch. Such running changes were almost never recorded and mattered little to the crew on the production line.

GT-350 suspension modifications included a thicker front sway bar, longer idler and Pitman arms, lowered upper control arms, over-ride traction bars, and Koni adjustable shock absorbers. Heavy-duty brake pads were added to the stock Mustang system.

Shelby modified the stock K-code V-8 engine with a "Cobra" aluminum high-rise intake manifold, 715-cfm Holley four-barrel carburetor, "Cobra" cast aluminum finned valve covers, a "Cobra" finned cast aluminum 6.5-quart oil pan, steel tubing "Tri-Y" exhaust headers, low-restriction mufflers, and dual side-exit exhaust pipes. Shelby advertised that his modifications resulted in 306 horsepower.

It was necessary to shore up the engine compartment with a "Monte Carlo" bar because of the engine's extra power. This device was simply a strong piece of steel that ran between the two shock towers to prevent torque twisting of the chassis under hard acceleration or cornering. Another change to the engine compartment on early GT-350s was the re-location of the battery to the trunk for better weight distribution, although customer complaints after 300 or so cars killed that modification.

Other mechanical hard parts included a heavy-duty shortened Galaxie rear end with a Detroit Automotive no-spin gear unit and an aluminum-cased Borg-Warner T-10 four-speed transmission. Befitting such a single-purpose vehicle, stock wheels were stamped steel 15 x 5 1/2-inch production pieces from Ford's big station wagons, painted silver and minus any type of hubcap. Because they looked so utilitarian, most buyers opted for the Cragar and American Racing optional rims produced to Shelby's specifications. Shelby, a Goodyear tire distributor, chose high-performance Goodyear Blue Dots to give the GT-350 the best street rubber available.

All GT-350s had fiberglass hoods, although several different versions were produced during the 1965-66 run as attempts were made to solve a problem with cracking. Initial hoods

1965 K-code 289-cid/4V V-8

1965 Shelby wood-rimmed steering wheel

1965 Shelby underhood identification plate

1965 Shelby optional wheel

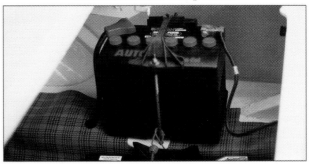

1965 Shelby relocated battery

were made entirely of fiberglass; later versions had metal framing. The hood latch mechanism was deleted and NASCAR-style pins were installed to lock everything down. A low-profile, but functional, scoop drew outside air into the air cleaner.

A fiberglass shelf sat where the stock Mustang rear seat would be, with the spare tire taking up the bulk of the useable room. This was done partly to qualify the car as a "sports car" in the SCCA racing series; it also helped reduce weight.

Each GT-350 received a tri-bar Guardsman Blue paint stripe along the rocker panel and door bottom. The stripes broke only for a "G.T. 350" logo rendered in 3M tape. Customers could also request twin, 10-inch-wide blue racing "LeMans" stripes—a popular option that ran from front to rear over the top of the car and was most often added by the dealership.

Part of the legend that intrigues collectors so is the Shelby-specific vehicle identification number for 1965 that was placed on a small plaque over the Ford VIN on the driver's side fender. The information breakdown initially told the owner that he or she had purchased a Shelby (S) Ford (F) Mustang (M) produced in 1965 (5), and that it was the 32nd (032) one to be converted that year. Even this system experienced changes during the production year when Shelby realized that there should be a way to differentiate between the street and race-prepared models. As of car number 032, an "S" or "R" appeared before the three-digit serial number, depending on whether the car was a street or race model. Cars already shipped were left with the old numbering system, although 001, 002 and 003 were retrofitted as they still belonged to Shelby American.

According to accounts from 1965, the GT-350 was the most brutal car ever built for the general public. Like a race-car, it was beastly fast and required a heavy foot and strong arms to drive it to its potential. Unlike a racecar, it could be purchased at Ford dealerships and came with a full warranty.

In all, only 526 GT-350s were sold in 1965 for an advertised base price of $4,547. Another 36 were special competition-only packages known as R-models that sold for $5,995 and produced between 325 and 350 horsepower.

SHELBY VIN DECODING

The Ford Vehicle Identification Number for 1965 is stamped on the top upper flange of the right and left front fender apron, not visible with the hood open. Shelby-specific VINs were located on a plate affixed directly over the Ford number. The numbers were also stamped onto the passenger-side inner fender panel in a location halfway between the firewall and radiator.

MANUFACTURER/MODEL

SFM – Shelby Ford Mustang

MODEL YEAR

5 – 1965

PURPOSE

S – street
R – race

CONSECUTIVE UNIT NUMBER

001 to 562

ENGINE

289-cid 4-bbl. High-Performance V-8

Valves . . . . overhead
Block . . . . cast iron
Displacement . . . . 289 cid
Bore and stroke. . . . . 4.00 x 2.87 inches
Compression ratio 10.5:1
Brake hp 306
Main bearings 5
Valve lifters . . . . solid
Carburetor. . . . . Holley 4-barrel 3259
Code . . . . K

OPTIONS LIST

Cragar wheels
LeMans stripes
Axle ratios (3.89:1 standard)

1965 SHELBY MUSTANG PRODUCTION CHART

Model	Doors/Body/Seating	Factory Price	Prod. Total
GT-350	2/fastback/2	$4547	526
GT-350R	2/fastback/2	$5995	36

NOTE 1: Total model year output was 562 units. This figure includes 521 GT-350s, 34 GT-350Rs, 4 drag racing versions (with street serial numbers), 2 R-model prototypes and 1 GT-350 prototype.

1965 Shelby deleted back seat

1965 Shelby racing mirror

**1966 Shelby GT-350
Owner: Earl Morris**

1966 Shelby

At the beginning of its second year, the GT-350 experienced several running changes thanks to a quirk of the mass production process. Ford Motor Company shut down every July for the annual new model changeover but Shelby American built cars year round based on the San Jose plant's output. Before the shutdown Carroll Shelby took delivery of 252 1965 fastbacks to be converted into 1966 models.

These last 1965s were immediately worked into the conversion process. Much of the first year's equipment was intended to carry over into 1966, but there were a few changes such as a plexiglass insert in place of the Mustang's rear air vents and a functional rear brake air scoop mounted just rearward of the door. The only thing the cars would have to wait for to be shipped was the redesigned 1966 stock Mustang grille—the only stock part that would change on the Shelby.

Early in this production cycle, executives and efficiency experts visited the plant to make changes to Shelby's car-building process. Some costly and time-consuming procedures performed on the 1965 GT-350 were the subject of customer and dealer complaints, such as the expensive, but clunky Detroit Locker rear axle and the super-stiff competition suspension.

Dealers wanted sporty, but comfortable, cars that could seat four people and be serviced by a regular Ford technician. In other words, they wanted a Mustang that was just a little bit faster than the factory's own GT option. They wanted more colors, an automatic transmission and a back seat, for starters. Dealers also requested a less-expensive conversion

as a stripped Mustang listing for nearly $1,000 more than a loaded Galaxie turned off many potential customers.

Proof that Shelby anticipated some of the requests in his plans for the 1966 GT-350 was the noisy Detroit Locker that was already listed as an option in 1966 literature. The 252 carryover cars were already in the process of having their A-arms lowered, but most GT-350s afterwards would retain stock factory geometry. Those race-ready traction over-ride bars were replaced by cheaper units that were easier to install. The Koni adjustable shocks were gradually phased out, as was the fiberglass shelf that had replaced the back seat on 1965 Shelbys. The expensive imported real-wood steering wheels were replaced with stock Mustang GT units wearing special GT-350 logos and the previous year's Guardsman Blue side stripes were now entirely a 3M tape product.

Once the GT-350 package was redesigned, the car actually retailed for less than the previous year's model at $4,428. It was also a more comfortable and customer-friendly package, with other amenities including Candy Apple Red, Sapphire Blue, Ivy Green, Wimbledon White and Raven Black paint; a C-4 high-performance automatic transmission option (a 595-cfm carburetor was specified when the automatic was ordered); and an AM radio that became a factory-installed option halfway through the year.

The most exciting option came toward the end of the model year when Shelby offered a Paxton supercharger for

$670, including factory installation. Shelby American claimed the option would produce up to 46% more horsepower from the 289-cid V-8. Apparently, Shelby wasn't too sure how much abuse the blowers could take from his customers because the warranty was only for 90 days or 4,000 miles. Only 11 GT-350s were ordered with this high-performance option.

Total GT-350 production for '66 was 2,378 cars—quite an increase over the previous year's sales numbers. Sales to the Hertz Sports Car Club accounted for nearly 40 percent of the 1966 run. A special run of 1001 GT-350H fastbacks was put into service as rental cars—mostly in black-with-gold paint schemes, but later in all 1966 Shelby colors. Early H-models were part of the 1965 carryover line and included all of the heavy-duty suspension modifications. Hertz later asked that all of its GT-350s come with automatic transmissions and a brake booster for the stiff competition-style brakes.

Receiving the Hertz order was probably the pivotal point in Shelby production. Guaranteeing nearly 1,000 cars (the original pitch to Hertz executives was for 100 units) put Shelby American in a better position to bargain with its suppliers. The sale also meant that the average traveler could be exposed to the GT-350, a point that no doubt increased non-Hertz sales for 1966 and later. Featuring the GT-350 in all of Hertz' national advertising didn't hurt, either.

SHELBY VIN DECODING

The Ford Vehicle Identification Number for 1966 is stamped on the top upper flange of the right and left front fender apron, not visible with the hood open. Shelby-specific VINs were located on a plate affixed directly over the Ford number. The numbers were also stamped onto the passenger-side inner fender panel in a location halfway between the firewall and radiator.

MANUFACTURER/MODEL

SFM – Shelby Ford Mustang

MODEL YEAR

6 – 1966

PURPOSE

S – street

CONSECUTIVE UNIT NUMBER

0001 to 2378

ENGINE

289-cid 4-bbl. High-Performance V-8

Valves . . . . overhead
Block . . . . cast iron
Displacement . . . . 289 cid
Bore and stroke . . . . 4.00 x 2.87 inches
Compression ratio 10.5:1
Brake hp 306
Main bearings 5
Valve lifters . . . . solid
Carburetor . . . (automatic transmission cars) Ford 4-barrel
. . . . (standard transmission cars) Holley 4-barrel
Code . . . . K

OPTIONS LIST

Paxton supercharger
LeMans stripes
15-inch Cragar five-spoke wheels
14-inch aluminum 10-spoke wheels
Detroit No-Spin rear axle
Rear axle ratio (3.89:1 standard)
Koni adjustable shocks (standard on early cars – dealer-installed later)
LeMans stripes
AM radio
Rear seat
Automatic transmission (Ford C-4, no charge)

1966 SHELBY MUSTANG PRODUCTION CHART			
Model	Doors/Body/Seating	Factory Price	Prod. Total
GT-350	2/fastback/4	$4428	2374
GT-350	2/convertible/4	N/A	4

NOTE 1: Total model year output was 2,378 units. This figure includes 1,369 GT-350s, 1,001 Hertz models, 4 convertibles, and 4 drag racing versions.

1966 Shelby 9000-rpm tachometer

1966 Shelby wheel

1967 Shelby GT-350
Owner: Glenda Yoder

1967 Shelby

If the GT-350's second year could be described as a step away from the original, hardcore sports car Shelby introduced in 1965, then the third year would be considered a giant leap away. For 1967, the GT-350 took on an appearance that distanced it from the stock Mustang; thereby fixing one complaint Shelby dealers had been repeating about the first-generation cars. Paradoxically, the Shelby Mustangs became mechanically more similar to their garden-variety cousins. Shelby dealers were happy with this change in direction because it created a visually exciting product to sell that had as much creature comfort as a basic Mustang, but without the need for specialized maintenance equipment and training.

Owing to the base Mustang's redesign for 1967, Shelby American created an entirely new appearance package that cleverly made the fastbacks look longer and lower than stock Mustangs by the tasteful use of more fiberglass than in previous years.

A fiberglass hood, wearing twin scoops and racing-style lock-down pins, reached farther than the Mustang's all-steel piece and gave the grille the appearance of a dark, menacing mouth. The grille housed the Shelby's two round high-beam headlights placed side-by-side in the middle. This style was not appreciated by some states' departments of motor vehicles and the lights were separated on later cars. The Mustang front bumper, minus the vertical bumperettes, looked like it was made for the Shelby. In front of each rear wheelwell were fiberglass, forward-facing scoops that channeled air into the rear brakes if the car was built on a day that Shelby's suppliers were keeping ducts in inventory. Stock Mustang rear vents were covered with a rear-facing scoop that helped draw air out of the passenger compartment. (Early 1967 cars had a red running light installed in this scoop, but the accessory was dropped later due to legal concerns.) A three-piece spoiler was applied to the rear of all 1967 Shelby-Mustangs and accented by the extra-wide taillights mounted in a flat panel.

Mustang's Deluxe Interior was the only choice for the more luxurious 1967 Shelbys, available in Black, White or Parchment. A sporty, two- or four-point rollbar was installed into every car. The bar was a mounting point for jet fighter-style inertia reel shoulder harnesses; the GT-350 marking the first time a production car came standard with a rollbar or such high-tech seatbelts. All Shelbys received a unique wood-rimmed steering wheel with GT-350 or GT-500 plastic horn buttons. Fold-down rear seats, once an option, were made standard equipment in 1967. Stewart-Warner gauges measuring oil pressure and amps were housed in a metal bezel under the middle of the dashboard. The Mustang's optional 8000-rpm tach sat next to a 140-mph speedometer.

Shelbys came standard that year with power steering and power-assisted brakes. Suspension enhancements were largely stock Mustang, including the special handling package, front disc brakes, thicker front stabilizer bar, export brace and adjustable Gabriel shock absorbers. Stock wheels were 15-inch stamped steel units with 1967 Thunderbird hubcaps (their identity changed with Shelby center caps); various sporty rims from Kelsey-Hayes were optional.

Shelby continued to use the 289-cid Ford K-code engine, with very few changes to the hot rodding formula. The tubular exhaust headers were dropped at the beginning of the year for Ford's high-performance cast-iron manifold, yet the factory continued to claim an output of 306 horsepower. Paxton's powerful supercharger remained on the option list, as did SelectAire air conditioning and the high-performance C-4 automatic transmission. For the second straight year, GT-350 prices decreased, perhaps explaining how Shelby dealers were able to part with 1,175 units for $3,995 apiece.

With the new looks came a new family member, in the form of the GT-500. While Ford started selling its 390-cid big-block V-8 in a Mustang in 1967, Shelby went one better by installing the 428-cid big-block V-8 in his top-line offering and the massive powerplant produced at least 50 more horsepower than the 390.

This "Police Interceptor" engine featured hydraulic lifters and an aluminum, medium-rise intake manifold wearing a pair of 600-cfm four-barrel Holley carburetors. Ford's four-speed "toploader" transmission was standard with the 1967s, with the stout "police spec" C-6 handling automatic shifting duties. The GT-500, available only in fastback form like the GT-350, retailed for $4,195 and sold 2,050 units.

SHELBY VIN DECODING

The Ford Vehicle Identification Number for 1967 is stamped on the top upper flange of the right and left front fender apron and is not visible with the hood open. Shelby-specific VINs were located on a plate affixed directly over the Ford number. The numbers were also stamped onto the passenger-side inner fender panel in a location halfway between the firewall and radiator.

MODEL YEAR

67 – 1967

ENGINE

2 – 289-cid 4-bbl. V-8
4 – 428-cid 4-bbl. V-8

TRANSMISSION

0 – four-speed
1 – automatic

VEHICLE COMPONENT

0 – base vehicle
1 – Ford air conditioning
2 – Thermactor exhaust emission
3 – air conditioning and Thermactor exhaust emission

BODY

F – fastback

EXTERIOR COLOR CODE

1 – Bronze	7 – Lime Green
2 – Dark Blue	8 – Brittany Blue
3 – Raven Black	9 – Red
4 – Wimbledon White	0 – Medium/Acapulco Blue
5 – Dark Moss Green	S – Yellow
6 – Medium Gray	

INTERIOR TRIM

A – Black
U – Parchment
White (no special Shelby code)

CONSECUTIVE UNIT NUMBER

00001 to 03225

ENGINES

289-cid 4-bbl. High-Performance V-8

Valves	overhead
Block	cast iron
Displacement	289 cid
Bore and stroke	4.00 x 2.87 inches
Compression ratio	10.5:1
Brake hp	306
Main bearings	5
Valve lifters	solid
Carburetor	Holley 4-barrel
Code	(Shelby/Ford) 2/K

428-cid 4-bbl. Police Interceptor V-8

Valves	overhead
Block	cast iron
Displacement	428 cid
Bore and stroke	4.13 x 3.98 inches
Compression ratio	10.7:1
Brake hp	355
Main bearings	5
Valve lifters	hydraulic
Carburetor	twin Holley 4-barrels
Code	(Shelby/Ford) 4/Q

OPTIONS LIST

Paxton supercharger (GT-350 only)
15 x 7-inch Kelsey-Hayes MagStar wheels
15 x 7-inch 10-spoke aluminum wheels
AM radio
Folding rear seat
Air conditioning
Tinted glass (mandatory when ordering air conditioning)
Automatic transmission (Ford C-4 on GT-350; Ford C-6 on GT-500)

1967 SHELBY MUSTANG PRODUCTION CHART			
Model	Doors/Body/Seating	Factory Price	Prod. Total
GT-350	2/fastback/4	$3995	1175
GT-500	2/fastback/4	$4195	2048

NOTE 1: Total model year output was 3,225 units. This figure includes 2,048 GT-500s, 1,175 GT-350s plus two GT-500 prototypes (a notchback and a convertible).

1968 Shelby GT-350 convertible with Paxton supercharger Owner: Don Perry

1968 Shelby

Although most customers never realized it, Shelby production was relocated halfway across the country before the beginning of the 1968 model year. The decision had been made for two primary reasons: quality fiberglass could not be found in quantity near Southern California; and Shelby American was losing its lease on the airport buildings.

Since GT-350s and GT-500s were being built with an increasing number of fiberglass components, locating a supplier in Canada that could keep up with a 5,000-unit annual pace made for an easy decision to move production to Michigan. The A.O. Smith Co., in Ionia, manufactured all 1968 Shelbys from Mustang fastbacks and convertibles assembled at Ford's Metuchen, New Jersey, plant. A.O. Smith had experience with large-volume conversions and had dealt extensively with fiberglass.

At the same time, the company that had been Shelby American was broken into three different concerns: Shelby Automotive Inc. built and sold the cars; the Shelby Racing Co. worked on competition projects for Ford and others out of a building in Torrance, California; and the Shelby Parts Co. handled aftermarket parts and accessories from the same Torrance facility. Later, the parts arm was relocated to Michigan under the operating name Shelby Autosports.

Shelby's GT-350s and GT-500s received some cosmetic changes, even though the base Mustang had not changed very much from the previous year. The most obvious upgrade for 1968 was the hood, which now featured twin

scoops running almost to the leading edge of the car. Unlike on early cars, the stock Mustang hood lock mechanism was retained, although external turn-knob fasteners were provided for more safety. An even larger "mouth" was created by way of an all-new fiberglass front valance panel. That mouth housed twin rectangular Marchal driving lights (later replaced with Lucas units after legal problems). The Marchals marked the first time an American production car came equipped with auxiliary driving lights from the factory. Wide, sequential taillights from the 1965 Thunderbird just about stretched the width of the car's rear panel.

Because Shelby's Cobra roadsters ceased production the year before, badges depicting the coiled serpent were used liberally throughout the 1968 GT-350 and GT-500 body and interior. Strangely, some cars had Ford's tilt-away steering column, but it was not possible to specifically order the option; you either received it or you didn't. Cars ordered with air conditioning received tinted glass, as this was the only way Ford would build them. All Shelbys were again equipped with the Mustang's Deluxe Interior and a padded armrest that did double duty as the lid for the console storage.

New under the hood for 1968 was Ford's 302-cid V-8 (another growth spurt for the 260/289 block), rated in Shelby trim at 250 hp—down 56 from the previous model. Early production cars breathed through a 600-cfm Autolite carburetor sitting on a cast-iron intake manifold; an aluminum Cobra intake went into the mix once certification was complete.

With a slight power boost over the 1967 model, the GT-500 got a 428-cid 360-hp version of Ford's Police Interceptor package (although a few 390-cid V-8s were installed when the 428 ran short). The 428 had a single 735-cfm Holley four-barrel carburetor, and it (and the GT-350) had air cleaners sporting two screw-down wingnuts suggesting there were still two carburetors hiding under there. The GT-500 received a special oil cooler.

Since the GT-series cars were now being built for comfort, luxury, and style rather than all-out performance, Shelby introduced one of its most popular options for 1968—a convertible. On top of the padded rollbar were two small rectangular rings that legend says was for the mounting of surfboards. One-third of all Shelby conversions for 1968 were performed on convertibles.

Although racetracks were no longer the intended habitat of Shelby's wildlife, horsepower proliferation was still very much evident when Shelby introduced a midyear model known as the GT-500KR as a replacement for the standard GT-500. The KR ("King of the Road" some books claim) managed to stuff Ford's new (unofficially rated) 400-hp 428 Cobra Jet between the fenders. To support such a powerful engine, extra bracing on the lower edge of the shock towers and staggered rear shocks were installed when the KR was equipped with a four-speed transmission. Wider rear brake shoes and drums, heavy-duty wheel cylinders and brake line fittings were installed for the sake of safety, as was a freer-flowing exhaust system. As with the standard GT-500, the KR was available in either fastback or convertible body style.

The Mustang's heavy-duty suspension did well for the Shelbys, although special coil and leaf springs were used that increased stiffness with compression. Gabriel adjustable shocks and a thicker front sway bar gave the GTs increased handling without sacrificing comfort.

At the end of Shelby's best-ever year, the company produced 4,451 cars. The breakdown included 1,027 GT-350 fastbacks (suggested retail $4,116), 404 GT-350 convertibles ($4,238), 1,046 GT-500 fastbacks ($4,317), 402 GT-500 convertibles ($4,438), 1,053 GT-500KR fastbacks ($4,472), 518 GT-500KR convertibles ($4,594) and 1 notchback prototype GT-500.

SHELBY VIN DECODING

The Ford Vehicle Identification Number for 1968 is stamped on the top upper flange of the right and left front fender apron, not visible with the hood open. It is also stamped on a plate riveted to the top of the dashboard on the passenger's side and on the warranty plate riveted into the driver's door. See Ford Mustang entries in this book for year-by-year breakdown of data plate. The Shelby-specific VIN is located on a plate affixed directly over the Ford number.

MODEL YEAR

8 – 1968

ASSEMBLY PLANT

T – Metuchen, New Jersey

1968 Shelby GT-350 interior

1968 Shelby GT-350 wheel

1968 Shelby GT-500KR scoops

1968 Shelby GT-500KR

BODY SERIAL NUMBERS

02 – fastback
03 – convertible

ENGINE CODE

J – 302-cid 4-bbl. V-8
S – 428-cid 4-bbl. Police Interceptor V-8
R – 428-cid 4-bbl. Cobra Jet V-8

CONSECUTIVE UNIT NUMBER

000001 (Ford number)
00001 (Shelby number, followed Ford number on VIN)

EXTERIOR COLOR CODE

A – Raven Black
D – Medium Blue
I – Lime Green
M – Wimbledon White
R – Dark Green
T – Candyapple Red
Y – Gold Metallic
Yellow (no color code on warranty tag)

INTERIOR TRIM

5AA – black ComfortWeave
6AA – Black vinyl
6FA – Saddle vinyl

ENGINES

302-cid 4-bbl. V-8

Valves . . . . overhead
Block . . . . cast iron
Displacement . . . . 302 cid
Bore and stroke . . . . 4.00 x 3.00 inches
Compression ratio 10.5:1
Brake hp 250
Main bearings 5
Valve lifters . . . . hydraulic
Carburetor . . . . Holley 4-bbl.
Code . . . . J

428-cid 4-bbl. Police Interceptor V-8

Valves . . . . overhead
Block . . . . cast iron
Displacement . . . . 428 cid
Bore and stroke . . . . 4.13 x 3.98 inches
Compression ratio 10.5:1
Brake hp 360
Main bearings 5
Valve lifters . . . . hydraulic

Carburetor . . . . Holley 4-barrel
Code . . . . S

428-cid 4-bbl. Cobra Jet V-8

Valves . . . . overhead
Block . . . . cast iron
Displacement . . . . 428 cid
Bore and stroke . . . . 4.13 x 3.98 inches
Compression ratio 10.6:1
Brake hp 335
Main bearings 5
Valve lifters . . . . hydraulic
Carburetor . . . . Holley 4-bbl.
Code . . . . R

OPTIONS LIST

427-cid V-8
15 x 7-inch 10-spoke aluminum wheels
Ram-Air hood (standard GT-500KR)
Traction-Lok rear axle (standard GT-500KR)
AM radio
AM/FM radio
AM radio w/8-track player
Automatic transmission (Ford C-4 on GT-350; Ford C-6 on GT-500)
Tilt-away steering wheel
Shelby performance and dress-up accessories

1968 R-code 428-cid/4V V-8

1968 SHELBY MUSTANG PRODUCTION CHART

Model	Doors/Body/Seating	Factory Price	Prod. Total
GT-350	2/fastback/4	$4116	1227
GT-350	2/convertible/4	$4238	404
GT-500	2/fastback/4	$4317	1046
GT-500	2/convertible/4	$4438	402
GT-500KR	2/fastback/4	$4472	1053
GT-500KR	2/convertible/4	$4594	518
GT-500	notchback prototype		1

NOTE 1: Total model year output was 4,451 units.

**1970 Shelby GT-500 convertible
Owner: Richard and Scott Wert**

1969-70 Shelby

For better or worse, the stylish, third-generation Shelby Mustang had gone full circle in relation to the stock Ford product. In 1965, the GT-350 looked exactly like a Mustang, but underneath beat the hot rod heart of a racecar; in 1969, the GT-350 didn't even resemble the stock pony car in silhouette, but its mechanical DNA was pure Mustang.

The 1969 Shelby's cosmetic camouflage act was accomplished through the extensive use of fiberglass—chosen for its lightweight nature and the cheapness with which whole body panels could be designed and produced. Fiberglass fenders, hood, and rear cap allowed Shelby designers to stretch the GT-350 another three inches past the already-elongated 1969 Mustangs.

The hood was festooned with a total of five recessed NASA-type hood scoops, while the leading edge of the hood was trimmed with a chrome strip that curved around and down at the outer edges to meet the unique-to-Shelby front bumper. A chrome strip formed a wide rectangle inside the car's "mouth" as it ran around the outside of the flat black grille. Just like in late 1968, Lucas driving lights were chosen to add a degree of nighttime safety and were attached to the underside of the bumper.

Traditional Shelby side stripes were larger and now sat in the middle of the body, where they ran the entire length of the car. Rear brakes were once again cooled through an air scoop mounted on the body just ahead of the wheelwell; on

convertibles it was in line with the body stripe, on fastbacks it sat just behind the door handle.

A set of 1965 Thunderbird sequential taillights—the same units used on the 1968 GT-350s and GT-500s—further removed the cars from their Mustang roots. Directly between the two taillight lenses sat a spring-mounted frame that displayed the license plate and concealed the fuel filler cap. A pair of rectangular exhaust tips, separated from the fuel filler only by the width of the rear bumper, were part of a fire-hazard recall later in the year.

Paint colors for 1969 offered the greatest choice in Shelby history, with all of Ford's "Grabber" hues available. Bright Blue, Green, Yellow, Orange and Competition Orange were added early in the year to Black Jade, Acapulco Blue, Gulfstream Aqua, Pastel Gray, Candy Apple Red and Royal Maroon. Shelby interior colors for 1969 included Black, White and Red (less than 80 built in this color), with high-back bucket seats, vinyl-covered "Rim Blow" steering wheel and center console appearing as part of the deluxe Mustang equipment. Door panels and the dashboard contained many fake wood inserts.

Suspension work on the 1969 Shelbys was minimal and included the ordering of heavy-duty Mustang components from the Ford factory. In order to keep the rear axle from suffering during the occasional hard launch, staggered shocks were standard on the GT-500. No longer was the

1970 Shelby shifter

Shelby Mustang a car that would be ordered with anything plain or uninspired; gone were the stamped steel wheels of earlier years. In their place was a five-spoke, 15x7-inch rim that mounted Goodyear belted E-70x15 wide oval tires (F-60x15 tires were optional). Some Shelbys wound up with Boss 302 "Magnum 500" wheels when a defect was discovered in the stock rim, forcing a recall.

Every GT-350 built in 1969 received Ford's new 351-cid 290-hp Windsor V-8 that breathed through a 470-cfm Autolite four-barrel carburetor and came standard attached to Ford's four-speed manual transmission. Optional gearboxes included a close-ratio four-speed and the FMX automatic.

No longer referred to by the "KR" suffix, the GT-500 retained the fire-breathing 428-cid Cobra Jet V-8 from the previous year. A close-ratio four-speed was standard, with the C-6 back as an optional automatic.

1970 Shelby wheel

Sales for 1969 were brisk, with 1,087 GT-350 fastbacks (retailing at $4,434), 194 GT-350 convertibles ($4,753), 1,534 GT-500 fastbacks ($4,709) and 335 GT-500 convertibles ($5,027) going to new owners.

In the fall of 1969 Carroll Shelby convinced Ford to end the Shelby GT program. Shelby could see that the American auto industry and federal government were tightening the screws on performance cars and

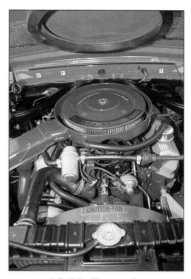
1970 R-code 428-cid/4V V-8

that there would soon be no market for the type of vehicles he wanted to produce. Also, Ford Motor Company was mass-producing cars that competed directly with the GT-350 and GT-500, such as the Mach 1, Boss 302, and Boss 429.

With several hundred Mustangs still in the pipeline, Shelby agreed to update 1969 leftovers into 1970 models with new vehicle identification numbers, a set of black hood stripes, a chin spoiler, and an emissions control unit required for that year. The hands-on work of converting from one year to the next was handled directly by the factory, under the watchful eyes of representatives from the Federal Bureau of Investigation. There is not an accurate count for how many 1970 Shelbys were created, although some reports say 789 units finished off the 1969 carryovers.

SHELBY VIN DECODING

The Ford Vehicle Identification Number for 1969-70 is stamped on the top upper flange of the right and left front fender apron, not visible with the hood open. It is also stamped on a plate riveted to the top of the dashboard on the driver's side and on the warranty plate on the driver's door. See Ford entries in this book for year-by-year breakdown of data plate.

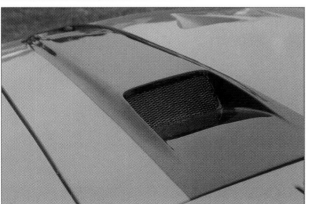
1970 Shelby hood scoop

1970 Shelby dual exhaust outlets

MODEL YEAR

9 – 1969
0 – 1970

ASSEMBLY PLANT

F – Dearborn, Michigan

BODY

02 – fastback
03 – convertible

ENGINE CODE

M – 351-cid 4-bbl. V-8
R – 428-cid 4-bbl. Cobra Jet V-8

SHELBY CODE

48 – only found on Shelby Mustangs

CONSECUTIVE UNIT NUMBER

0001 to 3295

EXTERIOR COLOR CODE

B – Royal Maroon
C – Black Jade
D – Acapulco Blue
F – Gulfstream Aqua
T – Candyapple Red
4 – Silver Jade
6 – Pastel Gray
_5 – Grabber Blue
_5 – Grabber Orange
_5 – Grabber Green
_5 – Shelby Yellow
MOR M5 – White

INTERIOR TRIM

3A – Black
3D – Red
3W - White

ENGINES

351-cid 4-bbl. V-8

Valves . . . . overhead
Block . . . . cast iron
Displacement . . . . 351 cid
Bore and stroke. . . . . 4.00 x 3.50 inches
Compression ratio 10.7:1

Brake hp 290
Main bearings 5
Valve lifters . . . . hydraulic
Carburetor . . . . Ford 4-bbl.
Code. . . . . M

428-cid 4-bbl.Cobra Jet V-8

Valves . . . . overhead
Block . . . . cast iron
Displacement . . . . 428 cid
Bore and stroke. . . . . 4.13 x 3.98 inches
Compression ratio 10.6:1
Brake hp 335
Main bearings 5
Valve lifters . . . . hydraulic
Carburetor. . . . . Holley 4-bbl.
Code . . . . R

OPTIONS LIST

Power ventilation
AM radio
AM/FM stereo
Stereo tape player (requires AM radio)
Folding rear seat (fastback models only)
Automatic transmission
Tilt-away steering wheel
Tinted glass
Drag package

Extra heavy-duty suspension package (includes F60 x 15 Goodyear tires)

**1969 GT-500 convertible
Owner: Steve Mason**

1969-70 SHELBY MUSTANG PRODUCTION CHART			
Model	Doors/Body/Seating	Factory Price	Prod. Total
GT-350	2/fastback/4	$4434	935
GT-350H	2/fastback/4	N/A	152
GT-350	2/convertible/4	$4753	194
GT-500	2/fastback/4	$4709	1534
GT-500	2/convertible/4	$5027	335
barrier test/pilot cars			3

NOTE 1: Total model years output was 3,153 units.
NOTE 2: Records indicate that 789 cars were sold as 1970 models. There is currently no accurate body style breakdown.

1984 Saleen #32 (Saleen)
Owner: Stu Akers

1984 Saleen

Due to rising insurance premiums, federal regulations, and environmental concerns, performance cars were all but extinct in the United States during most of the 1970s, with only the 139-hp King Cobra bringing any life to the Mustang party. American car companies were struggling to keep market share away from foreign companies such as Toyota, Datsun, and Volkswagen and adding a couple of gas crises to the technical hurdles facing the Big Three meant that no one placed high-performance at the top of the priority list. As Detroit poured money and resources into engine-management computer technologies, the industry was able to turn out a more stable product that was at once fuel-efficient and reliable, and tuning for performance was the next logical step.

Ford attempted to put some urgency into its pony cars by turbocharging the four-cylinder Mustang off and on between 1979 and 1986, but the car's high cost, relative lack of power when compared to the cheaper V-8, and reliability issues killed that program. It was the re-introduction of the 5.0-liter HO V-8 in the 1982 Mustang GT that put Ford (and its competition) back on the road to high-performance.

At the forefront of that movement was a young Californian whose last name would eventually hold a similar gravity among Mustang fans as the revered Carroll Shelby's had 15 years earlier. Steve Saleen, a business school graduate with a racing background in the Sports Car Club of America (SCCA) Formula Atlantic and Trans-Am series, was thrilled by Ford's first assault on the early 1980s horsepower war. Saleen (pronounced like the last two syllables of "gasoline") had owned '65 and '66 Shelby GT-350s and a '67 GT fastback with a 390-cid V-8, so he was personally quite aware of how Shelby's guiding hand had once turned a garden-variety Mustang into a world-class performance car.

Working within the confines of the federally regulated car industry, Saleen established a formula he would apply at least initially to all of his high-performance Mustangs. Rather than make a faster pony through engine modifications that would require expensive and extensive testing for emissions, fuel consumption, and warranty standards, Saleen elected to leave the engines bone stock and enhance performance by concentrating on suspension, brake, chassis, and aerodynamic improvements.

Saleen Autosport produced only three cars in 1984, each built from 175-hp Mustang hatchbacks. Saleen's own Racecraft suspension components, including specific-rate front and rear springs, Bilstein pressurized struts and shocks, a front G-load brace, and urethane swaybar bushings, lowered the car and improved the Mustang's handling to near racetrack levels. Those first three cars wore some of the largest high-performance rubber available at the time—Goodyear Eagle GTs measuring 215/60-15 wrapped around 15x7-inch Hayashi "basketweave" wheels. A custom front airdam, sideskirts, clear covers for the recessed headlights and a rather showy spoiler created a smoother aerodynamic package. The interior featured a Saleen-unique gauge package, Wolf Racing four-spoke steering wheel and Escort radar detector.

The rest of the standard equipment list included Saleen windshield graphic, decklid emblem, serial-numbered plaques, Ford Motorsport rear window graphic, tri-color racing stripes on the rocker panels, side window louvers, chrome air cleaner with Saleen graphic, 170-mph speedometer, Cal Custom Hawk leather-covered shift knob, Escort radar detector, and Cal Custom Hawk security system. The short options list included only a Sanyo AM/FM stereo cassette player with speakers. (Because these first three cars were essentially prototypes for what was to follow, it is interesting to note that the tri-color stripes were hand-painted on two of the cars and deleted altogether on the third. In 1985 and afterward, tape was used.)

For a sticker price of $14,300 ($4,526 more than a standard Mustang GT), the Saleen was quite reasonable when parked next to a comparably equipped Camaro Z-28 ($14,086), Pontiac Trans-Am ($15,100) or Toyota Supra ($16,853). Even Ford's own SVO Mustang was more expensive at $15,585.

Showing great faith that these would be the first of many cars to bear his name, Saleen took a lesson from the rabid Shelby Mustang culture and began assigning year-specific serial numbers to his Mustangs. Those first three cars were numbered 84-032, 84-051 and 84-052 because Saleen felt having higher numbers than 001, 002, and 003 would suggest a larger, more successful company and encourage orders. In succeeding years, Saleen's numbers would never begin with 001 and progress from there, which is why fans of the marque usually become very good detectives when ferreting out information about their particular cars.

Over the next few years, Saleen Mustangs evolved at a fast pace, with more or better equipment being worked into the recipe as it became available.

DATA PLATE DECODING

A 17-character Vehicle Identification Number is stamped on an aluminum tab on the instrument panel, viewable through windshield. A vehicle certification label is found on the body side of where the driver's door closes.

VEHICLE WARRANTY NUMBER
MANUFACTURER ID

1FA – Ford Motor Co.

RESTRAINT SYSTEM

B – active belts

VEHICLE CLASSIFICATION

P – passenger car

BODY SERIAL NUMBERS

28 – hatchback

ENGINE CODE

M – 302-cid (5.0-liter) 4-bbl. V-8 HO

CHECK DIGIT

for internal use

MODEL YEAR

E – 1984

ASSEMBLY PLANT

F – Dearborn, Michigan

CONSECUTIVE UNIT NUMBER

Begins at 100001 at each factory

CODE NUMBERS
BODY CODE

61B – hatchback

PAINT CODE

1C – Black
9C – Bright Copper Glow
9L – Oxford White

ENGINE

302-cid (5.0-liter) 4-bbl. V-8 HO

Block . . . . cast iron
Displacement. . . . . .302 cid/5.0 liters
Bore and stroke. . . . . 4.00 x 3.00 inches
Compression ratio 8.3:1
Brake hp . . . . 175 @ 4000 rpm
Carburetor. . . . . Holley 4-bbl.
Code . . . . M

SUSPENSION ENHANCEMENTS

Springs . . . . specific-rate front and rear coil
Shocks. . . . . Bilstein pressurized gas
Struts . . . . Bilstein pressurized
Bushings . . . . urethane swaybar pivot units, front and rear
Chassis reinforcements . . . . additional front crossmember
Wheels . . . . 15 x 7-inch Hayashi alloy
Tires . . . . 215/60HR-15 Goodyear Eagle GT

BODY ENHANCEMENTS

Rear spoiler
front airdam
side spats for rear
headlight covers

1984 SALEEN PRODUCTION CHART			
Body	Doors/Body/Seating	Price	Built
61B	3/hatchback/4	$14,300	3

1985 Saleen (Saleen)

1985 Saleen

Based on the new 210-hp Mustang, the 1985 Saleen featured larger 225/60-15 Goodyear and Fulda tires (brand depends on time of production year) and a slightly modified aerodynamics package. Metallic pads for the front brakes were standard on the $16,900 Saleen. Sales were definitely improved for the year, with 140 units going to new owners, including two in convertible form.

The Saleen conversion for 1985 cost $4,195 on top of the factory-ordered LX V-8 hatchback or convertible. Standard colors included Ford's Black, Canyon Red, Medium Regatta Blue, or Oxford White. Special-ordered paint cost an additional $150. Building the car on a Mustang GT was an additional $100.

Ford agreed to a bailment pooling arrangement with Saleen in 1985, meaning his cars could be sold through the company's established dealer network and were eligible for full warranty protection. Stock Mustangs were shipped from the Dearborn Ford factory directly to the Saleen conversion facility in California, then distributed to ordering dealers.

Participating dealers were advised to order cars intended for Saleen conversion in the following manner: with the M-code 5.0-liter V-8, 3.08:1 limited-slip axle, five-speed transmission, and 225/60VR-15 Goodyear Gatorbacks. Equipment not to be ordered for conversion included: lower two-tone paint treatment and cruise control.

Ford agreed to honor its full warranty on parts not altered or replaced by Saleen; Saleen established its own warranty system for the conversion equipment. Exterior fiberglass or plastic pieces, however, were only guaranteed as of delivery to the purchasing Ford dealership.

Because Saleen's production line was subjected to the same sort of component supply problems and customer demands Shelby had endured, running changes were common right from the start. Some 1985s were fitted with 16-inch wheels and German-made Fulda tires, and several early units were built using the blockier 1984 spoilers and dams. Cars converted early in the year were modified in a shop in Petaluma, California, whereas the remainder of 1985 production took place at the Burch Ford dealership at 201 North Harbor Boulevard in LaHabra.

DATA PLATE DECODING

A 17-character Vehicle Identification Number is stamped on an aluminum tab on the instrument panel, viewable through windshield. A vehicle certification label is found on the body side of where the driver's door closes.

VEHICLE WARRANTY NUMBER MANUFACTURER ID

1FA – Ford Motor Co.

RESTRAINT SYSTEM

B – active belts

VEHICLE CLASSIFICATION

P – passenger car

BODY SERIAL NUMBERS

27 – convertible
28 – hatchback

ENGINE CODE

M – 302-cid (5.0-liter) EFI V-8, automatic
M – 302-cid (5.0-liter) 4-bbl. V-8 HO, five-speed

CHECK DIGIT

for internal use

MODEL YEAR

F – 1985

ASSEMBLY PLANT

F – Dearborn, Michigan

CONSECUTIVE UNIT NUMBER

Begins at 100001 at each factory

CODE NUMBERS
BODY CODE

66B – convertible
61B – hatchback

PAINT CODE

1C – Black
2C – Canyon Red
3Y – Medium Regatta Blue
9L – Oxford White

ENGINES

302-cid (5.0-liter) EFI V-8,
automatic transmission models
Block . . . . cast iron
Displacement. 302 cid/5.0 liters
Bore and stroke. . . . . 4.00 x 3.00 inches
Compression ratio 8.3:1
Brake hp . . . . 165 @ 4200 rpm
Induction . . . . electronic fuel injection
Code. . . . . M

302-cid (5.0-liter) 4-bbl. V-8 HO,
manual transmission models
Block . . . . cast iron
Displacement. 302 cid/5.0 liters
Bore and stroke. . . . . 4.00 x 3.00 inches
Compression ratio 8.3:1
Brake hp . . . . 210 @ 4400 rpm
Carburetor. . . . . Holley 4-bbl.
Code. . . . . M

SUSPENSION ENHANCEMENTS

Springs . . . . specific-rate front and rear coil
Shocks. . . . . Bilstein pressurized gas
Struts . . . . Bilstein pressurized
Bushings . . . . urethane swaybar pivot units, front and rear
Chassis reinforcements . . . . additional front crossmember
Wheels . . . . 15 x 7-inch Hayashi alloy
Tires. . . . . 215/60HR-15 Goodyear Eagle GT

BODY ENHANCEMENTS

Rear spoiler
front airdam
side and rear skirts
headlight covers

OPTION LIST

Kenwood KRC 6000 AM/FM w/cassette. $559
Non-Saleen colors $150
GT conversions. . . . . (additional) $100

1985 SALEEN PRODUCTION CHART

Body	Doors/Body/Seating	Price	Built
61B	3/hatchback/4	$16,900	130
66B	2/convertible/4	$18,900	2

NOTE 1: Total output for 1985 was 140 units. The above figures do not reflect eight models listed with the compay as "unknown."
NOTE 2: Output included one competition model.

**1986 Saleen #72
Owner: Mark LaMaskin/
Performance Autosport**

1986 Saleen

The Mustang V-8 gained electronic fuel injection in 1986, and Saleen stepped up the standard equipment list for his custom-built versions. With Saleen Mustangs taking to the racetrack in Sports Car Club of America (SCCA) events, the cars saw high-performance improvements such as 16-inch wheels, a revised airdam and spoiler package, a short-throw Hurst shifter, three-spoke leather-covered Momo steering wheel, GT bucket seats, Koni adjustable gas rear shocks and a top-line Kenwood stereo system. A race-style "dead pedal" for the driver's left foot, such as what was offered in the SVO Mustang, became standard equipment in 1986.

Other standard equipment included 225/50VR-16 Fulda tires, specific rate front and rear coil springs, Saleen-specific strut mounting bearings, Koni quad shocks, urethane swaybar pivot bushings, Saleen aerodynamic kit (now built from urethane), Lexan headlight covers, 170-mph speedometer, leather-covered shift knob, Escort radar detector, articulated sport seats (with leather option) and a Saleen Mustang jacket.

The only option listed by the factory was a Kenwood KRC 6000 AM/FM cassette stereo system, although customers could make special requests such as automatic transmissions, sunroofs, and certain aftermarket performance enhancements. Running changes through the production year include many cars that were built without the Hurst shifter, a few shipped with 15-inch wheels and many wearing the 1985-spec aerodynamics package.

Exterior colors available were Black, Canyon Red, Medium Regatta Blue, and Oxford White. On red and white

cars the side louvers located just behind the triangular rear window were painted body color. The tri-color racing stripes were available in gold, silver or blue.

Participating Ford dealers were required to order cars for conversion with the following specs: LX hatchback or convertible, 5.0-liter V-8, five-speed manual transmission, 3.08:1 limited-slip axle, 225/60VR-15 tires, radio delete, articulated sport seats, GT dash panel, SVO driver's foot rest and pinstripe delete. Two-tone paint and cruise control were not to be ordered on cars receiving the Saleen treatment.

Magazine testers were impressed with the package's 6.0-second zero-to-60 mph time and top speed of 142 mph. Corvette-caliber handling was a measured .88g of lateral acceleration. Sales continued to increase, with 190 of the $17,900 coupes selling and 11 $19,900 convertibles going to new customers.

DATA PLATE DECODING

A 17-character Vehicle Identification Number is stamped on an aluminum tab on the instrument panel, viewable through windshield. A vehicle certification label is found on the body side of where the driver's door closes.

VEHICLE WARRANTY NUMBER
MANUFACTURER ID

1FA – Ford Motor Co.

RESTRAINT SYSTEM

B – active belts

VEHICLE CLASSIFICATION

P – passenger car

BODY SERIAL NUMBERS

27 – convertible
28 – hatchback

ENGINE CODE

M – 302-cid (5.0-liter) EFI V-8 HO

CHECK DIGIT

for internal use

MODEL YEAR

G – 1986

ASSEMBLY PLANT

F – Dearborn, Michigan

CONSECUTIVE UNIT NUMBER

Begins at 100001 at each factory

CODE NUMBERS
BODY CODE

66B – convertible
61B – hatchback

PAINT CODE

1C – Black
2C – Canyon Red
3Y – Medium Regatta Blue
9L – Oxford White

ENGINE

302-cid (5.0-liter) EFI V-8 HO
Block . . . . cast iron
Displacement. . . . . 302 cid/5.0 liters
Bore and stroke. . . . . 4.00 x 3.00 inches
Compression ratio 9.2:1
Brake hp . . . . 200 @ 4400 rpm
Induction . . . . electronic fuel injection
Code. . . . . M

SUSPENSION ENHANCEMENTS

Springs . . . . specific-rate front and rear coil
Shocks. . . . . Koni adjustable gas
Struts. . . . . Koni adjustable
Bushings. . . . . urethane swaybar pivot units
Chassis reinforcements . . . . shock tower brace

Wheels . . . . 16 x 7-inch Riken Racing Design alloy
Tires. 225/50VR-16 Fulda Y-2000

BODY ENHANCEMENTS

Rear wing
urethane front airdam
urethane side skirts
urethane rear valance
headlight covers

1986 Saleen headlight cover

1986 Saleen wheel

1986 SALEEN PRODUCTION CHART			
Body	Doors/Body/Seating	Price	Built
61B	3/hatchback/4	$17,900	190
66B	2/convertible/4	$19,900	11

NOTE 1: Total production was 201 units.
NOTE 2: There were three competition models produced in '86.

1986 Saleen Kenwood stereo

1986 Saleen seats

1986 M-code 5.0-liter/EFI V-8

1986 Saleen serial identification plate

1987 Saleen #245
Owner: Gary McCann

1987 Saleen

Ford restyled and re-engineered its Mustang for 1987. With a 225-hp V-8 under the slightly more aerodynamic hood, the LX and GT moved up a step on the high-performance ladder.

Saleen Autosport's products benefited from the improvements, then took the package into new territory, with the addition of disc brakes at all four wheels and stronger five-lug rotors that had originally been designed for the 1984-86 SVO Mustang. This labor-intensive change also required the addition of a heavy-duty master cylinder. When tested, the new brakes showed a five-foot savings when stopping the car from 60 miles an hour and exhibited far less fade under extreme conditions.

Alloy American Racing "basket weave" wheels, measuring 16 x 7 inches (front) and 16 x 8 inches (rear), were wrapped by 225/50VR-16 General XP-2000 high-performance tires. Saleen's Racecraft suspension system included specific-rate front and rear coil springs, Koni shocks all around, special strut mounting bearings, urethane sway bar pivot bushing and high-performance alignment specs. The chassis was tightened by a triangulated strut tower brace and a bar that ran under the engine's oil pan effectively making a strong box out of the front subframe.

The greatest boost to the Saleen's acceleration was the introduction in 1987 of the 3.55:1 rear axle ratio as an option. It was available to replace the standard Saleen

3.08:1 gearing and provided a substantial improvement in zero-to-60 mph and quarter-mile times.

Compared to previous years, there were very few running changes inflicted on the Saleen product line in 1987. A few cars built early in the year were fitted with side window louvers (similar to what had come stock from Ford prior to 1987), but problems with the adhesive used to affix them ended their use. The louvers could be seen in magazine ads and posters distributed throughout the year.

Interior upgrades included installation of articulated FloFit seats, a three-spoke Momo steering wheel, and a new Kenwood KRC 5001 AM/FM cassette six-speaker sound system. The Escort radar detector came off the standard equipment list and became an option as more states questioned the legality of such products. One two-door coupe was produced in Saleen trim for 1987 for Austin Craig, co-founder of the Shelby American Automobile Club and account manager for Ford Motorsports. This unusual car added a third bodystyle to the hatchback and convertible models. Sales of the $20,999 base Saleen were brisk at 280 copies.

The only option listed by the factory was the 3.55:1 rear axle, although customers could make special requests such as automatic transmissions, sunroofs, and certain aftermarket performance enhancements. Exterior colors available were Black, Canyon Red, Dark Grey Metallic, and Oxford White, although other colors could be arranged through the Ford dealer. The tri-color racing stripes were available in gold, silver, or blue.

1987 was also a good year for Saleen Mustangs on the racetrack, as it marked the company's first (of four) SCCA Manufacturer's championships.

DATA PLATE DECODING

A 17-character Vehicle Identification Number is stamped on an aluminum tab on the instrument panel, viewable through windshield. A vehicle certification label is found on the body side of where the driver's door closes.

VEHICLE WARRANTY NUMBER
MANUFACTURER ID

1FA – Ford Motor Co.

RESTRAINT SYSTEM

B – active belts

VEHICLE CLASSIFICATION

P – passenger car

BODY SERIAL NUMBERS

40 – coupe
41 – hatchback
44 – convertible

ENGINE CODE

M – 302-cid (5.0-liter) EFI V-8 HO

CHECK DIGIT

for internal use

MODEL YEAR

H – 1987

ASSEMBLY PLANT

F – Dearborn, Michigan

CONSECUTIVE UNIT NUMBER

Begins at 100001 at each factory

CODE NUMBERS
BODY CODE

66B – coupe, convertible
61B – hatchback

PAINT CODE

1C – Black
2D – Scarlet Red
9L – Oxford White
9R – Dark Grey Metallic

ENGINE

302-cid (5.0-liter) EFI V-8 HO

Displacement . . . . .302 cid/5.0 liters
Bore and stroke . . . . 4.00 x 3.00 inches
Compression ratio 9.2:1
Brake hp . . . . 225 @ 4000 rpm
Induction . . . . electronic fuel injection
Code . . . . M

SUSPENSION ENHANCEMENTS

Springs . . . . specific-rate front and rear coil
Shocks . . . . Koni adjustable gas
Struts . . . . Koni adjustable
. . . . special strut mounting bearings
Axle damper . . . . Koni
Bushings . . . . urethane swaybar pivot units
Chassis reinforcements . . . . strut tower brace
Wheels . . . . (front) 16 x 7-inch American Racing alloy
. . . . (rear) 16 x 8-inch American Racing alloy
Tires . . . . 225/50VR-16 General XP-2000
Brakes . . . . four-wheel discs, five-lug pattern

BODY ENHANCEMENTS

Rear wing
urethane front airdam
urethane side skirts
urethane rear valance
side window louvers (early cars only)

1987 SALEEN PRODUCTION CHART			
Body	Doors/Body/Seating	Price	Built
61B	3/hatchback/4	$20,999	246
66B	2/convertible/4	$22,999	33
66B	2/coupe/4	N/A	1

NOTE 1: Total production was 280 units. Additionally, Saleen Autosport produced two Ranger-based trucks for competition.
NOTE 2: There were seven competition models produced in '87.

1987 Saleen Escort radar detector

1987 Saleen wheel

1987 Saleen serial number

1987 Saleen interior

1987 Saleen door panel

**1988 Saleen notchback #690
Owner: Mark Turner**

1988 Saleen

1988 Saleens were essentially carryovers from the previous year, with minimal changes. Monroe shock absorbers replaced the Koni units after Monroes helped Saleen racecars turn faster lap times. American-built Pioneer got the nod to replace Kenwood as the official stereo supplier to Saleen Autosport. The Escort radar detector was dropped from the standard equipment list for '88.

Saleen's Racecraft suspension system included specific-rate front and rear coil springs, Monroe shocks all around, special strut mounting bearings, urethane sway bar pivot bushing and high-performance alignment specs.

Other standard equipment included 225/50VR-16 General XP-2000V tires, Monroe quad shocks, Saleen aerodynamic kit, 170-mph speedometer, leather-covered shift knob, Hurst quick-ratio shifter, articulated FloFit sport seats, three-spoke Momo steering wheel and a Saleen Mustang jacket. The standard stereo was comprised of a Pioneer KEH 6050 AM/FM system with cassette player, Pioneer BP 880 graphic equalizer and six speakers.

The only option listed by the factory was the 3.55:1 rear axle, although customers could make special requests such as automatic transmissions, sunroofs and certain aftermarket performance enhancements.

Running changes through the production year were minimal.

Exterior colors available were Black, Canyon Red, Dark Grey Metallic and Oxford White, although other colors could be arranged through the Ford dealer. The tri-color racing stripes were available in gold, silver or blue.

Participating Ford dealers were required to order cars for conversion with the following specs: LX hatchback, coupe or convertible, 5.0-liter V-8, five-speed manual transmission, 3.08:1 limited-slip axle, 225/60VR-15 tires, radio delete, Custom Equipment Group and rear window defogger. Cruise control was not to be ordered on cars receiving the Saleen treatment as it interfered with the addition of a custom steering wheel.

With enthusiasm and name-recognition building for Saleen's modified Mustangs, it was no surprise that 708 were sold in '88, including 137 convertibles and 25 coupes.

In an attempt to keep the Saleen production line busy during Ford's annual downtime for Mustang model switchover, the company experimented in '88 with building a Ranger-based Sportruck for the street. Since Steve Saleen and other drivers were already competing in four-cylinder, short-bed Rangers in SCCA events, a street version built around a V-6, long-bed model seemed like a good marketing idea. Unfortunately, interruptions in the component supply line and a total re-design of the Ranger killed the momentum for this project with only 24 examples produced at a list price of $16,500 each.

DATA PLATE DECODING

A 17-character Vehicle Identification Number is stamped on an aluminum tab on the instrument panel, viewable through windshield. A vehicle certification label is found on the body side of where the driver's door closes.

VEHICLE WARRANTY NUMBER MANUFACTURER ID

1FA – Ford Motor Co.

RESTRAINT SYSTEM

B – active belts

VEHICLE CLASSIFICATION

P – passenger car

BODY SERIAL NUMBERS

40 – coupe
41 – hatchback
44 – convertible

ENGINE CODE

M – 302-cid (5.0-liter) EFI V-8 HO

CHECK DIGIT

for internal use

MODEL YEAR

J – 1988

ASSEMBLY PLANT

F – Dearborn, Michigan

CONSECUTIVE UNIT NUMBER

Begins at 100001 at each factory

CODE NUMBERS BODY CODE

66B – coupe, convertible
61B – hatchback

PAINT CODE

1C – Black
2D – Scarlet Red
9L – Oxford White
9R – Dark Grey Metallic

ENGINES

302-cid (5.0-liter) EFI V-8 HO

Displacement . . . . 302 cid/5.0 liters
Bore and stroke . . . . 4.00 x 3.00 inches
Compression ratio 9.2:1
Brake hp . . . . 225 @ 4000 rpm
Induction . . . . electronic fuel injection
Code . . . . M

SUSPENSION ENHANCEMENTS

Springs . . . . specific-rate front and rear coil
Shocks . . . . Monroe Formula GP gas
Struts . . . . Monroe Formula GP gas
. . . . special strut mounting bearings
Axle damper . . . . Monroe
Bushings . . . . urethane swaybar pivot units
Chassis reinforcements . . . . strut tower brace
Wheels . . . . (front) 16 x 7-inch American Racing alloy
. . . . (rear) 16 x 8-inch American Racing alloy
Tires . . . . 225/50VR-16 General XP-2000V
Brakes . . . . four-wheel discs, five-lug pattern

BODY ENHANCEMENTS

Rear wing
urethane front airdam
urethane side skirts
urethane rear valance

1988 SALEEN PRODUCTION CHART

Body	Doors/Body/Seating	Price	Built
61B	3/hatchback/4	$21,500	546
66B	2/convertible/4	$24,950	137
66B	2/coupe/4	N/A	25

NOTE 1: Total production was 708 units. Additionally, Saleen Autosport produced 24 Ranger-based Sportrucks.
NOTE 2: There were three competition Saleen Mustangs produced in '88.
NOTE 3: There were three competition Ranger-based race trucks produced in '88.

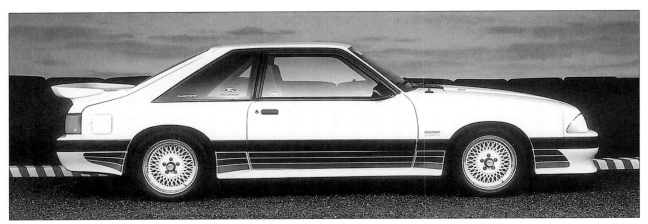

1988 Saleen (Saleen)

1988 Saleen #140
Owner: Mark Kemesky

1988 Saleen #191
Owner: Patti Sankey

1989 Saleen SSC #002

1989 Saleen

Big things were happening for Saleen Autosport in 1989 on several fronts. The company's plans included record sales of its popular Mustang conversion, another attempt at an SCCA championship, an IndyCar campaign, and the introduction of the highly anticipated Saleen SSC supercar.

1989 Saleen Mustangs were essentially carryovers from the previous year, with minimal changes. The Racecraft suspension system included specific-rate front and rear coil springs, Monroe shocks all around, special strut mounting bearings, urethane sway bar pivot bushing, and high-performance alignment specs.

The standard stereo was comprised of a Pioneer KEH 6050 AM/FM system with cassette player, Pioneer BP 880 graphic equalizer, and six speakers. Other standard equipment included 225/50VR-16 General XP-2000V tires, Monroe quad shocks, Saleen aerodynamic kit, 170-mph speedometer, leather-covered shift knob, Hurst quick-ratio shifter, articulated FloFit sport seats, three-spoke Momo steering wheel (in its final year, owing to the following year's debut of a driver's side airbag) and a Saleen Mustang jacket.

The only options listed by the factory were the 3.27:1 limited-slip differential, the 3.55:1 limited-slip axle, a heavy-duty radiator and cooling system and a Panhard rod; however, customers could make special requests such as automatic transmissions, sunroofs, and other aftermarket performance enhancements. Special five-spoke, 16-inch wheels became available early in the year. For the first time, Saleen buyers had the option of cruise control due to the availability of a custom bracket.

Available exterior colors were Black, Canyon Red, Dark Shadow Blue, and Oxford White, although other colors could be arranged through the Ford dealer. New rocker panel-affixed racing stripes (featuring the first re-design since their debut on the 1984 model) were available in gold, silver, or blue. 1989 marked the first year for the Saleen date tag to be affixed to the firewall with the last six digits of the Ford vehicle identification number.

Participating Ford dealers were required to order cars for conversion with the following specs: LX hatchback; coupe or convertible; 5.0-liter V-8; five-speed manual transmission; 3.08:1 limited-slip axle; 225/60VR-15 tires; radio delete; Custom Equipment Group; and rear window defogger. A Saleen Identification Code, 31S, gave the Ford factory in Dearborn a clear indication that a certain order was part of the unique bailment pooling/drop ship arrangement Saleen Autosport enjoyed. Sales for the standard conversion added up to 734 cars, including four specially-built hatchbacks for Pioneer (although standard Saleens, they resembled SSCs), two ordered by Eagle 1 for giveaways and one ordered by General Tire.

On the track, the SCCA campaign was still successful and continuing to build the high-performance image of the base Saleen Mustang. Unfortunately, Steve Saleen's attempt to move to the open-wheel IndyCar series ended quickly after the team failed to qualify for the Indianapolis 500.

The most memorable aspect of the year for fans of the Saleen-built cars was the introduction, on April 17, 1989 (the Mustang's 25th birthday), of the SSC. The SSC was the second huge step forward for Saleen Autosport as it was built around a 292-hp, 5.0-liter V-8 approved for sale by the Environmental Protection Agency in all 50 states—no mean feat for a small-volume automaker. Saleen's modifications to the 5.0 included a 65mm throttle body (up from the stock Mustang's 60mm), revised intake plenum, enlarged cylinder head ports, wider

1989 Saleen SSC #002

1989 Saleen SSC #002

rocker arm ratios, stainless steel tubular headers, heavy-duty cooling system, and Walker Dynomax mufflers.

A high-performance version of the Mustang's Borg-Warner T-5 transmission was installed behind the new powerplant and controlled by a Hurst short-throw shifter. Standard 3.55:1 gears were housed in an Auburn "cone clutch" differential for ground-scorching acceleration.

Three-way Monroe Formula GA electronic cockpit-adjustable shock absorbers were quite an innovation at the time and Steve Saleen had to have them on his flagship SSC. Massive 245/50-16 General XP-2000Z rubber sat on the rear, with the slightly narrower front receiving 225/50-16Zs. SSC wheels were beautiful five-spoke, 16x8-inch DP models. Mechanically, the car either benefited from the stock Saleen inventory or, in most cases, went one better with all-new equipment.

Saleen interiors had always been special places; the SSC cabin was a sacred shrine to the marriage of luxury and performance. Leather FloFit seats and matching door panels told the driver he was a very lucky person. The SSC speedometer showed 200 miles an hour. There was no back seat in the SSC; that area was taken up with 200 watts of Pioneer sound system, CD player and six speakers. A four-point interior chassis support system (known in the old, pre-litigious days as a "rollbar") further stiffened the Mustang platform.

Despite the incredible list of standard equipment, there were no options available. All 161 SSCs produced as 1989-only models were identical; all were white with white wheels and gray-and-white interiors. The only differences lay in running changes affected by component suppliers; for example, not all cars received the Momo steering wheel. The asking price for this "unofficial" 25th anniversary Mustang model was $36,500. Certifying, building, and selling a modified engine package made Saleen customers happy, but it also gave the company a broader product range that now included a constantly evolving "base" model as well as a high-end supercar.

DATA PLATE DECODING

A 17-character Vehicle Identification Number is stamped on an aluminum tab on the instrument panel, viewable through windshield. A vehicle certification label is found on the body side of where the driver's door closes.

VEHICLE WARRANTY NUMBER MANUFACTURER ID

1FA – Ford Motor Co.

RESTRAINT SYSTEM

B – active belts

VEHICLE CLASSIFICATION

P – passenger car

BODY SERIAL NUMBERS

40 – coupe
41 – hatchback (SSC exclusive)
44 – convertible

ENGINE CODE

M – 302-cid (5.0-liter) EFI V-8 HO

CHECK DIGIT

for internal use

MODEL YEAR

K – 1989

1989 SALEEN PRODUCTION CHART			
Body	Doors/Body/Seating	Price	Built
61B	3/hatchback/4	$23,500	549
66B	2/convertible/4	$26,450	165
66B	2/coupe/4	N/A	20
61B	3/hatchback SSC/2*	$36,500	161

NOTE 1: Total production was 734 standard cars in all bodystyles plus 161 SSCs.
NOTE 2: There were two competition Saleen Mustangs produced in 1989.
NOTE 3: There were three competition Ranger-based race trucks produced in 1989.
* One SSC, number 159, was built with a rear seat in place of the Pioneer speaker system.

ASSEMBLY PLANT

F – Dearborn, Michigan

CONSECUTIVE UNIT NUMBER

Begins at 100001 at each factory

CODE NUMBERS
BODY CODE

66B – coupe, convertible
61B – hatchback

PAINT CODE

1C – Black
2D – Scarlet Red
9L – Oxford White (SSC exclusive)
7N – Dark Shadow Blue Metallic

ENGINES

302-cid (5.0-liter) EFI V-8 HO Standard Saleen
Displacement . . . . 302 cid/5.0 liters
Bore and stroke . . . . 4.00 x 3.00 inches
Compression ratio 9.2:1
Brake hp . . . . 225 @ 4000 rpm
Induction . . . . electronic fuel injection
Code . . . . M

302-cid (5.0-liter) EFI V-8 HO Saleen SSC
Displacement . . . . 302 cid/5.0 liters
Bore and stroke . . . . 4.00 x 3.00 inches
Compression ratio 9.2:1
Brake hp 292
Induction . . . . electronic fuel injection
Code . . . . M

SUSPENSION ENHANCEMENTS

Standard Saleen
Springs . . . . specific-rate front and rear coil

Shocks . . . . Monroe Formula GP gas
Struts . . . . Monroe Formula GP gas
. . . . special strut mounting bearings
Axle damper . . . . Monroe
Bushings . . . . urethane swaybar pivot units
Chassis reinforcements . . . . strut tower brace
Wheels . . . . (front) 16 x 7-inch American Racing alloy
. . . . (rear) 16 x 8-inch American Racing alloy
Tires . . . . 225/50VR-16 General XP-2000V
Brakes . . . . four-wheel discs, five-lug pattern

Saleen SSC
Springs . . . . specific-rate front and rear coil
Shocks Monroe Formula GA electronic three-way adjustable
Struts . . . . Monroe Formula GP gas special strut mounting
bearings
Axle damper . . . . Monroe
Bushings . . . . urethane swaybar pivot units
Chassis reinforcements . . . . strut tower brace
Wheels . . . . 16 x 8-inch DP five-spoke alloy
Tires . . . . . . (front) 225/50ZR-16 General XP-2000Z
. . . . (rear) 245/50ZR-16 General XP-2000Z
Brakes . . . . grooved four-wheel discs, five-lug pattern

BODY ENHANCEMENTS

Rear wing
urethane front airdam
urethane side skirts
urethane rear valance

1989 Saleen (Saleen)

1989 Saleen SCCA race car

**1993 Saleen #66 with supercharger
Owner: Mark LaMaskin/
Performance Autosport**

1990-93 Saleen

Turning a Mustang into a world-class performance car made Steve Saleen a household name, but a national recession in the early 1990s nearly made his company one more footnote in automotive history. Rolling along on the success of the 1989 sales figures, Saleen Autosport looked poised to take its various products to an even larger audience. Unfortunately, that next level would have to wait a few years as a slow economy pulled the rug out from under the high-performance car market.

Displaying the same spirit that won him the 1987 SCCA championship, Saleen worked against the odds to develop and improve his two well-loved products. Considering the decline in sales from 1990 (243 regular Saleen Musangs) to a low not seen since the company's first year in business (17 cars sold in 1992), it's amazing the company was able to survive at all. One way Saleen survived was by subcontracting some of the conversion work; 1990-91 standard cars were built by Cars & Concepts in St. Louis, Missouri, while the SCs were assembled by Saleen Parts Inc. in California.

Because the Mustang on which it was based was not fundamentally different (driver's airbag and improved front suspension geometry the only obvious changes) 1990 Saleens were carryovers from the previous year. The Racecraft suspension system now included variable rate front and rear coil springs (gone were the stiff, specific-rate units), Monroe Formula GP gas shocks all around, special strut mounting bearings, urethane sway bar pivot bushing, and high-performance alignment specs. Due to changes made by Ford, Saleen modified the shock tower brace this year.

The standard stereo was again a Pioneer AM/FM cassette unit with six speakers, graphic equalizer and a remote control. Other standard equipment included 225/50ZR-16 General XP-2000Z tires on American Racing rims (16 x 7 inches in front, 16 x 8 inches in rear), Monroe quad shocks, four-wheel disc brakes, Saleen aerodynamic kit, 170-mph speedometer, leather-covered shift knob, Hurst quick-ratio shifter, articulated FloFit sport seats, and a Saleen Mustang jacket. New for 1990 were a "split" front air dam, two-piece rear wing and bolt-on subframe connectors.

The only options listed by the factory were the 3.55:1 limited-slip axle, Pioneer CD player and leather interior; however, customers could make special requests such as automatic transmissions, sunroofs and certain aftermarket performance enhancements.

As in years past, participating Ford dealers were required to order cars for conversion with the following specs: LX hatchback, coupe or convertible, 5.0-liter V-8, five-speed manual transmission, 3.08:1 limited-slip axle, 225/60VR-15 tires, radio delete, Custom Equipment Group and rear window defogger. A Saleen Identification Code, 31S, gave the Ford factory in Dearborn a clear indication that a certain order was part of the unique bailment pooling/drop ship arrangement Saleen Autosport enjoyed.

1993 Saleen Spyder package

For 1990, the upscale SSC became known as the "SC" and continued giving Saleen enthusiasts power, handling, and appearance upgrades. Continuous improvements and changes to the aerodynamic body pieces, wheels and tires, and various other equipment proceeded deliberately during this period. The 1990 SC received a special intake manifold, while the 1990-91 SC wore a new 77mm mass airflow sensor. Saleen's "Spyder" convertible package, featuring a soft tonneau cover that turned the rear

seats into a convenient storage area, was new for 1992. Saleen teamed with Vortech in 1992 to offer one of its superchargers as an option and Recaro came on board to supply its legendary seats. Seventeen-inch Stern rims—17x8 inches in the front and 17x9 inches in the rear—became standard Saleen equipment in 1992 at a time when the SVT Mustang Cobra was still one year away from such rolling stock.

As eager as the team was to put customers in cars, the demand for Saleen's products stalled. Only 243 Saleens were built in 1990; only 92 sold in 1991; only 17 in 1992. Outside the regular 1992 Saleen Mustang line were four non-serialized "entry level" GT Sport hatchbacks modified with the lowered suspension and a few body upgrades, and one Ranger pickup given treatment similar to the 1988 Sportrucks.

Production for 1993 was slow, but a remarkable improvement over the previous year. Saleen sold 87 of its base Mustang packages, five SCs and nine supercharged $37,995 SA-10 models commemorating Saleen's 10th year in business. Sticker for the base, original recipe Saleen hatchback was $27,490; list for the convertible ran $31,690 and either model could be pumped up with a $3,200 Vortech supercharger. Ordering the hot and spicy SC with standard supercharger and a never-ending list of high-performance goodies (including a Tremec heavy-duty five-speed transmission) would cost $39,990. Saleen even offered a convertible in the SC for the first time at $44,490.

Comedian Tim Allen's one-off Saleen supercar, known as the "R-R-R" model, was produced in 1993. The 576-hp 5.0-liter V-8 Saleen built for the all-white hatchback featured a balanced and blueprinted block, ported and polished aluminum heads, Saleen-spec upper and lower intake manifold, 65mm throttle body, 1.72:1 aluminum roller rocker arms, 38 lbs./hr. fuel injectors, ceramic headers, and a Vortech "B-trim" supercharger pumping out 13.5 pounds per square inch.

1993 E-code 5.0-liter/EFI V-8 with supercharger

Putting the R-R-R's massive power smoothly to the ground was a Tremec five-speed transmission, aluminum driveshaft, and an Auburn cone-clutch differential with 3.55:1 gears. Huge brake discs all around and four-piston calipers kept the horsepower from getting the comedian in trouble on the racetrack or street. A slew of other improvements, including entirely new fenders and hood and bumper fascia fashioned out of carbon fiber and urethane made sure Allen never found himself driving a car that looked or drove like someone else's.

Feeling optimistic about the future of his company (perhaps based on the improved sales figures for 1993) Steve Saleen produced a limited run of nine SA-10 models to celebrate the company's 10th anniversary. The SA-10

1993 Saleen interior

1993 Saleen wheel

hatchback, available only in Black, was powered by a modified and supercharged version of the 5.0-liter V-8. Each SA-10 was custom-ordered by the owner.

The special model featured many high-performance pieces first offered on the SSC and SC, such as sub-frame connectors, chassis support braces, a rear shock tower brace and a Panhard rod. The SA-10 was to be the last of the 5.0-liter Saleen Mustangs as the company's 1994 offerings would be based around a 5.8-liter/351-cid V-8.

DATA PLATE DECODING

A 17-character Vehicle Identification Number is stamped on an aluminum tab on the instrument panel, viewable through windshield. A vehicle certification label is found on the body side of where the driver's door closes.

VEHICLE WARRANTY NUMBER
MANUFACTURER ID

1FA – Ford Motor Co.

RESTRAINT SYSTEM

C – air bags, active belts

VEHICLE CLASSIFICATION

P – passenger car

BODY SERIAL NUMBERS

40 – coupe

41 – hatchback
44 – convertible

ENGINE CODE

M – 302-cid (5.0-liter) EFI V-8 HO – 1990
E – 302-cid (5.0-liter) EFI V-8 HO – 1991-'93

CHECK DIGIT

for internal use

MODEL YEAR

L – 1990   N – 1992
M – 1991   P – 1993

ASSEMBLY PLANT

F – Dearborn, Michigan

CONSECUTIVE UNIT NUMBER

Begins at 100001 at each factory

CODE NUMBERS
BODY CODE

66B – coupe, convertible
61B – hatchback

PAINT CODE

Various Ford colors were used an on a per-request basis.

1990 Saleen convertible (Saleen)

1991 Saleen (Saleen)

1990 Saleen SC (Saleen)

1991 Saleen SC (Saleen)

1993 Saleen RRR model (Saleen)

1993 Saleen SC (Saleen)

ENGINE

302-cid (5.0-liter) EFI V-8 HO Standard Saleen

Displacement. 302 cid/5.0 liters
Bore and stroke. . . . . 4.00 x 3.00 inches
Compression ratio 9.2:1
Brake hp . . . . 225 @ 4000 rpm
Induction . . . . electronic fuel injection
Code . . . . (1990) M
. . . . (1991-'93) E

SUSPENSION ENHANCEMENTS

Springs . . . . variable-rate front and rear coil
Shocks. . . . . (1990-'92) Monroe Formula GP gas
. . . . (1993) Racecraft
Struts . . . . (1990-'92) Monroe Formula GP gas
. . . . (1993) Racecraft
. . . . special strut mounting bearings
Axle damper . . . . (1990-'92) Monroe
. . . . (1993) Racecraft
Bushings . . . . urethane swaybar pivot units
Chassis reinforcements . . . . strut tower brace
. . . . subframe connector

Wheels. . . . .
   (1993 SC, SA-10 front) 17 x 8-inch Saleen three-piece,
     five-spoke
   (1993 SC, SA-10 rear) 17 x 9-inch Saleen three-piece,
     five-spoke
   (1992-'93 front) 17 x 7.5-inch Speedline five-spoke
   (1992-'93 rear) 17 x 8.5-inch Speedline five-spoke
   (1990-'91 front) 16 x 7-inch American Racing alloy
     five-spoke
   (1990-'91 rear) 16 x 8-inch American Racing alloy five-spoke
   (1990-'91 SC) 16 x 8-inch European Style five-spoke
Tires . . . .
   (1993 SC, SA-10 front) 225/45ZR-17 BFGoodrich Comp T/A
   (1993 SC rear) 255/40ZR-17 BFGoodrich Comp T/A
   (1993 SA-10 rear)
   (1990-'91) 225/50ZR-16 General XP-2000Z
   (1990 SC front) 225/50ZR-16 General XP-2000Z
   (1990 SC rear) 245/50ZR-16 General XP-2000Z
Brakes . . . . four-wheel discs, five-lug pattern

BODY ENHANCEMENTS

1990-91 two-piece rear wing   urethane side skirts
1992-93 one-piece rear wing   urethane rear valance
urethane front airdam

1990 SALEEN PRODUCTION CHART

Body	Doors/Body/Seating	Price	Built
61B	3/hatchback/4	$24,990	173
66B	2/convertible/4	$29,390	62
66B	2/coupe/4	N/A	8
61B	3/hatchback SC/4	$32,000	12

NOTE 1: Total production was 243 standard cars in all body styles plus 12 SCs.
NOTE 2: There were two competition Ranger-based race trucks produced in 1990.

1991 SALEEN PRODUCTION CHART

Body	Doors/Body/Seating	Price	Built
61B	3/hatchback/4	$25,990	58
66B	2/convertible/4	$29,990	30
66B	2/coupe/4	N/A	4
61B	3/hatchback SC/4	$34,750	10

NOTE 1: Total production was 92 standard cars in all body styles plus 10 SCs.
NOTE 2: There was one competition Ranger-based race truck produced in 1991.

1992 SALEEN PRODUCTION CHART

Body	Doors/Body/Seating	Price	Built
61B	3/hatchback/4	$26,990	12
66B	2/convertible/4	$30,990	5

NOTE 1: Total production was 17 standard cars of all body styles.
NOTE 2: Outside the regular 1992 Mustang line were four "entry level" GT Sport hatchbacks modified with the lowered suspension and a few body upgrades, plus a Ranger built similar to the 1988 Sportruck.

1993 SALEEN PRODUCTION CHART

Body	Doors/Body/Seating	Price	Built
61B	3/hatchback/4	$27,490	56
66B	2/convertible/4	$31,690	30
66B	2/coupe/4	N/A	1
61B	3/hatchback SC/4	$39,990	2
66B	2/convertible SC/4	$44,490	3
61B	3/hatchback SA-10/4	$37,995	9
61B	3/hatchback R-R-R/4	N/A	1

NOTE 1: Total production was 87 standard cars in all body styles, plus five SCs, nine SA-10s and one R-R-R.

**1992 Saleen #19 with supercharger
Owner: Mark LaMaskin/
Performance Autosport**

1992 Saleen spoiler

1992 Saleen rear valance

1992 Saleen wheel

**1992 E-code 5.0-liter/EFI V-8 with
supercharger**

1992 Saleen interior

1992 Saleen seat

1993 Saleen SA-10 #01 with supercharger
Owner: John McCauley

1993 Saleen SA-10
#01 with
supercharger

1994 V-6 Sport by Saleen
Owners: Keith and Pat Suddeth

1994 Saleen

There's nothing like an all-new model to put life back into a car line, as Steve Saleen discovered when he debuted the efforts of his rejuvenated car company during the Mustang's 30th anniversary show at Charlotte Motor Speedway in April of 1994. It calmed fears that Saleen Autosport (now Saleen Performance) had gone the way of Shelby American.

Ford's SN-95 (internal code for the 1994 Mustang) gave Saleen a fresh canvas on which to create masterpieces into the 21st Century with its better-engineered chassis and sportier styling. The redesign could not have come at a better time for small-volume manufacturer Saleen, who had spent 10 years making the Fox-platform Mustang into an exciting product for performance enthusiasts.

First to debut was Saleen's "entry level" V-6 Sport, a model that combined traditional Saleen equipment with a less-expensive powerplant. Boosted by a standard supercharger, the Sport's 3.8-liter V-6 was rated at 220 hp—just a bit more power than the heavier 5.0-liter V-8—and benefited from Racecraft suspension tuning, 17 x 8-inch wheels, and Saleen aerodynamic body pieces. A short-throw Hurst shifter and leather-grained shift knob were the only interior modifications. Listing for less than $22,000 put the V-6 Sport (official name: V-6 Sport by Steve Saleen) in the same price range as a loaded GT Mustang, but without the super-high insurance premium. Saleen saw this as a good entry-level car that would appeal to younger enthusiasts.

Saleen's next all-new product to debut, the S-351, took the previous SSC and SC concepts to the next level.

Powered by a 351-cid 371-hp V-8 built and EPA certified by Saleen Performance, the S-351 had the highest Saleen-unique content of any car to date. V-6 coupes and convertibles were delivered to the new Saleen factory in Irvine, California, where they were stripped to bare shells (except for certain components such as the dash).

The S-351 V-8 featured high-performance cylinder heads with bigger valves; hydraulic roller camshaft and lifters; 65mm throttle body; 77mm mass air sensor, and a slew of other high-tech goodies. The unique powerplant was then installed on relocated motor mounts (one inch rearward and one inch lower than stock) and entirely rewired to a new EEC-IV engine management system. Just about every part of the S-351 was replaced or massaged during a period of 120 hours, which made the coupe's $34,990 asking price ($40,990 for the convertible) quite remarkable.

The S-351 could be outfitted with any number of accessories, unlike the "no options" SSC of 1989. The stock 235/40-18 (front) and 245/40-18 (rear) BFGoodrich Comp T/A radials could be upgraded to Dunlop SP8000s measuring 255/40-18 and 285/40-18. Need more power? There was a Vortech supercharger option. Even stronger acceleration could be dialed in with a 3.55:1 rear axle. If stopping was as important as going, larger 13-inch brake discs could be ordered. The Speedster package, first seen as a 1992 option known as the "Spyder," was again offered, this time with a rollbar-like "sport bar" and hard tonneau cover.

If the S-351 was a home run—as several publications described it—then the third all-new Saleen model for 1994 was equivalent to winning the World Series. The SR ("Supercharged Racer" according to some) was the barely legal equipment package that dressed a Vortech-supercharged S-351 in FIA Group A competition clothing, including a dual-plane rear wing, carbon-fiber hood and scooped bodyside enhancements. Inside, the SR benefited from a rear race tray (taking the place of the back seat), four-point rollbar, four-point safety harness and racing Recaro seats. With its 351-cid supercharged V-8 rated at 480 hp, no one could say the SR was "all-show, no-go." Base price for the latest Saleen supercar was $45,990.

Adding to the excitement of the three-model Saleen lineup was the company's announcement that 75 Ford outlets were "stocking dealers," meaning they had agreed to keep a minimum of two cars on the floor at all times. With only a few months of real production time in 1994, those 75 dealers managed to sell 29 V-6 Sports, 44 S-351s and two SRs.

DATA PLATE DECODING

A 17-character Vehicle Identification Number is stamped on an aluminum tab on the instrument panel, viewable through windshield. A vehicle certification label is found on the body side of where the driver's door closes.

VEHICLE WARRANTY NUMBER
MANUFACTURER ID

1FA – Ford Motor Co.

RESTRAINT SYSTEM

L – air bags, active belts

VEHICLE CLASSIFICATION

P – passenger car

BODY SERIAL NUMBERS

40 – coupe
42 – convertible

ENGINE CODE

4 – 232-cid (3.8-liter) EFI V-6*
*removed from Saleen S-351s during conversion

CHECK DIGIT

for internal use

MODEL YEAR

R – 1994

ASSEMBLY PLANT

F – Dearborn, Michigan

CONSECUTIVE UNIT NUMBER

Begins at 100001 at each factory

CODE NUMBERS
PAINT CODE

Various Ford colors were used an on a per-request basis.

ENGINE

351-cid (5.8-liter) EFI V-8

Displacement	351 cid/5.8 liters
Bore and stroke	4.00 x 3.50 inches
Horsepower	(S-351) 371 @ 5,100
	(SR) 480
Heads	high-performance aluminum
Camshaft	hydraulic roller/lifters
Induction	electronic fuel injection
Injectors	(S-351) 30 lb/hr
	(SR) 36 lb/hr
Throttle body	65mm
Mass air sensor	77mm
Headers	Saleen ceramic-coated
Code	not assigned by Ford

SUSPENSION ENHANCEMENTS

Springs	progressive-rate front and rear coil
Shocks	Racecraft gas
Struts	Racecraft gas
	special strut mounting bushings
Quad shocks	Racecraft gas
Bushings	urethane swaybar units
Chassis reinforcements	strut tower brace
Wheels	

(S-351) 18 x 8.5-inch Saleen five-spoke
(S-351 upgrade, SR front) 18 x 8.5-inch magnesium
(S-351 upgrade, SR rear) 18 x 10-inch magnesium

1994 V-6 Sport wheel

1994 4-code 3.8-liter/EFI V-6 with supercharger

Tires . . . .
 (S-351 front) 235/40ZR-18 BFGoodrich Comp T/A
 (S-351 rear) 245/40ZR-18 BFGoodrich Comp T/A
 (S-351 upgrade, SR front) 255/40ZR-18 Dunlop SP8000
 (S-351 upgrade, SR rear) 285/40ZR-18 Dunlop SP8000
Brakes . . . . four-wheel discs, five-lug pattern

OPTIONAL EQUIPMENT (S-351 only)

T Code Package 13-inch rotors, four-piston calipers, 3.27:1
 rear axle, leather seats
Brakes 13-inch front rotors, four-piston calipers and grooved
 rear rotors
Tire upgrade . . . . (front) Dunlop SP8000 255/40-18
 . . . . (rear) Dunlop SP8000 285/40-18
Wheel upgrade . . . . (front) 18 x 8.5-inch magnesium
 . . . . (rear) 18 x 10-inch magnesium

Rear axle . . . . 3.27:1 gears
Brace support . . . . (coupe only) B-pillar chassis brace
Other individual options . . upgrade sound system, leather,
 twin gauge pod, custom paint, Speedster package (sport
 bar and tonneau)

BODY ENHANCEMENTS

Centrex rear wing
Saleen FIA rear wing (SR)
urethane front airdam
Centrex side skirts
rear brake duct scoops (SR)
urethane rear valance
carbon fiber hood (SR)
NOTE: some early 1994s had fiberglass body kits.

1994 SALEEN PRODUCTION CHART

Body	Doors/Body/Seating	Price	Built
40	2/coupe S-351/4	$34,990	30
42	2/convertible S-351/4	$40,990	14
40	2/coupe SR/2	$45,990	2

NOTE 1: Total production was 44 S-351s in all body styles plus two SRs.
NOTE 2: The V-6 Sport sold 29 units, but was not considered part of the regular Saleen numbering scheme.

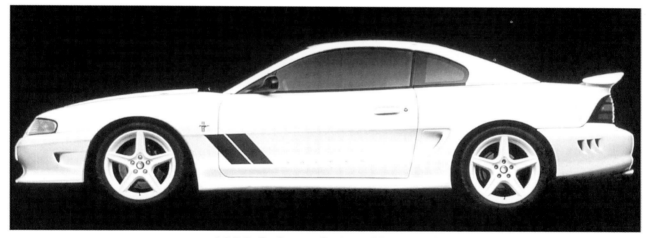

1994 Saleen S-351 (Saleen)

**1995 Saleen S-351 #021
with supercharger
Owner: Mark LaMaskin/
Performance Autosport**

1995 Saleen

Following Ford's example with the stock Mustang, Saleen made few changes to his offerings for the second year of the new style in 1995. The V-6 GT Sport was dropped from the line so the company could concentrate its resources on further development of the V-8 models.

Sales were picking up in 1995, with 126 S-351s and seven SRs going out the door.

DATA PLATE DECODING

A 17-character Vehicle Identification Number is stamped on an aluminum tab on the instrument panel, viewable through windshield. A vehicle certification label is found on the body side of where the driver's door closes.

VEHICLE WARRANTY NUMBER
MANUFACTURER ID

1FA – Ford Motor Co.

RESTRAINT SYSTEM

L – air bags, active belts

VEHICLE CLASSIFICATION

P – passenger car

BODY SERIAL NUMBERS

40 – coupe
42 – convertible

ENGINE CODE

4 – 232-cid (3.8-liter) EFI V-6*
*removed from Saleen S-351s during conversion

CHECK DIGIT

for internal use

MODEL YEAR

S – 1995

ASSEMBLY PLANT

F – Dearborn, Michigan

CONSECUTIVE UNIT NUMBER

Begins at 100001 at each factory

CODE NUMBERS
PAINT CODE

Various Ford colors were used an on a per-request basis.

ENGINE

351-cid (5.8-liter) EFI V-8
Displacement. . . . . 351 cid/5.8 liters

Bore and stroke. . . . . 4.00 x 3.50 inches
Horsepower. . . . . (S-351) 371
. . . . (SR) 480
Heads . . . . high-performance aluminum
Camshaft . . . . hydraulic roller/lifters
Induction . . . . electronic fuel injection
Injectors . . . . (S-351) 30 lb/hr
. . . . (SR) 36 lb/hr
Throttle body. 65mm
Mass air sensor 77mm
Headers. . . . . Saleen ceramic-coated
Code . . . . not assigned by Ford

SUSPENSION ENHANCEMENTS

Springs. . . . . progressive-rate front and rear coil
Shocks . . . . Racecraft gas
Struts . . . . Racecraft gas
. . . . special strut mounting bushings
Quad shocks . . . . Racecraft gas
Bushings . . . . urethane swaybar units
Chassis reinforcements . . . . strut tower brace
Wheels. . . . .
   (S-351) 18 x 8.5-inch Saleen five-spoke
   (S-351 upgrade, SR front) 18 x 8.5-inch alloy or magnesium
   (S-351 upgrade, SR rear) 18 x 10-inch alloy or magnesium
Tires . . . .
   (S-351 front) 235/40ZR-18 BFGoodrich Comp T/A
   (S-351 rear) 245/40ZR-18 BFGoodrich Comp T/A
   (S-351 upgrade, SR front) 255/40ZR-18 Dunlop SP8000
   (S-351 upgrade, SR rear) 285/40ZR-18 Dunlop SP8000
Brakes . . . . four-wheel discs, five-lug pattern

OPTIONAL EQUIPMENT (S-351 only)

R Code Package . . . . Vortech supercharger, 13-inch rotors, four-piston calipers, twin gauge pods (boost and fuel pressure), four-core radiator, dual high-flow fuel pumps and enhanced electronics

T Code Package 13-inch rotors, four-piston calipers, 3.27:1 rear axle, leather seats

Brakes 13-inch front rotors, four-piston calipers and grooved rear rotors

Tire upgrade. . . . . (front) Dunlop SP8000 255/40-18
. . . . (rear) Dunlop SP8000 285/40-18

Wheel upgrade. . . . . (front) 18 x 8.5-inch magnesium
. . . . (rear) 18 x 10-inch magnesium

Rear axle. . . . . 3.27:1 gears

Brace support. . . . . (coupe only) B-pillar chassis brace

Other individual options . . upgrade sound system, leather, twin gauge pod, custom paint, Speedster package (sport bar and tonneau), Recaro seats, 3.55:1 rear axle

BODY ENHANCEMENTS

Centrex rear wing
Saleen FIA rear wing (SR)
urethane front airdam
Centrex side skirts
rear brake duct scoops (SR)
urethane rear valance
carbon fiber hood (SR)

1995 SALEEN PRODUCTION CHART			
Body	Doors/Body/Seating	Price	Built
40	2/coupe S-351/4	$34,990	84
42	2/convertible S-351/4	$43,990	42
40	2/coupe SR/2	$59,990	7

NOTE 1: Total production was 126 S-351s in all body styles plus seven SRs.
NOTE 2: Three SR models were built to competition specs for drivers Steve Saleen, Bob Bondurant, and Tim Allen.

1995 Saleen SR (Saleen)

**1995 Saleen S-351 #021
with supercharger**

1995 Saleen S-351 hood vent, decal

1995 Saleen S-351 wheel

1995 Saleen S-351 convertible (Saleen)

1996 Saleen S-281 #331
with Cobra V-8
Owner: Lee Davis

1996 Saleen

The original Saleen formula made a dramatic return in 1996, in the form of the aggressive-looking S-281 that featured minimal upgrades to the engine and interior (a new shifter and gauge treatment), but maximum massaging of the suspension and aerodynamics. Ford's new modular 4.6-liter 281-cid V-8, with only minor tweaking from Saleen, provided motivation for the bespoiled coupes and convertibles. Massive 245/40-18 BFGoodrich rubber on 18-inch, five-spoke alloy wheels belied the fact that the S-281 was the "entry-level" Saleen at only $28,990 for the coupe. Options included 18-inch magnesium wheels, Recaro seats, a carbon fiber hood, 3.55:1 rear axle, and the convertible-only Speedster package, which featured a hard tonneau cover for the back seat and a two-point padded rollbar.

Although it was not listed as a separate model, customers could have SVT's Cobra taken to the next level with a Saleen S-281 conversion. Checking this option gave buyers the double overhead cam Cobra V-8 with the looks and handling of a Saleen. Supercharging, long a way to squeeze more air into a set amount of cubic inches, was available on the S-281, but not from the Saleen factory directly. Because the 4.6-liter engine's supercharger package was not approved for sale initially, it was up to dealers or aftermarket installers to meet the customer's higher-performance needs. It was not until 1999 models that Saleen could sell a factory-installed supercharger in a post-1993 Mustang.

Showing a crystal clear understanding of who the

company's most ardent supporters were, Saleen included one-year memberships in both the Mustang Club of America and the Saleen Owners & Enthusiasts Club with the purchase of an S-281. The S-281 proved to be the most popular Saleen model in many years, with 436 examples selling in the first year of production—30 of which were convertibles sold to the Budget rental car company for use at its premium locations such as Las Vegas.

Twenty S-351s were sold in 1996. The SR model was unofficially blended into the S-351 line on which it was based as the S-351 was now available with the same 500-hp rating when ordered with the Vortech supercharger option. 1996 S-351s received new Trick Flow heads in place of the previous Edelbrock units.

DATA PLATE DECODING

A 17-character Vehicle Identification Number is stamped on an aluminum tab on the instrument panel, viewable through windshield. A vehicle certification label is found on the body side of where the driver's door closes.

VEHICLE WARRANTY NUMBER MANUFACTURER ID

1FA – Ford Motor Co.

RESTRAINT SYSTEM

L – air bags, active belts

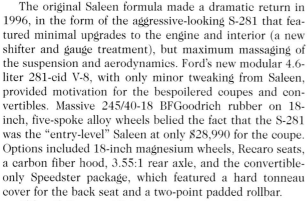

VEHICLE CLASSIFICATION

P – passenger car

BODY SERIAL NUMBERS

40 – coupe
42 – GT coupe
44 – convertible
45 – GT convertible
46 – Cobra convertible
47 – Cobra coupe

ENGINE CODE

4 – 232-cid (3.8-liter) EFI V-6*
W – 281-cid (4.6-liter) EFI V-8
V – 281-cid (4.6-liter) EFI V-8 Cobra
*removed from Saleen S-351s during conversion

CHECK DIGIT

for internal use

MODEL YEAR

T – 1996

ASSEMBLY PLANT

F – Dearborn, Michigan

CONSECUTIVE UNIT NUMBER

Begins at 100001 at each factory

CODE NUMBERS
PAINT CODE

Various Ford colors were used an on a per-request basis.

ENGINES

281-cid (4.6-liter) EFI SOHC V-8

Valves . . . . overhead
Camshaft . . . . single overhead cam
Block . . . . cast iron
Displacement . . . . 281 cid/4.6 liters
Bore and stroke . . . . 3.60 x 3.60 inches
Compression ratio 9.0:1
Brake hp . . . . 220 @ 4400 rpm

Torque . . . . 285 @ 3500 rpm
Induction . . . . electronic fuel injection
Code . . . . W

281-cid (4.6-liter) EFI DOHC V-8 Cobra

Valves . . . . 4 per cylinder
Valve size . . . . (intake) 37mm
. . . . (exhaust) 30mm
Camshaft . . . . double overhead
Block . . . . aluminum
Heads . . . . aluminum
Displacement . . . . 281 cid/4.6 liters
Bore and stroke . . . . 3.55 x 3.54 inches
Compression ratio 9.85:1
Brake hp . . . . 305 @ 5800 rpm
Torque . . . . 300 lb./ft. @ 4800 rpm
Induction . . . . electronic fuel injection
Intake manifold . . . . equal length thin-wall cast aluminum
    runners, cast aluminum plenum chamber
Throttle body . . . . dual 57mm
Port throttles . . . . . electronically actuated 34mm, open to
    secondary intake valves at 3250 rpm
Exhaust headers . . . . . cast high-silicon, molybdenum iron,
    manifold type
Code V

351-cid (5.8-liter) EFI V-8

Displacement . . . . 351 cid/5.8 liters
Bore and stroke . . . . 4.00 x 3.50 inches
Horsepower 400
. . . . (supercharged) 510
Heads . . . . high-performance aluminum
Camshaft . . . . hydraulic roller/lifters
Induction . . . . electronic fuel injection
Injectors . . . . 30 lb/hr
Throttle body 65mm
Mass air sensor 80mm
Headers . . . . Saleen ceramic-coated
Code . . . . not assigned by Ford

SUSPENSION ENHANCEMENTS

Springs . . . . . Racecraft progressive-rate front and rear coil
Shocks . . . . Racecraft gas

1996 Saleen S-281 wheel

**1996 V-code 4.6-liter/EFI DOHC V-8
with supercharger**

Struts . . . . Racecraft gas
. . . . special strut mounting bushings
Quad shocks . . . . Racecraft gas
Bushings . . . . urethane swaybar units
Wheels. . . . .
   (S-281/S-351) 18 x 8.5-inch Saleen five-spoke
   (S-281 upgrade/S-351 upgrade, front) 18 x 8.5-inch alloy
     or magnesium
   (S-281 upgrade/S-351 upgrade, rear)
   18 x 10-inch alloy or magnesium
Tires . . . .
   (S-281) 245/40ZR-18
   (S-351) 245/40ZR-18 BFGoodrich Comp T/A
   (S-281 upgrade, front) 255/35ZR-18
   (S-281 upgrade, rear) 285/35ZR-18
   (S-351 upgrade, front) 255/40ZR-18 Dunlop SP8000
   (S-351 upgrade, rear) 285/40ZR-18 Dunlop SP8000
Brakes. . . . . four-wheel discs, five-lug pattern

OPTIONAL EQUIPMENT

S-281

Brakes. . . Saleen/Alcon 13-inch rotors, four-piston calipers
Brace support . . . . two-point chassis brace
Twin-gauge pod. . . . . . manifold and fuel pressure readings

Sportbar . . (convertible only) includes special soft tonneau
Speedster package . (convertible only) includes hard speedster tonneau, sportbar,
. . . . special soft tonneau

S-351

R Code Package . . . . Vortech supercharger, 13-inch rotors,
   four-piston calipers, twin gauge pods (boost and fuel
   pressure), four-core radiator, dual high-flow fuel pumps
   and enhanced electronics
T Code Package. . . . . 13-inch rotors, four-piston calipers,
   3.27:1 rear axle, leather seats
Brakes . . . . . 13-inch front rotors, four-piston calipers and
   grooved rear rotors
Rear axle. . . . . 3.27:1 gears
Brace support . . . . (coupe only) B-pillar chassis brace
Other individual options . . upgrade sound system, leather,
   twin gauge pod, custom paint, Spyder package (sport bar
   and tonneau)

BODY ENHANCEMENTS

Saleen design front facia
Saleen design side skirts
Saleen design rear valance
Saleen S-281 rear wing (S-281 only)

1996 SALEEN PRODUCTION CHART

Body	Doors/Body/Seating	Price	Built
42	2/coupe S-281/4	$28,990	191
47	2/coupe S-281/4 Cobra	$38,900	5
40	2/coupe S-351/4	N/A	9
45	2/convertible S-281/4	$33,500	234
46	2/convertible S-281/4 Cobra	$41,000	6
44	2/convertible S-351/4	$47,990	11

NOTE 1: Total production was 436 S-281s in all body styles (including 30 Budget rental convertibles) plus 20 S-351s.

1996 Saleen S-281 (Saleen)

For 1997, Saleen continued offering its S-281 with either a 220-hp version of the 4.6-liter SOHC V-8, or a 310-hp 4.6-liter DOHC (the SVT Cobra's 32-valve engine introduced the previous year). A six-speed manual transmission became standard on the S-351. Optional equipment available on the S-351 included outrageous "Widebody" front fascia, fenders, rear quarter panels, rear valance, a carbon-fiber hood and dual-plane rear wing. All S-351s built in 1997 were supercharged. They also benefited from forged pistons, Saleen/Cosworth computers and 36 lbs./hr. injectors.

An extra-cost tire upgrade on the S-281 and S-351 were Michelin Pilots measuring 255/40-18 (front) and a super-wide 295/35-18 (rear). All S-351s came standard in 1997 with magnesium wheels. The company produced 327 S-281s and 40 S-351s in 1997.

DATA PLATE DECODING

A 17-character Vehicle Identification Number is stamped on an aluminum tab on the instrument panel, viewable through windshield. A vehicle certification label is found on the body side of where the driver's door closes.

VEHICLE WARRANTY NUMBER
MANUFACTURER ID

1FA – Ford Motor Co.

RESTRAINT SYSTEM

L – air bags, active belts

VEHICLE CLASSIFICATION

P – passenger car

BODY SERIAL NUMBERS

40 – coupe
42 – GT coupe
44 – convertible
45 – GT convertible
46 – Cobra convertible
47 – Cobra coupe

ENGINE CODE

4 – 232-cid (3.8-liter) EFI V-6*
W – 281-cid (4.6-liter) EFI V-8
V – 281-cid (4.6-liter) EFI V-8 Cobra
*removed from Saleen S-351s during conversion

CHECK DIGIT

for internal use

MODEL YEAR

V – 1997

ASSEMBLY PLANT

F – Dearborn, Michigan

CONSECUTIVE UNIT NUMBER

Begins at 100001 at each factory

CODE NUMBERS
PAINT CODE

Various Ford colors were used an on a per-request basis.

ENGINES

281-cid (4.6-liter) EFI SOHC V-8

Valves . . . . overhead
Camshaft . . . . single overhead cam
Block . . . . cast iron
Displacement. . . . . 281 cid/4.6 liters
Bore and stroke. . . . . 3.60 x 3.60 inches
Compression ratio 9.0:1
Brake hp . . . . 220 @ 4400 rpm
Torque . . . . 285 @ 3500 rpm
Induction . . . . electronic fuel injection
Code . . . . W

281-cid (4.6-liter) EFI DOHC V-8 Cobra

Valves . . . . 4 per cylinder
Valve size . . . . (intake) 37mm
. . . . (exhaust) 30mm
Camshaft . . . . double overhead
Block . . . . aluminum
Heads. . . . . aluminum
Displacement. . . . . 281 cid/4.6 liters
Bore and stroke. . . . . 3.55 x 3.54 inches
Compression ratio 9.85:1
Brake hp . . . . 310 @ 5800 rpm
Torque . . . . 300 lb./ft. @ 4800 rpm
Induction . . . . electronic fuel injection
Intake manifold . . . . equal length thin-wall cast aluminum runners, cast aluminum plenum chamber
Throttle body. . . . . dual 57mm
Port throttles . . . . electronically actuated 34mm,
. . . . open to secondary intake valves at 3250 rpm
Exhaust headers. . . . . cast high-silicon, molybdenum iron, manifold type
Code V
Transmission . . . . Borg-Warner T45 5-speed
Rear axle ratio 3.27:1

351-cid (5.8-liter) EFI V-8

Displacement. . . . . 351 cid/5.8 liters
Bore and stroke. . . . . 4.00 x 3.50 inches
Horsepower . . . . (supercharged) 510
Heads . . . . high-performance aluminum
Camshaft . . . . hydraulic roller/lifters
Induction . . . . electronic fuel injection
Injectors . . . . 36 lb/hr
Throttle body. 65mm
Mass air sensor 77mm
Headers. . . . . Saleen ceramic-coated
Code . . . . not assigned by Ford

SUSPENSION ENHANCEMENTS

Springs . . . . . Racecraft progressive-rate front and rear coil
Shocks . . . . Racecraft gas
. . . . (S-351) Bilstein N2
Struts . . . . Racecraft gas
. . . . (S-351) Bilstein N2
. . . . special strut mounting bushings
Quad shocks . . . . Racecraft gas
Bushings . . . . urethane swaybar units
Wheels. . . . .
   (S-281) 18 x 8.5-inch Saleen five-spoke
   (S-281 upgrade/S-351, front) 18 x 8.5-inch magnesium
   (S-281 upgrade/S-351, rear) 18 x 10-inch magnesium
Tires . . . .
   (S-281) 245/40ZR-18
   (S-351) 245/40ZR-18 BFGoodrich Comp T/A
   (S-281 upgrade, front) 255/35ZR-18
   (S-281 upgrade, rear) 285/35ZR-18
   (S-351 upgrade, front) 255/40ZR-18 Dunlop SP8000
   (S-351 upgrade, rear) 285/40ZR-18 Dunlop SP8000
Brakes . . . . four-wheel discs, five-lug pattern

OPTIONAL EQUIPMENT

S-281

Brakes. . . Saleen/Alcon 13-inch rotors, four-piston calipers
Brace support . . . . two-point chassis brace
Twin-gauge pod . . . . . manifold and fuel pressure readings
Sportbar . . (convertible only) includes special soft tonneau
Speedster package . . . . . . (convertible only) includes hard
   speedster tonneau, sportbar, special soft tonneau

S-351

Brakes . . . . . 13-inch front rotors, four-piston calipers and
   grooved rear rotors
Rear axle. . . . . 3.27:1 gears
Brace support. . . . . (coupe only) B-pillar chassis brace
Other individual options . . upgrade sound system, leather,
   twin gauge pod, custom paint, Speedster package (sport
   bar and tonneau), Recaro seats, 3.55:1 rear axle

BODY ENHANCEMENTS

Saleen design front facia
Saleen design side skirts
Saleen design rear valance
Saleen S-281 rear wing (S-281 only)

1997 SALEEN PRODUCTION CHART

Body	Doors/Body/Seating	Price	Built
42	2/coupe S-281/4	$29,500	113
47	2/coupe S-281/4 Cobra	$38,900	13
40	2/coupe S-351/4	$53,500	21
45	2/convertible S-281/4	$33,990	196
46	2/convertible S-281/4 Cobra	$39,500	5
44	2/convertible S-351/4	$57,990	19

NOTE 1: Total production was 327 S-281s in all body styles (including 88 Budget rental convertibles) plus 40 S-351s.
NOTE 2: One competition model was produced this year.

1998 Saleen

The 1998 Saleen models, based on a now five-year-old Mustang design, changed little. Saleen's efforts were aimed toward the Mustang facelift Ford was promising for the 1999 model year.

Sales of the S-281 slipped to 186 cars, and the super-fast S-351 only found 22 purchasers in 1998.

DATA PLATE DECODING

A 17-character Vehicle Identification Number is stamped on an aluminum tab on the instrument panel, viewable through windshield. A vehicle certification label is found on the body side of where the driver's door closes.

VEHICLE WARRANTY NUMBER
MANUFACTURER ID

1FA – Ford Motor Co.

RESTRAINT SYSTEM

L – air bags, active belts

VEHICLE CLASSIFICATION

P – passenger car

BODY SERIAL NUMBERS

40 – coupe
42 – GT coupe
44 – convertible
45 – GT convertible
46 – Cobra convertible
47 – Cobra coupe

ENGINE CODE

4 – 232-cid (3.8-liter) EFI V-6*
W – 281-cid (4.6-liter) EFI V-8
V – 281-cid (4.6-liter) EFI V-8 Cobra
*removed from Saleen S-351s during conversion

CHECK DIGIT

for internal use

MODEL YEAR

W – 1998

ASSEMBLY PLANT

F – Dearborn, Michigan

CONSECUTIVE UNIT NUMBER

Begins at 100001 at each factory

CODE NUMBERS
PAINT CODE

Various Ford colors were used an on a per-request basis.

ENGINES

281-cid (4.6-liter) EFI SOHC V-8
Valves . . . . overhead
Camshaft . . . . single overhead cam
Block . . . . cast iron
Displacement . . . . 281 cid/4.6 liters
Bore and stroke . . . . 3.60 x 3.60 inches
Compression ratio 9.0:1
Brake hp . . . . 220 @ 4400 rpm
Torque . . . . 285 @ 3500 rpm
Induction . . . . electronic fuel injection
Code . . . . W

281-cid (4.6-liter) EFI DOHC V-8 Cobra
Valves . . . . 4 per cylinder
Valve size . . . . (intake) 37mm
. . . . (exhaust) 30mm
Camshaft . . . . double overhead
Block . . . . aluminum
Heads . . . . aluminum
Displacement . . . . 281 cid/4.6 liters
Bore and stroke . . . . 3.55 x 3.54 inches
Compression ratio 9.85:1
Brake hp . . . . 305 @ 5800 rpm
Torque . . . . 300 @ 4800 rpm
Induction . . . . electronic fuel injection
Intake manifold . . . . equal length thin-wall cast aluminum
runners, cast aluminum plenum chamber
Throttle body . . . . dual 57mm
Port throttles . . . . electronically actuated 34mm,
. . . . open to secondary intake valves at 3250 rpm
Exhaust headers . . . . . cast high-silicon, molybdenum iron,
manifold type
Code V

351-cid (5.8-liter) EFI V-8
Displacement . . . . 351 cid/5.8 liters
Bore and stroke . . . . 4.00 x 3.50 inches
Horsepower . . . . (supercharged) 510
Heads . . . . high-performance aluminum
Camshaft . . . . hydraulic roller/lifters
Induction . . . . electronic fuel injection
Injectors . . . . 36 lb/hr
Throttle body 65mm
Mass air sensor 77mm
Headers . . . . Saleen ceramic-coated
Code . . . . not assigned by Ford

SUSPENSION ENHANCEMENTS

Springs . . . . . Racecraft progressive-rate front and rear coil
Shocks . . . . Bilstein N2
Struts . . . . Bilstein N2
. . . . special strut mounting bushings
Quad shocks . . . . Bilstein N2
Bushings . . . . urethane swaybar units
Wheels . . . .
(S-281) 18 x 8.5-inch Saleen five-spoke
(S-281 upgrade/S-351, front) 18 x 8.5-inch magnesium
(S-281 upgrade/S-351, rear) 18 x 10-inch magnesium
Tires . . . .
(S-281) 245/40ZR-18
(S-351) 245/40ZR-18 BFGoodrich Comp T/A
(S-281 upgrade, front) 255/35ZR-18
(S-281 upgrade, rear) 285/35ZR-18
(S-351 upgrade, front) 255/40ZR-18 Dunlop SP8000
(S-351 upgrade, rear) 285/40ZR-18 Dunlop SP8000
Brakes . . . . four-wheel discs, five-lug pattern

OPTIONAL EQUIPMENT

S-281

Brakes. . . Saleen/Alcon 13-inch rotors, four-piston calipers
Brace support . . . . two-point chassis brace
Twin-gauge pod. . . . . . manifold and fuel pressure readings
Sportbar . . (convertible only) includes special soft tonneau
Speedster package . . . . . . (convertible only) includes hard
speedster tonneau, sportbar, special soft tonneau

S-351

Brakes13-inch front rotors, four-piston calipers and grooved
rear rotors

Rear axle. . . . . .3.27:1 gears
Brace support . . . . (coupe only) B-pillar chassis brace
Other individual options . . upgrade sound system, leather,
twin gauge pod, custom paint, Spyder package (sport bar
and tonneau)

BODY ENHANCEMENTS

Saleen design front facia
Saleen design side skirts
Saleen design rear valance
Saleen S-281 rear wing (S-281 only)

1998 SALEEN PRODUCTION CHART

Body	Doors/Body/Seating	Price	Built
42	2/coupe S-281/4	$26,990	59
47	2/coupe S-281/4 Cobra	$36,990	14
40	2/coupe S-351/4	$56,990	10
45	2/convertible S-281/4	$32,990	91
46	2/convertible S-281/4 Cobra	$39,590	21
44	2/convertible S-351/4	$60,990	12

NOTE 1: Total production was 186 S-281s in all body styles (including 10 Budget rental convertibles) plus 22 S-351s.
NOTE 2: One competition model was produced this year.

1999 Saleen S-281 #104 with
Speedster package
Owner: Mark LaMaskin/
Performance Autosport

1999 Saleen

Ford's facelift for the Mustang in 1999 must have inspired Steve Saleen, because he added another 25 hp to the stock V-8's rating. The company found 285 hp in the SOHC 4.6-liter V-8 through the use of a new premium fuel calibration, special underdrive pulleys and a new exhaust system. Saleen offered a Roots-type supercharger option that boosted horsepower on the S-281 to an advertised 350. No longer the domain of the Ford service department, in 1999 the Eaton supercharger became a Saleen factory-installed option.

The S-351, again standard with a Vortech supercharger, claimed 495 horses for 1999—down from the previous year. The standard, quick-ratio, six-speed manual transmission sent power to a 3.27:1 rear axle (3.08:1 and 3.55:1 were optional). 1999 was the last year for production of the S-351; its replacement is promised for sometime in 2002.

While the S-281 came with the standard 15.4-gallon Mustang fuel tank, the 351-equipped Saleens were fitted with 22-gallon race-type fuel cells. The new Mustang design and more power in its base model gave Saleen a sales spike in 1999, with 373 S-281s and 45 S-351s finding new homes.

DATA PLATE DECODING

A 17-character Vehicle Identification Number is stamped on an aluminum tab on the instrument panel, viewable through windshield. A vehicle certification label is found on the body side of where the driver's door closes.

VEHICLE WARRANTY NUMBER MANUFACTURER ID

1FA – Ford Motor Co.

RESTRAINT SYSTEM

L – air bags, active belts

VEHICLE CLASSIFICATION

P – passenger car

BODY SERIAL NUMBERS

40 – coupe	46 – Cobra convertible
42 – GT coupe	47 – Cobra coupe
44 – convertible	
45 – GT convertible	

ENGINE CODE

4 – 232-cid (3.8-liter) EFI V-6*
X – 281-cid (4.6-liter) EFI V-8
V – 281-cid (4.6-liter) EFI V-8 Cobra
*removed from Saleen S-351s during conversion

CHECK DIGIT

for internal use

MODEL YEAR

X – 1999

ASSEMBLY PLANT

F – Dearborn, Michigan

CONSECUTIVE UNIT NUMBER

Begins at 100001 at each factory

CODE NUMBERS
PAINT CODE

Various Ford colors were used an on a per-request basis.

ENGINES

281-cid (4.6-liter) EFI SOHC V-8

Valves . . . . overhead
Camshaft . . . . single overhead cam
Block . . . . cast iron
Displacement. . . . . 281 cid/4.6 liters
Bore and stroke. . . . . 3.60 x 3.60 inches
Compression ratio 9.0:1
Brake hp . . . . 285 @ 5100 rpm
. . . . (supercharged) 350 @ 5000 rpm
Torque . . . . 315 @ 4100 rpm
. . . . (supercharged) 410 @ 3000 rpm
Induction . . . . electronic fuel injection
Code X

281-cid (4.6-liter) EFI DOHC V-8 Cobra

Valves . . . . 4 per cylinder
Valve size . . . . (intake) 37mm
. . . . (exhaust) 30mm
Camshaft . . . . double overhead
Block . . . . aluminum
Heads. . . . . aluminum
Displacement. . . . . 281 cid/4.6 liters
Bore and stroke. . . . . 3.55 x 3.54 inches
Compression ratio 9.85:1
Brake hp . . . . 320 @ 6000 rpm
Torque . . . . 317 @ 4750 rpm
Induction . . . . electronic fuel injection
Intake manifold . . . . equal length thin-wall cast aluminum
runners, cast aluminum plenum chamber
Throttle body. . . . . dual 57mm
Port throttles . . . . electronically actuated 34mm,
. . . . open to secondary intake valves at 3250 rpm
Exhaust manifold . . . . cast iron
Code V

351-cid (5.8-liter) EFI V-8

Displacement. . . . . 351 cid/5.8 liters
Bore and stroke. . . . . 4.00 x 3.50 inches
Horsepower . . . . (supercharged) 510
Heads . . . . high-performance aluminum
Camshaft . . . . hydraulic roller/lifters

Induction . . . . electronic fuel injection
Injectors . . . . 36 lb/hr
Throttle body. 65mm
Mass air sensor 77mm
Headers. . . . . Saleen ceramic-coated
Code . . . . not assigned by Ford

SUSPENSION ENHANCEMENTS

Springs . . . . . Racecraft progressive-rate front and rear coil
Shocks . . . . Racecraft gas
Struts . . . . Racecraft gas
. . . . special strut mounting bushings
Quad shocks . . . . Racecraft gas
Bushings . . . . urethane swaybar units
Chassis reinforcements . . . . strut tower brace
Wheels. . . . .
  (S-281/S-351) 18 x 9-inch Saleen five-spoke
  (S-281/S-351 optional rear) 18 x 10-inch Saleen five-spoke
Tires . . . .
  (S-281/S-351, front) 255/35ZR-18 Pirelli P7000
  (S-281/S-351, rear) 265/35ZR-18 Pirelli P7000
  (S-281/S-351 upgrade, front) 265/35ZR-18 Pirelli PZero
  (S-281/S-351 upgrade, rear) 295/35ZR-18 Pirelli PZero
Brakes . . . . four-wheel discs, five-lug pattern

OPTIONAL EQUIPMENT

S-281

Brakes. . . Saleen/Alcon 13-inch rotors, four-piston calipers
Brace support . . . . two-point chassis brace
Twin-gauge pod . . . . . manifold and fuel pressure readings
Sportbar . . (convertible only) includes special soft tonneau
Speedster package . . . . . . (convertible only) includes hard
  speedster tonneau, sportbar, special soft tonneau
Seats. . . . . Recaro
Rear axle. . . . . 3.55:1 gears
Other individual options carbon fiber hood, chrome wheels

S-351

Brakes . . . . . 13-inch front rotors, four-piston calipers and
  grooved rear rotors
Rear axle. . . . . 3.27:1 gears
Brace support . . . . (coupe only) B-pillar chassis brace
Other individual options . . . . upgrade sound system,
  leather, twin gauge pod, custom paint, Speedster package (sport bar and tonneau)

BODY ENHANCEMENTS

Saleen design front facia
Saleen design side skirts
Saleen design rear valance
Saleen S-281 rear wing (S-281 only)

1999 SALEEN PRODUCTION CHART			
Body	Doors/Body/Seating	Price	Built
42	2/coupe S-281/4	$27,990	183
47	2/coupe S-281/4 Cobra	N/A	8
40	2/coupe S-351/4	$49,990	19
45	2/convertible S-281/4	$31,790	170
46	2/convertible S-281/4 Cobra	N/A	12
44	2/convertible S-351/4	$54,490	26

NOTE 1: Total production was 373 S-281s in all body styles plus 45 S-351s.

1999 Saleen S-281 #104 with Speedster package

1999 Speedster package

1999 Saleen interior

1999 Saleen gauges

1999 X-code 4.6-liter/EFI SOHC V-8

1999 Saleen SA-15 #09
Owner: Rich Thacker

1999 Saleen S-281 #259
Owner: Mark LaMaskin/Performance Autosport

2000 Saleen S-281
Owner: Jimmy Morrison/Morrison Motor Co.

2000 Saleen

With the end of S-351 production in 1999 and the SVT Cobra's one-year hiatus to work out power output issues (see the Cobra entry elsewhere in this book), 2000 was a one-flavor season for Saleen, but what flavor!

The supercharged version of the S-281 became known as the S-281 SC, although the blower package was not considered a separate model. With a sticker price of $29,900, the S-281 coupe settled in as the lowest-priced Saleen model, but with few other changes.

In tests on the dragstrip, the $35,460 S-281 SC coupe bested the zero-to-60 mph time of the normally aspirated 281 by 0.4 seconds (4.8 vs. 5.2) and both models burned up the skidpad at .93g.

DATA PLATE DECODING

A 17-character Vehicle Identification Number is stamped on an aluminum tab on the instrument panel, viewable through windshield. A vehicle certification label is found on the body side of where the driver's door closes.

VEHICLE WARRANTY NUMBER
MANUFACTURER ID

1FA – Ford Motor Co.

RESTRAINT SYSTEM

L – air bags, active belts

VEHICLE CLASSIFICATION

P – passenger car

BODY SERIAL NUMBERS

42 – GT coupe
45 – GT convertible

ENGINE CODE

X – 281-cid (4.6-liter) EFI V-8

CHECK DIGIT

for internal use

MODEL YEAR

Y – 2000

ASSEMBLY PLANT

F – Dearborn, Michigan

CONSECUTIVE UNIT NUMBER

Begins at 100001 at each factory

CODE NUMBERS
PAINT CODE

Various Ford colors were used an on a per-request basis.

ENGINE

281-cid (4.6-liter) EFI SOHC V-8

Valves	overhead
Camshaft	single overhead cam
Block	cast iron
Displacement	281 cid/4.6 liters
Bore and stroke	3.60 x 3.60 inches
Compression ratio	9.0:1
Brake hp	285 @ 5100 rpm
(supercharged)	350 @ 5000 rpm
Torque	315 @ 4100 rpm
(supercharged)	410 @ 3000 rpm

Induction . . . . electronic fuel injection
Code X

SUSPENSION ENHANCEMENTS

Springs . . . . . Racecraft progressive-rate front and rear coil
Shocks . . . . Bilstein N2
Struts . . . . Bilstein N2
. . . . special strut mounting bushings
Quad shocks . . . . Bilstein N2
Bushings . . . . urethane swaybar units
Chassis reinforcements . . . . strut tower brace
Wheels . . . . 18 x 9-inch Saleen five-spoke
. . . . 18 x 10-inch Saleen five-spoke
Tires . . . . (front) 255/35ZR-18 Pirelli P7000
. . . . (rear) 265/35ZR-18 Pirelli P7000
. . . . (upgrade, front) 265/35ZR-18 Pirelli PZero
. . . . (upgrade, rear) 295/35ZR-18 Pirelli PZero
Brakes . . . . four-wheel discs, five-lug pattern

OPTIONAL EQUIPMENT

Brakes . . . Saleen/Alcon 13-inch rotors, four-piston calipers
Brace support . . . . two-point chassis brace
Twin-gauge pod . . . . . manifold and fuel pressure readings
Sportbar . . (convertible only) includes special soft tonneau
Speedster package . . . . . . (convertible only) includes hard
    speedster tonneau, sportbar, special soft tonneau
Seats . . . . Recaro
Rear axle . . . . 3.55:1 gears
Other individual options carbon fiber hood, chrome wheels

BODY ENHANCEMENTS

Saleen design front facia
Saleen design side skirts
Saleen design rear valance
Saleen rear wing

2000 SALEEN PRODUCTION CHART			
Body	Doors/Body/Seating	Price	Built
42	2/coupe S-281/4	$29,900	539
45	2/convertible S-281/4	$33,900	435

NOTE 1: Total production was 974 S-281s in all body styles. There is currently no breakdown between supercharged and normally aspirated models.

**2000 Saleen S-281
Owner: Jimmy Morrison/
Morrison Motor Co.**

**2000 Saleen S-281
Owner: Jimmy Morrison/
Morrison Motor Co.**

**2000 Saleen S-281
Owner: Jimmy Morrison/
Morrison Motor Co.**

**2000
Saleen
side
scoop**

2001 Saleen S-281 (Saleen)

2001 Saleen

2001 Saleen S-281 convertible with Speedster package (Saleen)

The S-281 and S-281 SC continued unchanged for 2001.

The biggest news for Saleen fans this year was the availability of an all-new SR model wearing a $158,000 price tag. The now-familiar 351-cid V-8 was rated at 505 horsepower and 500 lbs.-ft. of torque with a six-speed transmission sending all that power back to a 3.55:1-geared rear axle by way of a shortened driveshaft.

Independent rear suspension components sat where a live axle had been for more than 35 years of Mustang history. Braking occurred through 14.4-inch front rotors with four-piston calipers in front and 13-inch metallic discs with four-piston calipers in the rear.

Beneath the wildly styled, Saleen-unique composite body panels lay a complete roll cage and suspension reinforcement system. The SR, available in coupe form only, was wind tunnel tuned at Lockheed-Martin's full-size tunnel in Marietta, Georgia. Performance figures released by Saleen Performance claim the SR can reach 60 miles an hour from a standstill in 4.0 seconds flat and circle the skidpad at 1.09g.

The Cobra-based Saleen was once again offered, with the return of SVT's double-overhead cam 320-hp V-8. Saleen made no engine modifications to the Cobra package other than the addition of a performance exhaust system.

The standard S-281 coupe retailed for $32,099, with the convertible selling for $36,099. When the Cobra platform was ordered, prices were $41,600 (coupe) and $45,500 (convertible).

DATA PLATE DECODING

A 17-character Vehicle Identification Number is stamped on an aluminum tab on the instrument panel, viewable through windshield. A vehicle certification label is found on the body side of where the driver's door closes.

VEHICLE WARRANTY NUMBER MANUFACTURER ID

1FA – Ford Motor Co.

RESTRAINT SYSTEM

L – air bags, active belts

VEHICLE CLASSIFICATION

P – passenger car

BODY SERIAL NUMBERS

42 – GT coupe
45 – GT convertible

ENGINE CODE

X – 281-cid (4.6-liter) EFI SOHC V-8
V – 281-cid (4.6-liter) EFI DOHC V-8 Cobra

CHECK DIGIT

for internal use

MODEL YEAR

1 – 2001

ASSEMBLY PLANT

F – Dearborn, Michigan

CONSECUTIVE UNIT NUMBER

Begins at 100001 at each factory

CODE NUMBERS

PAINT CODE

Various Ford colors were used an on a per-request basis.

ENGINES

281-cid (4.6-liter) EFI SOHC V-8

Valves . . . . overhead
Camshaft . . . . single overhead cam
Block . . . . cast iron
Displacement. . . . . 281 cid/4.6 liters
Bore and stroke. . . . . 3.60 x 3.60 inches
Compression ratio 9.4:1
Brake hp . . . . 285 @ 5100 rpm
. . . . (supercharged) 365 @ 5800 rpm
Torque . . . . 315 @ 4100 rpm
. . . . (supercharged) 400 @ 3500 rpm
Induction . . . . electronic fuel injection
Code X

281-cid (4.6-liter) EFI DOHC V-8 Cobra

Valves . . . . 4 per cylinder
Valve size . . . . (intake) 37mm
. . . . (exhaust) 30mm
Camshaft . . . . double overhead
Block . . . . aluminum

Heads. . . . . aluminum
Displacement. . . . . 281 cid/4.6 liters
Bore and stroke . . . . 3.55 x 3.54 inches
Compression ratio 9.85:1
Brake hp . . . . 320 @ 6000 rpm
Torque . . . . 317 @ 4750 rpm
Induction . . . . electronic fuel injection
Intake manifold . . . . equal length thin-wall cast aluminum
   runners, cast aluminum plenum chamber
Throttle body. . . . . dual 57mm
Port throttles. . . . . . electronically actuated 34mm, open to
   secondary intake valves at 3250 rpm
Exhaust manifold . . . . cast iron
Code V

SUSPENSION ENHANCEMENTS

Springs . . . . . Racecraft progressive-rate front and rear coil
Shocks . . . . Racecraft gas
Struts . . . . Racecraft gas
. . . . special strut mounting bushings
Quad shocks . . . . Racecraft gas
Bushings . . . . urethane swaybar units
Chassis reinforcements . . . . strut tower brace
Wheels. . . . .
   18 x 9-inch Saleen five-spoke
   18 x 10-inch Saleen five-spoke
Tires . . . .
   (front) 255/35ZR-18 Pirelli P7000
   (rear) 265/35ZR-18 Pirelli P7000
   (upgrade, front) 265/35ZR-18 Pirelli PZero
   (upgrade, rear) 295/35ZR-18 Pirelli PZero
Brakes . . . . four-wheel discs, five-lug pattern

OPTIONAL EQUIPMENT

Brakes. . . Saleen/Alcon 13-inch rotors, four-piston calipers
Brace support . . . . two-point chassis brace
Twin-gauge pod . . . . . manifold and fuel pressure readings
Sportbar . . (convertible only) includes special soft tonneau
Speedster package . . . . . (convertible only) includes hard
   speedster tonneau, sportbar, special soft tonneau

BODY ENHANCEMENTS

Saleen design front facia
Saleen design side skirts
Saleen design rear valance
Saleen rear wing

2001 SALEEN PRODUCTION CHART

Body	Doors/Body/Seating	Price	Built
42	2/coupe S-281/4	$32,099	N/A
45	2/convertible S-281/4	$36,099	N/A
42	2/coupe S-281/4 Cobra	$41,600	N/A
45	2/convertible S-281/4 Cobra	$45,500	N/A

NOTE 1: Production figures were not available at the time of this printing.

**1993 SVT Cobra
Owner: Jimmy Morrison/
Morrison Motor Co.***

1993 SVT Cobra

Think of the 1993 SVT Cobra as a going-away present for the 14-year-old Fox-based Mustang platform—a four-wheeled, beefed-up bon voyage party that only 5100 special guests could enjoy.

Ford's Special Vehicle Team (SVT) was created with the same mission as the '80s Special Vehicle Operations (SVO) group—to raise the Mustang's performance bar by producing a limited run of factory-blessed supercars. Both SVT and the Special Vehicle Engineering (SVE) groups were formed late in 1991 to bring a new line of upscale high-performance products to Ford dealerships. SVT's role was to handle the marketing, training, and customer-relations chores; SVE was the arm devoted to developing and building the final product. In February of 1992, it was announced that the first two SVT vehicles would be introduced as 1993 models—a fast turnaround for any car company!

Increasing popularity of pickups convinced SVT that a short-wheelbase F-150 with a 351-cid/240-horsepower V-8 would help Ford establish itself as the leader in the small performance truck market. More conventionally, SVT's

other product was a hopped-up version of the Mustang built using many of the go-fast parts already sold through Ford's existing dealer network.

When it was announced the revered "Cobra" name would be making a comeback on the SVT Mustang, longtime ponycar enthusiasts feared the promised Camaro-killer might turn out to be just another tape-and-stripe job. The coiled snake emblem had meant little since Carroll Shelby stopped using it on his line of Ford-powered aluminum-bodied roadsters in 1967. The 1976-78 Mustang II Cobra II, 1978 King Cobra, and anemic Cobra models of the early 1980s had pretty much de-fanged the hooded serpent.

Fears were relieved when the Cobra hit showrooms mid-year, with enthusiast publications and Mustang fans declaring it to be a true successor to the hallowed name. For its freshman year the Cobra was available as a hatchback only; its sole powerplant offering was a 235-hp version of Ford's forever-young 5.0-liter V-8. The 30-hp boost over the GT's engine was due to new upper and lower intake manifold designs, revised "GT40" heads with larger intake and exhaust ports, larger valves and revised rocker arms. Throttle body and mass air sensor size were increased to 70mm and 65mm,

---

*This 1993 Cobra, from Jimmy Morrison's personal collection, has been stored since it was delivered from the factory. No dealer prep has ever been performed on the car.

respectively, for better flow, and a different cam spec was used. The intake manifold was a special two-piece GT-40 design cast from aluminum. Twelve percent smaller crank and water pump pulleys—a hot rod trick long used by late-model Mustang modifiers—were fitted to the Cobra. Block and heads were cast iron. Redline for the Cobra V-8 was a giddy 6000 rpm, with a fuel shut-off switch putting a damper on an overzealous driver's enthusiasm at 6250 rpm.

The Borg-Warner T-5 transmission was similar to the stock Mustang component, but with phosphate-coated gears and stronger bearings. A short-throw shifter made for more positive gear changes, and the 8.8-inch limited-slip differential was fitted with 3.08:1 cogs. The driveshaft was made of steel, with a hardened yoke.

Keeping a rein on all that new power were big disc brakes on all four corners—a setup not seen on a factory Mustang since the SVO's demise in 1986. The 10.84-inch front rotors were vented, with single-piston calipers; the 10.07-inch rears were also vented and wore calipers actuated by single pistons. Goodyear 245/45ZR-17 Eagle uni-directional tires were mounted on Cobra-unique 17 x 7.5-inch seven-blade alloy rims. The low-profile tires and lower body ride height gave the Cobra its great handling ability.

The suspension, surprisingly, was set up to ride softer than Ford's stock GT as part of SVT's "controlled compliance" philosophy. Front components included modified MacPherson struts, with separate springs on the lower arms, 400/505-pounds-per-inch variable rate coil springs and a 28.5mm stabilizer bar. Underneath the rear of the car is a rigid axle, upper and lower trailing arms, two leading hydraulic links, 160 pounds-per-inch constant-rate coil springs, shock absorbers and a stabilizer bar.

Despite its higher price tag and high-tech speed parts, the car's body was a fairly conservative package, free of the contrasting stripes and "look-at-me" badges that had adorned the 1980s Cobra Mustangs. The GT's lower grille and bumper were used, but with a slight grille opening

sporting a galloping pony. Side-mounted ground effects were smooth from one end to the other, in marked contrast to the GT's boy-racer design. In back was a one-piece fascia with dual stainless steel 2.25-inch exhaust pipes poking out beneath and a square-shouldered wing mated to the hatch lid. Modified SVO Mustang taillights gave the new car a link to its legendary past. If not standing close enough to see the small coiled-snake emblem on the front fender or subtle "SVT" initials just below the rear wing, the average car enthusiast would be hard-pressed to identify the Cobra.

Interiors drew mostly from the GT standard equipment list, differing only in the white-faced instruments that have since been used on all successive Cobras. Cobra drivers could watch the white-faced speedometer reach 60 mph in less than six seconds and a quarter mile in 14.5 seconds, while keeping the tachometer needle hovering around the stratospheric 6,000-rpm neighborhood.

With a list of standard equipment including driver's-side airbag, articulated sport seats, Premium Sound, Power Equipment Group, rear window defroster, air conditioning, cruise control, front floor mats and dual illuminated visor mirrors, the only options were leather seating surfaces, four-way power driver's seat, sunroof (after Feb. 1 build date), CD player, California emissions equipment and a high-altitude principle-use package. Available only in Performance Red, Teal or Black, the 1993 SVT Cobra was clearly the pinnacle of the Fox-bodied Mustang platform. To enhance collectability, each Cobra starting with the '93 went to its new owner with a signed certificate that documented the car's production number (from SVT) and VIN (from Ford).

Because it was common knowledge by mid-1993 that the Mustang was due for a major re-design within months, writers for the car magazines were curious as to why SVT would put out so much effort for a one-year-only model. Even though no official explanation was forthcoming, the consensus is that Ford wanted to draw attention away from General Motors' new-for-1993 275-hp Camaros and Firebirds.

1993 SVT Cobra grille

1993 D-code 5.0-liter/EFI V-8 – street version

**1993 SVT Cobra R
Owner: Jimmy Morrison/
Morrison Motor Co.***

1993 Cobra R

Rather than rest on the immediate success of the Cobra, SVT decided to send the Fox platform to its final resting place in style with a competition model. The Cobra "R" was released in the summer of 1993 to improve Ford's status in the International Motor Sport Association (IMSA) Firestone Grand Sport Series and Sports Car Club of America (SCCA) World Challenge Class B Series.

Race-ready Koni shock absorbers, an engine cooling kit, upgraded brakes, and five-lug wheels were added to the package, while non-necessities such as air conditioning, the back seat, sound deadening and auxiliary lights were removed to save weight. Special blacked-out wheels with three twin-spoke arms and chromed hub covers were installed.

SVT's goal of selling 5,000 Cobras was all but met by the end of the model year, with 4,993 of the $18,505 hatchbacks going to new owners. An additional 107 "R" models were sold for $25,692 apiece.

---

*This 1993 Cobra R, from Jimmy Morrison's personal collection, has been stored since it was delivered from the factory. No dealer prep has ever been performed on the car.

DATA PLATE DECODING

A 17-character Vehicle Identification Number is stamped on an aluminum tab on the instrument panel, viewable through windshield. A vehicle certification label is found on the body side of where the driver's door closes.

VEHICLE WARRANTY NUMBER MANUFACTURER ID

1FA – Ford Motor Co.

RESTRAINT SYSTEM

C – air bags, active belts

VEHICLE CLASSIFICATION

P – passenger car

BODY SERIAL NUMBERS

42 – hatchback

ENGINE CODE

D – 302-cid (5.0-liter) EFI V-8 Cobra

CHECK DIGIT

for internal use

MODEL YEAR

P – 1993

ASSEMBLY PLANT

F – Dearborn, Michigan

CONSECUTIVE UNIT NUMBER

Begins at 100001 at each factory

CODE NUMBERS
PAINT CODE

ES – Vibrant Red Clearcoat
EY – Vibrant Red
RD – Teal Metallic
UA – Black

DRIVETRAIN INFORMATION
ENGINE

302-cid (5.0-liter) EFI V-8 Cobra

Valves . . . . 2 per cylinder
Valve size. . . . . (intake) 1.84 inch
. . . . (exhaust) 1.54 inch
Camshaft. . . . . in block

Valvetrain high-lift roller camshaft, roller lifters, 1.7:1 roller rocker arms
Block . . . . cast iron
Heads . . . . cast iron GT-40 design
Intake manifold. . . . . . . aluminum two-piece GT-40 design
Displacement. . . . . 302 cid/5.0 liters
Bore and stroke. . . . . 4.00 x 3.00 inches
Compression ratio 9.0:1
Brake hp . . . . 235 @ 4600 rpm
Torque . . . . 280 @ 4000 rpm

1993 SVT Cobra R wheel

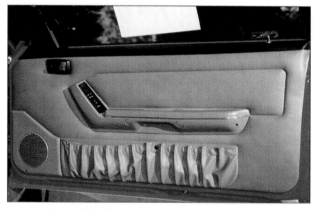

1993 SVT Cobra R door panel

1993 SVT Cobra R, mandatory rear seat delete

1993 D-code 5.0-liter/EFI V-8 – race

1993 SVT Cobra R front valance

Redline . . . . 6000 rpm
Induction . . . . electronic fuel injection
Throttle body 70mm
Fuel injectors . . . . 24 lbs/hr
Exhaust headers . . . . tubular stainless steel
Code . . . . D
Transmission
    . . . . Borg-Warner T5 5-speed w/phosphate-coated gears
Rear axle ratio 3.08:1

SUSPENSION

Front . modified MacPherson strut, with separate spring on
    lower arm,
    400/505 lbs./in. variable rate coil springs, 28.5mm stabi-
    lizer bar
Rear . rigid axle, upper and lower trailing arms, two leading
    hydraulic links,
    160 lbs./in. constant-rate coil springs, shock absorbers,
    stabilizer bar

BRAKES*

Front . . . . 10.84-inch vented disc, single-piston caliper
Rear . . . . 10.07-inch vented disc, single-piston caliper
*ABS not available

WHEELS AND TIRES

Wheels . . . . 17 x 7.5-inch 7-spoke
Tires . . . . 245/45ZR-17 Goodyear

OTHER SPECS

Wheelbase . . . . 100.5 inches
Length . . . . 179.6 inches
Height . . . . 56.6 inches
Track . . . . (front) 56.6 inches
    . . . . (rear) 57.0 inches
Head room . . . . 37 inches
Leg room . . . . 41.7 inches
Fuel tank . . . . 15.4 gallons
Weight distribution (front/rear) 57%/43%

SIGNIFICANT COBRA PRODUCTION DATES

Aug. 4, 1992 . . . . Cobra No. 1 produced
Dec. 17, 1992 . Cobra No. 19 produced (first customer car)
June 28, 1993 . . . . Cobra No. 5100 produced (last '93)

OPTION LIST

PEP Package includes Power Equipment Group (dual elec-
    tric remote control mirrors, power side windows, Power
    Lock Group, cargo tie-down net, front floor mats, speed
    control, AM/FM Radio w/cassette player and clock, styled
    road wheels), air conditioning, front floor mats . . $1455
Leather seating surfaces articulated sport seats $523
4-way power driver's seat $183
Rear window defroster $170
Engine block heater $20
Clearcoat paint $91
Flip-up open-air roof $355
AM/FM stereo radio w/CD player $629

1993 SVT COBRA PRODUCTION CHART

Model	Doors/Body/Seating	Factory Price	Shipping Weight	Prod. Total
42	3/hatchback Cobra/4	$18,505	3,255	4993
42	3/hatchback Cobra R/2	$25,692	3,195	107

NOTE 1: Exterior color breakdown includes 1,882 Vibrant Red Clearcoat, 1,854 Black, 1,355 Teal Metallic and 9 Vibrant Red. Total production was 5,100.
NOTE 2: Of the 9 Vibrant Red models produced, only one is known to have gone directly to a customer. The rest were used within Ford.

1993 SVT Cobra R

**1994 SVT Cobra
Owner: Mark LaMaskin/
Performance Autosport**

1994 SVT Cobra

Like its standard and GT Mustang stablemates, the Cobra was redesigned and updated to the "SN-95" platform for 1994. The hoodline was lowered; the deck height raised; the roof took on a gentle, uninterrupted curve and the new silhouette made the relatively square 1993 model look as aerodynamic as a barn door.

To distinguish the higher-priced Cobra from the GT on which it was based, SVT added a new bumper fascia incorporating perfectly round auxiliary lights (the GT lights were smaller and rectangular). Crystal clear, European-style reflector headlamps gave the Cobra the edge for nighttime high-performance driving, and the pedestal-mounted rear spoiler had an LED brake light built in. Emblems depicting coiled snakes replaced the GT fender badges, even though a galloping pony still took center stage in the grille opening. The Cobra's rear valance panel, lifted from Ford's V-6 model, read "Mustang."

Interior design touches included a steering wheel embossed with the word "Cobra," Cobra-unique floor mats and white-faced gauges (including a 160-mph speedometer). The stick shift knob and boot were wrapped in leather. A little-noticed upgrade is the switch from steel to magnesium for the front seat cushion frames.

Ford's move to the SN-95 model pared the Mustang family down to only two bodystyles, coupe and convertible, and SVT offered its Cobra as either starting in 1994. Although it was wrapped in an all-new design, the SVT Cobra powertrain and suspension formula were remarkably unchanged.

The heart of the beast, the 5.0-liter V-8, enjoyed some computer tinkering that boosted it to 240 hp and 285 lbs.-ft. of torque. While the GT used a lower-profile intake manifold (the same unit found atop the Thunderbird's 5.0-liter) to fit under the steeply sloped hood, SVT decided to retain the taller 1993 piece for more power. In order to fit everything under the hood, the strut tower-to-cowl brace was removed.

The brace was not missed by many Cobra buyers because the SN-95 coupe had gained a tremendous 44 percent in torsional rigidity over the previous model, and the convertible chassis was stiffer by 80 percent when compared to the 1993 offering.

For future swap meet parts chasers, SVT stamped the "Cobra" name on the intake manifold, valve covers, accessory belt and lower radiator hose. An engine oil cooler, first found on the previous year's Cobra R, became standard equipment in 1994.

Cobra springs were still softer than the production GT setup, aided by a smaller diameter sway bar in front (25mm vs. 30mm) and larger unit in the rear (27mm vs. 24mm). Front springs were changed from variable to linear units rated at 400 lbs./in., while rear springs stayed at the previous year's 160 lbs./in. rating.

Four-wheel disc brakes with a five-lug pattern became the standard Mustang setup for 1994; the Cobra went one better with larger ABS-equipped discs assigned to handle the extra horsepower. Front vented discs measured 13.0 inches in diameter and were fitted with twin-piston "Cobra"-embossed calipers; rears were vented discs measuring 11.65 inches. Bosch's three-channel, four-sensor ABS equipment was standard on all 1994 Cobras. Larger Goodyear tires than on the 1993—255/45ZR-17 uni-directional Eagle GS-Cs mounted on five-spoke, 17 x 8-inch alloy rims—were installed, and a 17-inch mini spare was tucked away in the trunk.

Ford chose to show off its new top-line Cobra convertible by having one pace the 1994 Indianapolis 500. Three cars were modified by Jack Roush for heavy-duty "real" pace car chores, while SVT turned out 1000 Rio Red replicas with saddle leather interiors and Saddle tops. As with most pace car knock-offs, decals were shipped to the dealers inside the cars (not on them) and left to the buyer's discretion to install.

The three race-day duty pace cars were modified at Roush's shop in Allen Park, Mich., with specially "tweaked" four-speed automatic transmissions, 15-gallon racing fuel cells, heavier rear springs (to accommodate the weight of television camera equipment), a Halon fire-extinguisher system, a rollbar with 50,000-watt strobe lights built in and special lights in the rear spoiler.

Regular Cobra standard equipment included dual airbags, articulated sport seats (with four-way power driver's seat), premium stereo, Power Equipment Group, rear window defroster, speed control, Cobra floor mats and dual illuminated visor mirrors.

Options for 1994 included leather interior, remote keyless entry system and the Mach 460/CD equipment. The pace car replica included all of these options as standard.

Colors included Rio Red, Crystal White and Black. Interior options were cloth or leather in Black or Saddle. SVT turned out 5009 copies of its high-performance Cobra coupe at $20,765 apiece and 1,000 convertibles (all red Indy Pace Car replicas) at $26,845 each.

DATA PLATE DECODING

A 17-character Vehicle Identification Number is stamped on an aluminum tab on the instrument panel, viewable through windshield. A vehicle certification label is found on the body side of where the driver's door closes.

VEHICLE WARRANTY NUMBER MANUFACTURER ID

1FA – Ford Motor Co.

RESTRAINT SYSTEM

L – air bags, active belts

VEHICLE CLASSIFICATION

P – passenger car

BODY SERIAL NUMBERS

42 – coupe
45 – convertible

1994 SVT Cobra wheel

1994 SVT Cobra interior

1994 D-code 5.0-liter/EFI V-8

ENGINE CODE

D – 302-cid (5.0-liter) EFI V-8 Cobra

CHECK DIGIT

for internal use

MODEL YEAR

R – 1994

ASSEMBLY PLANT

F – Dearborn, Michigan

CONSECUTIVE UNIT NUMBER

Begins at 100001 at each factory

CODE NUMBERS
PAINT CODE

E8 – Rio Red
UA – Black
ZF – Crystal White

DRIVETRAIN INFORMATION
ENGINE

302-cid (5.0-liter) EFI V-8 Cobra

Valves . . . . 2 per cylinder
Valve size. . . . . (intake) 1.84 inch
. . . . (exhaust) 1.54 inch
Camshaft. . . . . in block
Block . . . . cast iron
Heads . . . . cast iron GT-40 design
Displacement. . . . . 302 cid/5.0 liters
Bore and stroke. . . . . 4.00 x 3.00 inches
Compression ratio 9.0:1
Brake hp . . . . 240 @ 4800 rpm
Torque . . . . 285 @ 4000 rpm
Induction . . . . electronic fuel injection
Throttle body. 70mm
Exhaust headers. . . . . tubular stainless steel
Code . . . . D
Transmission . . . . Borg-Warner T5 5-speed
Rear axle ratio 3.08:1

SUSPENSION

Front . modified MacPherson strut, with separate spring on
lower arm, 400 lbs./in. linear rate coil springs, 25mm
anti-roll bar
Rear . . rigid axle four bar links, 160 lbs./in. linear rate coil
springs, 27mm anti-roll bar, vertical shock absorbers and
horizontal axle dampeners

BRAKES

Front . . 13.0-inch vented disc PBR twin-piston caliper with
embossed "COBRA" lettering
Rear . . . . 11.65-inch vented disc single-piston caliper
ABS. . . . . Bosch 3-channel, 4-sensor system

WHEELS AND TIRES

Wheels . . . . 17 x 8-inch 5-spoke
Tires . . . . 255/45ZR-17 Goodyear Eagle GS-C

OTHER SPECS

Wheelbase . . . . 101.3 inches
Length . . . . 181.5 inches
Height. (coupe) 53.4 inches
. . . . (convertible) 53.3 inches
Width. . . . . 71.8 inches
Track . . . . (front) 60.0 inches
. . . . (rear) 58.7 inches
Head room . . . . (coupe) 38.2 inches
. . . . (convertible) 38.1 inches
Leg room . . . . 42.6 inches
Fuel tank. . . . . 15.4 gallons

OPTION LIST

PEP Package includes air conditioning, rear window
defroster, front floor mats and speed control
. . . . (coupe) $1455

PEP Package includes air conditioning, rear window
defroster, front floor mats, speed control and remote
keyless illuminated entry . . . . (convertible) $2285
Power Group 3 includes remote keyless illuminated entry
and cargo net $310
Leather seating surfaces articulated sport seats
. . . . (coupe) $500
Mach 460 AM/FM stereo radio w/cassette $375
CD player (requires Mach 460 system). $475

1994 SVT COBRA PRODUCTION CHART				
Model	Doors/Body/Seating	Factory Price	Shipping Weight	Prod. Total
42	2/coupe Cobra/4	$20,765	3365	5009
45	2/convertible Cobra/4	$26,845	3567	1000

NOTE 1: Exterior color breakdown includes 2,908 Rio Red coupes/1,000 Rio Red convertibles, 1,795 Black
coupes and 1,306 Crystal White coupes. Total production was 6,009.

1994 SVT Cobra

**1995 SVT Cobra with removable
hardtop in place
Owners: Norm and Karen Demers**

1995 SVT Cobra

Given the effort it took SVT to produce the single-year 1993 Cobra and still turn out an all-new 1994 right behind it, the company can perhaps be forgiven for only making minimal changes to the 1995 model. SVT permanently added a convertible to the lineup this year; it was only available in Black, with a Black leather interior and Black top. Coupe colors were restricted to Rio Red, Crystal White, and Black.

An interesting collectible in the form of a removable hardtop was available briefly during 1995 for the convertible. Considering the high-dollar clientele of the Cobra line, it probably wasn't the option's $1,825 pricetag that killed it; instead, Ford's problems with the supplier and concerns about quality were more likely the culprits. Only 499 of the special tops were made, supposedly Cobras account for the majority of models so equipped—if not all models so equipped. (Unfortunately for Mustang owners looking to retrofit their convertibles with the removable top, it can't be done without major, expensive modifications to the car.)

One minor underhood addition was the placement of an identification label on the driver's-side valve cover. While the powerful 240-hp 5.0-liter was unchanged for 1995, it was enjoying its final year of life as a production power-plant. After 28 years of nearly uninterrupted service to the Mustang, the pushrod 302 was being retired; both the Cobra and GT would receive new "modular" V-8s in 1996.

Regular Cobra standard equipment included dual airbags, articulated sport seats (with four-way power driver's seat), premium stereo, Power Equipment Group, rear window defroster, speed control, Cobra floor mats and dual illuminated visor mirrors. Options for 1995 included leather interior, remote keyless entry system and the Mach 460/CD equipment.

1995 SVT Cobra with dealer-installed "light bar"

1995 SVT Cobra

1995 SVT Cobra wheel

1995 SVT Cobra spoiler

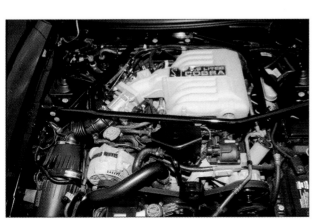

1995 D-code 5.0-liter/EFI V-8

1995 SVT Cobra removable hardtop

1995 Cobra R

The 1995 introduction of the Cobra's second-generation R model signified a new high-water mark for late-model Mustang performance. Not since 1973 had a Mustang been available with 351 cubic inches of small-block V-8; the R's slightly enlarged fiberglass hood hid just such a powerplant.

Because demand for the 1993 R had easily exceeded the 100-car run, SVT increased the availability to 250 units for 1995. Realizing that many of the first Rs had gone straight to collectors' garages (bypassing the racetracks they were built to compete on), Ford insisted that sales of the 1995 would be made only to licensed, active competitors in the SCCA and IMSA series.

Since the standard Cobra's 5.0-liter/302-cid V-8 and R-model's 351-cid V-8 were part of the same "family," emissions certification was easier than if a different powerplant had been chosen. A Ford marine block formed the basis for the super V-8, with a special camshaft, aluminum alloy pistons, forged steel connecting rods, GT-40 heads and lower intake and specially designed upper intake manifold making up most of the performance gains. Visually topping off the package was a "5.8 Liter Cobra" plate on the intake manifold. The greater displacement produced 300 hp and 365 lbs.-ft. of torque.

SVT dropped the usual Borg-Warner T-5 for a beefier Tremec five-speed, giving Ford's warranty department peace of mind concerning broken gears, and the 3.27:1 rear axle ratio generated neck-snapping acceleration. To increase its performance potential, the R was stripped of unnecessary components, including the air conditioning system, radio, rear seat, some soundproofing materials and fog lamps. Suspension components were chosen for ultimate road-holding with Eibach springs, Koni adjustable shocks, firmer bushings, five-spoke wheels measuring 17 x 9 inches and 255/45-17 BFGoodrich Comp T/As contributing to the competition-level handling.

Other race-oriented pieces included a fiberglass hood, 20-gallon fuel cell and radiators for engine oil and power steering fluid. All 250 cars were painted Crystal White and fitted with the Saddle cloth interiors.

Despite the addition of a hot-selling R-model, overall Cobra sales were down in 1995. The $21,300 coupe sold 4,005 units; the $25,605 convertible rang up 1,003 new customers and the $35,499 (plus $2,100 gas guzzler tax) R quickly pre-sold all 250 copies.

DATA PLATE DECODING

A 17-character Vehicle Identification Number is stamped on an aluminum tab on the instrument panel, viewable through windshield. A vehicle certification label is found on the body side of where the driver's door closes.

VEHICLE WARRANTY NUMBER MANUFACTURER ID

1FA – Ford Motor Co.

RESTRAINT SYSTEM

L – air bags, active belts

VEHICLE CLASSIFICATION

P – passenger car

BODY SERIAL NUMBERS

42 – coupe
45 – convertible

ENGINE CODE

D – 302-cid (5.0-liter) EFI V-8 Cobra
C – 351-cid (5.8-liter) EFI V-8 Cobra R

CHECK DIGIT

for internal use

MODEL YEAR

S – 1995

ASSEMBLY PLANT

F – Dearborn, Michigan

CONSECUTIVE UNIT NUMBER

Begins at 100001 at each factory

CODE NUMBERS PAINT CODE

E8 – Rio Red
UA – Black
ZF – Crystal White

DRIVETRAIN INFORMATION ENGINE

302-cid (5.0-liter) EFI V-8 Cobra

Valves . . . . 2 per cylinder
Valve size. . . . . (intake) 1.84 inch
. . . . (exhaust) 1.54 inch
Camshaft. . . . . in block
Block . . . . cast iron

1995 SVT COBRA PRODUCTION CHART

Model	Doors/Body/Seating	Factory Price	Shipping Weight	Prod. Total
42	2/coupe Cobra/4	$21,300	3365	4005
45	2/convertible Cobra/4	$25,605	3567	1003
42	2/coupe Cobra R /2	$35,499*	3280	250

NOTE 1: Exterior color breakdown includes 1,447 Rio Red coupes, 1,433 Black coupes/1,003 convertibles and 1,125 Crystal White coupes. All 250 R models were Crystal White. Total production was 5,258.
* Price does not include $2,100 "gas guzzler" tax.

Heads . . . . cast iron GT-40 design
Displacement. . . . . 302 cid/5.0 liters
Bore and stroke. . . . . 4.00 x 3.00 inches
Compression ratio 9.0:1
Brake hp . . . . 240 @ 4800 rpm
Torque. . . . . 285 @ 4000 rpm
Induction . . . . electronic fuel injection
Throttle body. 70mm
Exhaust headers. . . . . tubular stainless steel
Code . . . . D
Transmission . . . . Borg-Warner T5 5-speed
Rear axle ratio 3.08:1

351-cid (5.8-liter) EFI V-8 Cobra R
Valves . . . . 2 per cylinder
Camshaft. . . . . in block
Block . . . . cast iron
Heads . . . . cast iron GT-40 design
Displacement. . . . . 302 cid/5.0 liters
Bore and stroke. . . . . 4.00 x 3.50 inches
Brake hp 300
Torque . . . . 365 lb./ft.
Main bearings 5
Valve lifters. . . . . hydraulic
Induction . . . . electronic fuel injection
Exhaust headers. . . . . tubular stainless steel
Code C
Transmission. . . . . Tremec 5-speed
Rear axle ratio 3.27:1

SUSPENSION

Front. . . . modified MacPherson strut, with separate spring
on lower arm, 400 lbs./in. linear rate coil springs, 25mm
anti-roll bar
(R model) heavier springs and swaybars, Koni shocks
Rear. . . . . rigid axle four bar links, 160 lbs./in. linear rate
coil springs, 27mm anti-roll bar, vertical shock absorbers
and horizontal axle dampeners
(R model) heavier springs and swaybars, Koni shocks

BRAKES

Front. . . . . 13.0-inch vented disc PBR twin-piston caliper
with embossed "COBRA" lettering
Rear . . . . 11.65-inch vented disc single-piston caliper
ABS. . . . . Bosch 3-channel, 4-sensor system

WHEELS AND TIRES

Wheels. . . . .
17 x 8-inch 5-spoke
(Cobra R) 17 x 9-inch 5-spoke
Tires . . . .
255/45ZR-17 Goodyear Eagle GS-C
(Cobra R) 255/45ZR-17 BFGoodrich Comp T/A

OTHER SPECS

Wheelbase . . . . 101.3 inches
Length . . . . 181.5 inches
Height. . . . . (coupe) 53.4 inches
. . . . (convertible) 53.3 inches
Width. . . . . 71.8 inches
Track . . . . (front) 60.0 inches
. . . . (rear) 58.7 inches
Head room . . . . (coupe) 38.2 inches
. . . . (convertible) 38.1 inches
Leg room . . . . 42.6 inches
Fuel tank . . . . 15.4 gallons

OPTION LIST

PEP Package includes air conditioning, rear window
defroster, front floor mats and speed control
(coupe) $1260
PEP Package includes air conditioning, rear window
defroster, front floor mats, speed control, Mach 460 radio
and leather seating surfaces . . . . . (convertible) $2755
Power Group 3 includes remote keyless illuminated entry
and cargo net $310
Convertible hardtop. $1825
Leather seating surfaces articulated sport seats
. . . . (coupe) $500
Mach 460 AM/FM stereo radio w/cassette $375

**1996 SVT Cobra
Owner: Jimmy Morrison/
Morrison Motor Co.**

1996 SVT Cobra

1996 was a "hold-your-breath-and-wait" year for Ford Motor Company as it was replacing the Mustang's legendary 5.0-liter pushrod V-8 with an engine wearing single overhead camshafts and displacing only 4.6 liters. Although this "modular" powerplant was already in use in the company's Lincoln products—where it earned high marks for smoothness and efficiency—Ford wasn't sure how the rabid Mustang enthusiasts would take to it.

Because the SVT crew was assembled to create a new level of performance for the Mustang, they decided to install a motor in the 1996 Cobra that would really separate the snake from the pony. SVT leapfrogged over the GT's single overhead cam V-8 with a 32-valve, double overhead cam, handbuilt version of the new 4.6-liter.

The company developed an aluminum-block V-8 that produced 305 horsepower at 5800 rpm and 300 lbs.-ft. of torque at 4800 rpm. The block was specially cast by the Teksid company in Italy and shipped to Ford's Romeo, Michigan, engine assembly plant where it was fitted with four-valve heads, twin 57mm throttle bodies, an 80mm Mass Air Sensor and a German-built crankshaft. Twelve two-person teams assembled all 10,000-plus 1996 Cobra motors on the special "Niche Line," then personally autographed a metallic plate on the passenger-side cam cover. Redline jumped to 6800 rpm, with a fuel shutoff device limited revs to 7000.

In addition to being powerful and efficient, the Cobra V-8 was built to last, with six bolts used to retain each

nodular iron bearing cap. This cross-bolting results in a much stiffer assembly. A built-in engine water-to-oil cooler also increased the V-8's life expectancy.

The wider and taller V-code engine required changes in the Cobra's second crossmember and oil pan, as well as revising the car's steering geometry. It also made room for the return of the firewall-to-tower triangulated brace that had been absent since the 1994 Cobra.

Cobras received the same new Borg-Warner T-45 five-speed transmissions as standard 1996 GTs and these units were more than capable of handling the stump-pulling torque of the DOHC 4.6-liter. Rated to handle a maximum of 320 lbs.-ft. of torque, the T-45 design made the transmission casing and bell housing one piece for greater rigidity.

SVT modified its earlier suspension philosophy by installing '95 GT-spec variable-rate springs measuring 400/505 lbs./in. in the front and 165/265 in the rear. A larger, 29mm swaybar made for stronger handling in the front, while the previous year's 27mm bar was in place in back.

Another seemingly unusual decision was a slight downsizing in tires; the Cobra's BFGoodrich T/As measured 245/45ZR-17. Although the tire was only 10mm narrower, it weighed one pound less, which benefited the high-performance driver due to lower unsprung weight. Other than a more compact hydraulic unit replacing the previous model's vacuum system (across the board for Mustangs), brake components remained the same as 1995.

Exterior colors offered were Laser Red, Crystal White, Black, and an unusual "Mystic" paint scheme. Developed by GAF, Mystic was a combination of colors that show themselves from different angles—the green, purple, blue, and black hues reacted in different ways to the light and created a love-it-or-hate-it $815 option for 1996 Cobra coupes only. Controversial though it was, 1,999 customers happily drove home Mystic-painted coupes.

A slight dome was built into the Cobra hood starting in 1996 to clear the taller 4.6-liter engine. The new hood also contained simulated air scoops that distinguished it from the GT model. Other appearance changes included "COBRA" lettering stamped into the rear valance panel and a new rear spoiler (the GT-style spoiler became a "customer delete" option this year). A coiled snake emblem appeared at the mouth of the Cobra's grille this year in place of the 1995's galloping pony. Three-inch dual exhaust tips were fitted to the Cobra—an upgrade from the previous model's 2.75-inch units.

Standard equipment included dual airbags, ABS, articulated sport seats (four-way power for the driver), Premium Sound, Power Equipment Group, rear window defroster, air conditioning, cruise control, front floor mats, dual illuminated visor mirrors and remote keyless illuminated entry. The short options list included the Preferred Equipment Package, California emissions components, high-altitude principle-use equipment, and rear spoiler.

Although reliability of these cars under normal driving conditions was well above average, drivers who submitted their 1996 Cobras to extremes of accelerating, braking, and shifting identified a few problem areas while still under warranty. When pushed hard at high ambient temperatures, the 4.6-liter tended to overheat—a problem that was solved with a cooling upgrade Ford offered to Cobra owners. Many serpentine belt pulleys were replaced with later Cobra pieces when it was determined that the originals were prone to making squealing noises or coming off altogether. The new-for-'96 T-45 transmission weakened quickly when subjected to the full force of the Cobra's V-8, with reports of shift forks bending and synchronizer gears wearing excessively. Under license from Borg-Warner, Tremec began making the T-45 sometime in 1998 in order to correct this weakness.

In spite of these problems, enthusiasm for the new DOHC 4.6-liter engine helped to give SVT its highest production run in history. Customers drove home 10,006 of the high-performance Mustang Cobras. Coupes were the most abundant with 7,496 selling for $24,810 and convertible sales were also strong with 2,510 produced for a list price of $27,580.

DATA PLATE DECODING

A 17-character Vehicle Identification Number is stamped on an aluminum tab on the instrument panel, viewable through windshield. A vehicle certification label is found on the body side of where the driver's door closes.

VEHICLE WARRANTY NUMBER MANUFACTURER ID

1FA – Ford Motor Co.

RESTRAINT SYSTEM

L – air bags, active belts

VEHICLE CLASSIFICATION

P – passenger car

BODY SERIAL NUMBERS

47 – coupe
46 – convertible

ENGINE CODE

V – 281-cid (4.6-liter) EFI DOHC V-8 Cobra

CHECK DIGIT

for internal use

MODEL YEAR

T – 1996

ASSEMBLY PLANT

F – Dearborn, Michigan

CONSECUTIVE UNIT NUMBER

Begins at 100001 at each factory

CODE NUMBERS
PAINT CODE

E9 – Laser Red
LF – Mystic
UA – Black
ZR – Crystal White

DRIVETRAIN INFORMATION
ENGINE

281-cid (4.6-liter) EFI DOHC V-8 Cobra

Valves	4 per cylinder
Valve size	(intake) 37mm
	(exhaust) 30mm
Camshaft	double overhead
Block	aluminum
Heads	aluminum
Displacement	281 cid/4.6 liters

1996 SVT COBRA PRODUCTION CHART				
Model	Doors/Body/Seating	Factory Price	Shipping Weight	Prod. Total
47	2/coupe Cobra/4	$24,810	3446	7496
46	2/convertible Cobra/4	$27,580	3620	2510

NOTE 1: Exterior color breakdown includes 2,122 Black coupes/1,053 Black convertibles, 1,999 Mystic coupes, 1,940 Laser Red coupes/962 Laser Red convertibles and 1,435 Crystal White coupes/494 Crystal White convertibles. Total production was 10,006 units.

Bore and stroke. . . . . 3.55 x 3.54 inches
Compression ratio 9.85:1
Brake hp . . . . 305 @ 5800 rpm
Torque . . . . 300 lb./ft. @ 4800 rpm
Induction . . . . electronic fuel injection
Intake manifold . . . . equal length thin-wall cast aluminum
  runners, cast aluminum plenum chamber
Throttle body. . . . . dual 57mm
Port throttles . . . . . electronically actuated 34mm, open to
  secondary intake valves at 3250 rpm
Exhaust headers. . . . . cast high-silicon, molybdenum iron,
  manifold type
Code V
Transmission . . . . Borg-Warner T45 5-speed
Rear axle ratio 3.27:1

SUSPENSION

Front . modified MacPherson strut, with separate spring on
  lower arm, 400/505 lbs./in. variable rate coil springs,
  29mm stabilizer bar
Rear . rigid axle, upper and lower trailing arms, two leading
  hydraulic links, 165/265 lbs./in. variable-rate coil
  springs, shock absorbers, 27mm stabilizer bar

BRAKES

Front. . . . . . 13.0-inch vented disc PBR twin-piston caliper
  with embossed "COBRA" lettering
Rear . . . . 11.65-inch vented disc single-piston caliper
ABS. . . . . Bosch 3-channel, 4-sensor system

WHEELS AND TIRES

Wheels . . . . 17 x 8-inch 5-spoke
Tires . . . . 245/45ZR-17 BFGoodrich Comp T/A

OTHER SPECS

Wheelbase . . . . 101.3 inches
Length . . . . 181.5 inches
Height. . . . . (coupe) 53.4 inches
  . . . . (convertible) 53.3 inches
Width. . . . . 71.8 inches
Track . . . . (front) 60.0 inches
  . . . . (rear) 58.7 inches
Head room . . . . (coupe) 38.2 inches
  . . . . (convertible) 38.1 inches
Leg room . . . . 42.6 inches
Fuel tank. . . . . 15.4 gallons
Weight distribution (front/rear). 57%/43%

OPTION LIST

PEP Package includes Mach 460 stereo/CD player, leather
  interior, perimeter anti-theft system. . . . (coupe) $1335
Rear spoiler $215

**1995 SVT Cobra
with Mystic paint option**

1996 SVT Cobra hood scoop

**1996 SVT Cobra
brake caliper**

1996 V-code 4.6-liter/EFI DOHC V-8

**1997 SVT Cobra
Owner: Bob Cox**

1997 SVT Cobra

It was business as usual for SVT in 1997. The only noticeable change in the Cobra was a slightly larger grille opening, which was shared by the entire Mustang lineup due to a wider and taller radiator design across the board. The galloping horse emblem replaced the coiled serpent this year in the grille, but the rear valance panel retained the embossed "Cobra" lettering.

Standard equipment included dual airbags, ABS, articulated sport seats (four-way power for the driver), Premium Sound, Power Equipment Group, rear window defroster, air conditioning, cruise control, front floor mats, dual illuminated visor mirrors and remote keyless illuminated entry. The short options list included the Preferred Equipment Package, California emissions components, high-altitude principle-use equipment and rear spoiler.

For 1997, Pacific Green shared the Cobra paint chip chart with Rio Red, Black, and Crystal White.

SVT established another sales record for its Cobra in '97 by an additional 43 units. Of the 10,049 Cobras produced, 6961 were $25,335 coupes; 3088 were $28,135 convertibles.

DATA PLATE DECODING

A 17-character Vehicle Identification Number is stamped on an aluminum tab on the instrument panel, viewable through windshield. A vehicle certification label is found on the body side of where the driver's door closes.

VEHICLE WARRANTY NUMBER MANUFACTURER ID

1FA – Ford Motor Co.

RESTRAINT SYSTEM

L – air bags, active belts

VEHICLE CLASSIFICATION

P – passenger car

BODY SERIAL NUMBERS

47 – coupe
46 – convertible

ENGINE CODE

V – 281-cid (4.6-liter) EFI DOHC V-8 Cobra

CHECK DIGIT

for internal use

MODEL YEAR

V – 1997

ASSEMBLY PLANT

F – Dearborn, Michigan

CONSECUTIVE UNIT NUMBER

Begins at 100001 at each factory

CODE NUMBERS
PAINT CODE

E8 – Rio Red
PS – Pacific Green
UA – Black
ZR – Crystal White

DRIVETRAIN INFORMATION
ENGINE

281-cid (4.6-liter) EFI DOHC V-8 Cobra

Valves . . . . 4 per cylinder
Valve size . . . . (intake) 37mm
. . . . (exhaust) 30mm
Camshaft . . . . double overhead
Block . . . . aluminum
Heads . . . . aluminum
Displacement . . . . 281 cid/4.6 liters
Bore and stroke . . . . 3.55 x 3.54 inches
Compression ratio 9.85:1
Brake hp . . . . 305 @ 5800 rpm
Torque . . . . 300 lb./ft. @ 4800 rpm
Induction . . . . electronic fuel injection
Intake manifold . . . . . . equal length thin-wall cast aluminum runners, cast aluminum plenum chamber
Throttle body . . . . dual 57mm
Port throttles . . . . . electronically actuated 34mm, open to secondary intake valves at 3250 rpm
Exhaust headers
. . . . cast high-silicon, molybdenum iron, manifold type
Code V
Transmission . . . . Borg-Warner T45 5-speed
Rear axle ratio 3.27:1

SUSPENSION

Front . modified MacPherson strut, with separate spring on lower arm, 400/505 lbs./in. variable rate coil springs, 29mm stabilizer bar
Rear . rigid axle, upper and lower trailing arms, two leading hydraulic links, ... 165-265 lbs./in. variable-rate coil springs, shock absorbers, 27mm stabilizer bar

BRAKES

Front . . 13.0-inch vented disc PBR twin-piston caliper with embossed "COBRA" lettering
Rear . . . . 11.65-inch vented disc single-piston caliper
ABS . . . . Bosch 3-channel, 4-sensor system

WHEELS AND TIRES

Wheels . . . . 17 x 8-inch 5-spoke
Tires . . . . 245/45ZR-17 BFGoodrich Comp T/A

OTHER SPECS

Wheelbase . . . . 101.3 inches
Length . . . . 181.5 inches
Height . . . . (coupe) 53.4 inches
. . . . (convertible) 53.3 inches
Width . . . . 71.8 inches
Track . . . . (front) 60.0 inches
. . . . (rear) 58.7 inches
Head room . . . . (coupe) 38.2 inches
. . . . (convertible) 38.1 inches
Leg room . . . . 42.6 inches
Fuel tank . . . . 15.4 gallons
Weight distribution (front/rear) 57%/43%

OPTION LIST

PEP Package includes Mach 460 stereo/CD player, leather interior, perimeter anti-theft system . . . . (coupe) $1335
Rear spoiler $195

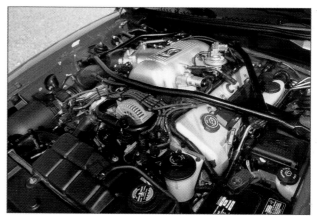

1997 V-code 4.6-liter/EFI DOHC V-8

1997 SVT COBRA PRODUCTION CHART				
Model	Doors/Body/Seating	Factory Price	Shipping Weight	Prod. Total
47	2/coupe Cobra/4	$25,335	3446	6961
46	2/convertible Cobra/4	$28,135	3620	3088

NOTE 1: Exterior color breakdown includes 2,369 Black coupes/1,180 Black convertibles, 1,994 Rio Red coupes/925 Rio Red convertibles, 1,543 Crystal White coupes/606 Crystal White convertibles and 1,055 Pacific Green coupes/377 Pacific Green convertibles. Total production was 10,049 units.

**1997 SVT Cobra
Owner: Bob Cox**

**1997 SVT Cobra
interior**

1998 SVT Cobra
Owner: Jimmy Morrison/
Morrison Motor Co.

1998 SVT Cobra

The Cobra went into 1998 with very few changes, the most noticeable being a switch to five-spoke wheels similar to what SVT put on the 1995 R models. The Cobra's firewall-to-tower triangulated brace disappeared again this year. Once again, the Cobra grille featured the stock Mustang's running horse emblem, and the rear valance panel read "Cobra."

Interior changes reflected the stock GT Mustang: the console was re-designed; the clock pod was removed from the instrument panel, leaving the radio in charge of telling time and a CD player became standard with the premium sound system. The console-mounted ashtray was replaced with cup holders.

At some point in the model year, Tremec began building the Cobra's T-45 transmission under license from Borg-Warner. Tremec's changes strengthened the five-speed and ended customer complaints about bent shift forks and ruined synchronizer gears. The Tremec name is stamped into the casings of the T-45s built by that company.

Standard equipment included dual airbags, ABS, articulated sport seats (four-way power for the driver), Premium Sound, Power Equipment Group, rear window defroster, air conditioning, cruise control, front floor mats, dual illuminated visor mirrors and remote keyless illuminated entry. The short options list included the Electronic Leather/Trim Group, California emissions components, high-altitude principle-use equipment, and rear spoiler.

Body color choices were the most numerous to date in 1998, including perennial favorites Laser Red, Crystal

White, and Black with the addition of Atlantic Blue and Canary Yellow. The 1998 carryover model sold in respectable numbers, with 8,654 overall sales for SVT. Coupe production measured 5,174 units (listing for $25,710 apiece); convertibles sold 3,480 models ($28,510 each).

DATA PLATE DECODING

A 17-character Vehicle Identification Number is stamped on an aluminum tab on the instrument panel, viewable through windshield. A vehicle certification label is found on the body side of where the driver's door closes.

VEHICLE WARRANTY NUMBER
MANUFACTURER ID

1FA – Ford Motor Co.

RESTRAINT SYSTEM

L – air bags, active belts

VEHICLE CLASSIFICATION

P – passenger car

BODY SERIAL NUMBERS

47 – coupe
46 – convertible

ENGINE CODE

V – 281-cid (4.6-liter) EFI DOHC V-8 Cobra

CHECK DIGIT

for internal use

MODEL YEAR

W – 1998

ASSEMBLY PLANT

F – Dearborn, Michigan

CONSECUTIVE UNIT NUMBER

Begins at 100001 at each factory

CODE NUMBERS
PAINT CODE

BZ – Canary Yellow
E9 – Laser Red
PS – Atlantic Blue
UA – Black
ZR – Crystal White

DRIVETRAIN INFORMATION
ENGINE

281-cid (4.6-liter) EFI DOHC V-8 Cobra

Valves . . . . 4 per cylinder
Valve size . . . . (intake) 37mm
. . . . (exhaust) 30mm
Camshaft . . . . double overhead
Block . . . . aluminum
Heads. . . . . aluminum
Displacement. . . . . 281 cid/4.6 liters
Bore and stroke. . . . . 3.55 x 3.54 inches
Compression ratio 9.85:1
Brake hp . . . . 305 @ 5800 rpm
Torque . . . . 300 lb./ft. @ 4800 rpm
Induction . . . . electronic fuel injection
Intake manifold . . . . . equal length thin-wall cast aluminum
runners, cast aluminum plenum chamber
Throttle body. . . . . dual 57mm
Port throttles . . . . . electronically actuated 34mm, open to
secondary intake valves at 3250 rpm
Exhaust headers
. . . . cast high-silicon, molybdenum iron, manifold type
Code V
Transmission
(later '98s were Tremec-built) Borg-Warner T45 5-speed
Rear axle ratio 3.27:1

SUSPENSION

Front . modified MacPherson strut, with separate spring on
lower arm, . . 400/505 lbs./in. variable rate coil springs,
29mm stabilizer bar

Rear . rigid axle, upper and lower trailing arms, two leading
hydraulic links, 165-265 lbs./in. variable-rate coil
springs, shock absorbers, 27mm stabilizer bar

BRAKES

Front . . 13.0-inch vented disc PBR twin-piston caliper with
embossed "COBRA" lettering
Rear . . . . 11.65-inch vented disc single-piston caliper
ABS. . . . . Bosch 3-channel, 4-sensor system

WHEELS AND TIRES

Wheels . . . . 17 x 8-inch 5-spoke
Tires . . . . 245/45ZR-17 BFGoodrich Comp T/A

OTHER SPECS

Wheelbase . . . . 101.3 inches
Length . . . . 181.5 inches
Height. . . . . (coupe) 53.4 inches
. . . . (convertible) 53.3 inches
Width. . . . . 71.8 inches
Track . . . . (front) 60.0 inches
. . . . (rear) 58.7 inches
Head room . . . . (coupe) 38.2 inches
. . . . (convertible) 38.1 inches
Leg room . . . . 42.6 inches
Fuel tank. . . . . 15.4 gallons
Weight distribution (front/rear). 57%/43%

OPTION LIST

Electronic Leather/Trim Group includes Mach 460 stereo,
leather seating surfaces, perimeter anti-theft system
. . . . (coupe) no charge
. . . . (convertible) $1040
Anti-theft system $145
Rear spoiler $195

1998 V-code 4.6-liter/EFI DOHC V-8

1998 SVT COBRA PRODUCTION CHART

Model	Doors/Body/Seating	Factory Price	Shipping Weight	Prod. Total
47	2/coupe Cobra/4	$25,335	3446	6961
46	2/convertible Cobra/4	$28,135	3620	3088

NOTE 1: Exterior color breakdown includes 2,369 Black coupes/1,180 Black convertibles, 1,994 Rio Red coupes/925 Rio Red convertibles, 1,543 Crystal White coupes/606 Crystal White convertibles and 1,055 Pacific Green coupes/377 Pacific Green convertibles. Total production was 10,049 units.

**1999 SVT Cobra
Owner: Mark LaMaskin/
Performance Autosport**

1999 SVT Cobra

Ford gave the Mustang a major facelift for its 35th anniversary year, as well as several chassis and engine improvements on the base and GT models. SVT took the new-and-improved Mustang platform and built one of the most awesome musclecars of the 20th Century.

The Cobra's 4.6-liter DOHC engine was given a different combustion chamber design and reconfigured intake port geometry that created a more efficient mixing of the air/fuel mixture. Improved combustion raised the Cobra V-8 to a factory-claimed 320 hp and 317 lbs.-ft. of torque. A coil-on-plug ignition system and new type of knock sensor contributed to the Cobra's reliability and smooth power delivery.

Handling all that power was the Borg-Warner-designed T-45 five-speed introduced on the 1996 Mustang and Cobra models, but for 1999 the Cobra unit was built by Tremec. These units can be identified from the Borg-Warner-built transmissions by the "Tremec" name stamped into the housing.

SVT's gift to the Mustang world was a long-awaited independent rear suspension (IRS) using short and long arms mounted on a tubular subframe. With an eye toward the

thousands of Mustangers who would want the same IRS system on their cars, SVT designed it to mount to the four very same points as the stock GT's solid rear axle. Although the IRS weighed 80 pounds more than the previous setup, it reduced the all-important unsprung weight by 125 pounds, resulting in sharper handling and a better ride. SVT applied much stiffer rear springs—470 lbs./in. versus 210 on the solid-axle GT—and a thicker swaybar than ever before at 26mm. Front springs were more traditional 500-lbs./in. units working in concert with a 28mm stabilizer bar.

The rear axle's differential case was made of aluminum, although the same gears as before were installed. The Mustang's optional all-speed Traction Control System (TCS) was standard on the Cobra, providing a great safety benefit as it worked with the car's ABS to limit wheelspin in slippery conditions.

SVT changed the Cobra's body to reflect the standard Mustang's new design, but left out the running horse's chrome surround and installed the traditional coiled serpent emblem in place of the stock car's 35th Anniversary logo. Even though the 1999 Mustang was quite blocky, the Cobra managed to have rounder features thanks to an SVT-designed front bumper cover and scoop-less hood.

A new 17-inch five-spoke, star-shaped wheel debuted on the 1999 Cobra, again offering a nearly unobstructed view of the large disc brakes at each corner. Brake sizes and specs were unchanged for '99, but Brembo became the supplier.

Standard equipment included dual airbags, ABS, articulated sport seats (four-way power for the driver), Premium Sound, Power Equipment Group, rear window defroster, air conditioning, cruise control, front floor mats, dual illuminated visor mirrors, and remote keyless illuminated entry. The short options list included the rear spoiler and a smoker's package.

Four exterior colors were offered: Ultra White, Ebony, Rio Red, and Electric Green. New upholstery patterns and colors were available, although only in leather as there were no cloth options for seats in 1999.

The Cobra's reputation for high-performance continued to grow in its seventh year of production, but with one glitch. Car magazines, while testing the supposedly more powerful 1999 4.6-liter, reported that their test cars seemed slower than the previous model. Consideration was given to the extra weight of the IRS system, but in the end dynamometer tests revealed the new Cobra was not reaching its advertised output. In a move that is extremely rare in the car business, Ford ceased the sale of unsold Cobras at dealerships on Aug. 6, 1999, and recalled those models already in private hands. SVT replaced the intake manifold, engine management computer and entire exhaust system from the catalytic converter back on every single '99 produced. An "Authorized Modifications" label was placed at the front of the engine compartment as each car was fixed. SVT's efforts impressed the media as well as its customers.

An unusual balance was reached for 1999, with coupe and convertible sales nearly equal. Of the 8,095 total cars sold, 4,040 were the $27,470 coupe; 4,055 were the $31,470 convertible.

DATA PLATE DECODING

A 17-character Vehicle Identification Number is stamped on an aluminum tab on the instrument panel, viewable through windshield. A vehicle certification label is found on the body side of where the driver's door closes.

VEHICLE WARRANTY NUMBER
MANUFACTURER ID

1FA – Ford Motor Co.

RESTRAINT SYSTEM

L – air bags, active belts

VEHICLE CLASSIFICATION

P – passenger car

BODY SERIAL NUMBERS

47 – coupe
46 – convertible

ENGINE CODE

V – 281-cid (4.6-liter) EFI DOHC V-8 Cobra

CHECK DIGIT

for internal use

MODEL YEAR

X – 1999

ASSEMBLY PLANT

F – Dearborn, Michigan

CONSECUTIVE UNIT NUMBER

Begins at 100001 at each factory

CODE NUMBERS
PAINT CODE

E9 – Laser Red
SW – Electric Green
UA – Black
ZR – Ultra White

DRIVETRAIN INFORMATION
ENGINE

281-cid (4.6-liter) EFI DOHC V-8 Cobra
Valves . . . . 4 per cylinder
Valve size . . . . (intake) 37mm
. . . . (exhaust) 30mm
Camshaft . . . . double overhead

1999 SVT Cobra gauges   **1999 SVT Cobra interior**

Block . . . . aluminum
Heads . . . . aluminum
Displacement . . . . 281 cid/4.6 liters
Bore and stroke . . . . 3.55 x 3.54 inches
Compression ratio 9.85:1
Brake hp . . . . 320 @ 6000 rpm
Torque . . . . 317 lb./ft. @ 4750 rpm
Induction . . . . electronic fuel injection
Intake manifold . . . . equal length thin-wall cast aluminum
   runners, cast aluminum plenum chamber
Throttle body . . . . dual 57mm
Port throttles . . . . electronically actuated 34mm, open to
   secondary intake valves at 3250 rpm
Exhaust manifold . . . . cast iron
Code V
Transmission . . . . Tremec-built Borg-Warner T45 5-speed
Rear axle ratio 3.27:1

SUSPENSION

Front . . . . . modified MacPherson strut, with separate 500
   lbs./in.spring on lower arm,
 . . . . 28mm stabilizer bar
Rear . multi-link independent, steel upper control arm, aluminum lower control arm, fixed toe-control tie rod, aluminum spindle, gas-charged tubular shock absorber,
   470 lbs./in. coil spring, 26mm tubular stabilizer bar

BRAKES

Front . . . . . 13.0-inch vented Brembo disc PBR twin-piston
   caliper with embossed "COBRA" lettering

Rear . . . . 11.65-inch vented disc single-piston caliper
ABS . . . . 4-channel, 4-sensor system
Traction Control System . . engine ignition timing, cylinder
   cut-off, brake application linked to ABS module and
   engine control module, driver has on-off switch

WHEELS AND TIRES

Wheels . . . . 17 x 8-inch 5-spoke
Tires . . . . 245/45ZR-17 BFGoodrich Comp T/A

OTHER SPECS

Wheelbase . . . . 101.3 inches
Length . . . . 183.5 inches
Height . . . . (coupe) 53.2 inches
 . . . . (convertible) 53.5 inches
Width . . . . 73.1 inches
Track . . . . (front) 59.9 inches
 . . . . (rear) 59.9 inches
Head room . . . . (coupe) 38.1 inches
 . . . . (convertible) 35.5 inches
Leg room . . . . 41.8 inches
Fuel tank . . . . 15.7 gallons
Weight distribution (front/rear) 55.5%/44.5%

OPTION LIST

Rear spoiler $195
Smoker's package $15

1999 SVT COBRA PRODUCTION CHART

Model	Doors/Body/Seating	Factory Price	Shipping Weight	Prod. Total
47	2/coupe Cobra/4	$27,470	3430	4040
46	2/convertible Cobra/4	$31,470	3560	4055

NOTE 1: Exterior color breakdown includes 1,619 Black coupes/1,755 Black convertibles, 1,292 Laser Red coupes/1,251 Laser Red convertibles, 794 Ultra White coupes/731 Ultra White convertibles and 408 Electric Green coupes/318 Electric Green convertibles. Total production was 8,095.

1999 SVT Cobra wheel

1999 V-code 4.6-liter/EFI DOHC V-8

2000 SVT Cobra R (FMC)

2000 SVT Cobra

In a move unprecedented in the auto industry, SVT cancelled its production of 2000 street-model Cobras in order to evaluate its gaff over the 1999 Cobra's power deficit and to fix all of the recalled cars.

This statement on the SVT Web site gave the official explanation:

The reason for the cancellation is simply that our top priority has been our 1999 Cobra owners. Our focus and resources—and those of our SVT dealers—have been directed to the 1999 Cobra owner notification program. Rather than rushing to produce a limited number of 2000 models—and risking production/manufacturing issues by hurrying—we're choosing to focus our efforts on the timely production of the 2001 SVT Mustang Cobra.

The company did, however, go ahead with plans to produce the most powerful, brutal Mustang since the Boss 429—the 2000 Cobra R.

Not wanting to repeat themselves, the engineers at SVT developed an all-new powerplant for the 2000 R. Digging into the modular family parts bin, they settled on a cast-iron 5.4-liter DOHC, 32-valve V-8 and tweaked until it turned out an awe-inspiring 385 hp and 385 lbs.-ft. of torque. The 5.4-liter's cylinder bore is identical to that of the 4.6-liter engine found in the street Cobra, but stroke is 15.8mm longer, which provides greater displacement.

A K&N cylindrical air filter fed fresh air into the single oval-bore throttle body and 80mm Mass Air Sensor. A lot of aluminum four-valve head work went into the creation of all that power; peak airflow was increased by 25 percent over standard Cobra components. Stainless steel short-tube headers led to a Bassani X-pipe, 1998 Cobra catalytic converters, Borla mufflers and dual, twin-pipe side exhausts.

New engine mounts and crossmember lower the engine in the compartment by 12mm. Competition conditions dictated the use of an extra-capacity Canton Racing Products oil pan filled with synthetic lubrication. Redline for the R 5.4-liter was 6500 rpm, with a dual-stage rev-limiter shutting off fuel at 6800 and ignition at 7000.

To appreciate the R's tremendous power (without benefit of a test-drive), realize that its 5.4-liter generates 71.3 hp per liter, compared with 51.7 for the 1995 Cobra R, and 69.5 for the 1999 4.6-liter Cobra. Even the 8.0-liter V-10 Dodge Viper only creates 56.3 hp per liter.

A Tremec T56 six-speed manual transmission—the first six-speed ever installed in a factory-built Mustang—was specified to handle the 5.4-liter's tremendous torque. An aluminum driveshaft measuring four inches in diameter led to the 8.8-inch aluminum-case differential. Induction-hardened GKN halfshafts are the final link to the rear wheels. Final drive ratio was a short 3.55:1 for increased acceleration.

Suspension tweaks included Eibach coil springs that lowered the car 1.5 inches in front and 1.0 at the rear and made the chassis 30 to 40 percent stiffer than the 1999 Cobra. Brembo four-wheel disc brakes were activated through four-piston aluminum calipers. Air inlets designed into the Cobra fog light openings were used to provide extra cooling for the R's front brakes, with air ducts shipped and installed by SVT dealers if requested by the customer.

Eighteen-inch five-spoke wheels were fitted with 265/40ZR-18 BFGoodrich g-Force tires, which contributed somewhat to the R's astounding 1.0g of lateral acceleration. The Cobra R's rear deck and fascia were from the base V-6 Mustang, as rear-exit dual exhaust cutouts were unnecessary with the R's side-exit setup.

The front of the R included a specially designed front air splitter that, in concert with the large rear wing, reduced front lift and increased rear downforce. Because it also reduced ground clearance to a few inches, the splitter was shipped with the cars and installed at the customer's request by the dealer.

Racing Recaro seats, a thickly padded steering wheel and a B&M Ripper shifter were the R driver's only points of contact during this Mustang's wild ride. Many stock Cobra pieces were left off of the R to reduce weight, including some soundproofing material, trunk trim, spare tire cover, rear seat, air-conditioning and power seats, but the standard equipment list was still very extensive. It included dual airbags, independent rear suspension, ABS, a 20-gallon Fuel Safe bladder-type fuel cell, full-size spare tire, front air splitter, seven-inch rear wing, power dome hood, SecuriLock passive anti-theft system, Recaro seats, tilt steering wheel, 180-mph speedometer, B&M Ripper shifter with leather-wrapped shift knob, Power Equipment Group (dual electric remote-control mirrors, power side windows, power door locks and power deck lid release), dual illuminated visor mirrors and keyless illuminated entry system.

How does all of this power and suspension engineering work in the real world?

Quite well, it seems. The 3,590-pound R can zip to 60 miles an hour in less than five seconds, with a top speed of more than 170. Speeds at redline for each gear are astounding—47 mph in first; 68 in second; 98 in third; 141 in fourth; 170-plus in fifth; and 160-plus in sixth.

At $54,995, the SVT Mustang Cobra R models sold all 300 units before the first cars hit dealer showrooms.

DATA PLATE DECODING

A 17-character Vehicle Identification Number is stamped on an aluminum tab on the instrument panel, viewable through windshield. A vehicle certification label is found on the body side of where the driver's door closes.

2000 SVT Cobra R suspension

2000 SVT Cobra R interior (FMC)

2000 SVT Cobra R spoiler (FMC)

2000 SVT Cobra R wheel (FMC)

2000 SVT Cobra R (FMC)

VEHICLE WARRANTY NUMBER MANUFACTURER ID

1FA – Ford Motor Co.

RESTRAINT SYSTEM

L – air bags, active belts

VEHICLE CLASSIFICATION

P – passenger car

BODY SERIAL NUMBERS

47 – coupe

ENGINE CODE

H – 330-cid (5.4-liter) EFI DOHC V-8 Cobra R

CHECK DIGIT

for internal use

MODEL YEAR

Y – 2000

ASSEMBLY PLANT

F – Dearborn, Michigan

CONSECUTIVE UNIT NUMBER

Begins at 100001 at each factory

CODE NUMBERS
PAINT CODE

ES – Performance Red

DRIVETRAIN INFORMATION
ENGINE

330-cid (5.4-liter) EFI DOHC V-8 Cobra R

Valves . . . . 4 per cylinder
Valve size . . . . (intake) 37mm
. . . . (exhaust) 32mm
Camshaft . . . . double overhead
Block . . . . cast iron

2000 SVT Cobra R (FMC)

Heads . . . . aluminum
Displacement . . . . 281 cid/4.6 liters
Bore and stroke . . . . 90.2mm x 105.8mm
Compression ratio 9.60:1
Brake hp . . . . 385 @ 6250 rpm
Torque . . . . 385 lb./ft. @ 4250 rpm
Induction . . . . electronic fuel injection
Ignition . . . . distributorless coil-on-plug
Exhaust headers . . . . stainless steel short-tube
Exhaust system . Bassani X-pipe, production '98 Cobra cat-
alytic converters, Borla mufflers and side-exit exhausts
Code . . . . H
Transmission . . . . Tremec T56 6-speed
Rear axle . . . . . . 8.8-inch ring gear with hydromechanical
differential, aluminum case, high-durometer front differ-
ential bushings
Rear axle gears 3.55:1

SUSPENSION

Front . . . . . . modified MacPherson strut, with gas-charged,
monotube Bilstein shocks, separate 800 lbs./in. Eibach
springs on lower arms, 28mm stabilizer bar
Rear . . . . . . dual A-arm independent with high durometer
bushings, steel upper control arms, aluminum lower
control arms, fixed toe-control tie rod, aluminum spindle, gas-charged Bilstein twin-tube shock absorber, 750
lbs./in. Eibach coil spring, 26mm tubular stabilizer bar

BRAKES

Front . . . . . 13.0-inch vented Brembo disc, PBR four-piston
aluminum caliper . . with embossed "COBRA" lettering,
Galpher pads, cooling ducts
Rear . . . . 11.65-inch vented disc single-piston caliper,
Akebono pads
ABS . . . . 4-channel, 4-sensor system

WHEELS AND TIRES

Wheels . . . . 18 x 9.5-inch 5-spoke, cast aluminum
Tires . . . . 265/40ZR-18 BFGoodrich Comp T/A

OTHER SPECS

Wheelbase . . . . 101.3 inches
Length . . . . (minus air splitter) 183.5 inches
Height . . . . 52.2 inches
Width . . . . 73.1 inches
Track . . . . (front) 59.7 inches
. . . . (rear) 59.7 inches
Fuel cell . . . . 20-gallon Fuel Safe bladder-type unit
Weight distribution (front/rear) 56.5%/43.5%

2000 SVT COBRA PRODUCTION CHART				
Model	Doors/Body/Seating	Factory Price	Shipping Weight	Prod. Total
47	2/coupe Cobra R/2	$54,995	3590	300
NOTE 1: All 300 Cobra Rs produced for 2000 were painted Performance Red with Dark Charcoal interiors.				

2001 SVT Cobra (FMC)

2001 SVT Cobra

As of this printing, the 2001 SVT Cobra has been pre-viewed by the press but is not available yet for testing and evaluation. According to the company's releases, the 2001 model will reflect basic changes in the Mustang line and will continue to offer the 320-hp 4.6-liter introduced in 1999.

Standard equipment includes dual airbags, ABS, Traction Control System, articulated sport seats (four-way power for the driver), Premium Sound, Power Equipment Group, rear window defroster, air conditioning, cruise control, front floor mats, dual illuminated visor mirrors and remote keyless illuminated entry. The short options list included the rear spoiler, floor mats and polished wheels.

Color availability is the broadest ever in the Cobra's history, with eight tones for the choosing: Zinc Yellow, Laser Red, Performance Red, True Blue, Mineral Grey, Black, Silver, and Oxford White. Leather is again the only seat material, available in either dark charcoal or medium parchment.

The coupe lists for $28,605 and the convertible is priced at $32,605.

DATA PLATE DECODING

A 17-character Vehicle Identification Number is stamped on an aluminum tab on the instrument panel, viewable through windshield. A vehicle certification label is found on the body side of where the driver's door closes.

VEHICLE WARRANTY NUMBER MANUFACTURER ID

1FA – Ford Motor Co.

RESTRAINT SYSTEM

F – air bags, active belts

VEHICLE CLASSIFICATION

P – passenger car

BODY SERIAL NUMBERS

47 – coupe
46 – convertible

ENGINE CODE

V – 281-cid (4.6-liter) EFI DOHC V-8 Cobra

CHECK DIGIT

for internal use

MODEL YEAR

1 – 2001

ASSEMBLY PLANT

F – Dearborn, Michigan

CONSECUTIVE UNIT NUMBER

Begins at 100001 at each factory

CODE NUMBERS
PAINT CODE

B7 – Zinc Yellow
ES – Performance Red
E9 – Laser Red
L2 – True Blue
TK – Mineral Gray
UA – Black
YN – Silver
Z1 – Oxford White

DRIVETRAIN INFORMATION
ENGINE

281-cid (4.6-liter) EFI DOHC V-8 Cobra

Valves . . . . 4 per cylinder
Valve size . . . . (intake) 37mm
. . . . (exhaust) 30mm
Camshaft . . . . double overhead
Block . . . . aluminum
Heads. . . . . aluminum
Displacement. . . . . 281 cid/4.6 liters
Bore and stroke. . . . . 3.55 x 3.54 inches
Compression ratio 9.85:1
Brake hp . . . . 320 @ 6000 rpm
Torque . . . . 317 lb./ft. @ 4750 rpm

2001 SVT Cobra wheel (FMC)

Induction . . . . electronic fuel injection
Intake manifold . . . . . equal length thin-wall cast aluminum runners, cast aluminum plenum chamber
Throttle body. . . . . dual 57mm
Port throttles . . . . electronically actuated 34mm, open to secondary intake valves at 3250 rpm
Exhaust manifold. cast iron
Code V
Transmission . . . . . Tremec-built Borg-Warner T45 5-speed
Rear axle ratio 3.27:1

SUSPENSION

Front . . . . . modified MacPherson strut, with separate 500 lbs./in.spring on lower arm, 28mm stabilizer bar
Rear . multi-link independent, steel upper control arm, aluminum lower control arm, fixed toe-control tie rod, aluminum spindle, gas-charged tubular shock absorber, 470 lbs./in. coil spring, 26mm tubular stabilizer bar

BRAKES

Front13.0-inch vented Brembo disc PBR twin-piston caliper with embossed "COBRA" lettering
Rear . . . . 11.65-inch vented disc single-piston caliper
ABS. . . . . 4-channel, 4-sensor system

WHEELS AND TIRES

Wheels . . . . 17 x 8-inch 5-spoke
Tires . . . . 245/45ZR-17 BFGoodrich Comp T/A

OTHER SPECS

Wheelbase . . . . 101.3 inches
Length . . . . 183.5 inches
Height. . . . . (coupe) 53.2 inches
. . . . (convertible) 53.5 inches
Width. . . . . 73.1 inches
Track . . . . (front) 59.9 inches
. . . . (rear) 59.9 inches
Head room . . . . (coupe) 38.1 inches
. . . . (convertible) 35.5 inches
Leg room . . . . 41.8 inches
Fuel tank. . . . . 15.7 gallons
Weight distribution (front/rear). 55.5%/44.5%

OPTION LIST

Polished wheels $395
Rear spoiler $195
Floor mats $25

2000 SVT COBRA PRODUCTION CHART				
Model	Doors/Body/Seating	Factory Price	Shipping Weight	Prod. Total
447	2/coupe Cobra/4	$28,605	3430	Note 1
46	2/convertible Cobra/4	$32,605	3560	Note 1
NOTE 1: Production figures not known at time of printing.				

2001 SVT Cobra convertible (FMC)

2001 V-code 4.6-liter/EFI DOHC V-8 (FMC)

Price Guide

1964

2d HT	940	2,820	4,700	9,400	16,450	23,500
Conv	1,320	3,960	6,600	13,200	23,100	33,000

NOTE: Deduct 20 percent for 6-cyl. Add 20 percent for Challenger Code "K" V-8. First Mustang introduced April 17, 1964 at N.Y. World's Fair.

1965

2d HT	940	2,820	4,700	9,400	16,450	23,500
Conv	1,320	3,960	6,600	13,200	23,100	33,000
FBk	1,120	3,360	5,600	11,200	19,600	28,000

NOTE: Add 30 percent for 271 hp Hi-perf engine. Add 10 percent for "GT" Package. Add 10 percent for "original pony interior". Deduct 20 percent for 6-cyl.

1965 Shelby GT

GT-350 FBk	2,320	6,960	11,600	23,200	40,600	58,000

1966

2d HT	940	2,820	4,700	9,400	16,450	23,500
Conv	1,360	4,080	6,800	13,600	23,800	34,000
FBk	1,200	3,600	6,000	12,000	21,000	30,000

NOTE: Same as 1965.

1966 Shelby GT

GT-350 FBk	2,120	6,360	10,600	21,200	37,100	53,000
GT-350H FBk	2,200	6,600	11,000	22,000	38,500	55,000
GT-350 Conv	3,040	9,120	15,200	30,400	53,200	76,000

1967

2d HT	860	2,580	4,300	8,600	15,050	21,500
Conv	1,200	3,600	6,000	12,000	21,000	30,000
FBk	980	2,940	4,900	9,800	17,150	24,500

NOTE: Same as 1964-65 plus. Add 10 percent for 390 cid V-8 (code "S"). Deduct 15 percent for 6-cyl.

1967 Shelby GT

GT-350 FBk	1,840	5,520	9,200	18,400	32,200	46,000
GT-500 FBk	2,040	6,120	10,200	20,400	35,700	51,000

1968

2d HT	860	2,580	4,300	8,600	15,050	21,500
Conv	1,200	3,600	6,000	12,000	21,000	30,000
FBk	980	2,940	4,900	9,800	17,150	24,500

NOTE: Same as 1964-67 plus. Add 10 percent for GT-390. Add 50 percent for 427 cid V-8 (code "W"). Add 30 percent for 428 cid V-8 (code "R"). Add 15 percent for "California Special" trim.

1968 Shelby GT

350 Conv	2,360	7,080	11,800	23,600	41,300	59,000
350 FBk	1,440	4,320	7,200	14,400	25,200	36,000
500 Conv	2,880	8,640	14,400	28,800	50,400	72,000
500 FBk	1,960	5,880	9,800	19,600	34,300	49,000

NOTE: Add 30 percent for KR models.

1969

2d HT	820	2,460	4,100	8,200	14,350	20,500
Conv	980	2,940	4,900	9,800	17,150	24,500
FBk	900	2,700	4,500	9,000	15,750	22,500

NOTE: Deduct 20 percent for 6-cyl.

Mach 1	1,040	3,120	5,200	10,400	18,200	26,000
Boss 302	1,600	4,800	8,000	16,000	28,000	40,000
Boss 429	2,480	7,440	12,400	24,800	43,400	62,000
Grande	860	2,580	4,300	8,600	15,050	21,500

NOTE: Same as 1968; plus. Add 40 percent for "R" Code. Add 30 percent for Cobra Jet V-8. Add 40 percent for "Super Cobra Jet" engine.

1969 Shelby GT

350 Conv	2,320	6,960	11,600	23,200	40,600	58,000
350 FBk	1,680	5,040	8,400	16,800	29,400	42,000
500 Conv	2,640	7,920	13,200	26,400	46,200	66,000
500 FBk	1,800	5,400	9,000	18,000	31,500	45,000

1970

2d HT	820	2,460	4,100	8,200	14,350	20,500
Conv	960	2,880	4,800	9,600	16,800	24,000
FBk	880	2,640	4,400	8,800	15,400	22,000
Mach 1	960	2,880	4,800	9,600	16,800	24,000
Boss 302	1,520	4,560	7,600	15,200	26,600	38,000
Boss 429	2,400	7,200	12,000	24,000	42,000	60,000
Grande	860	2,580	4,300	8,600	15,050	21,500

NOTE: Add 30 percent for Cobra Jet V-8. Add 40 percent for "Super Cobra Jet". Deduct 20 percent for 6-cyl.

1970 Shelby GT

350 Conv	2,240	6,720	11,200	22,400	39,200	56,000
350 FBk	1,680	5,040	8,400	16,800	29,400	42,000
500 Conv	2,640	7,920	13,200	26,400	46,200	66,000
500 FBk	1,800	5,400	9,000	18,000	31,500	45,000

1971

2d HT	640	1,920	3,200	6,400	11,200	16,000
Grande	660	1,980	3,300	6,600	11,550	16,500
Conv	960	2,880	4,800	9,600	16,800	24,000
FBk	880	2,640	4,400	8,800	15,400	22,000
Mach 1	960	2,880	4,800	9,600	16,800	24,000
Boss 351	1,600	4,800	8,000	16,000	28,000	40,000

NOTE: Same as 1970. Deduct 20 percent for 6-cyl. Add 20 percent for HO option where available.

1972

2d HT	640	1,920	3,200	6,400	11,200	16,000
Grande	660	1,980	3,300	6,600	11,550	16,500
FBk	800	2,400	4,000	8,000	14,000	20,000
Mach 1	880	2,640	4,400	8,800	15,400	22,000
Conv	920	2,760	4,600	9,200	16,100	23,000

NOTE: Deduct 20 percent for 6-cyl. Add 20 percent for HO option where available.

1973

2d HT	620	1,860	3,100	6,200	10,850	15,500
Grande	660	1,980	3,300	6,600	11,550	16,500
FBk	760	2,280	3,800	7,600	13,300	19,000
Mach 1	880	2,640	4,400	8,800	15,400	22,000
Conv	960	2,880	4,800	9,600	16,800	24,000

1974 Mustang II, Mustang Four

HT Cpe	240	720	1,200	2,400	4,200	6,000
FBk	252	756	1,260	2,520	4,410	6,300
Ghia	252	756	1,260	2,520	4,410	6,300

1974 Mustang Six

HT Cpe	240	720	1,200	2,400	4,200	6,000
FBk	256	768	1,280	2,560	4,480	6,400
Ghia	256	768	1,280	2,560	4,480	6,400

1974 Mach 1 Six

FBk	380	1,140	1,900	3,800	6,650	9,500

1975 Mustang

HT Cpe	240	720	1,200	2,400	4,200	6,000
FBk	252	756	1,260	2,520	4,410	6,300
Ghia	252	756	1,260	2,520	4,410	6,300

1975 Mustang Six

HT Cpe	244	732	1,220	2,440	4,270	6,100
FBk	256	768	1,280	2,560	4,480	6,400
Ghia	256	768	1,280	2,560	4,480	6,400
Mach 1	380	1,140	1,900	3,800	6,650	9,500

1975 Mustang, V-8

HT Cpe	364	1,092	1,820	3,640	6,370	9,100
FBk Cpe	368	1,104	1,840	3,680	6,440	9,200
Ghia	380	1,140	1,900	3,800	6,650	9,500
Mach 1	420	1,260	2,100	4,200	7,350	10,500

1976 Mustang II, V-6

2d	252	756	1,260	2,520	4,410	6,300
3d 2 plus 2	256	768	1,280	2,560	4,480	6,400
2d Ghia	268	804	1,340	2,680	4,690	6,700

NOTE: Deduct 20 percent for 4-cyl. Add 20 percent for V-8. Add 20 percent for Cobra II.

1976 Mach 1, V-6

3d	360	1,080	1,800	3,600	6,300	9,000

1977 Mustang II, V-6

2d	260	780	1,300	2,600	4,550	6,500
3d 2 plus 2	268	804	1,340	2,680	4,690	6,700
2d Ghia	276	828	1,380	2,760	4,830	6,900

NOTE: Deduct 20 percent for 4-cyl. Add 30 percent for Cobra II option. Add 20 percent for V-8.

1977 Mach 1, V-6

2d	368	1,104	1,840	3,680	6,440	9,200

1978 Mustang II

Cpe	244	732	1,220	2,440	4,270	6,100
3d 2 plus 2	252	756	1,260	2,520	4,410	6,300
Ghia Cpe	256	768	1,280	2,560	4,480	6,400

1978 Mach 1, V-6

Cpe	360	1,080	1,800	3,600	6,300	9,000

NOTE: Add 20 percent for V-8. Add 30 percent for Cobra II option. Add 50 percent for King Cobra option. Deduct 20 percent for 4-cyl.

1979 V-6

2d Cpe	248	744	1,240	2,480	4,340	6,200
3d Cpe	252	756	1,260	2,520	4,410	6,300
2d Ghia Cpe	260	780	1,300	2,600	4,550	6,500

1979 V-6

3d Ghia Cpe	264	792	1,320	2,640	4,620	6,600

NOTE: Add 30 percent for Pace Car package. Add 30 percent for Cobra option.

1980 6-cyl.

2d Cpe	212	636	1,060	2,120	3,710	5,300
2d HBk	216	648	1,080	2,160	3,780	5,400
2d Ghia Cpe	224	672	1,120	2,240	3,920	5,600
2d Ghia HBk	228	684	1,140	2,280	3,990	5,700

NOTE: Deduct 20 percent for 4-cyl. Add 30 percent for V-8.

1981 6-cyl.

2d S Cpe	196	588	980	1,960	3,430	4,900
2d Cpe	204	612	1,020	2,040	3,570	5,100
2d HBk	208	624	1,040	2,080	3,640	5,200
2d Ghia Cpe	208	624	1,040	2,080	3,640	5,200
2d Ghia HBk	212	636	1,060	2,120	3,710	5,300

NOTE: Deduct 20 percent for 4-cyl. Add 35 percent for V-8.

1982 4-cyl.

2d L Cpe	180	540	900	1,800	3,150	4,500
2d GL Cpe	184	552	920	1,840	3,220	4,600
2d GL HBk	188	564	940	1,880	3,290	4,700
2d GLX Cpe	196	588	980	1,960	3,430	4,900
2d GLX HBk	200	600	1,000	2,000	3,500	5,000

1982 6-cyl.

2d L Cpe	196	588	980	1,960	3,430	4,900
2d GL Cpe	200	600	1,000	2,000	3,500	5,000
2d GL HBk	204	612	1,020	2,040	3,570	5,100
2d GLX Cpe	212	636	1,060	2,120	3,710	5,300
2d GLX HBk	216	648	1,080	2,160	3,780	5,400

1982 V-8

2d GT HBk	256	768	1,280	2,560	4,480	6,400

1983 4-cyl.

2d L Cpe	184	552	920	1,840	3,220	4,600
2d GL Cpe	188	564	940	1,880	3,290	4,700
2d GL HBk	196	588	980	1,960	3,430	4,900
2d GLX Cpe	200	600	1,000	2,000	3,500	5,000
2d GLX HBk	204	612	1,020	2,040	3,570	5,100

1983 6-cyl.

2d GL Cpe	204	612	1,020	2,040	3,570	5,100
2d GL HBk	208	624	1,040	2,080	3,640	5,200
2d GLX Cpe	216	648	1,080	2,160	3,780	5,400
2d GLX HBk	220	660	1,100	2,200	3,850	5,500
2d GLX Conv	240	720	1,200	2,400	4,200	6,000

1983 V-8

2d GT HBk	360	1,080	1,800	3,600	6,300	9,000
2d GT Conv	400	1,200	2,000	4,000	7,000	10,000

1984 4-cyl.

2d L Cpe	188	564	940	1,880	3,290	4,700
2d L HBk	192	576	960	1,920	3,360	4,800
2d LX Cpe	192	576	960	1,920	3,360	4,800
2d LX HBk	196	588	980	1,960	3,430	4,900
2d GT Turbo HBk	212	636	1,060	2,120	3,710	5,300
2d GT Turbo Conv	260	780	1,300	2,600	4,550	6,500

1984 V-6

2d L Cpe	192	576	960	1,920	3,360	4,800
2d L HBk	196	588	980	1,960	3,430	4,900
2d LX Cpe	196	588	980	1,960	3,430	4,900
2d LX HBk	200	600	1,000	2,000	3,500	5,000
LX 2d Conv	280	840	1,400	2,800	4,900	7,000

1984 V-8

2d L HBk	200	600	1,000	2,000	3,500	5,000
2d LX Cpe	204	612	1,020	2,040	3,570	5,100
2d LX HBk	204	612	1,020	2,040	3,570	5,100
2d LX Conv	320	960	1,600	3,200	5,600	8,000
2d GT HBk	212	636	1,060	2,120	3,710	5,300
2d GT Conv	340	1,020	1,700	3,400	5,950	8,500

NOTE: Add 20 percent for 20th Anniversary Edition. Add 40 percent for SVO Model.

1985 4-cyl.

2d LX	196	588	980	1,960	3,430	4,900
2d LX HBk	200	600	1,000	2,000	3,500	5,000
2d SVO Turbo	240	720	1,200	2,400	4,200	6,000

1985 V-6

2d LX	204	612	1,020	2,040	3,570	5,100
2d LX HBk	208	624	1,040	2,080	3,640	5,200
2d LX Conv	396	1,188	1,980	3,960	6,930	9,900

1985 V-8

2d LX	220	660	1,100	2,200	3,850	5,500
2d LX HBk	224	672	1,120	2,240	3,920	5,600
2d LX Conv	420	1,260	2,100	4,200	7,350	10,500
2d GT HBk	400	1,200	2,000	4,000	7,000	10,000
2d GT Conv	560	1,680	2,800	5,600	9,800	14,000

NOTE: Add 40 percent for SVO Model.

1986 Mustang

2d Cpe	200	600	1,000	2,000	3,500	5,000
2d HBk	200	600	1,000	2,000	3,500	5,000
2d Conv	380	1,140	1,900	3,800	6,650	9,500
2d Turbo HBk	240	720	1,200	2,400	4,200	6,000

1986 V-8

2d HBk	240	720	1,200	2,400	4,200	6,000
2d Conv	420	1,260	2,100	4,200	7,350	10,500
2d GT HBk	400	1,200	2,000	4,000	7,000	10,000
2d GT Conv	560	1,680	2,800	5,600	9,800	14,000

NOTE: Add 40 percent for SVO Model.

1987 4-cyl.

2d LX Sed	200	600	1,000	2,000	3,500	5,000
2d LX HBk	204	612	1,020	2,040	3,570	5,100
2d LX Conv	360	1,080	1,800	3,600	6,300	9,000

1987 V-8

2d LX Sed	200	600	1,000	2,000	3,500	5,000
2d LX HBk	204	612	1,020	2,040	3,570	5,100
2d LX Conv	424	1,272	2,120	4,240	7,420	10,600
2d GT HBk	220	660	1,100	2,200	3,850	5,500
2d GT Conv	400	1,200	2,000	4,000	7,000	10,000

1988 V-6

2d LX Sed	160	480	800	1,600	2,800	4,000
2d LX HBk	168	504	840	1,680	2,940	4,200
2d LX Conv	360	1,080	1,800	3,600	6,300	9,000

1988 V-8

2d LX Sed	200	600	1,000	2,000	3,500	5,000
2d LX HBk	220	660	1,100	2,200	3,850	5,500
2d LX Conv	400	1,200	2,000	4,000	7,000	10,000
2d GT HBk	380	1,140	1,900	3,800	6,650	9,500
2d GT Conv	560	1,680	2,800	5,600	9,800	14,000

1989 4-cyl.

2d LX Cpe	180	540	900	1,800	3,150	4,500
2d LX HBk	188	564	940	1,880	3,290	4,700
2d LX Conv	420	1,260	2,100	4,200	7,350	10,500

1989 V-8

2d LX Spt Cpe	236	708	1,180	2,360	4,130	5,900
2d LX Spt HBk	240	720	1,200	2,400	4,200	6,000
2d LX Spt Conv	560	1,680	2,800	5,600	9,800	14,000
2d GT HBk	388	1,164	1,940	3,880	6,790	9,700
2d GT Conv	680	2,040	3,400	6,800	11,900	17,000

1990 4-cyl.

2d LX	184	552	920	1,840	3,220	4,600
2d LX HBk	192	576	960	1,920	3,360	4,800
2d LX Conv	380	1,140	1,900	3,800	6,650	9,500

1990 V-8

2d LX Spt	240	720	1,200	2,400	4,200	6,000
2d LX HBk Spt	248	744	1,240	2,480	4,340	6,200
2d LX Conv Spt	520	1,560	2,600	5,200	9,100	13,000
2d GT HBk	400	1,200	2,000	4,000	7,000	10,000
2d GT Conv	560	1,680	2,800	5,600	9,800	14,000

1991 4-cyl.

2d LX Cpe	180	540	900	1,800	3,150	4,500
2d LX HBk	200	600	1,000	2,000	3,500	5,000
2d LX Conv	360	1,080	1,800	3,600	6,300	9,000

1991 V-8

2d LX Cpe	220	660	1,100	2,200	3,850	5,500
2d LX HBk	240	720	1,200	2,400	4,200	6,000
2d LX Conv	400	1,200	2,000	4,000	7,000	10,000
2d GT HBk	380	1,140	1,900	3,800	6,650	9,500
2d GT Conv	540	1,620	2,700	5,400	9,450	13,500

1992 V-8, 4-cyl.

2d LX Cpe	200	600	1,000	2,000	3,500	5,000
2d LX HBk	220	660	1,100	2,200	3,850	5,500
2d LX Conv	400	1,200	2,000	4,000	7,000	10,000

1992 V-8

2d LX Sed	360	1,080	1,800	3,600	6,300	9,000
2d LX HBk	380	1,140	1,900	3,800	6,650	9,500
2d LX Conv	520	1,560	2,600	5,200	9,100	13,000
2d GT HBk	420	1,260	2,100	4,200	7,350	10,500
2d GT Conv	600	1,800	3,000	6,000	10,500	15,000

1993 4-cyl.

2d LX Cpe	220	660	1,100	2,200	3,850	5,500
2d LX HBk	224	672	1,120	2,240	3,920	5,600
2d LX Conv	408	1,224	2,040	4,080	7,140	10,200

1993 V-8

2d LX Cpe	360	1,080	1,800	3,600	6,300	9,000
2d LX HBk	368	1,104	1,840	3,680	6,440	9,200
2d LX Conv	552	1,656	2,760	5,520	9,660	13,800
2d GT HBk	400	1,200	2,000	4,000	7,000	10,000
2d GT Conv	620	1,860	3,100	6,200	10,850	15,500

1993 Cobra

2d HBk	700	2,100	3,500	7,000	12,250	17,500

NOTE: Add 40 percent for Code R.

1994 V-6

2d Cpe	320	960	1,600	3,200	5,600	8,000
2d Conv	440	1,320	2,200	4,400	7,700	11,000

1994 GT, V-8

2d GT Cpe	420	1,260	2,100	4,200	7,350	10,500
2d GT Conv	480	1,440	2,400	4,800	8,400	12,000

1994 Cobra, V-8

2d Cpe	560	1,680	2,800	5,600	9,800	14,000
2d Conv	640	1,920	3,200	6,400	11,200	16,000